J. Lee Thompson

D1430762

MANCHESTER
UNIVERSITY PRESS

BRIAN MCFARLANE, NEIL SINYARD *series editors*

ALLEN EYLES, PHILIP FRENCH, SUE HARPER,
TIM PULLEINE, JEFFREY RICHARDS, TOM RYALL
series advisers

BRITISH
FILM
MAKERS

already published

Jack Clayton   NEIL SINYARD

Lance Comfort   BRIAN MCFARLANE

forthcoming titles

Terence Fisher   PETER HUTCHINGS

Pat Jackson   CHARLES BARR

Launder and Gilliat   BRUCE BABINGTON

J. Lee Thompson

Steve Chibnall

Manchester University Press

MANCHESTER AND NEW YORK

distributed exclusively in the USA by Palgrave

For Kara, my favourite Deutscher star

Published by Manchester University Press
Oxford Road, Manchester M13 9NR, UK
and Room 400, 175 Fifth Avenue, New York, NY 10010, USA
http://www.manchesteruniversitypress.co.uk

Distributed exclusively in the USA by
Palgrave, 175 Fifth Avenue, New York, NY 10010, USA

Distributed exclusively in Canada by
UBC Press, University of British Columbia, 2029 West Mall,
Vancouver, BC, Canada V6T 1Z2

British Library Cataloguing-in-Publication Data
A catalogue record for this book is available from the British Library

Library of Congress Cataloging-in-Publication Data applied for

ISBN 0 7190 6011 7 *hardback*
     0 7190 6012 5 *paperback*

First published 2000

08 07 06 05 04 03 02 01 00   10 9 8 7 6 5 4 3 2 1

Typeset in Scala with Meta display
by Koinonia, Manchester
Printed in Great Britain
by Bookcraft (Bath) Ltd, Midsomer Norton

Contents

List of plates

All illustrations are from the author's collection, part of the British Cinema and Television Research Group's archive, De Montfort University

Series editors' foreword

The aim of this series is to present in lively, authoritative volumes a guide to those film-makers who have made British cinema a rewarding but still under-researched branch of world cinema. The intention is to provide books which are up-to-date in terms of information and critical approach, but not bound to any one theoretical methodology. Though all books in the series will have certain elements in common – comprehensive filmographies, annotated bibliographies, appropriate illustration – the actual critical tools employed will be the responsibility of the individual authors.

Nevertheless, an important recurring element will be a concern for how the oeuvre of each film-maker does or does not fit certain critical and industrial contexts, as well as for the wider social contexts, which helped to shape not just that particular film-maker but the course of British cinema at large.

Although the series is director-orientated, the editors believe that a variety of stances and contexts referred to is more likely to reconceptualise and reappraise the phenomenon of British cinema as a complex, shifting field of production. All the texts in the series will engage in detailed discussion of major works of the film-makers involved, but they all consider as well the importance of other key collaborators, of studio organisation, of audience reception, of recurring themes and structures: all those other aspects which go towards the construction of a national cinema.

The series will explore and chart a field which is more than ripe for serious excavation. The acknowledged leaders of the field will be reappraised; just as important, though, will be the bringing to light of those who have not so far received any serious attention. They are all part of the very rich texture of British cinema, and it will be the work of this series to give them all their due.

Sir John Mills in *Ice Cold in Alex* (1958)

Foreword by Sir John Mills

I have always thought that my great friend, J. Lee Thompson, has always been a very under-rated director. He is technically brilliant.

I have had the great pleasure of working with him twice. I worked with Lee on *Ice Cold in Alex*. One of the best scenes in the film was the crossing of the minefield. All it said in the script was: 'And they take Katie, the ambulance, through the minefield', but everything was in his head, down to the last detail. He always got the best out of the actors, and every performance in that film was superb – Anthony Quayle, Harry Andrews and Sylvia Syms. He launched my daugher, Hayley, on her career in the film *Tiger Bay*. He handled her superbly and she turned in a really marvellous performance. She thoroughly enjoyed making the film – in fact, she hardly believed it was a film! He would talk to her about the scenes she had to play and she was humming rather loudly all the time. So I said to Lee, 'Do you think I should try and stop her humming?', but he said, 'Absolutely not; as long as she keeps humming, we have a smash hit on our hands!'

I hope this book about him will also be a big success and I, personally, wish I was starting another film with him next week!

Sir John Mills, CBE

Acknowledgements

My thanks must go first to my interviewees: J. Lee Thompson, Joan Henry, Richard Best and Gilbert Taylor, whose comments and memories enriched my understanding of the films and their production enormously. I am grateful also to a number of people who helped to access obscure visual material or supplied useful printed documents. Richard Dacre, Richard Best, Marc Morris, Alan Burton and Ian Hunter all helped me to track down elusive films. James Robertson and Barraclough Carey kindly loaned me transcripts of unbroadcast interview material for *Empire of the Censors*. Andrew Clay gave me permission to quote from one of his research interviews, and Melanie Williams allowed me to read working papers for her thesis. Stephen Bourne supplied useful data on the British Academy Awards, and Eithne Quinn, Andrew Clay and Steve Holland located valuable information.

Among a range of sources for illustrative material, *Flashbacks* was of outstanding assistance. Like the staff at the British Film Institute (BFI) Library, those at *Flashbacks* demonstrated great patience and efficiency in dealing with my requests. The same is true of the De Montfort University (DMU) technicians John Mackintosh and Steve Gamble, who solved all the computer disk problems I could throw at them.

I am grateful to the Faculty of Humanities at DMU for granting me a semester's study leave, without which this book would have been much slower to reach the printers. It has also benefitted from discussions with colleagues in DMU's British Cinema and Television Research Group, notably John Cook, Robert Murphy, Andrew Clay, Alan Burton and Ian Hunter. Thanks are due also to my series editors and my publisher at Manchester University Press for their support and encouragement. And, finally, I must give a special thank you to Kara McKechnie for her helpful advice, unfailing support and great fortitude in the preparation of the typescript.

Introduction

> One really has to rack one's brains to find anything to say about a British film. One wonders why. But that's the way it is. And there isn't even an exception to prove the rule. Especially not *Woman in a Dressing Gown* anyhow, in spite of its acting prize at the recent Berlin Festival. That just goes to show that the Germans have no idea either. (Jean Luc Godard, *Arts*, 30 July 1958)

Godard's review of J. Lee Thompson's *Woman in a Dressing Gown* (1957) reveals rather more than simply the French film-maker's arrogance and chauvinism. He has not been alone in finding it difficult to say something positive about British films and film-makers. In spite of a recent revival of academic interest in the national cinema, much remains to be said and the work of important contributors to British film culture is still shrouded in silence. A handful of directors making movies in England have received a disproportionate share of attention – Lean, Hitchcock, Reed, Powell, Losey, Jarman, Greenaway in particular. Certain periods of film production have also been privileged, notably the 1940s and, to a lesser extent, the 1930s and the 1960s. This focus on the glamour boys and glamour years of British cinema is only now beginning to be shifted by a line of inquiry which combines a resurgent auteurist perspective on the work of neglected film-makers with a socio-historical interest in its conditions of production and consumption. This has been a significant part of the project of the British Cinema and Television Research Group at De Montfort University,[1] and is an aim shared by the volumes in this series. Contrary to Godard's dismissive assertion, there really is a great deal to say about British films and specifically about British films in the 1950s. This is especially true of those made by J. Lee Thompson.

Lee Thompson is not a name with household status. It even elicits slightly puzzled expressions from film buffs, until mention of *The Guns of Navarone* (1961) and the 'original' *Cape Fear* (1962) brings smiles of recognition. When these two central films are linked back to *Ice Cold in Alex* (1958) and *Tiger Bay* (1959) and then forward to the most challenging of the *Planet of the Apes'* sequels[2] and a string of Charles Bronson revenge thrillers, expressions shift from surprise to mild bewilderment. In fact, since his first directorial commission at Welwyn Studios in 1950, Lee Thompson has directed forty-five pictures for theatrical release, covering almost every genre of the cinema. His remarkable ability to adapt his style to suit the material has made him perhaps the most versatile director ever produced by Britain. In addition, his training in acting, editing and scriptwriting, and his appreciation of the possibilities of cinematography, have made him a complete, all-round, film-maker.

When he moved from London to Los Angeles in the early 1960s to begin thirty years of intensive work in Hollywood, Lee Thompson was one of the most controversial and highly regarded figures in the British industry. He had shown a commitment to frankness, innovation and socially conscious film making which the British studio system had struggled to accommodate and the British Board of Film Censors (BBFC) had tried to moderate. His reputation for making taut and intimate dramas about the problems of ordinary people – *The Yellow Balloon* (1953), *The Weak and the Wicked* (1954), *Woman in a Dressing Gown, No Trees in the Street* (1959) – predates the rise of the 'New Wave' school of 'kitchen-sink' northern realism; and his films *Yield to the Night* (1956) and *I Aim at the Stars* (1960) were of sufficient political significance for them to be shown to members of the British Parliament and the American Senate (respectively). Although he honed his abilities in small-scale Anglo-centric productions, when the opportunity arose he demonstrated that he could apply his talents to the big-budget, location-based, action movie that the international market demanded. It was principally his two lavish but ironic reworkings of the Korda-style empire film *North West Frontier* (1959) and the Second World War daring-do movie *The Guns of Navarone* that finally took him to Hollywood. When *North West Frontier* was released, the critic Leonard Mosley indicated the stature which Lee Thompson had achieved, when he wrote in the *Daily Express* (9 October 1959):

> A new name is added this week to the small and distinguished list of British directors who can not only make brilliant small films but are capable of producing exciting and spectacular big films too. Sir Carol Reed and David Lean were the two founder members of this exclusive club ... now they are joined by J. Lee Thompson.

Simultaneously, in the *Daily Mail* (9 October 1959), the experienced reviewer Fred Majdalany had no hesitation in describing Lee Thompson as 'the best of our younger generation of directors'. Between 1954 and 1959 no fewer than five of his pictures were nominated for the Best Film award by the British Academy (BAFTA),[3] and in 1961 he received a Best Director Oscar nomination for *The Guns of Navarone*, which received six other nominations, including Best Picture.

The films of this period bear a clear authorial signature in their concern with social issues and moral dilemmas, imaginative use of the camera, adroit handling of suspense and recursive thematic motifs, and are often distinguished by an attention to visual stylistics unusual in British studio films. But as someone who had begun his career in the acting profession, Lee Thompson never allowed visual *mise-en-scène* to overshadow the performances in his films. He was fortunate to work with some of the best actors on both sides of the Atlantic, but he gave them the opportunity to experiment and extend their techniques in more emotive ways than many directors would sanction. Yvonne Mitchell won a Silver Bear at the Berlin Festival for just such a heightened performance in *Woman in a Dressing Gown*, prompting the critic C. A. Lejeune to describe it as 'perhaps the finest performance on the screen ever given by an English actress' (*Observer*, 6 October 1957). When it came to the British Academy Awards, it was one of Mitchell's co-stars, Sylvia Syms, who was nominated for Best Actress.[4] Her other co-star, Anthony Quayle, received his nomination for Best Actor the following year for his role in Lee Thompson's *Ice Cold in Alex*. Mitchell, Syms and Quayle were respected actors who might be expected to give award-quality performances, but Lee Thompson was also able to coax remarkable pieces of acting from unexpected sources. In *Yield to the Night*, for example, Diana Dors, then thought more a pin-up than an actress, overcame her glamour-girl image to give a profoundly moving portrayal of a woman in the death cell. Then in *Tiger Bay* Hayley Mills made one of the most sensational debuts by a child actor in cinema history, comfortably securing the British Academy's award for Most Promising New-comer.

The burst of creative energy between 1955 and 1961 that produced J. Lee Thompson's most acclaimed work was a 'purple patch' comparable to the one Carol Reed had enjoyed ten years before.[5] In fact the films Reed made during that period were a source of considerable inspiration for Lee Thompson and there are frequent oblique references to them in his own pictures. The influence of Reed is evident in the atmosphere of alienation, the sense of dislocation and moral uncertainty present in many of Lee Thompson's early films, and in his choice of protagonist: often a flawed and suffering outsider, trapped in a situation from which he or she struggles to escape. He also shares with Carol Reed a facility for working effectively with child actors, and the threat to children and their progress from innocence to experience are also motifs in Lee Thompson's cinema, up to and including his latest film *Kinjite: Forbidden Subjects* (1989). Where Lee Thompson differs from Reed is particularly in his tendency towards over-statement and excess, and this may be linked to his reverence for Hitchcock.[6] From Hitchcock, Lee Thompson takes his fondness for melodrama as a way of dramatising emotional truths and his taste for theatrical irony, but most of all his meticulous crafts-manship in the generation and maintenance of suspense. *Cape Fear* and *Return From the Ashes* (1966) are each a homage to the only director prior to Lee Thompson successfully to make a permanent transition from the British cinema to Hollywood, and there are Hitchcockian devices in almost all his thrillers from *Murder Without Crime* (1951) onwards.[7] But whereas Hitchcock was given the freedom to focus on a single genre of film making, cultivating the obsessions and honing the techniques that made his movies so instantly recognisable, Lee Thompson was expected to cover a much broader field.

This process of diversification began during his time in the British studio system where Associated British required him to produce musical comedies as well as thrillers, but it mushroomed when he became an independent director in Hollywood. Encouraged by both his desire to stay in regular employment and his enthusiasm for new challenges, he scattered his talents around epic adventures, comedies, westerns, musicals, and fantasy films, losing in the process some of the intensity he had previously brought to his thrillers and intimate dramas. His versatility began to erode his reputation, just as the imprint of his individual style became fainter as his career progressed. As he freely admits, like Carol Reed he lost his way, producing his most incisive work early in his directorial career.

When I interviewed Lee Thomson for this book, he expressed his frustration that his initial Hollywood movie turned out to be his best: '*Cape Fear* was like my old style and I think it probably is the best American film I made, which is very regrettable considering it was my first American film. That was in the style of my early British films and I shouldn't have relinquished that style.'[8]

By the early 1990s, the inspiration and innovation he brought to his first decade of film making had been so obscured by his less distinguished later work that Alex Cox, presenting a screening of *Cape Fear* on the eve of Martin Scorsese's 1992 remake, could describe J. Lee Thompson as 'a straightforward, bread and margarine director, best known for *The Guns of Navarone* and Charles Bronson and Chuck Norris epics' (*Moviedrome*, BBC 2, 1992). The suggestion seemed to be that *Cape Fear* – a movie so influential that a great director wanted to remake it, and to which one of cinema's acknowledged innovators, Nic Roeg, insisted on paying homage in his *Track 29* (1988) – was a lucky accident by a hack of

limited talent. In contrast, when Raymond Durgnat wrote his
contemporary review of *Cape Fear* in *Films and Filming* (February
1963), he was able to relate the picture to a distinctive body of
work:

> [The] earlier films have more than a little directorial showmanship,
> like the up-the-flue camera angles of *Woman in a Dressing Gown*,
> and not infrequent clichés; but there is a splendid lack of the
> inhibiting English fear of violent emotion and they all have a
> sharp, stabbing integrity not altogether unlike the angry young
> men's ... I feel that somehow he hasn't quite sorted out his artistic
> personality and that in consequence he is sometimes content to
> settle for the cudgel when a greater artist would prefer the scalpel.
> Yet all his films have very short, but very sharp moments worthy of
> the great directors.

For Durgnat, Lee Thompson could never be described as a 'bread
and margarine' director. Whatever their imperfections, his films
were typically 'disturbing and intriguing' (ibid.).

Like Durgnat, those who were active in film making in Britain
in the 1950s remember the impact which Lee Thompson's films
made. Roy Boulting, for example, describes his contemporary as
'the best of the bunch at Elstree',[9] while the scriptwriter (and,
later, director) Brian Clemens pairs him with the film-maker who
is in some ways his American equivalent, John Sturges, as 'two
directors who don't figure on anybody's best directors' list' but
have made 'some of the films that give me the most pleasure'. Lee
Thompson, he insists, is 'a really fine director – you can see it in
his early work ... you can see a sort of mastery of the medium
waiting to be exploited and developed'.[10] But it is those who
actually worked with Lee Thompson who sing his praises loudest.
Sir John Mills, who has the widest possible experience of directors
in a career spanning seventy years, judges that 'Lee Thompson
was a wonderful director' who could 'make a scene out of nothing'
(MacFarlane 1997: 416). Richard Best, Lee Thompson's editor on
seven of his British films, believes he deserves to be placed in 'the
premier league, the top five British directors', together with Lean,
Reed, Powell and the Boultings:

'I thought he was a really brilliant director. He was so clever to work with. He was never at a loss. He was most imaginative. He could answer any questions you had, just like that. And you could tell from the rushes – never mind the finished film – his talent. His talent for acting, for writing, his talent for getting wonderful performances from his cast, and his talent for casting ... He's an unsung hero to my mind. He gets absolutely to the emotional truth of the scene, not just in the dialogue and the lighting, but in the performances.'[11]

The distinguished cinematographer Gilbert Taylor, who has made films with Hitchcock, Kubrick, Polanski and Lucas, photographed nine pictures for Lee Thompson and is equally generous in his assessment of his talent:

'He was the most modest man I ever worked with as a director and, I think, one of the most talented. I mean, I don't call anybody a genius that directs films or has anything to do with them, but I think I could say he was one of the best technicians I ever worked with. I can say that with all truth: he's right up there with the best.'[12]

Similar recognition has not been forthcoming from film academics, who have largely ignored Lee Thompson's films and completely failed to spot his significance in the neglected world of 1950s' British cinema. In spite of his unusual commitment to issue-based film making and his successful transfer to Hollywood, Lee Thompson (like his contemporaries Val Guest, Roy Baker and Jack Lee) has been dismissed as part of the roster of jobbing directors who tilled the fields of cultural production before the harvest of the New Wave. Unlucky enough to be making a large-scale war film[13] when the small-scale working-class drama he had pioneered came into fashion, and then departing for America when British film became *à la mode*, he has hardly featured in critical histories of the national cinema.

When films which he directed have been considered by writers like John Hill (1986) and Marcia Landy (1992), it has been in the context of other 'social-problem' films rather than as part of the director's oeuvre.[14] One searches the literature in vain for any analysis of *Ice Cold in Alex* or *The Guns of Navarone*, the two war pictures which *Empire* magazine (October 1998) grouped with *Lawrence of Arabia* (David Lean, 1962) as the best of all British offerings in the genre. And yet there should be much to interest researchers in Lee Thompson's output, particularly in his first decade of film making. Many of these films introduce strongly innovative elements into the staid formulae of British genre cinema, most notably the revisionist war and action films with their ironic and politically conscious approach; the domestic dramas with their sense of entrapment and experimental cinematography; and, to a lesser extent, the musical comedies like *As Long as They're Happy* (1955), *An Alligator Named Daisy* (1955) and *The Good Companions* (1957), which try to revive a cinematic form becoming increasingly moribund in Britain. Historically, the films are rich documents of their day, offering valuable insights into the attitudes and practices of post-war Britain from the perspective of a socially concerned film-maker who believed that cinema has the potential to influence political change. 'Films can change society to a certain extent', he once told a reporter (*Screen International*, 31 July 1976), 'because they reach so many people'. The films also offer fruitful possibilities for the study of gender representations. Not only is the violent dimension of masculinity explored from the earliest films right up to the rene-gade cop and lone-avenger movies of the 1980s, but, as Marcia Landy has appreciated, the social-problem dramas of the 1950s present their stories from a predominantly female perspective, providing an interesting contrast to Basil Dearden and Michael Relph's more male-oriented approach.[15]

Pre-eminently, though, Lee Thompson's is a cinema of moral dilemma. Almost all of his films have at their core knotty ethical problems which are revisited and reworked from one picture to the next. In what remains the most perceptive analysis of the films Lee Thompson made in Britain, Raymond Durgnat (1970: 243–4) points to the emphasis he gives to 'the psychological and emotional hinterland of moral decisions' and the way in which his use of melodrama is a consequence of his 'determination to ram right into the complacent spectator the full pain and terror of the emotional extremes against which moral principles must assert themselves'. The ethical course of action is a difficult one to choose and a harder one to follow, and the tension of visual suspense in so many of Lee Thompson's dramas is usually matched by the tension of moral decision making.

Troubled by the same sort of contradictory emotional responses to the ambiguities of moral philosophy that beset his one-time business partner Graham Greene, but without Greene's recourse to religious theology, Lee Thompson explores alternative answers in his films. 'I like to get hold of an idea', he wrote (Lee Thompson 1963). 'In every film I do, I hold on to something, some social problem.' Although he always thought of himself as a political radical, more orthodox socialist commentators, notably the firebrand freelance critic Derek Hill, regarded him with suspicion and a contempt reserved for the counterfeit and the charlatan.[16] The public opposition to the practices of the BBFC, which both men maintained, did not prevent Hill from regarding Lee Thompson as a phoney radical who consistently failed to advocate left-wing arguments with any conviction. Part of Hill's difficulty was that the questions Lee Thompson raises in his films are not usually drawn from the conventional socialist concerns of class and inequality but from a wider humanist portfolio: What obligations do people have to each other? How are individuals linked by their shared humanity? What happens to obligations and communality when conflict erupts? What duties and loyalties override individual conscience? Under what circumstances is the taking of life justified? How savage is human nature? These questions are most often embedded in the dilemmas of penal policy. There is a continuing preoccupation with the ethics and expediency of the due process of law and their antagonistic relationship to a more primitive and emotional 'natural' justice which they attempt to codify and interpret. The most intractable human emotion here is the righteous desire for revenge, whether it be by the implacable State or the passionate and obsessive individual.

Just as so many of Lee Thompson's films explore situations of entrapment and the battle to escape, so the film-maker himself seems to be locked into a spiral of moral contradictions without easy solutions. The early films like *Yield to the Night* and *Tiger Bay* express relatively unequivocal sympathy for the wrongdoer and condemn the repressiveness of the law. In these films criminality stems from weakness and the inability to deal with the emotions created by interpersonal relationships. As the director put it (Lee Thompson 1963): 'I think that in life people do crimes and they're not criminals at all. So it's fascinating to show somebody who does a murder, and see it sympathetically.' But the certainties of this liberal humanism are already giving way to ambivalence and doubt in *Cape Fear* and *Conquest of the Planet of the Apes*, and finally begin to reverse in the renegade-cop films of the 1980s with their vengeful and frustrated protagonists and irredeemable antagonists, and their contempt for the efficacy of due process. Instead of functioning as the repressive apparatus of *Yield to the Night*, the law in these films is the flimsiest of shields against the savagery of individuals whose psycho-sexual mechanisms have been thrown into disarray. Thus there is a slow shift of emphasis in Lee Thompson's cinema from the championing of the weak to the condemnation of the wicked, and from the virtues of tolerance to the need for retribution. In the later films the portfolio of humanist issues has been whittled down to one question which is posed obsessively: what should a man of honour do in the face of legal impotence?

The growing disillusionment and waning radical commitment of Lee Thompson's later films are likely the consequences of growing old and rich in Los Angeles, suspended over a cauldron of lawlessness and racial tension. As such, they are not really the concern of this study, which explores Lee Thompson's relationship to British cinema, primarily in his first decade of directing. What led up to this period and what followed will be discussed briefly, but the lion's share of the analysis will be reserved for the significant thrillers and domestic dramas that culminated in *Cape Fear*, a film that may be more fruitfully understood as the end of the first phase of his career rather than as the beginning of the second. The six pictures that Lee Thompson periodically returned to Europe to make with predominantly British casts and crews after his move to Hollywood will receive shorter consideration, as will the four comedies and musicals he made for British studios in the 1950s. Although, textually, the focus is primarily on only half of the twenty British films that Lee Thompson made, the industrial contexts and practices of the production of all twenty will be considered. So, too, will be their critical reception, which can tell us much about the normative expectations with which reviewers surveyed the field of cultural production in the 1950s and 1960s.

In its desire to rescue from critical neglect a film-maker whose work is not only powerfully innovative and distinctive but which shows remarkable continuities of style and theme, this study is unashamedly auteurist. However, as David Caute (1994: xv) points out in the Introduction to his book on Joseph Losey, a film is 'the outcome of a long process of collaboration and contingency – the writing, the financing, the available cast, the bad weather, the processing laboratories, the demands of the producers and distributors'. The collaborative nature of this process should be evident in the pages of this book, as should both the limits of the director's freedom of expression and the range of organisational skills required. Moreover, although the study of the processes of cultural consumption are limited to an analysis of newspaper and periodical reviews, I have tried to maintain, where possible, a sense of the general popularity of the films discussed. Overall, the intention is to plot the trajectory of a unique film-maker through the typical constraints and opportunities offered by British cinema as a dominant studio system gave way to independent production in the two decades after the Second World War. Unusually for the time, that trajectory took J. Lee Thompson beyond the boundaries of his national cinema, and the new forces operating on his later career will be noted in the final chapters of this book.

In 1960, British cinema lost two of its most unconventional and uncompromising directors. Both left under a cloud of critical disapproval occasioned by the films they released that year. One of these films was *Peeping Tom*, a work of unpalatable revelations which put Michael Powell beyond the pale of decent film making and provoked Derek Hill to recommend that the only satisfactory way to dispose of it 'would be to shovel it up and flush it swiftly down the nearest sewer' (*Tribune*, 29 April 1960). The other was *I*

Aim at the Stars, a picture which Hill suggested had made such a pathetic attempt to paint over the indelible guilt of the man whose V-2 rockets had killed hundreds of Londoners during the war that its maker had ended up 'with the whitewash bucket on his own head' (*Tribune*, 2 December 1960). This is the story of that film's director.

Notes

1 For film-makers see, for example, Burton, O'Sullivan and Wells (1997) and (2000), Chibnall (1998) and Aitken (2000). For television see Cook (1998).
2 *Conquest of the Planet of the Apes* (1972)
3 *For Better, For Worse* (1954), *Yield to the Night* (1956), *Ice Cold in Alex* (1958), *North West Frontier* (1959) and *Tiger Bay* (1959).
4 Sylvia Syms was nominated again in 1959 for Lee Thompson's *No Trees in the Street*.
5 Between 1947 and 1949 Reed released three films of exceptional quality: *Odd Man Out* (1947), *The Fallen Idol* (1948, USA: *The Lost Illusion*) and *The Third Man* (1949). For an examination of his career and the themes of his cinema see Moss (1987).
6 Lee Thompson was on the set of both Reed and Hitchcock films in the 1930s and was able to observe their directorial techniques at first hand.
7 His most blatant Hitchcock reference occurs in one of his last thrillers, *Murphy's Law* (1986), in which a man falsely accused of murder goes on the run to find the real killer, while handcuffed to a woman (*The 39 Steps*).
8 My interview with J. Lee Thompson took place over five hours in London on 10 April 1999 and was supplemented by subsequent phone conversations. All unreferenced quotations from the director are taken from this interview material and are introduced in the present tense (e.g. 'Lee Thompson recalls') to distinguish them from extracts from previously published interviews or articles written by Lee Thompson, which are introduced in the past tense.
9 In conversation with the author, Leicester, 21 February 2000.
10 Brian Clemens in an unpublished interview with Andrew Clay, Bedfordshire, 15 November 1999. Sturges excelled in action films like *The Magnificent Seven* (1960), *The Great Escape* (1963) and *The Eagle Has Landed* (1976), but showed in the Oscar-nominated *Bad Day at Black Rock* (1954) that he knew how to handle a suspense thriller.
11 Interview with the author, 31 January 1999. All subsequent remarks by Dick Best are taken from this source.
12 Interview with the author, 4 March 1999. All subsequent remarks by Gilbert Taylor are taken from this source, unless otherwise indicated.

13 *The Guns of Navarone.*

14 Landy, whose analyses of *The Yellow Balloon*, *The Weak and the Wicked*, *Yield to the Night* and *Woman in a Dressing Gown* constitute the most substantial writing on Lee Thompson's films, does make a token attempt to identify common themes among them. Hill considers *Dressing Gown* and *No Trees in the Street* as primarily Ted Willis-authored texts and unaccountably overlooks *Tiger Bay* entirely in his consideration of *Sex, Class and Realism in British Cinema 1956–1963.*

15 The significance of Lee Thompson's films in their representations of women has also been recognised by Viv Chadder (1999) and Melanie Williams, who is currently writing a PhD thesis on aspects of the director's cinema. Dearden and Relph's approach to the social-problem film is discussed in Medhurst (1984), Hill (1986: 68–96), Landy (1992: 462–82) and Burton, O'Sullivan and Wells (1997).

16 This attitude continues to puzzle Lee Thompson: 'I always liked to bring political viewpoints into my films and I was always strictly towards the Left ... I wasn't a member of the Communist Party or anything like that, but I had very left-wing views. But the other left-wingers in the business hated me. To this day I don't know why.'

From Jack of all trades ...

Our interest's on the dangerous edge of things.
The honest thief, the tender murderer,
The Superstitious atheist, demi-rep
That loves and saves her soul in new French books –
We watch while these in equilibrium keep
The giddy line midway.
(Robert Browning, *Bishop Blougram's Apology*,
Selected by Graham Greene (1971: 117)
as an epigraph for his own work)

John (Jack) Lee Thompson was born in Bristol just before the First World War (1 August 1914). His mother, Kathleen Lee Bowhill, was Scottish and his father, Peter Anthony Thompson, a Welshman from Penarth. Peter Thompson owned an engineering company and travelled widely, writing several books including one on his adventures in Siam (Thailand) called *Lotusland*, and a well-received critique of the management of the Great War, *Lions Led by Donkeys*. Kathleen Lee Thompson separated from her husband when Jack was still very young, taking her children first to Perthshire, where she herself had been brought up, and then to the south of England. Jack attended preparatory school at Seafield, Bexhill-on-Sea, before going to Dover College.

Throughout his boyhood Jack (or Lee, as he came to be known) was a keen fan of the silent screen. 'I used to love the cinema [he remembers] and I used to go many times a week even when I was very young. One of my favourite cinemas was a little one which is no longer there in Kensington High Street called the Royal Cinema. I used to go there with my brother.'

By the time J. Lee Thompson left school his ambition was to be an actor, and he joined Nottingham Repertory, making his debut in *Young Woodley* in 1931. Like his father, however, he also enjoyed writing, and before he was 19 had completed two plays for the stage. The first, *Murder Happens* was produced by his next repertory company, Croydon, and taken up by other provincial companies. His second play, *Double Error*, attracted the attention of the famous impresario Binky Beaumont who managed the H. M. Tennant company. Beaumont agreed to put the play on at the Fortune Theatre in London's West End, but did not want the author to take a leading acting role. Lee Thompson believes that his acceptance of Beaumont's terms revealed his lack of commitment to an acting career: 'From that moment on I realised I hadn't got the stuff of an actor in me if I hadn't got the guts to say: "You can't have the play unless you put me in the lead." My reneging on myself like that cured me of the acting bug. I never acted professionally again in the theatre.' But if *Double Error* effectively brought down the curtain on Lee Thompson's acting career, it gave him his first opportunity to explore dramatic themes and plot ideas which would become significant in his subsequent career as writer and director. The play concerns the blackmailing of a man who mistakenly believes he has committed murder, a plot he would return to (with variations) over the next twenty years. The deeper theme of entrapment and the desire to escape from a claustrophobic situation, however, would characterise Lee Thompson's work for much longer.

Double Error's West End run lasted 57 performances in the summer of 1935 but it had already been spotted by Walter C. Mycroft, the head of British International Pictures (BIP), who not only purchased the film rights, but offered Lee Thompson a job in Elstree's scriptwriting department on a basic wage of £5 per week. The salary may have been modest, but the chance to work in the British Hollywood was one that a starstruck and ambitious young man, still not out of his teens, could hardly pass up. By the time Lee Thompson joined BIP in 1934 its studios were producing a stream of light and glamorous musicals, operettas, romances and historical melodramas. The sort of thrillers in which Lee Thompson specialised were generally relegated to the status of supporting feature, but as a university of film making Elstree offered unique opportunities to learn the craft. A steady stream of gifted directors and technicians were beginning to arrive from the Continent, often as the result of the upheavals brought about by the rise of Fascism.

In the scriptwriting department, which boasted the indigenous talents of Frank Launder and Sidney Gilliat, J. Lee Thompson was paired with another young scenarist, Ruth Landon, to work on an adaptation of *Double Error* which was re-titled *The Price of Folly*.[1] The film was eventually made in 1936 by Walter Summers at Welwyn Studios, often used by BIP for the production of 'quota quickies' (Warren 1995: 180). Running just 52 minutes with a modest cast of jobbing actors, it is described by Quinlan (1984: 131) as 'a crudely radical crime story' and 'an inauspicious start to J. Lee Thompson's long association with the cinema'. In fact, his first 'association with the cinema' had been as an actor in Carol Reed's solo directorial debut *Midshipman Easy* (USA: *Men of the Sea*) made at Ealing Studios in the summer of 1935. Lee Thompson had landed a small (uncredited) part in the film through his friendship with its 16-year-old star Hughie Green.[2] It was a significant moment, not because it was Lee Thompson's only sortie into screen acting, but because it gave him a chance to observe the directorial technique of a film-maker who was to become one of his prime inspirations, Carol Reed.

At Elstree, Lee Thompson began to learn the craft of adaptation, working on Ivor Novello's Romany musical *Glamorous Night* (Brian Desmond Hurst, 1937) in a team of writers which also included Dudley Leslie who would become his collaborator on a number of stage plays.[3] Next came an adaptation (with Clifford Grey) of Stephen King-Hall and Ian Hay's nautical farce *The Middle Watch* (Thomas Bentley, 1939), a barnacled old tub which would later be refloated as *Girls at Sea* (Gilbert Gunn, 1958). *The Middle Watch* was notable for its star, the venerable musical comedy performer Jack Buchanan, whom Lee Thompson would later direct in *As Long As They're Happy* (1955). After writing for the stage, Lee Thompson relished 'the freedom to be able to move around' which the film medium allowed. He also benefited from Walter Mycroft's policy of moving apprentice screenwriters around the various jobs involved in film making in order to give them a wider appreciation of the craft. Two secondments were of particular significance to Lee Thompson's subsequent directorial career. The first was the cutting rooms at B&D Studios where he worked as an assistant to David Lean, then Elstree's star editor. 'It was Mycroft's idea that writers should learn more about the editing process because it would help in the writing of scripts', he recalls, and he could not have wished for a better teacher.[4] His apprenticeship in the cutting rooms helped Lee Thompson to develop both his visual acuity and his understanding of the technical requirements of his editors when he came to direct. Dick Best, who cut the majority of his early films, is full of praise for the way Lee Thompson's ability to visualise a sequence of shots made the editor's task a happy one. 'I can only say it was an absolute dream working for him, and satisfying.' To illustrate the director's capabilities, Best tells this anecdote about the shooting of *Ice Cold in Alex* (1958): 'One night [on location] Lee didn't appear for supper, and the next day the continuity girl asked him what the matter was, had he been ill? He said "Oh, I stayed in my caravan, I was running the film in my head." Now he could do that. He had a tremendous visual sense.' His visual memory was such that, on set, he had no need to consult a moviola to remind him of previous footage. He knew exactly how his shots would fit together even when they had been filmed weeks apart.

Lee Thompson's second significant assignment away from Elstree's scriptwriting department was as a 'dialogue coach'. It was, he admits 'a rather grandiose title for someone who is put on the [studio] floor and completely ignored by the actors'. The job boiled down to checking to see if the actors had memorised their lines, an intrusion which they would frequently resent. But, in spite of the occasional abusive comment, 'it was all good solid training, and I enjoyed every moment of it and learnt a great deal'. His cheerful acceptance of his thankless task undoubtedly had a lot to do with the film on which he worked, *Jamaica Inn* (1939), directed by the film-maker he most admired, Alfred Hitchcock, and made just prior to his departure to America. Most critics agree that *Jamaica Inn* is not one of Hitchcock's most artistically successful films and it was thoroughly detested by the author of the book on which it was based, Daphne du Maurier (Barr 1999: 241–2). Moreover, the production was a troubled one in which Hitchcock was 'denied the degree of control to which he had become thoroughly accustomed' (ibid.: 202), and was obliged to subordinate his auteurist inclinations to the needs of supplying a showcase for the film's star Charles Laughton (Harris and Lasky 1976: 75). For J. Lee Thompson, however, being on the studio floor with Hitchcock was an incredible learning experience.

> 'I saw the great master at work ... Of course I studied Hitchcock, all his films, very carefully, but it is one of my precious memories that I saw him closely at hand at work. He had everything plotted down to the last detail, so it wasn't a matter of actors coming on set and trying to improvise. He knew exactly what he wanted and, as he said himself: "I could shoot this from my office, I don't need to go down on the floor." Of course he did, but the theory was he worked every shot out, every move, and he didn't want any actors' suggestions.'

The Hitchcockian influence emerges clearly in the adaptation that Lee Thompson worked on immediately after his secondment to *Jamaica Inn. East of Piccadilly* (USA: *The Strangler*), produced by Walter Mycroft and directed by Harold Huth, was made at Welwyn Studios in 1939. Based on a story by Gordon Beckles serialised in the *Daily Express*, the screenplay was a collaboration between Lee Thompson and a fellow playwright at Elstree, Lesley Storm.[5] The plot is a product of the Edgar Wallace school of improbability, but its treatment is evidence of a certain decadence and sexual suggestiveness creeping into British crime thrillers just before the Second World War. Like predecessors such as *Murder in Soho* (Norman Lee, 1938, USA: *Murder in the Night*) and *A Window in London* (Herbert Mason, 1939, USA: *Lady in Distress*), the film trades on a prurient fascination with West End clubland and the lives of chorus girls and other female entertainers. It is a comedy drama that might have been described as 'sophisticated' in the days when that word, like 'American', was code for risqué and knowing. Certainly, *East of Piccadilly* pays passing homage to both the slick screwball comedy and the hard-boiled pulp thriller being exported from America at the time, but it tries to give them a distinctively British inflection as well as a London setting instantly recognisable to its potential transatlantic viewers. Its vision of a glittering Piccadilly Circus, swanky theatreland and sleazy Soho, peopled by supercilious policemen and dim-witted cockneys, and shrouded in fog, conforms faithfully to American expectations. But what makes the film more than simply a titillating glimpse beyond the façade of tourist London lies mainly in what it borrows from Hitchcock pictures of the period: notably, eccentric characterisation and an acute sense of its own theatricality.

Crime novelist Tamsie Green (Sebastian Shaw) and wise-cracking crime reporter Penny Sutton (Judy Campbell) team up to solve the murder of a Greek Street prostitute. They are told by a policeman that 'a lot of funny people live in Soho', and in the course of their investigations they come across a fair few of them, including an American millionaire leading a 'double life' (George Pughe) and a mad Shakespearian actor (George Hayes) who has a human skull as a candle holder and keeps effigies of his critics dangling from nooses behind a curtain in his rooms. He is a personification of the absurdity and melodramatic theatricality of contemporary crime fiction which the film constantly lampoons. 'This sort of thing can't happen', protests Penny as she feels the effects of a drink which she has already been jokingly told is doped. 'Bodies don't disappear, except in the thrillers you write', she tells Tamsie in an ironic reference to Lee Thompson's own stage plays. In an even more explicitly self-reflexive sequence, the pair actually go to the theatre to see a whodunit, and the film's detective inspector (a staple character of the murder mystery) points up the yawning plausibility gap between fiction and the reality of crime when he announces that he has 'learned to distrust the dramatic'.

Like the Hitchcock thrillers of the previous few years, *East of Piccadilly* reminds its audience that it is watching a theatrical construct with only a tenuous relationship to reality, but rewards the suspension of disbelief with shocks, humour and the kind of *frisson* afforded the male voyeur by a flash of stocking top.[6] This sort of knowing and conspiratorial address to the viewer would be a feature of J. Lee Thompson's directorial debut a decade later. Before that, however, there was a war to negotiate.

At the time war was declared, Lee Thompson was married with a son, Peter, and by the time his daughter, Lesley, was born in 1944 he had been serving in the Royal Air Force for four years. His roles as air-gunner and wireless operator were dangerous and stressful, but he still found the time and energy to write for the stage. He put his RAF experiences to creative use in *Thousands of Summers*, a play about the wives of fighter pilots written in difficult circumstances with Dudley Leslie. 'He was based in Sierra Leone in Africa and I was in the Air Force in England', Lee Thompson remembers, 'but we collaborated over this play'. The touring production starred Elizabeth Allan, a celebrated actress who had recently returned from Hollywood where she had made a number of films with MGM[7] but it failed to reach the West End stage. 'It was due to go into the Duchess Theatre', recalls Lee Thompson. 'Binky Beaumont was presenting it, but on tour they felt it didn't have enough success to bring it to London.' There was no lack of success, however, for the play Lee Thompson wrote in the same year (1942), *Murder Without Crime*, a reworking of ideas first developed in *Double Error*. It remained in the West End for two years and was also produced on Broadway. Two more plays followed in the immediate post-war years, but neither could match the popularity of *Murder Without Crime*. The first was a thriller called *The Curious Dr Robson*, which was tried out at the Q Theatre in 1946 with Peter Cushing in a starring role. The notices were encouraging, but the play was not transferred to the West End. The second play was *The Human Touch*, written with Dudley Leslie and produced at the Savoy Theatre by Firth Shepherd in 1949 after a successful try out at the Liverpool Playhouse. It starred Sophie Stewart (who had the distinction of appearing in the first televised play in 1936) and Alec Guinness, fresh from making *Kind Hearts and Coronets* (Robert Hamer, 1949). The play ran only a few months in the West End, for which Lee Thompson blames the change of director from John Furnell to the more in vogue Peter Ashmore:[8]

> 'The play was about the invention of chloroform. It was a deliberately rough play, a rough setting. And Peter Ashmore (who I greatly admired and who was a friend of mine), I regret to say, took all the guts out of the play, made it very soft and, as one critic said, "the anaesthetic, the chloroform swept from the stage, across the orchestra pit, and into the audience and put them all to sleep!"'

On his demobilisation from the RAF, J. Lee Thompson had returned to screenwriting, working on Associated British Picture Corporation (BIP's new identity) productions at Welwyn Studios.[9] One of his first projects was to work on the adaptation of Ernest Raymond's novel of low-life murder and false-imprisonment *For Them that Trespass* (1949). Lee Thompson's co-writer was William Douglas-Home, a well-connected ex-Etonian officer who had recently drawn on his experiences of imprisonment (for refusing to accept an order) to write a West End play, *Now Barabbas*.[10] Not one of the ABPC's in-house scriptwriters, Douglas-Home was presumably brought in to ensure authenticity in the film's prison scenes and, as a critic regarded as respectable by the Prison Commissioners (Nellis 1988: 10–11), because he might soothe the scenario's passage through the BBFC. The film's director, the celebrated documentarist Alberto Cavalcanti, had already encountered severe censorship difficulties with his film about an ex-serviceman caught up in the black market, *They Made Me a Fugitive* (1947, USA: *I Became a Criminal*) (Robertson 1999: 18–19).

The multiple authorship of *For Them That Trespass* makes it difficult to identify Lee Thompson's contribution. The themes of alienation, betrayal and unjust incarceration are close to the hearts of all the contributors, but there are many elements of the film that can be picked out as distinctive concerns for J. Lee Thompson. Most obviously, the film's central (but unsympathetic) character Christie Drew (Stephen Murray) is a playwright brought up in Sussex, like Lee Thompson himself. The film begins in the early 1930s when Christie (like Lee Thompson) is just beginning his writing career. Christie believes that if his writing is to have 'heart' he needs more 'experience of life'. He resolves to go out and look for the 'pain and power and passion' he has been sheltered from in his privileged upbringing. Like Graham Greene or Patrick Hamilton he wants to find the 'beauty' in the 'sordidness' of everyday life in the poorer parts of the city, and 'trespasses' in rough pubs and clubs, calling himself Kit Marlowe after another playwright fond of low dives.[11] The nightmare world of billowing smoke, cobbled streets and begging urchins which he discovers in the environs of *The Wild Swan* tavern looks to have changed little since Elizabethan times. Observation quickly gives way to participation, and Christie develops a relationship with 'sorry-for-nothing' Frankie (Rosalyn Boulter), the promiscuous girlfriend of a violent railwayman named Heal (Michael Laurence). Christie fools himself that he values Frankie's 'gay and generous' side but she is perceptive enough to realise that he is excited by 'rotten girls'. The lure of the transgressive and the enigma of another class is represented by the stone sphinx that stands outside Frankie's lodgings. When, in a scene that anticipates the crime of passion in *Tiger Bay*, Heal murders Frankie in a jealous rage, Christie proves to be more concerned with his reputation than the conviction of an innocent man. When suspicion for the murder falls on Frankie's other love Herb Logan (Richard Todd), an Irish ex-convict, Christie conceals his involvement in the case and allows Logan to be convicted.[12]

The film's centre of attention now shifts to Logan, a recognisably Lee Thompson anti-hero in a confining situation of entrapment, as well as a classic film noir fall guy. The scenes in the condemned cell at Pentonville as Logan plays board games with the warders, listens to the chiming of the clock and receives visits from the Governor, would have their unmistakable echo a decade later in *Yield to the Night*. Here, however, the reprieve does come, and Logan serves fifteen years' penal servitude while Christie has the first of a string of hit plays based on his research at *The Wild Swan*.[13] Unknowingly, Logan even lends out the published play in his role as prison librarian. Lee Thompson himself, of course, had already written two plays (*Double Error, Murder Without Crime*) in which the protagonist is made to suffer for a 'murder' he has not committed as a result of the playwright's ability to keep the full truth hidden.

Logan's ordeal continues even after his release when all but the most menial of work is denied him, but he eventually identifies the author Christopher Drew as Kit Marlowe when he recognises that one of the characters in his play, 'Sorry-for-nothing-Millie', is clearly based on their mutual lover Frankie. Christie is confronted by Logan when, like a personification of poverty, the ragged-trousered revenger gate-crashes the fashionable dramatist's dinner party. Christie, however, continues to resist involvement in Logan's attempt to clear his name, until, having survived an attempt on his life by the real murderer,[14] Logan tricks Christie into revealing to the police his role in Frankie's death and (unlike the conclusion of the more downbeat *They Made Me a Fugitive*) all comes to a happy and conventional closure.

Although the look and style of *For Them that Trespass* is un-mistakably Cavalcanti's, its self-reflexivity, colourful character-isations, ironic tone and unashamed wallowing in excess also link it to *East of Piccadilly* and *Murder Without Crime*. A writer on the fringes of the underworld, who exploits his knowledge of crime for profit; a discourse on authorial practice and ethics; overt and covert interpretations of a woman's murder; a man falsely accused of the crime – all these are motifs familiar from Lee Thompson's previous work. But, if Lee Thompson brought much that was relevant to *For Them that Trespass*, he also took away with him much he had learned from Cavalcanti. 'Working with him was a great experience', Lee Thompson feels. 'He was a very accomplished and clever director.' The influential Cavalcanti style would later be evident in films like *The Yellow Balloon* and *Yield to the Night*.

Themes and concerns that would later surface in films directed by J. Lee Thompson are apparent also in his first solo screenplay *No Place For Jennifer* (1949), which was filmed by Henry Cass, the director of the successful stage production of *Murder Without Crime*. After working on wartime documentaries, Cass had joined ABPC, directing the romantic *The Glass Mountain* (1948). *No Place For Jennifer* was based on the novel by Phyllis Hambledon and was part of a spate of films in the late 1940s which high-lighted 'youth' as a social problem. However, unlike the documen-tary *Children on Trial* (Jack Lee, 1946) or the dramas *Good Time*

Girl (David MacDonald, 1948) and *The Boys in Brown* (Montgomery Tully, 1949), it was not concerned with the threat posed by working-class juvenile delinquency, but rather with the consequences for the middle-class family of wartime disruption and the weakening of moral sanctions. The problem discussed here is the effect on children of their parents' divorce. By 1947, the divorce rate had climbed to 60,000 per year, ten times its pre-war level, prompting fears that the institution of marriage was facing a crisis (Hopkins 1964: 202–3).[15] Lee Thompson would not have found it difficult to empathise with 9-year old Jennifer (Janette Scott), the child of a broken marriage, as he had experienced a similar situation in his own childhood. He tells the story very much from Jennifer's point of view, while observing the conventions of the liberal social-problem film that suggest a range of opinions and approaches should be represented. This does not mean that the film fails to have a point of view. Divorce is clearly shown as an undesirable (if sometimes necessary) solution to relational problems, one which is likely to have severe consequences for a child's mental well-being and emotional and academic development. But, like the best of Lee Thompson's subsequent work, it largely avoids explicit moralising or the allocation of blame. There may be an impli-cation that Jennifer's mother (Beatrice Campbell) is irresponsible in leaving her husband for a composer (Guy Middleton) but her status as 'the guilty party' in the subsequent divorce proceedings is a legal more than a moral one. There is no suggestion that she does not love Jennifer, nor is a lack of love Jennifer's problem. The child's difficulties stem from a natural emotional immaturity which leaves her unable to cope with her divided loyalties to her parents and from her inability to impose her own normative expectations on her parents' relationship. This causes her to seek out the security represented by the film's model family, the Marshalls, and to covet the 'secret room' which the Marshall's son Martin (Brian Smith), an aspiring scientist, wants to use as a laboratory. She refers to it as his 'lovely safe little room', which is evidently a metaphor for the mental refuge she craves.

As the tug-of-love over Jennifer intensifies, her academic performance deteriorates, and her head teacher warns that she has become 'silent, secretive and nervy', reminding Jennifer's parents, and the audience, that 'the security of home' is 'a child's whole world'. No child, she advises, wants two homes. When Jennifer learns that her father's new wife is pregnant, she moves closer to a breakdown; she is referred to a child psychology clinic where children construct physical models of their experiential world. Jennifer's is prowled by the wild animals that represent her anxieties. 'We all have these wild animal feelings', she is reassured, 'especially when we are tugged two ways at once, like you are ... But you've been making friends with your wild animal feelings, so they need not frighten you any more'. Eventually she responds to the treatment and eliminates the tiger from her model world, leaving it 'a happy sort of place'. Although it borders on the parodic, the work of the psychologists is endorsed by Lee Thompson's script, as, broadly, is the view expressed by one doctor: 'It's the parents who ought to be in the clinics, not the children.'

The build up of tension between Jennifer's parents eventually comes to a head when her mother's attempts to take custody of her child result in her being summonsed for contempt of court. Jennifer is sickened to see her mother's humiliation in court and flees the building, finding herself alone on the dark streets of London. Henry Cass shoots the sequences which follow in expressionist style, using dramatic lighting contrasts and subjective camera angles to indicate the fear and alienation Jennifer experiences. Lee Thompson would use similar techniques in *The Yellow Balloon* when its diminutive protagonist Frankie is on the run, pursued by a killer. Both children, in fact, find the London Underground a place of terror, and the city itself is constructed, in typical noir fashion, as a shadowy jungle full of exploiters. This, it seems, is the natural habitat of the tiger in Jennifer's model. Having been conned out of her money and chased by a paedophile, Jennifer reaches the sanctuary of the Marshalls' house where she hides in her 'secret room' and contemplates suicide. Her distress is such that her parents finally recognise that 'between us, we've torn Jenny to pieces', and they agree to her staying with the harmonious Marshall family where she feels happy and secure.

No Place For Jennifer was the first of a number of studies of childhood trauma by J. Lee Thompson. Children under threat and coping with their fears can be found in *The Yellow Balloon, Tiger Bay, North West Frontier* and *Cape Fear*. Although Jennifer is a child, her predicament is typical of so many other Lee Thompson protagonists: trapped in adversity and desperately seeking escape. In this case, her perilous flight from a situation she cannot tolerate returns her to a womb-like haven of security, the secret room. For the protagonists who follow her, the haven will take different forms; but, be it the sea, the night or even a glass of ice-cold beer, its meaning will be much the same.

There is another protagonist *in extremis* and another haven in *Last Holiday* (1950), the last film Lee Thompson helped to script before he began his directorial career. The film is usually attributed solely to the celebrated author who devised and produced it, J. B. Priestley,[16] but in fact he was closely assisted by Lee Thompson. The film's director Henry Cass, having just filmed a Lee Thompson script, probably suggested that he would be the ideal writer to help realise the cinematic potential of Priestley's work.[17] Lee Thompson jumped at the opportunity to collaborate with an author for whom he had enormous admiration:

'I went down to the Isle of Wight where J. B. Priestley lived in those days, and spent about six weeks down there with him doing the script. I thought it was an excellent, tight, little film. It was a tremendous experience for me to work with Priestley. He didn't have much idea of film, and it was so interesting working with him because he was such a master of dialogue and of character, but it was difficult to get him to see the filmic sense of a scene, if you know what I mean. He was always more or less thinking in stage terms. But, of course, he was in his own way a genius. To sit with him and watch him map out a scene in dialogue was for me a fantastic experience because I had written plays – including West End plays – myself and I always had to struggle over dialogue – to re-write it and hack away at it just to get what I considered a competent stage performance from it. But here was this man who would sit down and tackle a scene, and he would write it in three or four different ways. I found this very depressing (*laughs*), that he had such a wonderful brain for dialogue and the gift of being able to put speakable words in the mouths of actors ... But, of course, it did have the feel sometimes of a stage play, because that was the way he wrote. My only real contribution to that film was an effort to keep it moving filmically and just to put in what scenes I could with some movement to them, and not always interiors ... I learnt so much from him. The main thing I learnt was if you're not happy with a scene don't hack away at it too long, just put a pencil through the whole scene and start again from a different angle. It was a lesson I cherished.'

This lengthy extract from interview material not only sheds light on the way *Last Holiday* was constructed, and on Priestley's writing method, but illuminates what Lee Thompson felt were his own strengths and weaknesses as a playwright and scenarist. It shows, too, his continuing willingness to learn from the finest craftsmen in his field. A few years later he would be able to pay back his debt to Priestley by producing and directing an adaptation of his famous play *The Good Companions*.

Last Holiday is the story of George Bird (Alec Guinness), a solitary salesman from the north of England who is told he has only a few weeks to live. He decides to spend them by the seaside. With little time left to make friends and contribute to the community, he sets about breaking down the British reserve he encounters at his hotel. When the staff of the hotel go on strike he inspires a spirit of self-help and co-operation among the other guests, bringing the ideals of the Labour Movement to middle-class individuals who discover the benefits of 'mucking-in' together. The irony added by the rather unsatisfactory twist ending – whereby George is pronounced well and then dies in a car accident – does little to undermine George's status as a martyr whose mission has been to rekindle the flames of wartime community feeling from the ashes of austerity Britain.

Unlike *No Place For Jennifer*, which had been a considerable box office success, *Last Holiday* fared badly with the critics and struggled to find an audience. Lee Thompson, however, hardly had time to notice, because the chance he had been preparing for since he had entered film making fifteen years earlier had come. He had always wanted to direct, and the opportunity came when he received an offer from Hollywood for the film rights to his play *Murder Without Crime*. Robert Clark, the shrewd head of ABPC's studios, reacted quickly. He had attended the first night of the play and realised that it was a redrafting of *Double Error* to which ABPC already owned the rights. Rather than allow the property to go overseas he offered Lee Thompson a directing contract and a bonus payment (reputedly £8,000) for the screenplay of *Murder Without Crime*. But before Lee Thompson could step onto the floor of Welwyn Studios, he was faced with a dispute that nearly shut down the whole operation:

> 'There was an effort to stop me directing because I wasn't a member of the ACT [Association of Cinematograph Technicians]. It came down to a battle where Robert Clark actually said he would close Welwyn Studios unless I was allowed to direct the film because, for some reason, the ACT wouldn't allow me to become a member. There were certain people who didn't want new directors to start up. One of these people was a very famous director himself, and a very fine one, Thorold Dickinson ... but for some reason he led the anti-Lee Thompson brigade. I don't know why – I mean, we'd never even met. It caused quite a sensation at the time, and Robert Clark stood by his threat that he'd close down Welwyn Studios for production if he wasn't allowed to choose his own director. So they gave me my membership ticket in the ACT and I went on to direct.'

Robert Clark's hard line was made easier by his knowledge that the studios at Welwyn were to be sold off in any case, and industry speculation about the concentration of production at Elstree probably fuelled ACT opposition to Clark's new boy. In any case, *Murder Without Crime* was one of Welwyn's last productions.[18] Lee Thompson still vividly recalls the terror of taking his first directing steps:

> 'It's really a very frightening thing to make your first film. I remember being full of confidence that I would be able to direct, and I would have no fears, but on that first morning of walking on the floor where everyone knows this is your first film, and you're on your own, and everybody is really wanting you to show your ignorance – especially when there was this anti-new director feeling which was around in those days – it really was one of my

most horrifying experiences. You know, all the crew is waiting for you, now where do you put the camera? I'd worked it all out like Hitchcock used to do. Hitchcock never deviated from his plan, and I would draw little sketches which only I could decipher on what I was going to shoot and how I would shoot it – a form of story-boarding which nobody else could understand, because I'm not an artist, I don't draw beautiful pictures. But this got me through. I knew exactly, shot for shot, what I was going to do, and I kept that method for quite a long time, until I felt it was hampering me.'

Notes

1 Lee Thompson joined BIP's scriptwriting department shortly before Launder and Gilliat were instrumental in the foundation of the Screen-writers' Association (1937). The SWA sought to improve the institutional position of scenarists and establish its members as what Sue Harper (1994:125) describes as 'a kind of aristocracy of labour'.

2 It was indeed the same Hughie Green who went on to become a television personality and hosted the (in)famous talent show *Opportunity Knocks*.

3 After graduating from Oxford, Dudley Leslie pursued a career in journalism before joining BIP as a screenwriter about the same time as J. Lee Thompson. He contributed to the screenplays of *Ourselves Alone* (Brian Desmond Hurst, 1936, USA: *River of Unrest*), *Living Dangerously* (Herbert Brenon, 1936), *The Tenth Man* (Brian Desmond Hurst, 1936), *Sensation* (Brian Desmond Hurst, 1936), *The Housemaster* (Herbert Brenon 1938), *Black Limelight* (Paul Stein, 1938), *Jane Steps Out* (Paul Stein, 1938), and wrote (adapted) *The Outsider* (Paul Stein, 1939) and *Hell's Cargo* (Harold Huth, 1939, USA: *Dangerous Cargo*). During the Second World War he was the Royal Navy Film Section's officer in charge of production, and on demobilisation he returned to Elstree before specialising in television scriptwriting.

4 Lean himself acknowledged the value of experiencing a number of film-making roles, a possibility restricted by the spread of trades-unionism in the film industry: 'The greatest advantage to those times, which was also the greatest disadvantage, was, of course, there were no unions ... I went around every department, and people laugh when I say I was a one-time wardrobe mistress' (Silverman 1992: 25–6)

5 Scottish-born Lesley Storm was one of a number of female writers with whom Lee Thompson collaborated in the first twenty years of his career. She had a number of her plays filmed, including *Great Day* (Lance Comfort, 1945), *Tonight and Every Night* (Victor Saville, 1945; based on *Heart of a City*) and *Personal Affair* (Anthony Pelissier, 1953; based on *The Day's Mischief*).

6 Like *The 39 Steps* (Alfred Hitchcock, 1935), the film tacitly acknowledges more secret forms of fetishism with the inclusion of a 'bondage' sequence.

7 Elizabeth Allan appeared in *David Copperfield* (George Cukor, 1935) and *A Tale of Two Cities* (Jack Conway, 1935). British screen acting credits included Cavalcanti's *Went the Day Well?* (1942).

8 Firth Shepherd's (alleged) affair with Furnell's wife, Coral Browne was undoubtedly a factor in the decision to replace Furnell with Ashmore.

9 Having been requisitioned as the Royal Army Ordnance Corps depot during the war years, the BIP/ABPC studios at Elstree did not re-open until September 1948. Lee Thompson, however, stayed with Welwyn productions until the studios were sold to a tobacco company in 1951.

10 *Now Barabbas* ran in London, first at Boltons Theatre, Kensington, and then at the Vaudeville Theatre between February and July 1947 (Nellis 1988). Accounts of its writing and staging are given in Douglas-Home (1954: 199–200 and 1979: 63–70). The play was filmed in 1949 by Gordon Parry.

11 In his biography of Patrick Hamilton, Sean French (1993: 1–2) quotes an essay written by Cyril Connolly (1985: 101) in 1935 which discusses the paucity of experience on which middle-class writers were able to draw in the period:

> English life is on the whole without adventure or variety, 90 per cent of English authors come from the mandarin class, the experiences from which both sexes can draw are limited to three or four – a peaceful childhood, a public school education, a university, a few years in London or the provinces in which to get a job, a wife, a house, and some children. Material for one book, perhaps, which publishers and the need to earn one's living will drag out to three or four. A rigorous class system blankets down all attempts to enlarge these barriers. The English mandarin simply can't get at pugilists, gangsters, speakeasies, negroes, and even if he should he would find them absolutely without the force and colour of the American equivalent.

12 Driven by guilt, he does anonymously try to secure Logan's reprieve and release.

13 Lee Thompson's script cannot resist a dig at the critics: when one reviewer announces 'I'm going to tell the public it's a first class play', another quips: 'Then it's bound to be a flop.'

14 Again, this scene of the innocent attacked in a railway tunnel by a killer will reappear in J. Lee Thompson's later film *The Yellow Balloon*.

15 A Royal Commission on Marriage and Divorce was eventually appointed in 1951. It offered few concrete proposals beyond those aimed at securing the position of children of the marriage before allowing a decree absolute.

16 Robert Murphy (1992: 217), for example, asserts that *Last Holiday* was 'the first film script he [Priestley] wrote single-handedly'.

17 The film's star Alec Guinness was, of course, also familiar with Lee Thompson's work, having just appeared on stage in *The Human Touch*.

18 The other two were *Talk of a Million* (John Paddy Carstairs, 1951, USA: *You Can't Beat the Irish*) and *The Franchise Affair* (Lawrence Huntington, 1950) (see Warren 1995: 182).

Murder Without Crime (1951)

> So many stories, some curious, all true, and most infinitely trivial
> – blacks and whites, shake 'em all together and see what comes
> out. Toss the coin, spin the wheel. Take off the lid. Slit open the pie
> crust ... (The Narrator, *Murder Without Crime*)

Based closely on his own successful stage play, Lee Thompson's
Murder Without Crime is a confident but largely unadventurous
first step in film making. Rather than anticipating the taut,
socially-concerned, realism which would become a trademark of
the director's best films, this is another story of death in Soho
which looks back to the rarefied hokum of earlier theatre work and
adaptations like *East of Piccadilly*. Again, the protagonist is a
writer, Stephen (Derek Farr), living in central London. This time
he has a fractious marriage and a dandified landlord, Matthew
(Dennis Price), who is a few degrees saner but no less malicious
than Mark Struberg, the deranged actor in *East of Piccadilly*. When
one of their quarrels drives his wife Jan (Patricia Plunkett) to
spend the night at an hotel, Stephen picks up a good-time girl,
Grena (Joan Dowling), in a nightclub. When they return to his
apartment, Stephen gets cold feet, provoking a row with Grena
and a tussle, which results in her receiving an apparently fatal
blow to the head. A visit from his landlord and his imminent
reconciliation with his wife panics Stephen into hiding Grena's
body in a convenient ottoman chest in his living room. It is a

familiar J. Lee Thompson scenario of entrapment and the frantic search for a means of escape.

What follows is largely a cat-and-mouse game between the dazed-and-confused Stephen and his cynical, blackmailing landlord who has discovered the secret of the ottoman. When he can stand Matthew's goading no longer, the accidental 'killer' prepares a suicide cocktail – an overdose of the drug which he has confiscated from the reckless Grena. But Matthew, suspicious that his blackmail victim might be desperate enough to poison him, switches glasses and downs the deadly draught. In a final twist, the dying Matthew reveals that there is no body in the ottoman. Grena had merely been knocked unconscious and, on recovery, had been helped out of the apartment by Matthew while Stephen had been away attempting to cover his tracks. The landlord's malevolent interventions had all been 'a terrible joke' that backfired with fatal consequences.

The film itself is rather better than 'a terrible joke', but never takes itself too seriously. For an apprentice piece it is surprisingly knowing and self-reflexive, as if Lee Thompson, realising that the theatrical origins of his text could never be disguised, decided to turn up the histrionics to just short of parodic excess. If it were only the performances that were ostentatious, one might suspect that the rookie director was struggling to make the transition from stage to screen acting, but everything in the concoction seems consciously over-cooked, from the florid dialogue to Don Ashton's marvellously baroque sets. The film's characters continually draw attention to their own theatricality: 'stop dramatising yourself' Stephen orders Grena, who unsheathes an ornamental dagger like a silent-movie vamp before collapsing decoratively onto the carpet like a cover-girl from a cheap crime novelette. On a number of occasions, Stephen is likened to a 'waxwork', anticipating the placement of his effigy in 'the Chamber of Horrors' where murder is recreated as a theatrical tableau. But, most of all, it is the cash-strapped sybarite Matthew, played with the supercilious disdain that was Dennis Price's forte, that embodies the film's drive for excess. A brother-in-acid to Waldo Lydecker of *Laura* (Otto Preminger, 1944) and coded as gay by his clothing, demeanour and furnishings, he stalks the capacious rooms of his town house in an exaggerated state of ennui, clad in bow-tie and brocade dressing gown. His censor-pacifying expression of frustrated desire for Stephen's wife does little to dispel the impression of campness. His conversation is loaded with sonorous phrases. He describes champagne as 'the drink for the madly gay', observes of the ottoman coffin 'to think, when we are all turned to dust this monstrosity will still be standing', and looks towards the time when 'my degradation will be complete'. But his statements also emphasise the absurdity of the proceedings and expose their trading in the clichés of the murder mystery. He plays 'Sherlock Holmes', looks for 'a clue', reads a book titled *Crime and its Consequences* and talks of 'the perfect murder' and a corpse that 'has to be disposed of'. On seeing the trunk into which Stephen (true to the conventions of British body disposal) plans to transfer Grena's body, Matthew exclaims: 'The proverbial trunk! How grim it looks, all ready to receive the mangled remains.' Although there is a perfunctory attempt to explain Matthew's lugubriousness as a consequence of his fear of his father,[1] he is never intended to be 'real'. Like the other roles in this drama, he is a stock character, in this instance a standard exotic, cultivated in the hothouse of his rococo domicile, and exuding about as much authenticity as an ormolu telephone.[2]

Lee Thompson clearly signposts *Murder Without Crime* as a tall story, a macabre entertainment with enough *Grand Guignol* to grip the spectators in the stalls and enough ironic self-awareness to please the more intellectual patrons in the circle. He even supplies a narrator – an American barfly with a 'perverted vein of impish humour', idling away an hour before his plane leaves for home – whose world-weary tones and ready use of hyperbole echo Matthew's. 'Oh, I know you've heard it all before, seen it all too', he acknowledges before beginning his tale of 'someone who is for a calamitous, climactic night, someone whose waxen image is destined to grace – or is it disgrace? – the Chamber of Horrors', adding that 'such are the perils of destiny'. His voice-over is an unmistakable echo of the narrator who opens the British version of *The Third Man* – sardonic and anonymous, an intriguing character whom we never meet.[3] Both narrators introduce a protagonist who is naive, vulnerable and out of his depth, and at the same time distance him from the audience. In this case, the film's prologue goes even further, systematically eliminating any hint of naturalism as the characters are introduced as *dramatis personae* rather than flesh-and-blood people.[4]

Of course, the Yankie narrator, like the noir touches in Bill McLeod's cinematography,[5] has the primary function of making a thinly disguised London stage play palatable to American cinema audiences, but he helps to keep the film's tongue wedged in its cheek. By his own admission, Lee Thompson 'may have exaggerated things a little', but the result stays just short of parody, offering an affectionate, post-Patrick-Hamilton pastiche of the tropes and conventions of the mystery thriller. Its campness is more Alfred Hitchcock than Frankie Howerd, aimed at provoking the sophisticated smile rather than the brash belly laugh. It strives to be a chic, *à la mode* version of a tried-and-tested genre with more than a nod to American film noir in its canted camera angles, tortured protagonists and nocturnal urban setting – a West End take on *The Woman in the Window* (Fritz Lang, 1944), complete with unwanted corpse. Lee Thompson describes it as 'a sort of Gothic melodrama' which 'wasn't meant to be taken too seriously'. He had hoped that 'the sense of humour of those situations would come across on film', but confesses that he was 'a little disappointed in the final result', not least because of the difficulties in treating the subject cinematically:

> 'I didn't open it up. It was, if you like, very near a photographed stage play, although I like to feel that my angles and the way I shot it – learning from the great master Hitchcock – ... was the only way to make that film. It was about a body in an ottoman, like *Rope*, yes, very much. I owe a lot to *Rope*, there's no doubt about that. Therefore it was confined and you couldn't start going to the south of France or Italy in a tight little stage play like this. If I made it again today, I'd make it even tighter. I'd really get a claustrophobic feeling to it. But this was my first film and it gave me confidence.'

Although he willingly shoulders the blame for the deficiencies of *Murder Without Crime*, he believes that Dennis Price in the pivotal role 'did not quite capture ... the evil comedy that was intended'. This, he believes, was brilliantly achieved by Raymond Lovell, the actor who had played Matthew in the play's West End run:

> 'He used to get laughs with practically every line. He never forgave me for not playing [i.e. casting] him in the film, and I mean that literally – he would never speak to me again, and felt that I had done a very bad thing in casting Dennis Price instead of himself. Good as Dennis Price was – and he became a great and dear friend of mine – I must admit that I made a grievous mistake in not playing Raymond Lovell in his original part. On the other hand, Robert Clark naturally wanted Dennis Price, because he was then a lead actor of British films.'

Price, fresh from his performance in *Kind Hearts and Coronets* (Robert Hamer, 1949), certainly does a creditable job and, with Patricia Plunkett, takes the acting honours. Derek Farr struggles to find the right pitch of hysteria, perhaps because Lee Thompson was never certain how the part should be played. Farr, in any case, is a little too old for the role, just as he had been when he played the young killer in *Bond Street* (Gordon Parry, 1947). At 38, he was a few years older than Dennis Price who was playing the patriarchal figure of the house. Lee Thompson, however, had very little control over the casting of Farr and Joan Dowling, another ABCP contract played who he felt was 'wrong for the part' (of the good-time girl): 'Derek Farr was a very charming person but, I have to say, he was rather a dull British actor. But he was under contract to ABC at the time and so we used him ... I had my arm twisted to use ABC contract stars. It was my first film. I hadn't got the power to say no.' Farr's character Stephen, however, allows Lee Thompson to satirise authors in much the same way he had done in *East of Piccadilly* and *For Them that Trespass*, but with increased bitterness.

Authors are described by Matthew as 'a positive epidemic, a plague' and Stephen justifies his own moodiness as a trait of his profession. His wife calls him 'a self-centred little weakling' and claims he has not written a word in years, and, by his own admission, he is able only to 'dish up a transparent hoax'. The phrase is an important one both because it hints at the attitude of the film's author towards his creation and because it registers a failure of the writer's imagination to move beyond the standard conventions of theatrical storytelling. The value of imagination to Lee Thompson is evident, ironically, in the way it is dismissed by his characters. Unable himself even to foresee the consequences of his actions, Stephen castigates his wife for having 'too much imagination' which he calls a 'millstone around her neck'. But it is the misanthropic Matthew who comes closest to voicing the credo which Lee Thompson would henceforth set out to challenge: 'I can think of no worse disease than imagination except, perhaps, conscience.' For the remainder of his time in the British film industry, imagination and conscience would be hallmarks of Lee Thompson's cinema.

Murder Without Crime created only the smallest of stirs in the piranha pool of film criticism when it began its London run at the Tivoli and Astoria cinemas early in 1951. Most critics found it a little too wordy and theatrical for their taste, but confessed to finding some entertainment value in the jaunty excesses of the production. The *Daily Mail* (1 February 1951) thought it a 'reasonably slick thriller when it stops being pseudo American', while the *Evening News* (1 February 1951) felt that, although it was a 'modest production, it might have enough to satisfy the seeker after thrills and mystery'. The *Star* (2 February 1951) was perceptive enough to realise that 'Mr Lee Thompson' did not intend the film 'to be taken very seriously', commenting that 'on its own highly theatrical level it is good fun'. *The Times* (5 February 1951) took rather more convincing that the transition from stage play to movie had been adequately accomplished, regretting that 'Mr Lee Thompson knows Mr Hitchcock's tricks, but not the secrets which so often makes them successful'.

Lee Thompson's debut box (or ottoman) of tricks went out on the ABC circuit as a double bill with an American film about a GI finding romance in Europe, *Four Days Leave* (Leopold Lindberg, 1950). Any chance of a romance that *Murder Without Crime* might have had with American audiences, however, was effectively nipped in the bud on St Valentine's Day 1951 when the influential trade paper *Variety* declared the film 'not good enough for the US market'.

The method

Murder Without Crime was a well-enough crafted film, but its mannered performances, studied theatricality, and restricted *mise-en-scène* gave few clues about the capabilities of its director once he was allowed to stretch his legs. Lee Thompson's second directorial outing, *The Yellow Balloon*, would reveal a good deal more of his potential. Crucial for realising this potential was the assembly of a creative team sympathetic to the director's aims and working practices. The team that came together for *The Yellow Balloon* would be a key component of Lee Thompson's success at Associated British over the next six years. Three figures were to be of particular significance: Gilbert Taylor, the innovative director of photography, then in the early stages of an illustrious career which would eventually see him immortalised as the man who photographed *Star Wars* (George Lucas, 1976), Richard Best, an editor of consummate skill who had worked on some early films of the Boulting Brothers and would cut his last film for Lee Thompson (*The Most Dangerous Man in the World*) as late as 1969; and Robert Jones, a gifted art director, respected for the meticulousness of his research and his ability to turn tiny budgets into impressive but practical sets. These three men would be crucial in the visualisation of Lee Thompson's concepts and constituted, as he puts it, 'a very comfortable and talented team'. Director of photography, Gilbert Taylor, recalls how closely knit the team was:

> 'We didn't make films like they do today with directors and cameramen as strangers. We were into every nut and bolt and paper on the wall and everything else. Lee took a big interest in the way I was going to treat things and the art director was always in our laps – not only that but wardrobe and every mortal thing ...'.

The team's members may have been comfortable with one another, but there was nothing comfortable about the level of security of Lee Thompson's career as he struggled to establish himself as a director. The hostility of other film-makers keen to maintain a 'closed shop', a debut feature which had attracted little attention and an employer with a reputation for ruthlessness – all placed him in a vulnerable position. The signs and consequences of stress were evident to his new director of photography Gilbert Taylor:

> 'Lee had these little idiosyncrasies, or whatever you like to call them, when I first worked with him, when he came out of the writing department. You know, he was very unsure of the situation because ABPC were a lethal mob to work for, and if you did anything wrong at all you'd be out, you see. So he did have these funny little things from the start.'

Gil Taylor prefers to obscure the issue in euphemism, but the 'idiosyncrasies' and 'funny little things' refer to the substance use and abuse which helped Lee Thompson manage the demands of his profession. The heavy consumption of alcohol has, of course, long been endemic among actors and writers. By the early post-war years, alcohol was being supplemented by the use of amphetamines, often first encountered in the services as a way of resisting combat fatigue. Charles Drazin's book on the making of *The Third Man* indicates that by 1948 the use of benzedrine among the film making community was quite widespread, extending from the producer David Selznick to director Carol Reed and his crew on location in Vienna (Drazin 1999: 22–3 and 56). Making movies in the studio system was a high-stress activity that needed to be conducted at pace to strict schedules. A production company like Associated British ('a very mean mob', in Gil Taylor's words) judged their directors on their efficiency almost as much as their artistic ability and, from the outset, Lee Thompson developed methods of delivering his product at speed.[6] Chemicals may well have played a part in this, but meticulous preparation was the key, as Gil Taylor explains:

> 'You see, Lee was a very unusual director. I don't think there was another director in the country who worked on his scripts the way that Lee did, and worked out the way he was going to do whole sequences, so that we used to average about 26 set-ups a day ... We started at half-past-eight in the morning and finished at twenty-past-five on a five-day week, and an enormous amount of work was done in a day because we did have big crews.'[7]

Lenses would be discussed and camera angles negotiated between the two men, with Lee Thompson making frequent use of the viewfinder.[8] In the same way, 'he would work closely with his production designer on the structure of the sets', remembers his editor Dick Best,

> 'and he would discuss every detail of style, but also how he was going to shoot it so that the set absolutely fitted his idea of angles. He never went on to the set and said: "Right, what shall we do today, boys?" In his head it was all planned. He would be deep in his script and He would have discussed everything with the cameraman and the designer, and the designer would have added his own ideas.'

When it came to the editing process, however, Best was allowed more freedom:

> 'In those days the director didn't come into the cutting room, unless you asked them, or they came in socially when they had finished shooting; or if there was a hold-up on the set they might wander over and have a little chat. But they didn't come and look at the moviola and you didn't cut under their direction. You cut what you saw in the rushes. This was the way it worked. You were the editor and you edited it. ... You chose from the selection of shots in the coverage that you thought were the best to get over the dramatic impact ... You chose between alternative camera angles, but Lee, of course, chose which take he wanted when we saw the rushes. And there were some dialogue scenes where Lee, or any director, would say: "I want you to use that line of dialogue from take four, and use take three for the rest of it." I would look at the rushes twice, because the producer usually saw them at lunchtime and Lee saw them with the unit after shooting at half-past-five. When they were all numbered, logged and broken down into their separate shots, I would start to cut them – usually the day after rushes had been viewed. Then I would usually show my complete cut to Lee and the producer within three days of the end of shooting. They would give notes on changes, and many would relate to tightening, as it would obviously be a long cut.
> There would be other ideas, such as: "I think that line should be in close up" or "Have you got a bit of reaction to go in there which would tighten things up?", and you would get quite a copious

> number of small notes ... With Lee's films, mostly, the actual
> selection of coverage was not altered dramatically, if at all, and
> probably only altered in small detail after he saw it. Then people
> have ideas, right up to dubbing, really, about things to do, but I
> would hope that 75 per cent of what I did is there.'

Although the cutting room remained sacrosanct, directors of Lee
Thompson's generation had more influence over the final cut of a
picture than their predecessors. Producers and the studio head
retained the final authority, but directors' voices were louder in
the editing process than, for instance, Carol Reed's had been when
he made films for Gainsborough before the war. 'It was such a
different business then', Reed once recalled. 'The chief editor at
the studios was inclined to resent directors. Very often I wasn't
even invited to see the editing' (quoted in Wapshott 1990: 115) For
Reed, as for Lee Thompson, the director was the vital link between
the author or screenwriter and the editor.

The practices described above constitute the method developed
by the group of film-makers which first assembled for *The Yellow
Balloon* and would stay together for a number of Elstree productions which followed. It is time now to examine the group's first
product, not simply in terms of its technical proficiency, but also
in the context of the emergent concerns and dominant discourses
of British society under a new Conservative government.

The Yellow Balloon (1953)

> It is time the community decided to sanitise itself. For if we do not
> root out this moral rot it will bring us down as inevitably as it has
> brought down every nation in history that became affected by it.
> (Editorial, *Sunday Express*, 25 October 1953)

There was nothing particularly original about the concept of *The
Yellow Balloon*, which came from Lee Thompson's fellow toiler in
the script department at Associated British, Anne Burnaby.[9] The
idea of a boy who witnesses a killing being pursued by criminals
had recently been effectively realised in RKO's *The Window* (Ted
Tetzlaff, 1949) and Independent Artists was already working on a

tale about a boy on the run with a spiv (*Hunted*, Charles Crichton, 1952). In fact, the opening of *The Yellow Balloon* was to stray uncomfortably close to Crichton's film. Both have a child running through the streets of London to a bomb site where he encounters a stranger in a trenchcoat beside a dead body. Each boy is duped into believing that he has committed a crime, with the intention of blackmailing him. Although the parallels between the two films' premisses are striking, the similarities recede as the narratives unfold. Crichton's intentions are to offer a sustained character study of a fugitive, to explore the contradictions between the constraints of moral conscience and the demands of self-preservation, and to show the redeeming quality of unselfish love.[10] His focus is on the adult killer (Dirk Bogarde) rather than his young companion (Jon Whitely). Lee Thompson, on the other hand, sets out to make a suspense thriller in which we are invited to empathise with a child in peril. As *The Yellow Balloon*'s publicity put it: 'Frankie was just a boy ... could have been anybody's boy ... your boy, perhaps. But fate and a yellow balloon threw him into the clutches of a murderer ... sent him running for his life tormented with fear ... You'll live with him every moment of heart-breaking panic ... But above all, you'll ache to join in the race to save him.'[11] Working again with the producer of his previous film, Victor Skutezky,[12] and this time drawing on the expertise of casting director John Redway,[13] Lee Thompson assembled an outstanding cast for *The Yellow Balloon*. It was headed by 13-year-old Andrew Ray (Frankie), son of successful radio comedian Ted Ray, and already himself an audience favourite after his performance in *The Mudlark* (Jean Negulesco, 1950). For Frankie's parents Emily and Ted, Lee Thompson had the services of Kathleen Ryan, who had been discovered by Carol Reed for *Odd Man Out* (1947) and was recently returned from Hollywood after working on Cy Endfield's anti-McCarthyist *The Sound of Fury* (1951), and Kenneth More, who was about to make his breakthrough to stardom in *Genevieve* (Henry Cornelius, 1953). American interest was represented by the casting of William Sylvester as the spiv, Len,[14] and box-office potential was further boosted by the presence of the well-known ENSA performer Hy Hazell as Mary, a kind-hearted woman of 'questionable virtue' who befriends Frankie.

The Yellow Balloon is a suspense melodrama with more than a few pretensions to realism and social comment. In a rare sustained analysis of the film, Marcia Landy has characterised it as a piece which explores the 'repressive' nature of family life and the ambivalent and exploitative attitudes of adults towards children (Landy 1991: 450–2). She presents a highly schematic reading in which Frankie's moral development is trapped in a vice whose jaws are constituted by 'the repressive agents of the family linked to law and religion' and 'the equally repressive forces of criminality'. It could hardly be disputed that criminality is presented as a disruptive force which might be encountered at any time in almost any situation, but much more contentious is Landy's identification of the nuclear family as 'a site of conflict and contradiction'. To describe *The Yellow Balloon* as 'a critique of family life (451) makes it sound like a libertarian tract by R. D. Laing, when its intention seems to be to expose the vulnerability of the post-war family to threats from the increasingly lawless environment beyond its protective boundaries. Hardly the disciplinary ogres Landy depicts, Frankie's parents are a well-meaning and responsible couple who are attempting to raise their son in a rule-governed but loving and secure household. Their resort to physical punishment comes only when the cohesion of familial bonds is threatened by a severe violation of trust (Frankie's theft of the family's holiday savings). Ted Palmer's amiable nature is put under strain by the sudden need to re-establish paternal authority, and rather than supporting her husband's action, as the puritanical disciplinarian of Landy's account, Emily's instinct is to protect her child. Far from looking on while he is beaten by his father, as Landy asserts, she shuts herself away from the scene of the chastisement and suffers with every blow. By the standards of 1952, the Palmers are an 'ordinary' upper-working-class family with legitimate aspirations for their son and the sort of moral and disciplinary codes which identify them as 'respectable'. Frankie's parents are presented sympathetically and their reluctant use of corporal punishment is understandable within the mores of their time. The film never shares with its close contemporary *Cosh Boy* (Lewis Gilbert, 1953) the celebration of a 'leathering' or the advocacy of its effectiveness in curing juvenile delinquency.

Although *The Yellow Balloon* avoids the reactionary rhetoric of *Cosh Boy*, it is still a film steeped in the conservatism of its time, one of the most repressive moments of post-war cultural history. The period 1952–54 in Britain is usually thought of as one of social tranquillity, its consensual underpinnings evidenced in the coronation celebrations which mark its mid-point.[15] But although Britain may have appeared immune from the MacCarthyite conflicts which continued to rend the American cultural fabric at the time, there were strains and upheavals which were prevented from surfacing only by blanket suppression. The sources of strain are not hard to detect – more than a decade of rationing and austerity restrictions which acted like the lid of a pressure cooker on simmering consumer aspirations; a hegemonic disapproval and disabling of American cultural products in the face of widespread demand; an ideology of welfare collectivism which submerged the desires of individualism; extensive social dislocation and the legacies of wartime trauma; housing shortages and privations; the disruption of expectations and gender relations forced by rapid cultural change; the continuing attempt to impose pre-war morality in changed circumstances ... the list could go on and on. The response of the Conservative government to rising social pressure was gradually to let off the economic steam but to screw the lid down tighter on the pot of cultural discontent. Thus, while rationing disappeared after 1952, restrictions on American imports remained, justified by a discourse of national debt and balance of payments, but informed by a deeper cultural prejudice and paranoia.

Governmental enthusiasm for cleansing any traces of Americanisation was largely matched by the Labour Party and exceeded by the zealots of the British Communist Party.[16] This bizarre trinity's most notorious alliance was in the successful persecution of British reprints of American horror and crime comics,[17] but there were many further acts of cultural purification (both public and discreet) which, backed by a highly censorious popular press, passed without challenge in the attempt to make the new Elizabethan State a more wholesome realm.[18] Homosexuals, prostitutes and the producers and distributors of salacious and pseudo-American gangster novelettes all experienced the wrath of Home Secretary Sir David Maxwell Fyfe and Director of Public Prosecutions Sir Theobald Mathew (Holland 1993; Higgins, 1996: 151–293). Maxwell Fyfe's public enemy number one, however, was the 'cosh boy', a crepe-soled, drape-suited embodiment of the deleterious effects of transatlantic influence untempered by parental control. By the late autumn of 1952, the fears of politicians, newspapermen and moral guardians of all kinds about the collapse of disciplined society had crystallised around the image of the young thug (Chibnall 1977: 51–60; Selwyn 1991: 8–12). In November the thug acquired a name: Christopher Craig, a 16-year-old accused with his older but intellectually backward friend Derek Bentley, of the murder of a police officer in south Croydon. *The Yellow Balloon* was to have its release immediately after their trial, and while Bentley waited in Wandsworth's death cell for a reprieve that never came, in spite of the recommendations for mercy made by his judge and the jury.[19] Bentley's execution was to be an offering from an authoritarian regime to the even more reactionary elements in Fleet Street and beyond which were baying for the return of the birch and other draconian measures to eradicate criminality in the young (Yallop 1971).

In such a climate, the concern of Lee Thompson's film with the vulnerability of the child to corrupting influences on the street and its plea for parental vigilance are part of the preoccupations of its time. Its sceptical attitude to the efficacy and legitimacy of corporal punishment place it as a relatively liberal contribution to the debate about youthful crime, but the film offers a largely conventional understanding of social organisation at the dawn of the new Elizabethan age. Above all, its demonising of the young spiv and its espousal of respectability and the primacy of familial bonds maintain an adequate compatibility with the doctrines of Maxwell Fyfe. In *Hunted*, Dirk Bogarde plays the kind of sympathetic and sensitive outsider who would become a familiar feature of Lee Thompson's texts, but while William Sylvester wears the same type of raincoat as Bogarde, the cool and violent confidence trickster he plays in *Balloon* more closely resembles the predatory Max Cady from *Cape Fear*. Len steps out of the very shadow world of spivvery that gives meaning to the Palmers' striving for respectability. His is a world in which easy money is squandered on pinball machines, where lounging wideboys complain that 'the bottom has dropped out of the nylon-racket' and 'the mugs aren't as trusting as they used to be'. In contrast, thrifty Mrs Palmer keeps her savings in a teapot, eschews dance-band tunes in favour of classical music, runs her home to a strict timetable, and reminds her hard-pressed husband that 'we've got a lot to be thankful for'. The nest egg in the teapot epitomises British respectability as readily as Len's tough-guy drawl and talk of 'Uncle Sam' identify him with disreputable Americanism. In fact, it is unnecessary to try to determine Len's actual nationality because there is such an apparent affinity between his social type and an American style of masculine performance. If William Sylvester was unable to disguise his transatlantic accent, it made little difference because he simply sounded like one of the multitude of 'mock Martins' who affected American accents and dress styles as part of their disaffection with British culture (Chibnall 1996).[20] Young men like these normalised a cultural masquerade 'passing' daily as their adopted identity, exchanging the prosaic for the exotic in a reversal of the feat of passing which most gay men felt obliged to perform in those pre-Wolfenden days.[21] But dissident and unattached hetero men like Len were thought to pose almost as great a moral threat as the homosexual to the hegemony of family life. Len is closely associated with places of corruption and liminality, like the amusement arcade, the milk bar and the bomb site. The proliferation of these places of temptation seemed to be turning the safe streets of pre-war days into danger zones.

The sense of paranoia engendered by the narrowing parameters of security in the post-war city is one that pervades *The Yellow Balloon* from its beginning. We first see Frankie, in the cocoon of safety that the nuclear family represents, looking out of his window.[22] His innocent consumer desires inflamed by the most childish of commodities, a colourful balloon, he begs sixpence from his father and runs from his inner zone of security, his tenement block, into a more unstable outer zone, his immediate neighbourhood. As he does so, the camera shows us that his home is called 'Victory Buildings', a name which suggests both the investment of human suffering which has gone into the construction of a stable post-war society and the work still needed to secure peace and prosperity. If we have seen Fritz Lang's child-murder policier *M* (1931), the itinerant balloon-seller Frankie is running towards should be enough of an omen to indicate that all is not well, and the boy immediately falls and sends his sixpence down the nearest drain. The reassuring presence of a kindly local bobbie (Bernard Lee) cannot dispel the impression that the streets have become hazardous. But greater danger lies ahead for Frankie when he covetously grabs the balloon of a playmate and heads off for the adventurous terrain provided by a blitzed building. The pursuit of his precious balloon by Frankie's friend ends tragically when he loses his footing in the crumbling shell of the building and falls to his death.[23] As Frankie stares guiltily at his friend's corpse in what was once the basement of the house, Len is lurking in the subterranean shadows. The association of neglect and criminality hardly need spelling out by Mrs Palmer's concerned neighbour: 'It's a scandal, Emily ... these places [bombed buildings] ought to be boarded up ... I shan't ever feel like letting the kids play in the street again.'

The implications of *Balloon*'s early scenes are clear: pre-war security has been eroded, like the extended family, and to the blight of poverty has been added physical danger. In a world in which, as Frankie's father moans, 'tanners' still 'don't grow on trees' the neighbourhood is becoming a place where money (literally) goes down the drain and children risk being killed. That the 'New Jerusalem' may become a haunt of fears is constantly underlined in the remainder of the film by recurrent shots of Frankie wide-eyed in apprehension or terror. Len takes advantage of the boy's confusion, infusing him with the spiv's occupational paranoia ('spies everywhere') and convincing him that 'Uncle Sam's on your tail'. The language and frame of reference of the fantasy Len peddles to Frankie is that of American crime films –

fall guys on the lam – and they contrast strikingly with the cosy British domesticity of the Palmer household, where mum dusts and darns and browns the toast while dad tackles the *News of the World* crossword.

Frankie's parents pack him off to Sunday School where he listens with mounting horror to the story of Cain and Abel whose *idée fixe* – 'Am I my brother's keeper? – magnifies his guilt and shame about the death of his playmate. Like Cain, Frankie has fallen from a state of grace – the innocence of childhood, albeit, as his father remarks, a savage innocence: 'Kids is proper little savages, even the best of 'em. Nothing bothers them much at least until they get their own kids to look after.' The metaphor of the fallen occurs repeatedly in the film: Frankie stumbles and loses his sixpence; his friend misses his footing and plummets to his death; Frankie falls again as he steals the family savings; and, finally, Len completes his own descent into the underworld when he plunges down a lift shaft. The implied moral lessons are as unequivocal as the biblical parables Frankie hears in Sunday school. Frankie failed to be his brother's keeper and was cast out of the Eden of childhood innocence. His East of Eden became the amusement arcades and spiv cafés where the serpents of temptation ply their trade. A similar fate awaits the fledgling post-war society if it abandons the collectivist values of the new socialist Eden and embraces the individualist values of materialism – not so much East of Eden as Anthony Eden.

As the film progresses, Frankie's descent into moral and physical danger becomes ever deeper. A typically entrapped Lee Thompson protagonist, he is unable to break away from Len, and helps him in a pub robbery in which the publican is killed. From being his accomplice, Frankie now becomes a witness whom Len must eliminate. Fearful to go home and hiding from Len, Frankie (like Jennifer before him) is a fugitive on the streets until, in a further biblical allusion, he is taken in by Mary, a Good Samaritan 'dance teacher' (Hy Hazell),[24] who feeds him and listens to his tearful confession before returning him home. Len, however, intercepts him and takes him to an abandoned tube station. The critically acclaimed scenes that follow strongly recall the subterranean chase at the end of *The Third Man*, generating an intensity rare in British cinema at that time and revealing in Lee Thompson a precocious talent in the handling of suspense, as Len first tries to push Frankie down a lift shaft and then pursues him down stairways and though deserted tunnels. It is a *tour de force* for the production team from Gil Taylor's canted-angle expressionist photography to Dick Best's tight editing and, most of all, to Bob Jones's thoroughly convincing sets. As Gil Taylor explained: 'We only did one shot in the real Tube. It was all shot in the studio. We had two tunnels built and we had to do fifty-six set ups in those tunnels.' Taylor's lighting ensures that there is a perfect match between studio and location shots. Lee Thompson recalls slightly more location shooting but pays tribute to the remarkable effects achieved by Jones and Taylor, particularly in the recreation of the London Underground lift shaft: 'I remember when Robert Jones finished building the lift shaft on the set, Victor Skutezky said: "I don't think this is going to work. I don't think this is going to look at all like a real lift shaft." But it did.'

Kinematograph Weekly (11 December 1952) called it a 'seat-gripping climax' and it is kept taut by sudden changes of pace, unexpected twists, and the close attention to detail which those fifty-six set ups evidence. The most memorable examples are the moments during the tense hunt in the tunnels, when first Frankie is alerted to Len's presence by spotting his feet protruding from behind a wall, and then, when the situation is reversed, Len grabs for Frankie when he thinks he has spied his feet only to discover that what he actually saw was a pair of discarded shoes. But although feet would be a strong *leitmotif* in Lee Thompson's *Yield to the Night*, it is eyes in *Balloon* that are the objects of most attention from Gil Taylor's camera.[25] It was a preoccupation emphasised in the film's poster, which is dominated by Andrew Ray's almost hypnotic stare and a tagline which assures the viewer that *The Yellow Balloon* 'will hold you wide-eyed in amazement'. The lidless look would become a trademark in Lee Thompson's attempts to express childish innocence and vulnerability, as he explains: 'You see this is really the beginning of how I dealt with child actors ... these big eyes that Andrew Ray has I made great use of in the film as I did with Hayley Mills in *Tiger Bay*. I used to dwell on the eyes a lot of those two child actors.'

The climax of *Balloon* may have a noir intensity experienced only occasionally in 1950's British cinema, but contemporary codes would inevitably ensure a conventional closure to its narrative. Again, the film is true to its collectivist sentiments by showing Frankie's deliverance to be a community effort from the helpful dance teacher and the vigilant train driver to the resolute police officers he alerts. Together they see that Frankie is returned to his relieved parents. The message is that the private world of the nuclear family can flourish only with the support of a concerned and public-spirited wider community.[26] Such liberal communitarianism might seem like a commendably humanitarian creed were it not for the questions it leaves unasked and the aspirations for change it fails to acknowledge. It leaves unchallenged the suffocating dullness of a culture in which every innovation was suspect and every dissident act condemned as a threat to wholesome social order. It was this climate of grey circumscription which, as Francis Selwyn (1991) so effectively argues, produced both Craig and Bentley and the reaction to their disastrous attempts at self-assertion; and it was the same climate that might have nurtured Len's spivery and marginalised an unmarried woman like Mary.

The Yellow Balloon may be frustratingly limited in its social critique, but as a piece of film making it was rightly praised for its performances and technical proficiency.[27] *Picturegoer* (17 January 1953) described Andrew Ray as 'a young actor of staggering awareness', while *Kinematograph Weekly* (11 December 1952) remarked on the naturalness of his performance. Some credit, however, must go to his director who coped patiently with the pronounced stutter which made Andrew's scenes, in Gil Taylor's words, 'an awful job to get done'.[28] Taylor, too, helped enormously in the angling of shots which help the impression that Frankie is younger than 13-year-old Andrew Ray. There was acclaim also for Ryan and More who, for *Kinematograph Weekly*, 'never put a foot wrong as Frankie's harassed parents'. *Picturegoer*'s Lionel Collier (24 January 1953) agreed that Ray was 'outstanding' and supported by some fine playing by the other actors, but has no doubt that the contribution made by the director was a crucial one, beginning his review: 'This unusual and compelling thriller rebounds credit on director J. Lee Thompson.' In describing *Balloon* as 'a picture that is right out of the rut', Collier was representing a substantial critical consensus which stretched from the reviewers of the popular press to the discriminating pages of the *Monthly Film Bulletin*.[29] The *MFB* (January 1953) was particularly impressed with the 'effective photography' which 'makes many routine situations fascinating', and with the striking 'absence of "phonyness"' which it attributed to 'everyone's close attention to how human beings really react under emotional strain'.

For Lee Thompson, the change of mode and tone from the camp histrionics of *Murder Without Crime* to the more critically approved realism of *Balloon* had been both remarkable and revealing. *The Yellow Balloon* began to demonstrate the versatility and assurance which would make him ABPC's premier director. His fellow professionals were already appreciating what *Kinematograph Weekly* (11 December 1952) called his 'resourceful direction', even if the prospect of financial success for *Balloon* was handicapped by an uncharitable response from the censor. Concerned about its potentially disturbing effect on young viewers, the BBFC classified the film as 'X' certificate. It was only the second British production to receive this classification since the certificate was introduced two years previously,[30] and it was the first Elstree film to be rated 'X' (Aldgate 2000). Associated British must have been dismayed by the blow dealt to *Balloon*'s box office prospects by the loss of the crucial family audience. As Elisabeth Forrest put it in *Picturegoer* (17 January 1953): 'Public and critics may admire the film's uncompromising quality. But maybe its distributors are wishing now that they had rationed that quality's quota to just an "A" certificate's worth.'

Only days before the Board announced its decision, Jack Goodlatte, managing director of Associated British Cinemas, had declared that he would be happier without 'X' films, adding that the good ones could play in key cities but that they had a bad effect on business as a whole as soon as they reached the neighbourhood cinemas. The ABC circuit, he said, would adopt a more cautious policy, booking only outstanding pictures with an 'X' certificate. (*Kinematograph Weekly*, 2 October 1952). Lee Thompson confirms that an 'X' certificate was a 'disaster' which meant 'death at the box office': 'We fought very hard to have the certificate removed but ... they said that this was a film of child terror and therefore couldn't be anything but an "X" certificate.'

ABPC decided to make the best of things for *Balloon*'s West End release, emphasising the 'X' in 'eXciting' on the film's posters and adding *Evening News*' critic Jympson Harman's comment that 'X' stands for 'excellent' to trade advertisements for the film's premiere at Studio One, Oxford Circus (8 January 1953). *Balloon*'s press book, however, suggests how unprepared ABPC was for the exclusion of children from the film's audience. Street stunts, toy shop displays, road safety campaigns and balloon give-aways and competitions had to be rapidly rethought to target adult patrons. Standard Brands Ltd, the makers of Royal Dessert ('Fully sweetened with sugar!') and the film's primary promotional partner ('Royal Desserts are smashing' says Andrew Ray), must have been less than thrilled to be associated with an 'X'-certificated movie. However, the film's stress on the value of parental responsibility and love at least gave the publicity department a rationale with which to persuade a variety of retailers to display pictures of a grinning Andrew Ray with a caption encouraging parents to make their sons happy and healthy by buying an appropriate product – toothbrushes, bicycles, watches, school uniforms, etc. In London's West End, where *Balloon*'s box office results 'exceeded all expectations' (*Kinematograph Weekly*, 5 February 1953), the novelty of a British film with an 'X' certificate pulled in the crowds, while the irony of its 13-year-old star being banned from its audience garnered publicity. But its distributor knew that it would struggle on general release. APBC's lobbying eventually persuaded the BBFC to show leniency and change *Balloon*'s certificate to an 'A', but not before its national run[31] had been severely handicapped. 'It went on general release as an "X" certificate' remembers Lee Thompson, 'and it didn't do good business. I think the certificate was changed later on because, I mean, by today's standards it's ridiculous.'

Notes

1 'My father understood the meaning of fear', he tells Stephen as they stand in the room that was once his father's study – 'a place of awe and terror and fear'. He envies Stephen's terror of the gallows as an emotion he no longer seems capable of experiencing, and his bullying of his tenant might be read as an attempt to replay the drama of his childhood, this time in the role of patriarch.

2 On the other hand, Matthew does appear to be based on the flamboyantly gay film director Brian Desmond Hurst with whom Lee Thompson had collaborated as a scenarist on *Glamorous Night* and for whom Dennis Price had starred in *Hungry Hill* (1947). Hurst occupied an ostentatious studio in an artists' quarter of Knightsbridge. According to Diana Dors (1979: 99), who described him as 'one of the most wonderful characters I have ever met', he lived in great splendour amid wealth inherited from his Irish ancestors with, among other things, carved wooden saints around his bedhead, and stained glass windows depicting religious scenes in the bedroom'. One of the numerous young actors he propositioned recalled 'walls covered with paintings. Very expensive statues and a profusion of objets d'art' (Roach 1993: 98). For a more extensive discussion of Hurst's lifestyle and career, see Bourne (1996: 26–32).

3 Differences in the prologue in the British and American versions of *The Third Man* are discussed in Drazin (1999: 123–6)

4 Grena, for example, is described as 'dainty as a piece of Dresden china with all the sauce of Worcester', and Matthew as 'a pompous, indolent lover of luxury' whose words are thought by his friends to be 'the mumblings of a distorted brain in the throws of hallucination'.

5 Bill McLeod had previously shot *No Place For Jennifer* from a script by Lee Thompson who remembers their collaboration with some ambivalence:

> 'That's right, Bill McLeod, a mad Scotsman. A great friend of [studio head] Robert Clark, but he was completely mad. I remember once telling him I thought he was too slow. We were waiting around a lot and suddenly he switched off a lamp and said: "I'm ready." We filmed the whole scene and, in rushes the next day, we could hardly see anything. And Bill McLeod said: "That serves you right for trying to rush me." He was a little mad, which I must say I loved.'

McLeod's tactics were probably designed to bring the new director down a peg or two, and Lee Thompson shed no tears about never working with him again.

6 Although the pre-war ethos of industrial production may have undergone some relaxation at the new Elstree, conformity to budgets and shooting schedules was of paramount importance, just as they had been for the directorial work of the 1930s, as described by Carol Reed:

> 'You were handed a script and told you had to shoot so many scenes a day. And you got on with it. If you hadn't finished by 6 o'clock you

broke for supper and went back to work until the day's job was done. It was a six day week and you were seldom through before eight any night. If, at the end of the first week of production, you were a day behind schedule you were told to pull your socks up. If you were, say, two days behind at the end of the second week, you were very unpopular indeed [...] If you didn't make up your lost time you were liable to be taken off the picture and somebody put in who *could* push it through on time.' (Quoted in Wapshott 1990: 99)

7 By the 1950s the growth of union power had increased the size of crews and shortened the working day and week, but restrictions on overtime increased the pressure on the director to arrange the shooting schedule for maximum efficiency.

8 Taylor later worked with Hitchcock, the director on whom Lee Thompson modelled many of his methods and techniques. He found the two directors similar in the way they thought out shots in advance but, at least towards the end of his career, Hitchcock gave his cinematographer greater autonomy: 'Hitchcock never looked through the camera once on *Frenzy*, not even remotely. He never suggested a lens. He did nothing – he just left it to you. He'd say "Make this a bit intimate" or "Make this a bit loose", and that's all there would ever be. He trusted you as a professional to do it, which you did.'

9 Anne Burnaby, daughter of the comedy actor Dave Burnaby (a member of the Co-optimists) was a young recruit to the script department. Lee Thompson recalls that her ambiguous sexuality was merely one of the factors that made her one of the more exotic blooms in the ABPC hothouse: 'Anne was, of course, a little off the wall ... She was a great character and we had lots of fun, and she was a good writer. There isn't any question that she was a really excellent writer.'

10 As Marcia Landy observes in her sympathetic analysis of *Hunted*, it brings together a boy and an outlaw, dramatising 'their bonding through their marginality' and offering 'an unusual image of male tenderness and nurturing which heightens the sense of these characters' difference from the hostile, uncaring world which they must inhabit'. (Landy 1991: 74)

11 *The Yellow Balloon* campaign book (Associated British–Pathe, 1952).

12 *Balloon* was produced by Victor Skutezky's company, Marble Arch. ABCP producers had been encouraged by their studio head to form their own companies in order to take advantage of funds offered by the British Film Finance Corporation to productions with guaranteed distribution.

13 Redway had been casting director for the Boulting Brothers before moving to ABPC.

14 Sylvester had already worked with Kathleen Ryan on his first film, the Depression drama *Give Us This Day* (Edward Dmytryk, 1949). He would eventually star in perhaps the most dissident of all British crime films, *Offbeat* (1960), directed by *The Yellow Balloon*'s assistant director Cliff Owen. Sylvester's wife Veronica Hurst played the prim Sunday school teacher in Lee Thompson's film.

15 One need look no further than Jeffrey Richard's rosy description of the period:

> 'The first half of the 1950s was an era of peace, prosperity and order. The crime rate was falling. There was full employment and rising productivity. The greater availability of consumer durables blunted out class antagonism. The coronation of Queen Elizabeth II in 1953 was seen as ushering in a new Elizabethan age, as Empire was transmuted into the Commonwealth, a world-wide brotherhood of nations...'. (1998: 135)

A society so tranquil and harmonious, then, that it would hardly require the judicial murder of a 19-year-old with severe learning difficulties (Derek Bentley) or the tragic illiterate dupe of a mass murderer (Timothy Evans).

16 See, for example Harry Hopkins' discussion (1964: 68) of anti-Americanism.

17 Martin Barker (1984) has produced an exemplary account of the campaign, which began in earnest in 1952 and culminated in The Children and Young Persons (Harmful Publications) Act 1955.

18 A realm fit for the happy national family mythologised in Humphrey Jenning's Festival of Britain film *Family Portrait* (1950).

19 Craig was convicted of the murder but was too young to be hanged.

20 'Mock Martins' is rhyming slang: Martins Bank = Yank. Dirk Bogarde played one of these counterfeit Yanks in *The Woman in Question* (Anthony Asquith, 1950).

21 Frankie pays tribute to Len's exoticism when he presents him with that most alien of objects in austerity Britain, a (stolen) pineapple.

22 The semi-autonomous nuclear family, increasingly loosening its attachments to extended kin networks and buffeted by the winds of austerity, was looked to as the cradle of the new post-war society.

23 The yellow balloon of the film's title can be read as representing the fragile aspirations and innocent yearnings of childhood. A child's vulnerability to exploitation is suggested when Len cements Frankie's trust by buying him the balloon he craves.

24 Lee Thompson confirms that her original identity as 'a good-time girl' fell foul of the BBFC, but she remains, like Anne Burnaby her creator, one of 1950's British cinema's least stereotypical women. Mary has her precursor in Rose (Dora Bryan), the prostitute in *The Fallen Idol* who comforts young Filipo when he runs away from an intolerable situation.

25 The concentration on Andrew Ray's eyes in *Balloon* perfectly expresses Taylor's lighting philosophy. As he told me: 'In films then ... you had to see their eyes ... you lit the artist so that you got their full performance, because you can't act without seeing eyes and mouth, and so I used to say "Keep the light on the money" because you had to light the actors' faces.'

26 Landy (1991: 452) remains unconvinced by the film's reinstallation of familial and societal order in its closure, regarding it as little more than a papering-over the problems of sexuality and family repression which the film has previously exposed: 'The film's ending only reinforces the

disparity between the problems posed and the solutions adopted, it functions as closure rather than resolution.'

27 The task of surveying press responses to the film is made more difficult by the lack of an appropriate microfiche at the BFI's library.

28 Lee Thompson recalls of the stutter: 'Sometimes I let it go, other times it was too much and I had to cut; but it lent a certain attractiveness to him, this slight stutter.' The director also gives credit to William Sylvester and Kathleen Ryan for helping to put young Andrew Ray at ease.

29 Associated British–Pathe selected some of the most complimentary comments for its press book, including: 'A tense yarn – brilliantly told ... spine-chilling ... realistic and gripping!' (Reg Whitely, *Daily Mirror*); 'Beautifully acted, beautifully photographed and filled with thrills' (Ray Nunn, *Daily Sketch*); 'An extremely tense thriller' (Dick Richards, *Sunday Pictorial*).

30 The first British 'X' certificate film, Romulus' *Women of Twilight* (Gordon Parry, 1952), actually went on general release shortly after *Balloon*.

31 Stickers were applied to the film's press book announcing the change of classification, but it was too late to re-orientate the campaign.

4

Women who lie in gaol

You may say with some confidence that in the present stage of English culture, a great many serious subjects cannot be treated at all. We cannot treat human justice truthfully as America treated it in *I Am a Fugitive from a Chain Gang*. No film ... which described the punishment cells at Maidstone would be allowed. (Graham Greene 1938: 66–7)

In his study of Lance Comfort, also in this series on British Film-makers, Brian McFarlane (1999) has applied Bordieu's ideas about the positioning of agents with 'systems of dispositions' ('habitus') within the 'field of cultural production' to a director working in post-war British cinema. McFarlane traces the career trajectory of Comfort from the 1940s when his habitus – his talent and disposition for making melodramas – was fashionable enough to allow him almost a privileged position in the field of cultural production to the 1960s when his ability to accumulate economic and symbolic capital had been severely compromised by his occupation of a subordinate position within the field. Problems with attracting both critical cachet (symbolic capital) and popular acceptance (economic capital) had transformed him, in Bourdieu's terms, from an autonomous producer with relatively unfettered creativity to one of those heteronomous cultural producers 'who can offer the least resistance to external demands, of whatever sort' (Bourdieu 1993: 41).

Bourdieu's taxonomies allow McFarlane to skirt around the mono-attributions and limited problematics of auteur theory, and to locate Comfort's work in the flow of post-war film production. One might apply them equally effectively to the career of J. Lee Thompson. By the spring of 1953 it was clear that British cinema had found a film-maker who could handle the technical demands of the thriller in a cinematic rather than a purely theatrical fashion. With *The Yellow Balloon*, Lee Thompson had demonstrated an aptitude for visual storytelling and a flair for imaginative shot composition while coaxing compelling performances from his actors. These were qualities not found in abundance among ABPC's directorial roster. Inspired by the provocative imagination of Hitchcock and the dark atmospherics of Carol Reed, Lee Thompson saw himself as a natural heir to the fiefdom of the British thriller. 'There was a time', he suggests 'when I wanted to become like a second Hitchcock and only do thrillers, but that went by the board ... if you are under contract you are pressured to do other films'.

Although he was establishing a more exalted place within the field of cultural production, he had not yet accumulated enough economic and symbolic capital to secure for his disposition for thrillers a niche position within the field. He remained subject to the dominant strategies of diversification practised by his studio. However, for the time being, his credit with Robert Clark remained good enough to allow him some autonomy in his choice of project. Late in 1952 he noticed a new book from Victor Gollancz which was causing a stir, reaching its fifth impression within two months of publication. It may be a worn-flat cliché, but this was to be the book that changed Lee Thompson's life. He tells the tale very simply:

> 'I read the book called *Who Lie in Gaol* by Joan Henry and I went to Robert Clark and said: "We've got to buy this book." And I went to see Joan Henry and I fell in love with her, and I divorced my wife for her, and we eventually married. Before we married I made *The Weak and the Wicked*, which was the film of her book. It became a huge hit.'

Joan Henry was born in London just before the First World War. Her cousin was the philosopher Bertrand Russell, and she could number two British prime ministers among her ancestors – Lord John Russell and (ironically, in the light of later events) Sir Robert Peel, the founder of the Metropolitan Police. Henry was brought up with her twin sister by their grandparents, first in Ireland and than at Ascot, and for many years her life faithfully followed the pattern expected of a woman of her class: 'coming out' into London society as a debutante, marriage to an army officer and the birth of a daughter in 1940. Six years later, however, her life was in disarray. Prolonged separations caused by military service had left her marriage on the rocks and she had become a persistent and reckless gambler, known on the racetracks of south east England as 'the lady in red' because of her penchant for scarlet suits. A wild bet on the last race at Windsor had incurred a huge debt to her bookmaker, which she was unable to repay, and she had been 'more or less warned off the turf'.[1] To aid the reconstruction of her life, Henry took up writing 'very light novels', engaging top agents Curtis Brown and publishing successfully with Cassell. *This Many Summers* (1947) and *Commit to Memory* (1948) both received good reviews, but by the time *Crimson Lake* (1950) was published its author was behind bars. She had been sentenced to twelve months for fraud, although she still protests her innocence of the charge, which may have related to her earlier gambling losses.

After spending eight months of 1950 in Holloway and the new 'open' prison at Askham Grange in Yorkshire, she reluctantly wrote a memoir of her experiences, *Who Lie in Gaol* (1952), at the insistence of her literary agents: 'They said "It's ridiculous – I mean, you're a novelist anyway, and it is an extraordinary experience to have [for a woman like you]", because in those days, whether you believe it or not, in a woman's prison there were hardly any educated people at all.' Although the book is a first-person account, it is not intended to be the story of Joan Henry so much as 'the story of any woman, innocent or guilty, who has the misfortune to go to prison' (Henry 1952: 7).[2] The opinions about the penal system expressed in the book are, for the most part, liberal humanist, but they are coloured by personal loss and discomfort:

During the first week in prison, the average prisoner forms a revulsion against authority that in normal circumstances would take a lifetime of mismanagement to acquire; a revulsion born of bitterness and self-pity, and nurtured by being in the power of uneducated people, who for the most part should not be in charge of animals, far less human beings. The majority of women in prison are weak characters who have become victims of circumstance. (1952: 48)

Henry goes on to condemn the way in which Holloway Prison fosters 'a life that saps initiative and encourages lethargy' (120), and to contrast its corrosive effects with the more positive results of the progressive regime at Askham Grange. The book's call for a more humanitarian treatment of offenders was bound to arouse controversy on its publication amid the 'cosh boy' panic in the autumn of 1952, garnering rave reviews and providing a rallying point for liberal and radical consciences alike. Lee Thompson immediately saw its dramatic potential, but Joan Henry maintains that his first thought was to turn it into a play, presumably because of the restricted settings imposed by an account of prison life. Joan believes that her memoir predisposed Lee Thompson to become romantically attached to her ('I think he fell in love with me, before he knew me, through that book'). Her own reactions to their initial meeting were far more mixed:

'He was under contract to Elstree and he wasn't supposed to do any plays. So anyway we arranged to meet. I went to his house. He was married and had two children. We had the most extraordinary meeting where he never stopped talking and pouring down gin and everything and behaving the way he always does when he describes how he's going to do a film ... and I thought he was really a bit round the bend to tell you the truth. And I rang up Curtis Brown and said: "I don't think I can work with this man, he's round the bend!" And they said: "Oh well, you know all film people are rather strange."'

It didn't take long, however, for Lee Thompson's boss Robert Clark to get wind of his idea for turning *Who Lie in Gaol* into a play and he quickly snapped up the film rights as Lee Thompson's next cinema project. In British cinema, prison stories had never constituted the flourishing sub-genre they did in Hollywood. Before the war, draconian censorship by the BBFC and an acutely suspicious attitude on the part of the Home Office had restricted prison subjects to convicts on the run, foreign jails and a single Will Hay comedy, *Convict 99* (Marcel Varnel, 1938). Although a number of prison memoirs appeared in the 1930s, their filming was heavily discouraged (Nellis 1988: 6–7). After the war, the subject of false imprisonment was raised by Cavalcanti in *They Made Me a Fugitive* and *For Them that Trespass*, and the Home Office and the Prison Commissioners began to offer tentative co-operation, first to the Crown Film Unit for its drama–doc *Children on Trial*, and then to Anatole de Grunwald to make the first British drama of prison life, *Now Barrabas* (1949).

If penal institutions for men had received some cinematic exploration by the early 1950s, the subject of women in prison remained a fresh one. Although the treatment of the theme by Hollywood dated back to the close of the silent era with Cecil B. de Mille's *The Godless Girl* (1929),[3] there was no depiction of a British penal institution for women until 1948 when David MacDonald filmed Arthur la Bern's *Good Time Girl,* partly set inside a girls' reformatory.[4] The first glimpse inside a women's prison had to wait until 1953 when the governor of Holloway offered limited co-operation for the opening scenes of Jack Lee's *Turn the Key Softly.* By then, the women in prison sub-genre had been given a new currency by the critical and popular success of Warner Bros' *Caged* (John Cramwell, 1950) which secured three Academy Award nominations (including Best Screenplay) for its uncompromising dissection of brutality and sexuality behind bars. Bev Zalcock (1998: 19) rightly identifies the films as a watershed, 'marking the end of the first phase of female prison movies with their mix of melodrama, social realism and a *frisson* of titillation, and the beginning of the next, the exploitation film with its formulaic plots, stock characters and erotically charged scenarios'. Joan Henry's book, with its muted plea for better conditions, never matched the intensity of *Caged,* but its adapting would require further moderation to satisfy the nervous watchdogs of Soho Square.

The Weak and the Wicked (1954)

> I know not whether laws be right
> Or whether laws be wrong
> All that we know who lie in Gaol
> Is that the wall is strong;
> And that each day is like a year
> A year whose days are long.
>
> (Oscar Wilde, *The Ballad of Reading Gaol*)

Lee Thompson quickly set to work with Joan Henry and Anne Burnaby to develop from *Who Lie in Gaol* a screenplay which would blend social criticism and melodrama with the leavening ingredient of comedy. Although ABPC was part-owned by Warner Bros, it did not have the American studio's track record in pioneering social-problem pictures. Apart from the odd gloomy crime melodrama like *Guilt Is My Shadow* (Roy Kellino, 1950) they liked to keep things 'light' at Elstree. The screenplay would emphasise the comedic passages of Henry's book and sandpaper some of the rougher textures of what was already a somewhat sanitised account, particularly in the reporting of speech. As the author recalls:

> 'The slang is very much like men's prisons', and the language! It rather amazes me that there were all these working-class women who I'm sure never use the word "fuck" or anything like that [normally], never used anything else. It was like the ranks in the army ... I think I had to put dots for the word. But I said pretty well a lot of things. There were some things I couldn't say.'

In the screenplay, prison officers could not be referred to as 'screws' and the incident where one officer has a slops pail emptied over her (Henry 1952: 48) had to be removed, together with discussions about sanitary towels. Nor could there be any explicit suggestion of lesbianism, which Henry singles out as 'a very difficult problem for the prison authority' (83), not least, as she now emphasises, because of its widespread incidence among prison officers. The book devotes a number of pages to the discussion of what it calls, in the parlance of the time, 'unnatural practices' between women, with Henry again avoiding a condemnatory approach:

> I have known women who are madly in love with prison officers and vice versa. I have been in contact with women who, having experienced no sexual satisfaction with men, consider they have fallen in love for the first time in their lives in prison and the liaisons very often become permanent when the prison sentence is finished. (48)

These were experiences that Anne Burnaby would herself authenticate when, remarkably, she also served a term in prison later in life. In the early 1950s, however, depictions of such experiences were unlikely to endear themselves to censorship bodies on either side of the Atlantic.[5] The requirements of realism, however, necessitated some acknowledgement of homosexuality and this could only be rendered censor-proof by connoting lesbian desire in the biases of a brutal prison officer, just as *Caged* had. The consequence, as Stephen Bourne (1996: 117) points out, would be to leave an impression of lesbianism as predatory and vindictive. On the other hand, the enduring nature of heterosexual love, which is hardly to the fore in Henry's book, would be pressed into service to provide satisfactory closure in the screenplay.[6]

While the adaptation of *Who Lie in Gaol* was being developed, a mood of patriotic fervour was being stoked up for the coronation of Elizabeth II. The summer of 1953, therefore, was not the most auspicious time to show the Home Office a screenplay that was critical of a national institution like the prison service. Unsurprisingly, official approval was withheld and co-operation denied. Luckily, the progressive governor of Askham Grange, Mary Size, had recently retired, and she was signed up as an advisor on the film. Miss Size, a devout Roman Catholic for whom Joan Henry had enormous respect, apparently fretted about the possible effect on her pension if the film offended the Home Office. Sitting at Lee Thompson's right hand on the thoroughly convincing prison sets which were constructed to Robert Jones' design on the Elstree floor, she would scrutinise the depiction of the prison regime. 'She nearly drove Lee mad', recalls Henry 'because she was always dashing up and saying that a warder didn't look nice just as he was shooting'.

The disapproval of the Home Office did *The Weak and the*

Wicked no harm as far as publicity was concerned. The *Daily Mirror* (17 August 1953) called the project 'bold and provocative', congratulating Associated British on the decision not to make 'a fawning, flattering picture' and describing Lee Thompson as 'that promising young director' – 39 was considered a tender age for a director in those days. But what also caught the *Mirror*'s eye was the film's casting. It was not so much the casting of Glynis Johns as Joan Henry (changed to Jean Raymond for the film) or John Gregson, fresh from his success in *Genevieve*, as her boyfriend Michael, but the opportunity given to Diana Dors to extend her acting range in drab prison garb. Filming began only a few weeks after Dors had been convicted in a Blackpool court of stealing some bottles of alcohol from a friend's house.[7] The irony of the situation was not lost on cinemagoers who reportedly hailed Dors' first appearance in prison uniform with 'gales of laughter' wherever the film was shown (Dors 1959: 100). Dors' first 'deglamorisation' became *The Weak and the Wicked*'s key publicity motif.[8] She plays one of 'the weak', Betty, an impressionable young woman who is in gaol because of misplaced loyalty to her larcenous boyfriend. The part is a highly sanitised version of the book's Betty Brown, a young blonde recidivist with two young children, tuberculosis, venereal disease and no time for the 'f— screws' (Henry 1952: 14).

Although the Jean Raymond character is made less recognisable as Joan Henry by changing her family circumstances and the details of her fraud conviction, she retains an emotional affinity with the woman who had so recently been imprisoned. Glynis Johns made sure of this by adopting Joan Henry as her advisor on set, as Lee Thompson recalls: 'Glynis Johns was a big star at the time, and I remember we grew very fond of her because she consulted my wife [Joan Henry] a lot ... Glynis Johns became our close friend.'

Personal ties, worries about offending the Home Office, and the censor combined with the problems of interpreting the personality of a literary narrator to make the Jean Raymond character rather more bland than Joan Henry would have liked:

'Glynis Johns ... played what was supposed to be me, but writing in the first person sounds a terribly good part in the book, but when you come to play it in a film it's not nearly such a good part because, you know, you [the author/narrator] are observing the other people all the time. I felt it made me seem awfully sort of goody-goody, when I wasn't the least bit goody-goody ... She was a very good actress but, except for one moment in the cell when she was near to breaking down, she made me seem a bit like Florence Nightingale.'

For Jean Raymond and, by implication, hundreds of other women, prison is the consequence of a wilful and self-centred recklessness which blinds an offender to danger, and the random selection of fate. In the film both recklessness and fate are represented by a spinning roulette wheel. However, as Marcia Landy (1991: 454) argues, there are deeper well-springs to the misfortune of Jean and her fellow inmates which have their origins in gender relations. Clearly, Betty is in gaol because of her attachment to an inappropriate male who has manipulated her and abused her love ('He's rotten through and through, but he's mine'), but Jean's relationship with her medical man, Michael, is ambivalent and more complex. Her downfall results from her lack of commitment to Michael, denying her destiny as a colonial wife and chancing her freedom at the gaming tables; or, as Landy puts it, 'By refusing respectability, she is marked as a loser in life' (454). Part of the rehabilitative role of prison is to end her selfishness and help her to appreciate the importance of devotion to her romantic duty. As she confides to the kindly prison chaplain: 'To live for somebody else is the finest thing in the world and there isn't a single wretched person in the whole of this wretched place that hasn't helped me to understand that. I want to help Michael to forget all the unhappiness I have caused him. I want to make him a good wife.'[9]

What preoccupies the inmates of this prison – in which, as the film's publicity suggestively put it, women are 'barred from men!' – is not the loss of freedom or even of sexual satisfaction but a loss of role, of the supportive relationships to men which allow them to make sense of themselves as women. In prison, even their babies, the tangible fruits of their heterosexual relationships, are taken away nine months after birth (mostly for adoption by respectable couples). They are reduced to an unnatural and undesired (but temporary) state of individualism. The women's reaction to the savage environment in which they find themselves locates them on a continuum on which femininity and recidivism are posed as polar opposites. The hard-bitten con played by Rachel Roberts sums up the loss of 'womanliness' experienced by the criminal individualist when she advises: 'You don't want to waste no sympathy in a place like this.' The line between compassion and selfishness is the one which separates 'the weak' from 'the wicked'. It is this realisation which will ultimately make Cambridge drop-out and inveterate gambler Jean into a woman who is truly marriageable. This, presumably, is the reason why Michael is not in Rhodesia but (almost magically) waiting in his sports car when Jean is released.

The responsibility for this trite ending and the whole sub-plot involving Jean's boyfriend lies squarely with the conceptions of commercial film making shared by Lee Thompson, Anne Burnaby and ABPC. Joan Henry still distances herself from the embellishments added to her narrative:

> 'I think they just thought that – I mean Glynis was an attractive girl and she would have had a boyfriend or someone – it was the sort of thing they thought of. I never thought of it ... It seemed to me rather a silly story, you know, why she went to prison and Michael, but it had to be something, so it didn't make much difference.'

Marcia Landy prefers to side-step the unpalatable sexual and cultural politics of the film's conventional closure, emphasising instead the tearful farewell between Jean and Betty which precedes Jean's surprise reunion with Michael. For Landy, the bond that develops between Jean and Betty epitomises the way in which the film successfully explores women's relationships with each other in the context of 'resistance to the status quo' and rebellion against a good home. Michael's 'totally unmotivated' reappearance is seen as 'gratuitous' (1991: 455). There seems an understandable degree of wishful thinking about this. This is not to deny that the film makes strenuous efforts to explore the emotional and redemptive qualities of relationships between women. And it is not as if male partners are presented in a particularly favourable light – Landy accurately describes them as 'insensitive, excessively moral, or exploitative' (455). It is not even that relations between the sexes are seen as necessarily positive – the problem for both Betty and Babs (Jane Hylton), the mother who fatally neglected her baby while she went out for a good time, is that they 'like men too much'. The elements of sisterhood which Landy celebrates are certainly present in *The Weak and the Wicked*, but ultimately, they are offered as moderating considerations in the recommendation of women's selfless and compassionate commitment to a stable heterosexual relationship. So Michael's return may be disappointing to anyone who holds dear the cause of female independence, but one has to read the film against the grain to find it 'gratuitous' and 'unmotivated'. *The Weak and the Wicked* may be more a discursive than a didactic text, with its rhetorical flourishes largely concentrated on the inhumanity of prison regimes, but its radicalism stops just short of the toleration of sisterhood over patriarchal marriage. One has only to observe the type of labour which the film appears to endorse as therapeutic in the open prison – consisting as it does of dressmaking, rug-making, leather work, knitting and cleaning – to appreciate that the world for which these women are being 'fitted' is a primarily domestic one. The impression persists that prison – open or closed – is a means of punishing and re-educating women for their gender transgressions as much as for their infringements of the law. Marriage may be, as one middle-aged inmate describes it, an act of 'martyrdom', but it is ultimately the only route to a state of grace. This reluctance to advocate opposition to problematic conditions is further evident in the film's attitudes towards the penal system. Although the brutality of prevailing prison conditions may be deplored, overt resistance to authoritarian regimes is not endorsed, and is even subtly coded, when it is depicted, as un-British.[10] Jean and Betty's transfer to 'a prison without bars' which the film's rhetoric advances as the future of imprisonment, suggests the system's ability and motivation to reform itself. We have nearly served our time under the old regimes; soon we may expect a change.

Even if Landy's interpretations of *The Weak and the Wicked*'s gender politics may be a little optimistic, she is not mistaken in identifying progressive elements within its discourses on prison life. In the process of imprisonment it is evident that some of the barriers of class, temperament, and cultural awareness which atomise women in everyday life are dissolved. A sense of commonality is a by-product of communal incarceration. The airs and graces of Mrs Skinner (Mary Merrall), 'a British subject born in Salisbury', cut no ice in the melting pot of the prison where the screws enforce a universally harsh regime and wealth is a packet of cigarettes. Gentlewoman and hard-hearted harridan share the same predicament, and under such abnormal conditions, as the governor of the Grange assures us, 'ill assorted pairs' can be 'valuable to each other'. Lee Thompson's socialist beliefs show through in the film's treatment of class and its advocation of mutuality and trust, just as Anne Burnaby's talent for comedy writing is apparent in some of the flash-back sequences which extend and embroider Joan Henry's original text. The most whimsical of these episodes, the arsenic-and-old-lace tale of poisoning featuring the comic talents of Sybil Thorndike and Athene Seyler, has all the macabre gentility of Ealing but its position within a social-problem drama raised eyebrows among the critics. Reviewers in the heavyweight newspapers were particularly displeased with *The Weak and the Wicked*'s 'sudden somersaults from tragedy into farce', which left the film lacking in 'form and discipline' (*The Times*, 8 February 1954). Campbell Dixon in the *Daily Telegraph* (6 February 1954) agreed that the treatment of the subject 'wavers between the realistic and anything-for-a-laugh', and David Granger in the *Financial Times* (8 February 1954) condemned the film's wavering as producing a 'meritricious' result which he felt obliged to dismiss as 'merely trumpery'. Although the performances of Seyler and Thorndike, in particular, were well liked, most reviewers thought them inappropriate to so serious a topic – 'more suited to a Ben Travers farce or to an Angela Brazil school story', as V. Graham put it in the *Spectator* (5 February 1954). Lee Thompson, however, still defends the inclusion of comedy elements which were based on incidents recorded in Henry's book: 'I think drama and comedy go together in all phases of life. But of course we did have a lot of comedy in *The Weak and the Wicked* ... But this was part of the story of life in gaol.'

In incorporating humour into his conception of social realism, Lee Thompson was doing no more than an acclaimed writer like *Saturday Night and Sunday Morning*'s Alan Silitoe would do only a few years later, but for *The Weak and the Wicked*'s critics the film's use of comedy betrayed its attitude of compromise which, according to Jympson Harman in the *Evening News* (4 February 1954), 'rears its ugly head' in the 'penny novelette style of the picture'. The *Daily Mail*'s Fred Majdalany (3 February 1954) summed up the feelings of most when he suggested that the film's 'gay revue sketches' were 'doubtless in keeping with the requirements of a popular entertainment', but were hardly 'the right substitutes for the starker details of the book'. Lee Thompson, in fact, almost concedes as much when, in maintaining that he did see his film as 'being of some value', he readily admits that it 'was made primarily for entertainment'.

Joan Henry argues that the heightened comedy was necessary to placate the censor, who might otherwise have denied a certificate or called for more cuts. She regards the dilution of her original message as par for the course: 'I've worked on films and I knew that all films do turn out differently, and somehow I'd had my say in the book and so many people had read my book ... There was nothing I could do about it really.' The mistake, perhaps, was to compartmentalise the comedy and drama instead of letting the one inform the other in a more fluid and organic way. This type of structural loosening of the film, coupled with a more subtle approach to the handling of its humour, might have avoided Roy Nash's complaint that 'the film itself quickly becomes a prisoner behind the box-office grille' (*Star*, 5 February 1954).[11]

The adverse comments on *The Weak and the Wicked*'s passages of humour were linked to a second theme in its reviews: the deodorising of prison and the domestication of some of its wilder inmates. Some critics thought the film much too 'nice'. Donald Douglas' review in the *Daily Worker* (6 February 1954) was headed 'Jail can be such a jolly place' and likened the film to a 'pleasant romantic drama'. The 'problem' for Douglas was the film's tendency to sit on the fence with regard to penal reform, a criticism which was a little unfair in the light of its evident support for the introduction of open prisons. More cogent were William Whitebait's accusations of 'sentimental journalising' (*New States-man*, 13 February 1954) and Paul Dehn's assertion (*News Chronicle*, 5 February 1954) that he could not really 'believe or enjoy this contrived cross-section of convict life'.

It was left to Caroline Lejeune (*Observer*, 7 February 1954), however, to relate the concerns about realism and sentimentality to the issue of gender representation. Conceding that the film 'gets a point home here and there', she went on to argue that its unintentional effect was 'to make crime committed by women seem a bit of a freak, a loveable eccentricity or lark, or at the very worst, an error of judgement'. Lejeune undoubtedly pinpoints a tendency of both book and film to operate with an essentialist conception of gender in which female criminality is cast as an aberration, an unfortunate failure to conform to a 'natural' model of law-abiding and nurturing femininity. The film might more accurately have been titled 'The Weak and the Weaker' because wickedness (at least among prisoners) is largely absent from its Christian Socialist discourse. Malevolence and maliciousness are traits confined largely to the custodial staff who separate mothers from their babies, and to the system of incarceration which disciplines and punishes with a minimum of compassion. To modern viewers, Gil Taylor's shots of spartan cells, metal lockers, supervised ablutions and piles of regulation shoes seem chilling. The barked orders of the warders challenge a freedom of action and an independence the rest of us take for granted. To contem-porary audiences inured to service life and the privations of rationing, however, the prison regime might have seemed less threatening, if not quite the 'Cushy Number' referred to in the title of the *Sunday Chronicle*'s review (7 February 1954).

Critical opinion may have deplored the genre compromises

and sanitised representations of *The Weak and the Wicked*, but audiences responded positively to its shrewd populism. By the time it went on general release, *Kinematograph Weekly*'s commercial seer Josh Billings was delighted to be able to 'crow' about his predictions for the film and confirm that it had 'definitely caught on' with the public, a success he attributed to the way 'it artfully plays down to the gallery without depriving the stalls of rattling good entertainment' (8 April 1954). For Lee Thompson, it was the hit he was looking for to ensure his career as a director. 'I needed that success', he says with relief, after two films he had 'loved very much' but which had performed only moderately at the box office.

A view on a death cell

'I go to the prison the day before, shake them by the hand and say, "Now you know who I am, do as I say and you'll be quite all right." Yes, I've had some lovely letters from mothers, thanking me for taking care of their sons.' (Albert Pierrepoint, Official Hangman, in conversation with Diana Dors 1978:98)

'When I saw myself with that revolver in my hand shooting him five times, I knew that I was another person from the one I am.' (Ruth Ellis speaking in the condemned cell at Holloway to Rt Rev. Joost de Blank, Bishop of Stepney, *Daily Mail*, 3 November 1955)

By the time *The Weak and the Wicked* premiered not only had the collaboration between J. Lee Thompson and Joan Henry developed into a romance, but the couple were already planning another prison film that would make a strategic intervention in the debate about penal policy. The genesis of *Yield to the Night* is recalled by Joan Henry:

'Lee and I were talking one day, and he was against capital punishment like me, and he said, "I've always wanted to write a book or a play about a man in a death cell." I said, "Well, I couldn't write about a man, but I might be able to do that about a woman." So he really gave me the idea, and then I showed him a plan.'

Lee Thompson was insistent that, if the story was to present an effective case against the death penalty, there should be 'no mitigating circumstances' to the woman's crime. Henry threw herself into the project, completing the book in one intensive period of writing. 'I wrote the book in six weeks, very, very quickly', she remembers, 'and I was in tears most of the time and had quite a lot to drink ... I felt very moved when I wrote it, I felt that it was me almost.' When she took it to her publisher, Victor Gollancz, he was at first shocked by its brevity, but found it such an affecting read that he wrote to Joan Henry asking her not to 'add one single word'.

The book was published in 1954 in the aftermath of a Royal Commission that had been given the brief of recommending more humane means of execution but which had suggested in its report that the 'real question now is whether capital punishment should be abolished or retained' (Hopkins 1964: 214). The subject of Henry's novel was clearly a timely one, and Lee Thompson was desperate to turn it into a film. His problem was to persuade the hard-nosed businessmen at ABPC that it would be a viable investment. Well-versed in the imperatives of commercial movie making, he knew that Henry's story possessed the same 'unfilmable' qualities that Graham Greene (1950: 145) had noted in his own story 'The Basement Room' when Carol Reed had proposed filming it as *The Fallen Idol*: 'a murder committed by the most sympathetic character and an unhappy ending'. Equally, the precedent was there, not just in *The Fallen Idol* but in the very touchstone of Lee Thompson's cinema, Reed's *Odd Man Out*. Chronicling the long journey into night of a shop girl who, in Reed's phrase, 'had done something wrong for the right reasons' (quoted in Wapshott 1990: 179) would be Lee Thompson's *Odd Woman Out*. It would posses the same elegaic sadness, the same nobility of suffering, the same feeling of persecution and martyrdom.

The executives remained to be convinced, but Lee Thompson could at least point to the success of *The Weak and the Wicked* to suggest that another excursion into the women-in-prison genre might be in order. He could also trade his agreement to direct more bankable comedies like *For Better, For Worse* (1954) in return for studio backing for his own chosen project. In the end, three factors probably won over his bosses at ABPC. The first was the money earned by hiring Lee Thompson to Rank to make two musical comedies (see Chapter 5); the second was the enthusiasm of Kenneth Harper to produce the film; and the third was the sudden box office potential given to the project by a highly publicised murder which closely resembled the fictional events in Henry's book. Her novel is the first-person narrative of Mary Hilton, a sexually adventurous shop assistant who deserts her dull husband to pursue an affair with a night-club pianist. Their relationship, however, is blighted by her lover's obsession with a rich society woman. When unrequited love leads him to suicide, Mary avenges the death by shooting her ex-rival, and spends three weeks in the condemned cell at Holloway awaiting execution. Those events were uncannily paralleled by the case of Ruth Ellis, a young night-club manager and model who shot her faithless lover David Blakely on Easter Sunday 1955 and was herself executed in Holloway that July (Hancock 1993). The two narratives are so similar that *Yield to the Night*, with its attractive blonde protagonist who so resembles Ellis in both her looks and motivations, is often mistaken for a Ruth Ellis 'bio-pic', even though the book was published the year before Ellis fired the fatal shots in Hampstead.[12] Just how closely life imitated art can be seen in the following comparisons: in both cases a long and brooding obsession with an unreliable man results in a young woman being driven to a residential part of London where she intercepts her target, takes a revolver from her bag and determinedly fires a volley of bullets into her victim, who dies by a motor car in full view of the bystanders.[13] Both women have recently experienced a failed marriage; both kill people from a higher social class, are summarily convicted and spend three Sundays in Holloway before execution.

Lee Thompson strenuously denies any connection between the Ruth Ellis case and his own film, to the extent that he now believes the film was finished *before* the execution of Ellis. Joan Henry believes that the film was being shot at Elstree when the execution took place.[14] In fact, Ruth Ellis was hanged on 13 July 1955, three months before *Yield to the Night* went before the camera. The script for the film held in the BFI's library is dated 9 August. This is *not* to suggest that the film is actually based on the Ellis case, but that its makers have spent so long refuting the idea that they were cashing in on the notoriety of a real crime that the sequence of events has become distorted in their memories. As Henry complains: 'Kenneth (Harper) and Lee were always denying it, but no one seemed to take any notice.' The accusation of exploitation dogged the film from the very beginning, as Lee Thompson relates:

> 'A famous London critic of the time, C. A. Lejeune, was going to write a very bad review of *Yield to the Night* because she thought that we had taken the Ruth Ellis case and twisted it around. And another film critic, Elspeth Grant, knew that Joan had written this before the Ruth Ellis case, so she got hold of Lejeune and very kindly said: "You're absolutely wrong. This is not a matter of trying to cash in on it."'

The hanging of Ruth Ellis is a milestone event in the abolition of capital punishment because the adverse public reaction[15] ensured that she would be the last woman to be executed in Britain. In February 1955, two months before Ellis killed Blakely, an anti-hanging bill was defeated in the House of Commons by thirty-one votes. A year later, Sidney Silverman's Abolition Bill passed its first reading. By that time, *Yield to the Night* was in the can and almost ready to make its own contribution to an ongoing debate which 'generated the sort of intense moral fervour that had scarcely been seen in Britain since the great days of Free Trade' (Hopkins 1964: 217).

From the beginning, the film had been conceived by Joan Henry and J. Lee Thompson as, unashamedly, a propaganda drama in the campaign against hanging. By eschewing the portrayal of a wrongly convicted innocent in favour of depicting a calculating killer, the pair hoped to mount a more comprehensive argument for abolition. As Lee Thompson told *Kinematograph Weekly* (10 November 1955): 'We are not making this film a special case. If hanging is essential to our civilisation then the heroine of our picture deserves to hang. If anything, we're loading the dice against the girl; she is not really a sympathetic character.' If the

film could evoke revulsion for the execution of even an unrepentant murderer, then the grounds for retaining the death penalty
would be severely undermined: 'If the person is so completely
unsympathetic and you still feel sorry for her – then the point is
made, and made more effectively than had she been presented as
a milk-and-water innocent' (*Films and Filming*, January 1956).

The success of this argument hinged on the studio's agreement to accept the book's bleak and gloomy ending, with Mary
Hilton denied a reprieve and going to her death. The profound
sadness that this would provoke in the audience was vital to
subsequent protest against the death penalty, but had always been
considered commercial suicide by British movie executives. In
1939 Carol Reed had said: 'The work of any director making
pictures in this country is conditioned absolutely by the happy
ending. I am sure that this is a wrong-minded policy and keeps
many intelligent people out of the cinemas...' (quoted in Wapshott
1990: 122). Reed had challenged this convention with *The Stars
Look Down* (1940) and *Odd Man Out*, but had acknowledged its
power by softening the ending of Greene's 'The Basement Room'
when making *The Fallen Idol*. Lee Thompson was determined that
Yield to the Night would not pull its final punch, whatever pressure
was applied by nervous executives. Joan Henry remembered
'terrible trouble at Elstree', with the director standing firm: 'Lee
said before the film started: "They're going to try to make me have
a happy ending, but I'm not going to. I'll shoot the ending first."'
The conservative and glib closures of *Balloon* and *The Weak and
the Wicked* were now to be resisted at all costs.

With Henry and Lee Thompson so close to the material,
producer Kenneth Harper engaged a screenwriter named John
Cresswell to bring an outside perspective and help with the
writing of dialogue. Cresswell had written effectively for Dirk
Bogarde in *The Woman in Question* (Anthony Asquith, 1950, USA:
Five Angles on Murder) and *Cast a Dark Shadow* (Lewis Gilbert,
1955) and it was hoped that he would be useful in developing the
part of Michael, Mary Hilton's lover. The move was not a successful one, as Joan Henry confirms: 'Lee couldn't stand him, and
tried to strangle him at one of our meetings at Kenneth Harper's

flat. He never came back again, although, of course, he had his name on the script ... So Lee and I really did it all.' The incident gives an insight into the passion and intensity with which Lee Thompson approached the filming of *Yield to the Night*. As the project progressed his commitment to it, and to its author Joan Henry, became increasingly exclusive, and his demand for creative control became more insistent – not least in the casting of the film.

The part of Mary Hilton was seen as a rare opportunity by actresses working in a film culture that was increasingly dominated by light comedies and war films. 'Everybody wanted the part', remembers Joan Henry. 'Olivia de Havilland wanted it. But I said she [i.e. whoever was selected] must not be a very smart sort of actress ... I wanted a much rougher person.' She and Lee Thompson never really doubted their choice, although to outsiders it looked highly controversial: Diana Dors was to play Mary Hilton. The casting would underline Mary's worldliness as well as attracting enormous publicity to the film. Although the acting potential of Dors had already been partially demonstrated by her supporting role in *The Weak and the Wicked* and recognised by her prominent casting in Carol Reed's *A Kid For Two Farthings* (1955), she was still better known for her scandalous private life than her screen performances. Now she was offered the chance to transcend her public persona and demonstrate her dramatic prowess alongside the established 'serious' actress Yvonne Mitchell, whose roles on the West End stage had already brought her critical acclaim, and the veteran character actress Athene Seyler, who was making an appearance in a Lee Thompson film for the third time.[16] The principal casting was completed only a few days before the filming began with the role of Jim going to ex-merchant seaman Michael Craig, who had spent five years in repertory before landing a role in *Passage Home* (Roy Baker, 1955).

Shooting on *Yield to the Night* began in late October 1955 at Elstree. With location work ruled out by the nature of the subject matter, art director Robert Jones was obliged to design an 18-foot by 12-foot 'death cell' to accommodate the principal action of the film. The authenticity of the design had to be established without the benefit of a co-operative Home Office, which refused to disclose any details. The production had to rely on information bought from a prison officer at Pentonville who had been present at executions.

Clearly, filming in such a confined space for such a substantial part of the film's running time posed considerable technical difficulties. Lee Thompson required an active approach to the cinematography which would allow the tense atmosphere of the condemned cell to be probed and interrogated and which would supply a continuity with the visual language of other scenes. Lighting cameraman Gilbert Taylor's solution was to use a light-weight Arriflex. Normally a hand-held camera used in docu-mentary filming, the blimped and mounted version used on *Yield to the Night* was highly manoeuvrable and could 'almost look round corners'. Fitted with a Cook 18-mm panchro lens, it also gave wide-angled pictures with little distortion, enabling Taylor to 'preserve the intimate atmosphere without lack of variety' (*Kinematograph Weekly*, 10 November 1955).

Yield to the Night's macabre theme and the adventurous casting of Diana Dors awoke press interest, which Elstree's head of publicity, Leslie Frewin, was quick to exploit. He issued a special invitation for journalists to visit the studio on the first day of filming on the condemned cell set. *Picturegoer*'s reporter Derek Walker questioned the wisdom of obliging Dors to perform before an intimidating bunch of 'acid penned writers', but Lee Thompson expressed total confidence in his leading actress: 'A lot of stars wouldn't do it. But with Dors it's different. I think she is, if anything, better with an audience. She likes to have some reactions to her performance' (*Picturegoer*, 17 December 1955). Gil Taylor remembers that Diana Dors had already stunned the film's technicians with an impromptu performance that none of them had expected:

> 'We had twenty-two electricians, and she came on the floor the first day in a scarlet and silver beaded dress, and she stood there in front of them and pulled it down and showed them her tits and said, "Well, boys, have a bloody good look. This is what I've got. Now when I'm giving my emotional performances you won't be all

round me watching." So she just showed them her tits and that
was it, nobody bothered after that.'

Dors wanted no distractions from a performance she saw as the
opportunity she had been waiting for:

> 'After ten years of vamping, I have got what I originally wanted to
> do – a really strong dramatic role ... This is the portrayal of a
> tortured woman, a bitter woman, a woman torn between the sense
> of justification for her crime and the price she may have to pay. It's
> a wonderful part, I love it.'[17] (*Photoplay*, January 1956)

The part was certainly a wonderful opportunity for Dors, but the
intensity of the role and the authenticity of the sets and costumes
quickly affected her, as she told the *Daily Mail's* reporter Maurice
Wiltshire: 'I keep telling myself this is only a film. But it's no good.
I shudder every time I have to go into that cell, even though it's
only a film set. I think it's the clothes. I keep thinking about the
wretched women who have to wear them' (*Daily Mail*, 3 November
1955). Dors' ability to convey distress and anxiety so powerfully
was evidently a response, in part, to the dreadful verisimilitude of
her surroundings, but may also have been deepened by events in
her personal life. The gambling and womanising of her husband
Dennis Hamilton was a constant cause of concern (Dors 1959:
140–1), but her role as a murderer was given a deeper poignancy
by the knowledge that Hamilton had recently persuaded her to
abort the child she was carrying, a decision she experienced as 'a
blight on our conscience' (139). In these circumstances, her role as
Mary Hilton, the condemned woman, can be seen as a form of
atonement.

Frewin's move to garner early publicity for the film turned out
to be a shrewd one, with photographs of the new-look Dors creating
a splash in the fan magazines and arousing public curiosity and
expectation. Diana's transformation from pin-up to actress fascin-
ated those journalists who had thought that, as she put it, 'Diana
Dors would never be capable of doing anything more accomplished
than climbing into a negligée' (*Photoplay*, April 1956). She used
her own column in *Picturegoer* to express her irritation at having
continually to answer the question 'What are you trying to prove?',

but confessed that, in addition to enhancing her earning power, the role of Mary Hilton was important for her self-esteem: 'I didn't have to work for my looks and my figure. I inherited them. And I get no kick at all out of being told that I'm gorgeous. But tell me I'm an actress and you'll make my day' (*Picturegoer*, 14 April 1956).

Dors would not have long to wait for the jury to return their verdict on her acting prowess. *Yield to the Night* was chosen as Britain's only official entry at the Cannes Film Festival after the festival authorities had requested the withdrawal of Rank's *A Town Like Alice*, lest it upset national sensibilities. With its Cannes' premiere scheduled for 4 May 1956, and its ten-week shooting schedule having taken production up to the start of the new year, time for post-production on *Yield to the Night* was tight.

In the run up to the Festival ABPC's publicity people continued to promote Diana Dors' image as a love goddess. During filming they had featured her flashing her legs as a sexy Santa on the cover of their own *ABC Film Review* (December 1955) and, on the eve of the Festival, she was called to Elstree for an all-day photo shoot, which was covered as an event in itself by the popular weekly *Illustrated*. Under the title 'Canned glamour' the magazine's reporter Cyril Kersh told readers that Dors was being sent to France 'to compete with the Continental lovelies' (*Illustrated*, 21 April 1956). Diana was shown dutifully posing for Frank Buckingham – in a clingy woollen dress for conservative British publications but wearing a cinching black basque for European magazines. The irony of using these pin-up shots to promote the grimmest of realist dramas was not lost, however, on Cyril Kersh, who concluded: 'Britain's film industry, the studio hopes, will be given a shot in the arm by this film – yet the film will be plugged by Hollywood-style pictures' (*Illustrated*, 12 April 1956). The criticism was well made, and it may have looked as if ABPC knew of only one way to sell a film, no matter what kind of drama it was, but Frewin's strategy seems to have been to market the contrast between the two 'Dianas'. The glamorous Diana implicitly invited cinemagoers to discover the real woman beyond the nyloned veneer. What *would* she look like without the make-up and peroxide? How would we be able to relate to her without her winsome smile or coquettish pout?[18]

Thus, the advance publicity for *Yield to the Night* may have aroused curiosity, but it may also have stimulated in its audience fantasies which would only handicap the film's attempts to win sympathy for its protagonist. After all, a film that shows a beautiful woman being punished (a key component of the women-in-prison genre), whatever the motivation of its creators, offers wish fulfilment to misogynists, and retributive satisfaction to women who feel threatened by overtly feminine displays. Her marketing as Britain's first Hollywood-style 'sex bomb', and her scandalous private life, marked out Diana Dors as a prime object of vindictive fantasy.[19] Her 'come-uppance' in *Yield to the Night* would offer succour to critics of both Americanisation and sexual licence, although they might find themselves recoiling from the sadistic spectacle of the 'blonde bombshell' stripped to her emotional essence and clinging desperately to life.

Hitchcock had challenged the persona of Madeline Carroll in a similar way. 'Nothing gives me greater pleasure than to knock the ladylikeness out', he said; 'that is why I deliberately deprived Madeline Carroll of her glamour and dignity in *The 39 Steps*. I have done the same thing with her in *Secret Agent* in which the first shot of her you see is with her face covered with cold cream' (Spoto 1983: 152). Lee Thompson did not approach the process of deglamorisation with quite such relish, but his film and the publicity which promoted it would probe the contradiction at the heart of audience perceptions of sex symbols during the first stirrings of the sexual revolution. In particular, they would (melo)dramatise that which Christine Geraghty (1986) has pointed to as 'the crux' of the construction of the 1950s sex symbol: the contradiction between 'knowingness' (exemplified in erotic display) and a redeeming vulnerability. While the publicity, partly driven by a wider imperative of demonstrating the sex appeal of British actresses to foreign markets, largely emphasised knowingness, the film itself would present a relentless examination of vulnerability.

Yield to the Night (1956, USA: *Blonde Sinner*)

> SIR WILLIAM JONES You said that women, when they are going to be hanged, are quite brave?
> MR PIERREPOINT Very brave.
> SIR WILLIAM What is the attitude of the women officers who have to attend them?
> MR PIERREPOINT The women don't see the execution. The men take over out of the cell, just before the execution.
> (Evidence to the 1949 Royal Commission on Capital Punishment, quoted in Koestler and Rolph 1961: 15–16)

Associated British sent to Cannes 'the biggest and most attractive party ever to represent the company at any festival' (*Kinematograph Weekly*, 3 May 1956). In addition to the producer, the director and the star of *Yield to the Night*, it included directors Michael Anderson and Mario Zampi and actors Richard Todd, George Baker and Yvonne Furneaux. There was always likely to be a jarring contrast between the melancholy mood of *Yield to the Night* and the film's ritzy marketing, in what Dilys Powell called an atmosphere of 'flashy, steamy, orchid-house luxury' (*Sunday Times*, 17 June 1956). The screening of Lee Thompson's bleak examination of a woman's suffering followed a lavish cocktail party. Dors drew up in a powder-blue Cadillac and swept into the festival palace in a dramatic matching-blue ballgown. She recalled (Dors 1978: 253):

> Inside the atmosphere was electric! The director J. Lee Thompson was sitting beside me, and tears were unashamedly rolling down his face, for he had lived and breathed this film for so long, and we all knew it was *good*. At the end the audience rose, applauding and cheering,[20] but in the midst of it, a tight-lipped John Davis [head of the Rank Organisation] strode past me with not a word of praise or congratulations.

Miffed by the success of a performance he felt Dors should have reserved for one of his own films (under her one picture a year contract with Rank), Davis denied her a place at the dinner which his company gave after the screening. There was no snub, however, from French distribution companies, which quickly snapped up the film in spite of its downbeat tone (*Kinematograph Weekly*,

10 May 1956). British critics, on the other hand, were more concerned about its sombre mood and the controversial nature of its message. However, the reviews that followed *Yield to the Night*'s opening at London's Carlton cinema on 13 June[21] were predominantly laudatory, particularly where the film's performances and direction were concerned. Most of the critics of the popular press seemed genuinely amazed at the qualities Diana Dors had demonstrated in her role. Peter Burnup in the *News of the World* (17 June 1956) proclaimed 'the emergence of an actress in her own right'. H. Deans in the *Sunday Dispatch* (17 June 1956) agreed that she 'stormed away with the picture', while Emery Pearce in the *Daily Herald* (15 June 1956) offered his congratulations on a 'truly great performance'. Others were more guarded in their praise, suggesting that Yvonne Mitchell stole the acting honours in a supporting role. Jympson Harman of the *Evening News* (14 June 1956) would concede only that Dors 'does quite well', while Edward Goring in the *Daily Mail* (15 June 1956) was prepared to admit that the film 'proves she can act' and that 'she gives as much as she has got', but added, acidly, 'unfortunately it is not quite enough'. The critics of the high-brow press were equally cautious. For Campbell Dixon in the *Daily Telegraph* (16 June 1956) it was a 'memorable performance'. For D. Granger of the *Financial Times* (18 June 1956) it was 'a commendable attempt'; but *The Times* (18 June 1956) was harsh in its judgement, noting the 'failure of Miss Dors to touch the more subtle of the emotions' and the substitution of 'a series of set poses' for 'true creative acting'. Not surprisingly, given the tacit criteria of 'quality' which so many of these reviewers shared (Ellis 1996) the aspects of the performance most praised were its obedience to directorial wishes and its emotional understatement. It was, remarked Caroline Lejeune (*Observer*, 17 June 1956), 'played with a decent reserve'.

This same quality of reserve was also valued in the film as a whole, and a number of reviewers contrasted its dignity with what Campbell Dixon (*Daily Telegraph* 16 June 1956) called 'the hysterical sadism' of an earlier French film about capital punishment, Andre Cayatte's *Nous sommes tous des assassins* (1953). Declaring *Yield to the Night* the 'most harrowing' film he had seen in years, Roy Nash (*Star*, 15 June 1956) told readers that, although it was three days since he had seen the film, 'the faces of Miss Dors and the wardresses in the final scenes haunt me still'. Again, it was understated emotion that most affected him: 'without mawkishness, with an almost clinical restraint, it brings home the full grisly ghastliness of the death cell'. Leonard Mosley (*Daily Express*, 16 June 1956) agreed that the film was 'compelling, gripping and left me shaken'. Harold Conway (*Daily Sketch*, 15 June 1956) was also pleased that the film 'never sensationalises' and confessed that 'during the entire second half ... my nerves were jangling in almost physical pain'. And, while crediting the performances of Yvonne Mitchell and Diana Dors, he was in no doubt that the reason the film 'grips you in a vice of horror is ... J. Lee Thompson's brilliant direction'. D. Granger (*Financial Times*, 18 June 1956) declined to go quite that far, however, describing Lee Thompson's directorial approach as one of 'rough, journalistic decency'.

It is curious that contemporary reviewers felt able to use so many of their favourite terms of appreciation – 'decency', 'restraint', 'dignity', 'reserve' – to describe a film which is certainly no *Brief Encounter* (David Lean, 1945). Rather than endorsing the social mores which elevate institutional imperatives above the gratification of personal desires, *Yield to the Night* exposes at the core of institutionalised order an inhumanity which coarsens and corrupts the lives it touches. Gone is David Lean's cosy vision of a hearth and home which may be dull, but which offers loving security. In Lee Thompson's film the hearth is no longer a place of safety, but a venue for suicide by gas heater in a lonely bedsitter. Home is not a comfy armchair in a suburban semi but an austere prison cell. The family which *Brief Encounter* championed as the bastion of 'decent' social arrangements has all but disappeared in *Yield to the Night*.[22] Mary Hilton has done what *Brief Encounter*'s Laura Jesson (Celia Johnson) could never bring herself to do: she has left the stifling confines of her marriage and moves among the unattached. In gaol, she grudgingly tolerates her husband's visits and is uncomfortable with her mother and brother. The comfort she receives is chiefly from strangers like Mrs Bligh, her visitor

(Athene Seyler), and state functionaries like the warders who give care and companionship in a death cell ensemble that constantly mocks the family group.

It might be tempting to read these inversions as a warning about the dangers of abandoning the normative world of *Brief Encounter*, were it not for the perverse purposes to which its sober conceptions of love and duty are applied. In *Yield to the Night*, the State's representatives demonstrate their commitment to loving compassion by ensuring that Mary Hilton goes to the gallows in the best possible health, and to duty by their unwavering dedication to hanging her. In other words, the finest of ideals are put to the basest of ends: the extinction of a life which has long ceased to be a danger to others. What the film offers is not a critique of deteriorating moral standards among the wayward, glamour-conscious, young, but an indictment of a continuing ethical failure by those older and more powerful. The film grants the demands of youth to fashion its own morality, however shallow or unsatisfactory it may appear, but it rejects the hypocrisy of a state which punishes an act of revenge with its own mortal vengeance.

Yield to the Night's polemic was an extraordinarily brave one by the conservative standards of 1950s' film making. Even with the radicalising influence of Hollywood exiles like Joseph Losey and Cy Endfield, British pictures of the era rarely deal with the institutionalisation of violence, let alone attempt to enlist our sympathy for a convicted murderer. But *Yield to the Night* achieves its aims without overt didacticism, and with a visual sophistication and unity worthy of Michael Powell. The aesthetic language of the film is established in its dynamic pre-credits' sequence, and it is worth looking at this scene in detail.

The sequence is a small masterpiece of narrative economy which, in three minutes of gripping cinema, shows how much Lee Thompson had learned from both David Lean and Alfred Hitchcock. In those three minutes, the visual and aural languages of the film are established and used to show the murder for which Mary Hilton is condemned. After fifty years of film making it remains the sequence of which Lee Thompson is most proud, having devised every camera angle and movement. His conception is perfectly realised by Gilbert Taylor's cinematography and Dick Best's razor-sharp editing. We are shown the preparation and enactment of an assassination in what is essentially a compression of the film's entire narrative structure. *Yield to the Night* begins and ends with the execution of a woman. The first takes three minutes of rapid-fire montage. The second is stretched over an almost unendurably poignant ninety minutes.

In the opening shots we are shown Trafalgar Square, a familiar tourist landmark, but this is not the picture-postcard view we usually see in movies.[23] From the outset, the expressionist cinematography positions us as voyeurs. We see the square from a disquieting pecking-pigeon angle or from behind ornamental balustrades and iconographically significant barred gates secured with a padlocked chain. Our surveillance camera follows the woman we will soon know as Mary Hilton as she strides purposefully through the pigeons towards the National Gallery. The canted camera angle contributes to the sense of dislocation as we view Mary from behind as she ascends the steps leading out of the Square. The mood is set by the foreboding sounds of Ray Martin's score, timpani-saturated and augmented only by the steady clicking of Mary's high-heels. As Viv Chadder (1999) has noted, the iconography of women's feet is a *leitmotif* of the post-war crime film, and in *Yield to the Night* it becomes an obsessive fixation. As she hails a taxi, we see Mary only from the waist down, her heels forming the point of a stiletto formation stabbing from the top of the frame. It is again her feet we see as she climbs into the vehicle. There are more locked gates and, as Taylor's camera tracks the taxi, we view from behind the naked foot of a statue along the route. As the taxi arrives (in canted long shot) in a busy street in west London the score is fractured by the diegetic sound of a veterans' harmonica band. As she leaves the taxi, there is a tight, fetishistic close-up of Mary's shoes and seamed stockings which is immediately contrasted with a close shot of the driver's hand as it swivels the 'for hire' sign back into position with a loud ring. Like feet, hands will become a prominent part of the film's visual rhetoric. The harmonica band dominates the frame as Mary moves resolutely on her way. As London goes about its daily business, we become increasingly aware that something untoward is about to happen.

Cut to a sniper's view of a Chelsea mews. From our position on the rooftop we can see the tiny figure of Mary striding down the quiet residential street. Suddenly the stillness is shattered by the thunderous roar of a motorbike as the frame is filled by another foot kick-starting the engine. The bike moves off to reveal Mary moving determinedly on. The woodwind and timpani soundtrack returns while we watch Mary through the windows of a sedan as it is cleaned by its driver. Mary at last arrives at her destination and we cut to a close shot of her gloved hand trying a key in the lock of an ornate door. She is disturbed by the noisy arrival of an American-styled car. In the foreground, Mary withdraws the key as, in deep focus, the car pulls to a halt. We see only the knee-length skirt and stockings of its driver as she turns off the ignition on the ostentatiously chromed dashboard. The camera dwells on her feet as she slips them erotically into elegant high-heeled courts and then quells the sound of lounge music on the car's radio. As she steps out of the car, a low-angle shot shows her to be expensively attired in an A-line coat with fur trim. We have still not seen her face as she crosses the front of the car, removing her gloves, heels click-clacking on the cobbles.[24] The camera follows her to the passenger window and, as we cut to a view of the car's front seat, we see that she has leaned through the open window to collect packages. As she takes the packages to her front door we watch her through the window of the valeted sedan. She unlocks the same door that Mary had tried to open moments earlier, and we glimpse her in profile before the camera pans to the watching Mary.

As the timpani begin to build on the soundtrack, there is an inspired cut to the newly polished hub-cap of the sedan in which we see Mary's distorted reflection, before the camera pans from the shiny metal to the soft fabric of her coat and up to rest on her clutch-bag. Up to this point, the cinematography has rhetorically suggested the seductive femininity and mystique of the two women. The building tension is sexually charged, but there is a sudden *frisson* of anticipated violence as Mary's hand reaches into her handbag to extract a revolver, before concealing it behind the bag. As we cut to her intended target (returning from depositing her packages) the soundtrack begins to swell. As her victim reaches her car to collect the remaining parcels, Mary uncovers her gun and begins to fire from the hip.

At the first shot, the incidental music is cut off and we watch through the windows of the victim's car as her hand, in involuntary spasms, throws a package in the air and then grasps despairingly at her passenger seat, pulling it forward as she is hit repeatedly by Mary's bullets. As her victim sinks to the ground we cut back to a point-of-view shot of Mary firing, her face registering only the effort of pulling the trigger and the loud report of the gun. As the final bullet is expelled the camera looks under the victim's car at her hand as the jewellery on her wrist hits the sandy cobbles. We see a wedding ring on her finger. Mary disgustedly tosses away the empty gun and, in a shot from her point of view, we watch it land between the feet of her victim. Immediately there are voices on the soundtrack as people crowd over the victim's body. One of them, the sedan's valet, looks up at Mary in fear and disbelief, the camera showing us his point of view as it closes in on Mary's face. The timpani music rises once again as Mary's quivering lip reveals her mounting anguish. Quickly the close-up becomes so tight that her face blurs and we understand that her mind, too, has lost its focus. The timpani's crescendo breaks dramatically into the film's elegiac theme and the screen is geometrically divided by stylised prison bars as the title sequence begins.

We have viewed one of the most arresting openings of any British film. Without a word of dialogue, and employing film-making techniques which were strikingly progressive for British cinema in the 1950s, we have been shown the crime for which Mary Hilton will be incarcerated. With almost forty edits and hardly a naturalistic shot, the sequence has eloquently expressed the distanciated state of mind of the protagonist and introduced the visual language and motifs which the rest of the film will use. These include mediated shots in which foregrounded objects break up the frame, distance the viewer from the action and register the intrusive and voyeuristic gaze; high, low and canted angle shots to further disturb the audience's complacent viewpoint; strong attention to geometric design within the frame with particular emphasis on verticals suggesting entrapment; keys and locks as emblems of a situation from which the protagonist craves release; and the detailed observation of body parts – particularly feet and hands – which will be used both to suggest a heightened state of consciousness and to express key states of mind.[25]

This iconographic system is evident in the very first shot that follows the title sequence: a key turned in a lock. Our first view of Mary Hilton in prison is a low-angle shot of her hand, recalling the shot of her victim's hand from beneath her car, a viewing point further echoed in a sequence which begins the de-eroticising of Mary and, by extension, of Diana Dors. We are again invited to gaze at her legs, but now they are loosely clad in coarse Lisle rather than sheathed in fine-denier nylon. She no longer wears her sexually aggressive high-heels, and she pulls off her hosiery and climbs into bed without a hint of allure. Gilbert Taylor's camera explores a woman stripped, not to the nubile flesh but to the emotional bone; and there is something distinctly embarrassing about viewing Mary – or more pertinently Dors – in this condition. We almost feel we should turn away to allow Diana to paint her face and cantilever her bosom, to reconstruct the 'glamour babe' persona on which her confidence and sense of self appear to rest. Without it, there is no sparkle in her eyes:[26] the light within has been extinguished just as she craves the switching off of the bulb that continuously illuminates her cell. 'Put out the light', she implores her gaolers, but instead she is given an eye shade, a piece of black fabric which must resemble the black cap her judge wore when pronouncing the sentence of death.

The light in her cell, of course, symbolises both Mary's own life and the surveillance which she is constantly under both from her warders and, extra-diegetically, from the film's audience. As in Michael Powell's *Peeping Tom* we, the audience, are obliged to watch the moments leading up to death and are invited to acknowledge our complicity in what is happening on screen. But, whereas

Powell shamelessly implicates us in a lurid Eastman-colour fantasy, Lee Thompson offers us monochromed realism in which the claustrophobic settings increase our discomfort with the role of voyeur. Our unease is intensified by the positioning of the camera. The agile Arriflex continually shuns the direct shot, preferring to adopt a furtive, sheltered position, behind furniture, low to the ground, or (quintessentially scoptophilic) peering though the cell window. The camera's intrusion may be softened by the mediation of fixtures and furnishings but is merciless in its interrogation. It records every nuance of Mary's relationship to her environment as if gathering data for an ergonomic study. Rarely in film is a setting quite so crucial or so closely observed as it is in *Yield to the Night*.[27] The bleak cell reflects back Mary's despair as pitilessly as the endless desert mocks human endeavour in *Ice Cold in Alex*. 'I know every mark and blemish in this cell', Mary's voice-over tells us, and Taylor's camera shows us with microscope clarity 'every crack in the walls; the scratches on the wooden chairs; the place where the paint has peeled off the ceiling; and the door at the foot of the bed, the door without a handle'. Mary remarks that she knows it 'better than any room I've ever lived in' and it begins to have the same oppressive familiarity for the audience. We may not have experienced the terrors of the death cell but, as Mary's unwed lover (Michael Craig) remarks about marriage, 'you don't have to go down a coal mine to know it's dark and deadly'.

But what *Yield to the Night* shows us with the greatest clarity is the collapse or dislocation of human relationships in the face of death. Lee Thompson uses the metonym of eye contact to eloquently express the emotional disengagement which prefigures death. When Mary's mother (Dandy Nichols) visits and tells her how she cannot look the signatories of the reprieve petition in the face it is evident that Mary cannot meet the gaze of her mother. In a shot which becomes a rhetorical trope of the film, her profile on the left of the frame is contrasted with the full face of her conversational partner on the right – a 'two shot' which quotes the dual-angle police 'mug shot'. This compositional practice complements the use of hands and feet as signifiers. In her bath, for

example, a disengaged Mary is seen in profile while her finger-
nails are clipped by a gaoler. She has not requested this service,
and it may be read as a metaphor for the submission of her
feminine vanity to the disciplinary regimes of the prison as well as
for the curtailment of her growth (life). There is also constant
reference to the condition of feet and shoes, from Mary's heightened awareness of one warder's 'flat, sensible shoes with iron
studs in the soles' (illustrated in hyper-real close-up), to her
problems with a blister on her own foot.[28] The blister 'matters',
she is told, and clearly the condition hobbles her, just as prison
restricts her bodily freedom and shackles her to its routines. We
are shown a close-up of Mary's bandaged foot and, in a scene
where she angrily sweeps a chess set from its board, the camera
creeps below the table to reveal the carpet slippers Mary wears. In
stark contrast to her youthful, high-heeled, pomp this is the
footwear of the aged, as if imminent execution had accelerated the
ageing process. She is certainly cared for as the old or sick are
cared for – her mattress is turned and she is weighed, bandaged,
manicured and generally tended – by her uniformed companions
who frequently talk distractedly among themselves. The banality
of their conversations strikes an ironic counterpoint to the
profundity of Mary's situation, a difference of depth which is
sometimes given visual expression in the use of deep-focus
photography – notably when Mary is seen with a warder knitting
in the foreground like a tricoteuse before the guillotine. When
death is close and predictable the most casual and unremarkable
of actions or phrases can take on a chilling new meaning: 'There's
a bitter east wind', a warder warns Mary in the exercise yard, 'you
could catch your death.'

In such an unbearable present and with such an unthinkable
future, it is inevitable that Mary should retreat into the past, and
Lee Thompson uses the standard noir technique of flash-backs
which reveal how his protagonist arrived at her doomed situation.
Although they reproduce the narrative order of Henry's book,
some critics felt that these sequences unnecessarily interrupted
the build up of tension in the death cell scenes.[29] Without them,
however, the contrast between the two Marys/Dianas would be

thoroughly muted, and with the use of a classical narrative structure the element of mystery would be removed. In telling the story of Mary's tragic relationship with her lover Jim, the flashbacks adopt the same visual codes and practices as the rest of the film. For example, when Mary first encounters her rival for Jim's affections and her eventual victim, Lucy (Mercia Shaw), a dangerous sexuality is suggested by the shot of her feet from Mary's point of view: 'That was the first thing I noticed about Lucy, her legs and feet – the beautiful shoes she had on, black suede with very high heels.' At the inquest after Jim's suicide, Mary's perception of Lucy as rich, spoilt and indifferent to the suffering of others is encapsulated in a close up of Lucy's ostentatiously bejewelled hand, its fingers impatiently strumming on the witness-box rail.

Diegetic music from radios is used to comment ironically on Mary's feelings,[30] and our view is constantly mediated by the foregrounding of mundane objects – tables, cupboards, benches, radios, etc. – in banal counterpoint to the depth of emotion beyond them in the frame. These directorial flourishes bring a vitality to what might otherwise be a conventional enough melodrama. Alan Brien writing in the *Evening Standard* (14 June 1956) called them 'irritating mannerisms', but conceded that at least they constituted 'a style which is personal and individual'. Peter John Dyer in *Films and Filming* (June 1956), however, had fewer reservations. Applauding *Yield to the Night*'s 'integrity, balance and grim refusal to alleviate its distress to box office tastes', he judged that its director revealed 'a fine sense of style, resourceful and very rarely mannered'. Lee Thompson's 'sense of detail in sound and vision', he felt, carried 'great weight and intuition', while the lighting and camerawork were 'masterly'.

Editor Dick Best concurs:

> 'I think *Yield to the Night* is tremendous in the way it's shot. There was a power. There are scenes in that film – on her [Mary's] last night when she's in bed – that are shot terribly ominously. They're low angle and you get an amazing feeling of gloom. ... It's shot in such an unorthodox way. If it had been cut, cut, cut, you wouldn't have got a feeling of impending doom, but he shot it in those semi-master shots with a moving camera ... *Yield to the Night* needed

very little editing – it is nearly all single planned master shots. I know when I viewed the rushes, it was nearly all cut or fade or dissolve from this master shot to that master shot. There was some cutting, but very little compared to most films.'

Gil Taylor remembers the challenge that this unconventional approach to the visual structuring and linking of scenes posed for him:

'Lee did masters at both ends of every sequence. He was terrible, he used to catch you out by saying, "I must have a reverse master on this", and you had to set all the bloody lights up again in reverse, which was terribly difficult, but I knew he was going to do it, although he promised he wouldn't ... And we also used to tie up one sequence with another so that it blended in nicely. The workings between cutting, and the lighting between cuts, was important, and we did it so that it cut right from one scene to another. If you were doing an interior and you had to cut outside to sunshine you would control the light so it wouldn't hit you in the face.'

When the full ensemble of technical expertise, acting talent and directorial sensitivity work together within the codes of the film's symbolic system, the effect is stunning. The finest example is the sequences in which Mary learns that there will be no commutation of her sentence. By the eve of her execution we have witnessed Mary's slow disintegration into abjection and paranoia, sharing her embittered anguish and the embarrassed compassion of her warders. She wakes to a sound montage of disciplinary commands before her voice-over breaks in to tell us that she hears the governor's footsteps in the corridor.[31] Her apparent prescience is attributable to a state of heightened perception which the closeness of death appears to bring. She stands, in medium shot, wide-eyed as she realises that she will 'know in a minute'. We cut away to the corridor, the warder's key chain in the foreground and the governor walking in deep focus towards the camera. Cutting back to an immobile Mary we hear her thought: 'I don't want to know', and then back to the corridor where a pensive governor nods to the warder to open the door. Editor Dick Best cuts between Mary's fear-filled eyes and her view of the cell door before the most arresting set-up of the sequence shows Mary in low-angle long shot as the door swings into the foreground, momentarily (and symbolically) blacking her out before swinging back to reveal the governor's woollen skirt and glistening walking shoes. A reverse camera angle from a position just behind Mary shows a silent tableau of the governor and the two warders. As the tension heightens uncomfortably the governor tells Mary that she 'must have courage', causing the two warders to avert their eyes from the doomed woman's gaze. As soon as the governor, in tones as flat as her shoes, has informed Mary that 'the Home Secretary has not seen fit to recommend a reprieve', the camera zooms in on her stupefied expression before cutting back and forth in a short series of reverse shots while the governor pledges to facilitate any last requests 'in accordance with the regulations'. As the governor leaves the cell, her 'painful duty' done, Lee Thompson reverts to the low-angle shot of Mary, who is again momentarily lost in the swing of the door.[32] When she re-appears standing in long shot like a ghost in her white night-dress, she knows that she too will 'swing'. It is one of the most profound shots in British cinema, and the director holds it, maintaining a discreet distance as Mary, alone and desolate, sinks slowly into a sitting position. Her staring eyes and limp arms already suggest a corpse and, although she does not have the composure of *The Blue Lamp*'s (Basil Dearden, 1949) Mrs Dixon (Gladys Henson), who reacts to the news of her husband's death by putting flowers in water, her silent response is within the British theatrical tradition of emotional continence exemplified by *Brief Encounter*. As Richard Dyer (1994) has commented, 'some of the great emotional moments in British cinema occur when the performance allows the pressure of feeling to be felt beneath a flatness of expression', and here the flatness shades into insensibility. Harold Conway (*Daily Sketch*, 15 June 1956) singled out this sequence and 'Miss Dors' expression of mute, numbed dread' as the film's most 'unforgettable moment', but although its dramatic impact is undeniable, we should not rush to equate its power with authenticity. In the real situation, Ruth Ellis' reaction on being told by the governor of Holloway that she would not be reprieved was apparently that she had hysterics and lay on her bed screaming 'I don't want to die' (Hancock 1993: 176).

Mary Hilton, however, stares at the unforgiving cell walls as a warder first takes her *hands* and closes them around a mug of tea before reaching down to place Mary's *feet* in her slippers. As the warder kneels, she looks up at Mary with a compassion that borders on adoration and whispers: 'I'm so sorry. I'm so dreadfully sorry.' Thus the scene ends in a tableau which resembles a Renaissance *pietà* in which the white-clad Mary Hilton plays the sacrificed Christ and the warder replaces his grieving mother.[33] Women's love, it seems, passeth all understanding in the weird sisterhoods of this film. Lucy is punished by Mary for her lack of compassion, while Mary herself struggles to accept the compassion of warder–companions who preside over her own punishment. The devotion comes principally from McFarlane (Yvonne Mitchell) whose empathy with Mary is deepened by the problems of her own home life. Their mutual unhappiness draws them towards each other in a way that transcends sexual orientation.[34] One might interpret the bonds that develop in this isolated and pressurised environment between Mary and her warders (particuarly Yvonne Mitchell's McFarlane) as an alliance against a repressive masculine apparatus of justice, but this would be simplistic and misleading. Although there is a suggestion that McFarlane is as much a prisoner of circumstance as the woman she guards,[35] and there is evident affection between them, Mary's emotional responsiveness is restricted by her dismissal of her gaolers as 'smug' overlaid with a (rational?) paranoia which implicates McFarlane in the conspiracy against her: 'You're in league with the others; you want to kill me', she rants at McFarlane. 'I hate you, I hate you all.' There is little feminist solidarity in the death cell, only a collusion in the act of murder. As Mary puts it, her warders 'all have a funny look in their eyes – like I had once – but they're going to kill someone too; only this time it's legal'. They encourage her not to fight for life but to 'accept' her punishment, making it 'easier to bear'. To see Mary's preparation for extinction in the condemned cell as a stark metaphor for the fate of female transgression under the Law of the Father glosses over too much.[36] Mary may have broken the bonds of domesticity and threatened patriarchal stability with her sexuality, but her wrath is directed principally against other women, and it is they who endorse her punishment.[37] Indeed, it was her sexuality that was implicitly offered as grounds for reprieve in the film's promotional campaign, which was dominated by an alluring portrait of Diana Dors – lips full and open, eyes closing in ecstasy – accompanied by the largely rhetorical question: 'Would *You* Hang Mary Hilton?'[38]

I have argued elsewhere (Chibnall 1999) that the crisis of masculinity evident in so many British genre films in the twenty years following the Second World War was marked by an unresolved ambivalence towards the sexually assertive woman.[39] In *Yield to the Night*, that ambivalence is apparently resolved by the de-sexualising of Dors/Hilton and the (justifiable?) homicide of the predatory Lucy, but resurfaces in the film's publicity which enlists male desire in the campaign against the noose. Nor is it an inappropriate strategy for a film which laments the violent repression of libidinous impulses by a vengeful and puritanical state. Raymond Durgnat, in discussing the 'punitive streak' in British Puritanism which is exemplified by a 'fascination with the condemned cell', has suggested that *Yield to the Night* appeared at 'a kind of junction of liberalism and severity'. He refers to an identification with 'suffering passivity' (1970: 165) which, one might argue, is an inchoate state of social criticism. Lee Thompson's film begins to move British cinema beyond sympathy for the underdog and into the realms of active critique. It opens the door not only to the liberal–humanist social-problem films of Dearden and Relph, but also to the bitterness of *Look Back in Anger* (Tony Richardson, 1959) and *Saturday Night and Sunday Morning* (Karel Reisz, 1961). Like Durgnat, Dilys Powell has argued that *Yield to the Night* marks a transition point in the replacement of a strict morality by a less censorious one,[40] and perhaps it is not over-fanciful to see Mary's condemned cell as an image, not simply of an imprisoning social order, but also of the stifling restrictions imposed on British film making.[41] When the prison doctor (Geoffrey Keen) advises Mary to 'conform to the routine however hard and futile it may seem', he could be offering a credo to all toilers in a national film industry shackled by gentility, euphemism and banality. Either way, there is a compelling case for interpreting the overwhelming identification with Mary's suffering which the film encourages as a vital expiation of guilt before the slow acceptance of more progressive moral, legal and artistic frameworks. Or to express this idea of necessary catharsis more flippantly: Mary Hilton had to swing before the 1960s could.

In the end, we identify with a woman who atones for her sins without the customary display of remorse. Although she knows she has 'done wrong', she regrets nothing, is 'not ready to die', and she rejects a hearty breakfast on the day of her execution. As she smokes her final cigarette[42] before praying with her gaolers she remains recalcitrant and, as the camera closes in on a neck that will soon feel the touch of hemp, she still refuses to endorse the legitimacy of her fate. When she is led to the gallows she leaves with dignity,[43] and as she fixes the viewer with her eyes before moving into shadow, any lingering desire for retribution we might harbour is swept away by a profound sense of tragedy. And as contemporary audiences watched the final frames of the film, with a bell tolling solemnly and the smoke coiling up symbolically from Mary's abandoned cigarette, they would have needed no reminder of Mrs Blight's prediction that the burden of Mary's sin would pass from her 'to those who have to go as usual about their daily business'. It is the final transfer of a film in which tragedy has been passed in a relay from one recipient to another. Its progress has been motivated by the dynamic set up when obsession meets rejection – Jim's indifference to Mary's desire; Lucy's rebuff of Jim's infatuation; Mary's refusal to legitimise the pious ministration of her gaolers; and, ultimately, the audience's rejection of the obsessive rituals of a criminal justice system bent on retribution.

J. Lee Thompson regards *Yield to the Night* as 'very much one of the best' films of his career. It is, he says, 'always very close to my heart'. For this, he feels, much of the credit must go to Diana Dors:

'I thought she was magnificent in it. She was noted for being a light comedienne. She hadn't done many dramatic roles. She knew it was the part of a lifetime, and it was one of the best experiences I've ever had working with her on that film; especially in the death cell as she got more and more drab looking and more and more worried. I knew at the time I was getting a very good performance from her, and I think she was underestimated by the critics. She didn't get the acclaim she should have had.'[44]

For Joan Henry, too, Diana Dors' performance is the abiding memory of a film which had faithfully reflected the spirit and mood of her story ('no author could have been more pleased'): 'I thought Diana was absolutely marvellous and Lee was marvellous in getting the performance out of her. I can see her now, walking towards the door in the wall, and she looked really as if she was already dead.' The film-makers may have been satisfied with their achievement, but the British Board of Film Censors felt that *Yield to the Night* succeeded rather too well in distressing its audience and decreed that the under-16's should not be exposed to its horrors. Lee Thompson was mortified by the 'X' certificate, as he told a television interviewer in 1994: 'I did everything I could to try and persuade Watkins [the Board's secretary] that he was wrong, but nothing would alter his opinion ... What the censors objected to was the whole premise, not any one particular scene – the torment of a woman in the death cell.'[45]

The censors' fears were given some substance when the film went on general release in the late summer of 1956. In Hove, Rosemary Vale, the 19-year-old daughter of a solicitor returned home after seeing *Yield to the Night* in Brighton and, like the love-lorn Jim Lancaster in the film, gassed herself. Insisting that Rosemary was 'a happy, normal girl', but admitting that she was also 'rather lonely', her mother denounced 'the ghastliness of such films' (*Daily Express*, 6 September 1956). Movies have always been a ready scapegoat for the grieving parents of troubled adolescents, but it does not require a monkey-see-monkey-do model of media effects to recognise that Lee Thompson's film is a disquieting and harrowing experience. As Caroline Lejeune (certainly not the most sentimental of critics) remarked: 'it is impossible for anyone with an imaginative turn of mind not to be moved' (*Observer*, 17 June 1956). We cannot know what despair predated the viewing of *Yield to the Night* by a lonely girl from Hove, but, if isolation was tipped into suicide, it is tragic testimony to the emotional power of the film. It is indicative, too, of the film's social penetration that its story of the torments of a shop girl from bedsit-land could reach so devastatingly into the well-heeled comfort of Hove, that most complacent of bourgeois citadels.

Lee Thompson prefers to stress the positive rather than the negative effects of his picture, pointing out that *Yield to the Night* was screened for members of parliament on more than one occasion, 'and I like to think that it had some small part in removing the death penalty'. The direct influence of the film is harder to establish. The last execution of a woman (Ruth Ellis) in Britain took place a year before *Yield to the Night* premiered. The film was already an elegy for a departed method of dealing with the unruly female. Two days after its West End release in June 1956, the House of Commons voted to retain the death penalty only for murders committed by prisoners already serving life sentences. When the Abolition Bill was debated by the Lords the following month, leading supporters Arthur Koestler and Gerald Gardiner QC arranged a special screening of Mary Hilton's ordeal for their lordships. Only six peers turned up to the National Film Theatre screening. Their reactions were mixed. One of them, 71-year-old Lord Burden, voted for the Bill while another, 28-year-old Lord Denham, voted against (*News Chronicle*, 20 August 1956). Denham was in the majority and the Bill was defeated in the Lords. The death penalty lingered on into the next decade, but the moral order it symbolised was already being given its last rights. While *Yield to the Night* went on general release Bill Haley and Elvis Presley dominated the pop charts and Britain's nostalgic attempt to flex its muscles as a world power ended in the military fiasco of Suez.

In the week *Yield to the Night* premiered and unexpectedly large crowds flocked to see Dors *sans* glamour, the mass circulation tabloid *Tit-Bits* (16 June 1956) carried a front page pin-up of Diana in a strapless evening gown dramatically slashed to the hip and stilettos that would have made Lucy envious. Inside, 'famous TV personality' Jeanne Heal assured her women readers that it was no longer necessary 'to keep on being British at all costs'. With the days of empire-building over, she suggested that 'we might now relax and enjoy ourselves in the manner of other people'. Rather than 'Why foreigners find *us* attractive', her piece might easily have been titled 'Yield to the Europeans', which, in a way, Lee Thompson's film already had: a British picture with a continental-style 'X' certificate, a British actress promoted like a foreign sex symbol; a British woman rejecting her dull husband and taking a younger lover; a British shop girl showing contempt for her 'social betters' in committing a continental crime of passion; and, finally, a British film-maker relishing what *Picturegoer* (30 June 1956) called 'cunning French-type direction'. Mary Hilton may never have escaped her prison cell, but her death was a significant moment of liberation for British cinema. Lee Thompson, too, had staged his own moment of liberation, leaving his wife for Joan Henry. His loss of wifely support left him, in Gil Taylor's words, 'much neglected' during the filming of *Yield to the Night*. 'I used to buy his shirts and do his laundry and have it all done for him', recalls his cinematographer. 'I used to send a boy out with ten bob to get him a clean shirt and stuff to wear.'

Notes

1 Interview with the author, 21 July 1999. All subsequent quotations from Joan Henry are taken from this interview, unless otherwise indicated.
2 The page number refers to the 1958 edition of the book, published in London by Four Square Books.
3 Zalcock (1998) identifies at least fourteen American films dealing with the subject of women in prisons and reform schools before 1952. See also Parish (1991).
4 The screenplay was by Muriel Box and a writer who would later become an important collaborator with J. Lee Thompson: Ted Willis. Two other British films had told the stories of incarcerated women, but both were set in France: Brian Desmond Hurst's *Prison Without Bars* (1938) and Frank Launder's *2000 Women* (1944).
5 The implied lesbianism in *Prison Without Bars*, for example, had already

provoked action from the American Producer Code Administration (Slide 1999:120).

6 The sanitising of Henry's book was a source of disappointment to some of its readers among the critics. For example P. Wilsher in the *Sunday Chronicle* (7 February 1954) complained: 'All the vice, squalor, sex and life has been smoothly pressed out, and a pale cloying "niceness" injected in its place, till you feel it should have been retitled *Mrs Dale's Gaol*.'

7 The theft had been intended as a joke and the 'technical' nature of Dors' conviction was reflected by her absolute discharge (Wise: 1998: 75–7).

8 See, for example Andrew Walton, 'Dors deglamorized', *Picturegoer*, 6 February 1954. Remarkably, both Diana Dors and Glynis Johns had appeared in previous women-in-prison films: *Prison Without Bars* (Johns) and *Good Time Girl* (Dors).

9 Jean demonstrates her new commitment to altruism, first by not standing in the way of her beau when he is given the opportunity of a job in Rhodesia; and then standing in the way when one of her fellow inmates tries to attack a vindictive prison officer. She is hospitalised with a stab wound as a result.

10 The attack on the warder, which Jean intercepts, is by a woman of Latin appearance (Simone Silva).

11 Not every critic disliked the film's use of comedy. Ross Shepherd (*People*, 7 February 1954) approved of the lightening of 'a grim enough subject' by 'some broad and brilliant comedy'. The *Daily Mirror*'s Reg Whitely (5 February 1954) also enjoyed 'some very good laughs' in a 'superbly acted' and 'first-rate film'; and Beverly Baxter in the *Evening Standard* (4 February 1954), while showing some concern at the film's lack of emotional depth, complimented it on its lightness of touch: 'it does not preach. [It] tells its story with both sad and amusing half-lights and only touches tragedy with gentle fingers.'

12 *Dance With a Stranger* (Mike Newell, 1985) *is* a bio-pic of Ruth Ellis.

13 The location of the murder in Lee Thompson's film is one of only two significant changes to Henry's novel which increase its resemblance to the Ellis case. The film moves the murder of Lucy from the interior of her flat to the street outside and reduces Mary Hilton's age from mid-30s (the age of the book's author) to mid-20s. Ruth Ellis was 28 when she killed Blakely.

14 Henry's recollection is as follows:

> 'Everybody thought my book was written about Ruth Ellis. It had nothing to do whatsoever with Ruth Ellis. It was out here, published by Gollancz, and it was out in America, published by Doubleday. I should say it was just over eighteen months before Ruth Ellis did the crime, and then it all took a long time. When she was sentenced to death, *Yield to the Night* was on the floor at Elstree. I remember Lee and I asked, when it happened, if we could stop because it all seemed so awful.'

15 A Mass Observation poll published in the *Daily Telegraph* in January 1956 revealed that of those asked, only 8 per cent actively approved of her execution (*Murder Casebook*, 11, 1990: 3 75).

16 She had previously appeared in *The Weak and the Wicked* (with Dors) and *For Better, For Worse*.

17 Interestingly, as Dors willingly embraced the deglamorising of her image, her co-star, the 'serious' actress Yvonne Mitchell, was reportedly yearning to play a 'really glamorous' role (*Films and Filming*, January 1956).

18 This marketing strategy is made explicit in the film's press book which encouraged exhibitors to display contrasting images of its star, together with the invitation to 'Meet the new Diana Dors'.

19 Harper and Porter's researches on fan magazines of the period suggest (1999: 73) that among teenage girls, in particular, Diana Dors was 'the most loathed' female star. The misogyny that her image provoked was still evident in comments on *Yield to the Night*, even after Dors' death. Gilbert Adair (1985: 61–2), for example, having made the common mistake of describing the film as being based on Ruth Ellis, has this to say: 'But even if Diana Dors ... with her chrome-gloss hair, her tawdry volupté and her mask-like, floury white, unbreakably porcelain face – a face like a breast on which someone has pencilled a face – was oddly effective in a stagey, posturing fashion, the treatment seemed intent less on "indicting" an unjust penal system than on voyeuristically leering at its heroine's degradation.' One need look no further for an example of the distortion of perception by the unconscious need for wish fulfilment.

20 Dilys Powell, however, detected a 'lukewarmness' in the audience response: 'Although surprised by such a lack of compromise from a British film, a Festival audience claps violence and gimmicks and the story which J. Lee Thompson has so ably directed has little of either' (*Sunday Times*, 6 May 1956).

21 The BBFC refused the 'A'-certificate Lee Thompson had wanted and classified the film as an 'X'.

22 The film's sympathetic attitude to the dissolution of marriage is probably a consequence of Lee Thompson's and Joan Henry's desires to abandon previous relationships and to establish a new partnership with each other.

23 The script produced in August 1955 begins in a mews in Belgravia. The sequence in Trafalgar Square was probably added for its visual expansiveness, but it also acts as a homage to the opening of Carol Reed's *A Kid For Two Farthings* released that year.

24 This repeated emphasis on the fetishised sound of footwear recalls Robert Hancock's description of Ruth Ellis in court: 'Ruth walked with a high-heeled clicking from the dock to the witness box' (1993: 58).

25 This close observation of hands and feet is taken directly from Henry's original novel. The implications of this fragmentation of body parts in a feminist theory of representation are clearly significant, signifying the destruction and dehumanising of the female body and a refusal to see women as complete individuals. Thus Landy (1991: 456) concluded of *Yield to the Night*:

> At stake is the familiar destruction of the female body by the authorities (and by the camera) ... From the perspective of the camera, the

woman's body become a site of conflicting images with which to read the nature of her motivation and responses to her impending death. From the perspective of the prison guards and the physician, her body is the symptom of her deviance.

26 Joan Henry had seen eyes like these during her time in prison, first in the face of a woman remanded on a murder charge, and then a woman serving five years for manslaughter: 'she had a strange, impassive kind of face, and her eyes were those of someone walking in her sleep, unblinking and void' (Henry 1952: 167).

27 Perhaps Polanski's *Repulsion* (1965), also photographed by Gil Taylor, offers a still more expressionistic examination of the psychological disintegration within a confined space of its tragic blonde protagonist.

28 Joan Henry had received treatment in prison for a foot condition.

29 For example, Harold Conway (*Daily Sketch*, 15 June 1956).

30 Lee Thompson remembers that even this use of diegetic music was controversial at the time:

> 'I wanted some jazz music to play against the drama, and I selected a lot of my own record collection, like *The Very Thought of You*, and used that every now and then in the film, much to Louis Levy's disgust. Louis Levy was the musical director at ABPC in those days, and he thought it was very wrong to use already recorded music. Studios liked to use their own orchestra and write the music themselves. I had quite a battle to use the jazz music we did.'

31 The sequence showcases the wonderfully detailed work of sound recording director Harold King and dubbing editor A. Southgate.

32 In *Odd Man Out*, Carol Reed and his cinematographer Robert Krasker had also used frequent low-angle shots of James Mason. Wapshott (1990: 185) suggests that this was 'a subliminal device' to elevate the character of Johnny, 'thereby giving him the dignity of a public monument or a political orator'.

33 The sequence deviates significantly from the script of 9 August 1955, scenes 143–5, adding the sound montage and voice-over and bringing forward the warder's offer of a mug of tea from a later scene (154). The treatment of Mary's emotional response has also been altered from the highly subjective original: 'The Governor goes on talking but her voice becomes faint and Mary sees her as a blurred image ... She seems to slide back or recede into the distance.' The scene was initially intended to end with a growing sound of traffic and a shock cut to a newspaper seller tearing down a hoarding proclaiming 'Mary Hilton to Hang' and replacing it with 'All the Latest Winners'.

34 The McFarlane character was based on a nursing sister who showed Joan Henry kindness when she was in Holloway's hospital ward with a foot complaint: 'I'm about the least lesbian person you could ever think of, but when you're in a very unhappy state and somebody is slightly kind to you ... At first it did seem rather lesbian really, but it's just that you must turn to somebody.'

35 This is made explicit in Henry's novel, in which Mary says of MacFarlane: 'In a way she was a prisoner too, or at least, I like to think so' (1954: 65).

36 Landy's contention that 'the film can be read as a broader allegory of society's retaliation against female desire through all of its institutional channels' (1991: 458) is guilty of glossing over some important complexities and contradictions in the film.

37 Viv Chadder's discussion of Ruth Ellis suggests she may have been 'hung for her transgressive image' and goes on to refer to contemporary surveys which revealed that women were less inclined than men to pardon her (Chadder 1999: 72–3).

38 Physical attractiveness was also an important element in the opposition to Ruth Ellis' execution. It is significant that the death sentence passed only a few months previously on Mrs Styllou Christofi, a Cypriot woman in her 50s, and rather plain, elicited a far lower level of public protest.

39 Dilys Powell hinted at the depth of this ambivalence when, interviewed on the television documentary series *Fifties' Features* (1986), she tried to make sense of the public reaction to *Yield to the Night*: ' I just don't know whether people ... thought it was a good idea for this girl who looked so pretty, and had worn such lovely clothes, and had had such a jolly good time, whether they thought it was a good idea for her, in particular, to be hanged.'

40 Ibid..

41 The restrictions were imposed not only by the British Board of Film Censors but by the American Production Code Administration (PCA) which, as Anthony Slide (1999) has documented, was still exerting a censorious influence on British film scripts until the end of the 1950s. *Yield to the Night* was released by Allied Artists in the USA, without a PCA seal of approval, as *Blonde Sinner*. It was cut by nearly thirty minutes, with many of the prison sequences removed.

42 This final image of the smouldering cigarette was not specified by the script of 9 August. It was added by Joan Henry after speaking to the prison officer who acted as an anonymous informant on the execution process:

> 'I said to him, "As you've done so many of these executions, what struck you most?" And he said, "Well, actually, the quickness of it. They nearly all had a cigarette before they went, and by the time we came back into the cell, the cigarette was often still burning in the ashtray." And I put that in the end of the film.'

43 Dignity was not necessarily a feature of the process of a real execution. Edith Thompson, for instance, had to be carried to the gallows in 1923 (*Murder Casebook*, 11, 1990: 391). Joan Henry's prison officer informant told her that as the moment of execution approaches, most prisoners experience the need to urinate and defecate, but they would, if necessary, be dragged to the scaffold with their pants down. They were obliged to wear their own clothes so that prison garments would not be soiled. On 20 August 1955, the *Lancet* disclosed that condemned women were made to put on waterproof underwear on the morning of the execution (Koestler and Rolph 1961: 67). *Yield to the Night*'s audience is spared these realities,

although the script of 9 August has Mary dressed for execution in her own clothes and asking who polished her shoes.

44 Gil Taylor agrees that Lee Thompson got a wonderful performance from Dors, adding: 'He fancied her like hell, of course, but he was terrified of her boyfriend – you could get your throat cut there.'

45 From unpublished transcripts of a 1994 interview by J. Lee Thompson for *Empire of the Censors*, broadcast on BBC 2 in May 1995. Comparison of the 9 August script with the finished film suggests that the censor may also have been concerned about a bedroom scene (scene 76) and Mary's comments about the Home Secretary – 'Does he lie awake at night – like me – thinking?'

1 A comedy of errors. Dennis Price takes one drink too many and Derek Farr contemplates the poisoned chalice in *Murder Without Crime*

2 Inflated claims? The poster for *The Yellow Balloon* (1953) tries hard to turn the film's certification to its advantage

3 The cool and the crazy: Glynis Johns is the object of the male gaze in *The Weak and the Wicked* (1954)

4 Kitchen-sink comedy: Susan Stephen discusses the problems of domestic management with her cheerless char (Thora Hird) in *For Better, For Worse* (1954)

5 Artist and model: Jack Buchanan discovers the pleasures of bohemian existentialism with Diana Dors in *As Long As They're Happy* (1955)

6 'Crocodile crawl': Donald Sinden watches as Jean Carson demonstrates how to handle a reptile in *An Alligator Named Daisy* (1955)

7 Woman behind bars: Diana Dors in a publicity photograph used for both *The Weak and the Wicked* and *Yield to the Night* (1956)

8 Writer's cell block: author of *Yield to the Night* Joan Henry (right) chats to a journalist on the set of the film

9 On the set 1: J. Lee Thompson (centre) discusses his work during the production of *Yield to the Night*

10 On the set 2: J. Lee Thompson directs Michael Craig and Diana Dors in one of
Yield to the Night's flashback sequences

11 Who lie in gaol: compassionate warder MacFarlane (Yvonne Mitchell) presents
Mary (Diana Dors) with a cup of kindness in *Yield to the Night*

12 Musical sophistication: Janette Scott and Irving Davies in a dance sequence from *The Good Companions* (1957)

Family entertainment

5

'I hate this sort of stuff. Melodrama is the only thing I can do.'
(Alfred Hitchcock on the set of his 1934 *Waltzes from Vienna*)[1]

'You know, when you are under contract to a studio it's difficult to
refuse everything they give you.' (J. Lee Thompson)

In the 1950s, 'family entertainment' was still the cinema's core
business, and it was inevitable that a promising new director
would be pressed into the service of the mass market for
insubstantial comedy and undemanding music. After all, even
'the master of suspense', Alfred Hitchcock, had been obliged to
interrupt his thrillers with a musical – *Waltzes From Vienna* – and,
twenty years later it was time for J. Lee Thompson to pay his dues
to light entertainment. He had already demonstrated a talent for
comedic drama in the flash-back sequences of *The Weak and the
Wicked*, and between 1954 and 1956 he stoked the boilers of British
musical comedy by making four colour films, relieved only by the
dark intensity of *Yield to the Night*. Although these four pictures,
*For Better, For Worse, As Long As They're Happy, An Alligator
Named Daisy* and *The Good Companions*, are now easily dismissed
as ephemeral box-office fodder which contribute little to Lee
Thompson's reputation, they marked, at the time, the British film
industry's growing recognition of his significance. While established film-makers from the 1940s like Lawrence Huntington,
Lance Comfort and Arthur Crabtree were forced to ply their trade
in the back-street bazaars of the 'B' movie studios, Lee Thompson's

burgeoning talent was given bright showcases in cinema's high street. The movies he was offered may not have been lavish by Hollywood standards, but colour stock, higher budgets and star actors were all indicative of Lee Thompson's growing ascendancy in the field of cultural production. Having demonstrated his abilities as a thriller director, this disposition was largely kept on 'hold' while studio bosses tested his virtuosity (the transferable nature of his habitus, in Bourdieu's term) across wider areas of the production field. Although he was as yet not even a relatively autonomous agent, like David Lean or Carol Reed, Lee Thompson's career trajectory was being given an opportunity to find a more commanding position in the field by accumulating a broader range of symbolic capital. There are two other indicators of Lee Thompson's developing position of privilege: the confidence with which he is given the job of launching new stars (like Jean Carson, Susan Stephen and a post-pubescent Janette Scott); and the demand for his services from Britain's dominant studio, Rank. The films themselves are not among J. Lee Thompson's most distinguished, but they reveal a good deal about how the genres of light entertainment functioned within the studio system of the 1950s. Perhaps surprisingly, they also exhibit features which relate them directly to the rest of Lee Thompson's cinema. These common features will be noted after the films have been considered individually.

For Better, For Worse (1954, USA: Cocktails in the Kitchen)

While J. Lee Thompson was producing his first trio of decidedly unglamorous melodramas for ABPC, Elstree's studios were home also to a string of Technicolor comedies, some with period settings (*Where's Charley?*, David Butler, 1952; *Isn't Life Wonderful?*, Harold French, 1952) and others dealing with contemporary domestic problems (*Father's Doing Fine*, Henry Cass, 1952; *Will Any Gentleman*, Michael Anderson, 1953). Their critical reception and box office returns clearly indicated that colour and undemanding situation comedy were a promising combination, an insight finally confirmed by the runaway success of Rank's *Genevieve* in 1953.

Anxious to catch the wave, ABPC secured the rights to a successful West End stage comedy about the problems of a young couple, from comfortable homes, struggling to make ends meet in a one-room flat. *For Better, For Worse* had been written soon after the end of the war when the housing crisis created by bomb damage was at its height. By the mid-1950s a large-scale house-building programme was already turning the play into a period piece. Moreover, its claustrophobic setting – a single room – while convenient for the stage, hardly offered much scope for the more expansive medium of film. There were, however, certain advantages to its production. First, it enabled a continuation of the theme of domestic disaster, which ABPC had recently developed with *Young Wives' Tale* (Henry Cass, 1951).[2] Second, the play's author was the secretary of the British Board of Film Censors, A. T. L. Watkins (writing under the nom-de-plume Arthur Watkyn), an important figure for any studio to cultivate. Third, the cast of the West End production had included Dirk Bogarde, one of the 'hottest properties' in the British cinema at the time, having just completed what would become the top-grossing British film of 1954, *Doctor in the House* (Ralph Thomas). The presence of Bogarde, on loan to Elstree, persuaded J. Lee Thompson to accept the offer of what he calls 'a run-of-the-mill comedy'. The conflict of interest in having a censor script the film meant that producer Kenneth Harper also asked Lee Thompson to adapt the play himself.[3] His faithful translation for the screen was received benignly by the BBFC, which objected only to the use of 'bloody' before granting a 'U' certificate.

Dirk Bogarde was teamed with a young ABPC contract player, Susan Stephen, who had already established her comedy credentials in *Father's Doing Fine*, and a strong supporting cast including the reliable talents of Cecil Parker, Athene Seyler and Thora Hird. However, Bogarde found Elstree a less congenial working environment than Pinewood and, annoyed with not being treated as respectfully as he believed his status required, he was in no hurry to return. He gives a typically assured performance in a genre for which he had little natural affinity, but, like his co-star Stephen, he is required to play second fiddle to a series of virtuoso cameos by the film's consummate comedy actors: notably, Dennis Price as a supercilious estate agent, Freddy Jones as a sentimental car dealer and James Hayter as a Trotskyite plumber.

Rather like a Hitchcock thriller of the 1930s, *For Better, For Worse* begins with a London audience watching a performance. In this case the venue is the ABC-Ritz and the film is a musical called *Forever More*, into which Sam Coslow's cheesy theme song is diegetically incorporated. Its lyrics celebrate a romanticised conception of marriage which clearly holds cinemagoer Anne (Susan Stephen) in thrall. When her boyfriend Tony (Bogarde) successfully 'pops the question' as he sits next to her in the stalls, the cinema's role in mythologising matrimony is cleverly evoked.[4] This is a promising start: the way in which the film self-reflexively mirrors its audience's experience of the romantic comedy genre and positions its viewers, suggests that *For Better, For Worse* may provide satirical comment on cinematic representations as well as on love and marriage. Unfortunately, the promise is not fulfilled. Mild satire evaporates in a fluffy cloud of light comedy that stifles all but the most inoffensive of situation humour.

What humour there is in the situations of *For Better, For Worse* derives from the newlywed couple finding themselves out-of-place in a world in which everyone else seems to be firmly in theirs. Sons and daughters of the bourgeoisie, like Tony and Anne, should be preparing to bring up a family in a nice semi in Metroland. Unfortunately, Oxford graduate Tony's determination to be financially independent and to resist the aid of his city gent father-in-law (Cecil Parker) forces the couple into a cramped flat in inner London. According to pre-war matrimonial codes, Tony, who continues to believe that 'a wife's place is in the home', should have postponed his marriage until he could afford to keep his spouse in the manner to which she had become accustomed, but as he complains to Anne's father, times have changed:

> A chap wanting to get married these days needs three things: a job, cash, and a house. His chance of getting any one of these three things is practically nil. So what does he do? He says 'I'll wait', and

> he waits. And the years go by and he gets older and older and older; and by the time that he has got the right job and saved up for a house, the girl has got fed up waiting for him and married somebody else. Honestly, sir, there's only one thing to do: get married first and think about it afterwards.

This must have sounded fairly hollow in the new Elizabethan climate of full employment and growing affluence, but the film carries on regardless, pitting the impetuosity of youth against a succession of long-suffering middle-aged tradesmen and artisans drawn lazily from stock. The practised ease and immaculate comic timing with which these proletarian roles are played cannot disguise the fact that they have been written by a bourgeois hand. They are working-class parts created by an outsider for the entertainment of well-heeled theatregoers. There may be superficial resemblances to the genuine articles, but the artificiality of the characters is revealed in their insufferable 'niceness'. Neither the meddlesome char nor the misogynist plumber evinces real maliciousness, and even the apparently unscrupulous estate agent and the used-car salesman turn out to be 'good sorts' in the end.

As far as the plot goes, it is hard to be truly concerned about a young couple with so many social advantages. Their financial insolvency is clearly only temporary and would be easily remedied by a parental loan. As Tony himself puts it: 'People like us don't go broke, we can't afford it. We just haven't got enough to live on that's all.' Anne's response, 'We'll have to go to Daddy', is almost superfluous. Like other young people in Elizabeth's 'new realm'[5] they are burdened with a legacy from the past, but there must have been many in the audience who had more to worry about than how to accommodate a great aunt's antique piano, let alone how to impress parents by giving a dinner party. To describe such a genteel activity, as the plumber does, as the decadent pursuit of 'bloated capitalists' might be an exaggeration, but as the principal source of dramatic tension it is hardly a matter of life or death.

In the unobtrusive anonymity of J. Lee Thompson's direction one can detect the embarrassment of a craftsman who realises that his commission is unworthy of his talents. He keeps things moving at a jaunty pace, and makes a token attempt to give a stage play cinematic appeal with some travelogue scenes of London, but the slightness of the material confounds all efforts to make this comedy any more than pleasantly disposable. Depressingly, most of the critics found *For Better, For Worse* a likeable little diversion from more significant cinema. Their taste for the insipid (endorsed, it must be said, by large sections of the cinema audience) had been developed by a steady diet of wholesome comedy ensured by the vigilance of the BBFC. In fact, they were so surprised at Lee Thompson's daring step of showing a newly married couple sharing a bed that the absence of any further suggestion of sexuality in *For Better, For Worse* seems to have passed without comment. Peter Burnup (*News of the World*, 3 October 1954) summed up the general feeling when he called the film 'well mannered, well-bred and well-made'. Fred Majdalany (*Daily Mail*, 1 October 1954) thought it quietly 'sneaked up on one' and 'made one like it'. It was enjoyable, he felt, because 'the participants are so pleasant'. Roy Nash (*Star*, 1 October 1954) also found it 'very easy to enjoy', recommending it as a 'jolly, charming, cosy little tale ... the sort of thing any child could safely take its parents to see'. If these warm responses from Fleet Street's male critics seem just a little patronising, it might have had something to do with the trade's perception of *For Better* as 'a neatly-tailored woman's film' which, *Kinematograph Weekly* (30 September 1954) predicted, 'the fair sex' would welcome 'with a glad eye'.

It is clear too, that *For Better, For Worse* did little harm to J. Lee Thompson's directorial reputation, his efforts winning the approval of the influential Dilys Powell (*Sunday Times*, 3 October 1954) and praise from the *Daily Telegraph*'s Campbell Dixon (2 October 1954) for 'avoiding the forcing of laughs which is the curse of domestic English comedy'. Only the critics of *The Times*, the *Evening News* and the *Sunday Express* expressed any serious reservation, questioning the freshness of the script and blaming Lee Thompson for indecision about whether he was making a farce or a comedy. But in critical circles, there was as much good will all round as there is among the film's characters. Remarkably, *For Better* even brought Lee Thompson his first recognition from the British Academy, with a nomination for Best Film in the annual Awards.

As Long As They're Happy (1955)

Even before the release of *For Better, For Worse* the services of J. Lee Thompson had been requested by Rank, Britain's premier studio. Producer Raymond Stross had been impressed with *The Weak and the Wicked* and wanted its director to take charge of two comedies at Pinewood Studios. For Lee Thompson, the proposition was attractive both financially and professionally: 'Of course, they were paying much better than Robert Clark at ABC, but the difference I had to split with Robert Clark, so I was still really working for him. I wanted to start making films outside Elstree to get experience in other studios, so I was happy to make these two films for Rank.'

For the first, *As Long As They're Happy*, Lee Thompson took with him cinematographer Gil Taylor and one of the co-stars of *For Better, For Worse*, Susan Stephen. A script based on Vernon Sylvaine's hit stage play had already been prepared by Alan Melville, but as always the director made his own revisions in pre-production. This time, the theatrical origins of the text were more convincingly disguised, but the star of the stage play was again retained. Indeed, Lee Thompson would have it no other way, as the star was the veteran Scottish entertainer Jack Buchanan. By 1954, Buchanan had been singing and dancing his way through West End and Broadway reviews, many of them his own productions, for more than forty years. Lee Thompson had known him since the 1920s and had scripted one of his numerous film roles, the misogynistic naval captain in the comedy *The Middle Watch*:

> 'I always looked on Jack Buchanan as my uncle. He went back years and years with me. When I was a small boy I first met him and I used to call him Uncle Jack. I used to see all his shows at the Hippodrome [1926–1934]. He used to give me seats for his musicals there. And suddenly here I am directing him. It was a strange experience – this great star of the musical comedy stage, that I had sort of worshipped from the theatre seats, I was now directing.'

Buchanan plays John Bentley, a city stockbroker whose life is built on the strict observance of convention and routine. Each weekend he commutes to work from his genteel Wimbledon home and returns to his excitement-starved wife (Brenda De Banzie) with the monotony of a metronome. Each weekend he tends his garden with a passion he rarely lavishes on human relationships. His English suburban idyll, however, is about to be disrupted by his three daughters and the bizarre foreign elements which they introduce into Bentley's well-ordered regime. Suddenly he has to accommodate a cowboy, an existentialist and a crooning teenage heart-throb. The cowboy (Hugh McDermott) flicks cigarettes from the housemaid's lips with a bullwhip while his horse tramples the lawn. The hard-drinking existentialist (Nigel Green) turns Bentley's living room into the Latin Quarter. And the crooner (Jerry Wayne) has all the women of the household hanging on his every note while his schoolgirl fans trash Bentley's flower beds.

Bentley's ordeal provides a fascinating index to patriarchal anxieties in the early 1950s. Vernon Sylvaine's play had been written during the period of cultural repression from 1952 to 1953 when a whole herd of scapegoats attested to the attempt to make Britain a suitably wholesome realm for a tender new monarch (see Chapter 3). The hysteria created by this censorious climate is abundantly evident in As Long As They're Happy's tone of crazed urgency. As Bentley tries vainly to maintain his routine and sense of self he is continually assailed by shibboleths of Englishness. The lure of American popular culture is personified in both its traditional form, the cowboy, and its new guise, the crooner. Only in a period as paranoid as the early 1950s could the visit of an apparently clean-cut young man in sports jacket and flannels and singing The Little White Cloud that Cried provoke such fear and loathing. When Johnny Ray, 'the Nabob of Sob' toured Britain in 1952, his willingness to express un-English and unmanly emotion and his ability to release the pent-up sexuality of his female audience caused consternation among fathers across the land. In 1954, when the Reithian guardians of public morals could stand the embarrassment no longer, the BBC banned the sultry number one record Such a Night by 'The Prince of Wails' from its airwaves. Ray recalled the shock he caused to the British system thus:

They [female fans] would smash automobiles and stage doors and everything else. It was not uncommon for little girls to fall down and for other fans to step on them trying to get to me. What amused me more was the press. They were sending psychiatrists into the audience to try to analyse why people were so hysterical; but I imagine at that time I was probably the first performer to go out and lay his emotions right out on his sleeve and just cry to an audience.[6]

The film's Bobby Denver is a slightly sanitised version of Ray, provoking the same reactions in women and a similar recourse to psychiatric help in Bentley. He wants to know why his world seems to have gone 'stark, staring, raving mad' and seeks the advice of Herman Schneider (David Hurst), a stereotypical Austrian shrink. Dr Schneider's reasonable explanation – that crooners are 'cardboard lovers for disappointed wives' and 'emotional outlets for frustrated adolescents' – only deepens Bentley's paranoia and feelings of impotence. His beatnik son-in-law's favourite term of abuse is 'a landseer' and, appropriately, Bentley is a British 'stag at bay', trapped between the banality of American mass culture and the inscrutability of European intellectualism. Both forms of cultural expression threaten to weaken the subordination of his wife and daughters by liberating their libidos. In his indignant despair he rails against the crooner to his spouse Stella:

'This degenerate product of so-called modern civilisation, this perishing weeper, barges into my house, wails his unadulterated muck into a microphone, and what happens? The maid faints all over the linoleum. My youngest daughter says she's in love with this nit-wit and you, Stella, go round goggle-eyed.'

But where he looks for apology he finds only defiant home truths, as his wife replies that for the past eighteen years 'I've put up with your drab, dreary, dull, dismal routine', implying that now she craves some glamour and excitement. It is Bentley's daughters, however, who pose the most intransigent challenge to his patriarchal authority. Representing, as they do, the impertinent rebeliousness of a new generation, they have filled Bentley's house with foreign contagion. He sees the failure of their socialisation as a symptom of the impossible demands made on men in his position: 'The father's always to blame. Give the children money and you spoil them. Give them no money, you handicap them. Expect much from them and you set too high a standard. Expect nothing and you give them an inferiority complex. There is no answer.' His youngest daughter, the 16-year-old Gwen (Janette Scott), is responsible for the arrival of the crooner, having fooled him into believing that she is J. Arthur Rank's secretary and that her house in Acacia Avenue is the mogul's office. When she justifies her youthful infatuation with Bobby Denver by reminding her father that Juliet was only 14 when she fell for Romeo, he can only utter the exasperated reply: 'They were foreigners.' Pin-striped and bowler-hatted, the true-blue Bentley is always ready to blame other countries for the failures of patriarchy in his own. Their iniquitous influence becomes his cipher for the more intangible forces of social change that are turning him into an anachronism. In a final bid for sympathy, he packs his bag to leave, announcing 'I don't fit into the scheme of things anymore', but his ridiculousness is evident from the pyjamas hanging from his suitcase. 'My tragedy has been robbed of dignity', he adds histrionically.

Jack Buchanan conveys his character's bewilderment effectively. His confused oscillations between petulance and pomposity are eventually mirrored in his lampooning of the crooner's theme song *I Don't Know Whether to Laugh or Cry*. Actor and director, however, make sure that Bentley remains a faintly ridiculous figure and thus prevent the film from wallowing in reactionary rhetoric. That we are being offered a gentle critique of repression is underlined by Dr Schneider's advice that Bentley must 'stop being respectable' if things are to improve. His response is to take advantage of his womenfolk's absence at a Denver television broadcast to throw a wild bachelor party. Clad in beret and silk dressing gown, like a Left Bank Noel Coward, he drinks whisky from an old boot and lasciviously snuggles up with a showgirl (played by 'guest star' Diana Dors in the sauciest of black basques).[7] It is a refreshing moment of transgression in the tight-buttoned world of 1950s' light entertainment, punctuated deliciously by a nosy neighbour (again played by Athene Seyler) peering through her leaded window and declaring 'It's an orgy!'. Unsurprisingly, however, the transgression of the moment is not sustained and the film opts for compromise and conformity in the best traditions of Rank. The existentialist couple renounce their commitment to radical philosophy and return to conventional dress with a decisive 'I just want to live an ordinary normal life with ordinary normal people'. The emotional expression of the crooner turns out to be bogus, his tears faked with the aid of an onion. Gwen transfers her affection from Denver to the more deferential persona of Norman Wisdom.[8] Stella reconciles herself to her matrimonial responsibilities with the help of her husband's rediscovered sense of fun; and finally Bentley, still bewildered but rejuvenated by his flirtation with bohemianism, returns to the stability of his commuting routine.

As Long As They're Happy was given a much rougher ride by the reviewers than For Better, For Worse. The Times (14 March 1955) complained about its wealth of talented performers being 'put to so little effect' in this 'good-natured, if somewhat feeble, piece of nonsense', while the Financial Times (14 March 1955) thought the film 'just about as dishevelled and unfunny as the play'. Campbell Dixon of the Daily Telegraph had praised Lee Thompson's previous effort at comedy, but this time found himself 'like Victoria the Good, unamused' (12 March 1955).[9] The film fared a little better among the reviewers of the popular press. Harold Conway in the Daily Sketch (11 March 1955) thought it 'livelier and much funnier than the play'. Jympson Harman (Evening News, 10 March 1955) praised its 'splendid show of talent' and a number of critics recommended it, albeit rather half-heartedly, as 'fun'. What they generally liked most about the film was the energetic performance of Jean Carson as Pat, the beatnik who disavows her existentialism. The flame-haired singer and dancer from Yorkshire was already a rising star of musical comedy in the West End and was being groomed by Rank as 'Britain's answer to Judy Garland'. As Long As They're Happy, her first screen appearance, was hardly the most appropriate showcase for her abilities.[10] Although one critic described her fantasy dance sequence as 'like a sudden blaze of winter sunset, both surprising and exciting'

(P. Holt, *Daily Herald*, 11 March 1955), it clashes awkwardly with the style of the rest of the film where songs are used diegetically. Whether their role is entertainment or parody, however, is unclear. To the modern listener, the banality of Sam Coslow's Tin-Pan Alley ditties may match the satirical intent of the film as a whole, but contemporary publicity suggests that they were intended as 'gay tunes to start you patrons humming' (campaign book) and published as such in sheet-music form. *Picturegoer* (2 April 1955) thought the musical offerings 'hit parade class', and *Kinematograph Weekly* (24 March 1955) also considered the 'catchy tunes' a vital part of the film's successful formula when it opened at the Odeon, Leicester Square, just before Easter.

Whatever the merits of its songs, *As Long As They're Happy* has aged rather better than Lee Thompson's other comedies and musicals of the 1950s. Although no one quibbled at the time, modern audiences may be less sympathetic to the indulgence granted to Jack Buchanan, but might find the zaniness and madcap of the humour both familiar and involving.[11] Much of the credit for the paciness of the film must go to its editor John Guthridge whose efforts were even acknowledged by Derek Hill (*Films and Filming*, May 1955) as disguising many of the film's weaknesses. This is perhaps as close as British cinema got to the comic-book style of Hollywood's Frank Tashlin, but it still falls a long way short of *The Girl Can't Help It* (1956).

An Alligator Named Daisy (1955)

After *As Long As They're Happy* J. Lee Thompson stayed at Pinewood for his next picture, although without Gil Taylor as his cinematographer. Having just contracted Jean Carson, Rank was keen to develop her as a musical comedy star. *An Alligator Named Daisy*, however, was again not the ideal scenario to showcase her vivacity, nor was Donald Sinden (by then in his mid-30s) the perfect partner for a romantic comedy. Things must have looked good on paper. The story, about a composer who receives an alligator as an unwanted gift but cannot finally part with the creature, was penned by novelist Charles Terrot and had been adapted by Jack Davies, one of Lee Thompson's close friends from his days at the script department at Elstree before the war. With Diana Dors, James Robertson Justice, Margaret Rutherford and Stanley Holloway in supporting roles, everything was set for a great screwball comedy in the style of *Bringing Up Baby* (Howard Hawks, 1938). Film making is never so predictable. Jean Carson's singing and dancing had to be incorporated, but the script offered few natural opportunities for musical interludes. In the end, she sings only two numbers, although one is the memorable (if incongruous) *In Love For the Very First Time* by Paddy Roberts.

On set, Lee Thompson found Carson 'difficult to work with' and lacking in self-confidence in spite of the acclaim her performances had received from critics. She was, Lee Thompson agrees, 'very talented', but 'she needed nursing a great deal.' Her confidence may have suffered from the atmosphere created on set by the domineering James Robertson Justice. Not content with parading his friendship with the Duke of Edinburgh by inviting him to visit the production, Robertson Justice became very antagonistic towards producer Raymond Stross. 'Whenever Raymond Stross came on the set', remembers Lee Thompson, 'and Robertson Justice was on the set, he would chase poor Raymond off!' Diana Dors had to cope with the death of her mother immediately before filming began (Wise 1998:95). And then there was the alligator, which, as Lee Thompson puts it, 'was very naughty'. In fact, several alligators were used (as well as an animatronic replica), but Daisy was played principally by an unashamedly male 'gator, as Donald Sinden discovered to his embarrassment during a scene in which he carries Daisy through a crowded ballroom. 'I looked down and saw that, in the region of her belly, a pair of "bomb doors" had opened and from them was hanging a long thing like a banana, but pink ... Nothing would make her/him retract it and we had a hundred and fifty "extras" and all the principals hanging around waiting' (Sinden 1982: 213). Lee Thompson suggested that Sinden conceal the reptile's offending member by putting his hat over it, but there was certainly nothing in Sinden's contract that called for such heroism. 'Daisy could have taken it as a token of affection, but "he" might have been outraged and turned nasty', reasoned the worried actor. 'We just had to wait' (213). The alligator's aggressive instincts had been dulled by keeping him cool and away from water, but under the hot studio lights he had already come close to biting the nose of Harry Kendall, the actor playing the butler who lifts Daisy from a drawer. Immediately after filming was completed, the alligator seized the arm of his keeper, a female circus performer known as Koringa, fracturing it in seventeen places. The reptile was undoubtedly a hazard on the set, but the real problem was that he was neither very loveable nor very funny – not the ideal accessory for a romantic comedy.

Sinden's character, Peter Weston, is a struggling composer who finances himself by working as a salesman in a music department. He acquires Daisy on a ferry from Dublin when an old soak who has brought her from Rio, leaves her in his care. He is about to toss the creature overboard when he is stopped by Moira (Carson), a feisty keeper at a London zoo. Although he is engaged to Vanessa (Dors), the voluptuous daughter of media tycoon Sir James Colebrook (Robertson Justice), Peter is quite smitten with Moira and drives her to London in his vintage car.[12] They stop at a garage on the way for Jean Carson to do a spot of flamenco dancing among the oil drums as she sings the hit song *In Love For the Very First Time*.

Thereafter, the comedy revolves around Peter's attempts to conceal, or dispose of, his unwanted reptile, and the consternation its discovery causes to others. When Daisy is rejected at the police station, he tries to sell her to an eccentric pet-shop proprietor (Margaret Rutherford), who listens to Daisy via a stethoscope and informs Peter that the alligator communicates in English and thinks him 'very attractive to the female sex'. The pet-shop owner, however, will never 'buy animals against their will', and Peter is reduced to releasing Daisy into Regent's Park lake; but, goaded by guilt and fearful of Moira's disapproval, he is forced into retrieving her.

Daisy is eventually taken to Colebrook Manor, the imposing country seat of Sir James, where Peter and Vanessa's engagement is to be celebrated with family and friends. It is no surprise when the alligator goes on the loose in the ballroom, scuttling menacingly around like Ridley Scott's *Alien* on the good ship *Nostromo*. Thankfully we are spared the sight of her materialising from the bubbles of Diana Dors' ridiculously opulent sunken bath. Miss Dors is sight enough. Vanessa finds it impossible to understand how anyone could 'possibly like an alligator' but Peter is now firmly attached to his pet, which is associated with Moira in his affections. In a desperate attempt to save his daughter's engagement, Sir James uses the power of his newspapers to try to convince the public that the alligator is really 'man's best friend'. He promotes this batty idea with an alligator beauty pageant in the grounds of his home, providing an opportunity for cameo appearances from Frankie Howerd, Jimmy Edwards and the ubiquitous Gilbert Harding. For a moment, the bizarre garden party, with its morning-suited guests, suggests that the notion of Ascot with alligators might not be so crazy after all, but the reptiles are soon giving their keepers the slip and heading for the lake. They are quickly followed into the water by guests and keepers when a bridge collapses. After some wild thrashing around in the ensuing mêlée, a bedraggled Peter eventually emerges with Moira, and Vanessa is carried to safety by a substitute suitor, Moira's brother (Stephen Boyd). Peter and Moira drive off to a lifetime of happy escapades with Daisy.

The film is an unpretentious piece of cinema. Its comedy eventually succumbs to knockabout farce, but there are a couple of engaging minor performances along the way – from Stanley Holloway as Peter's grandfather, a retired Indian Army general who loathes 'muggers' (crocodiles) and believes that 'shoot 'em on sight' is the best policy, and from Harry Green as a sentimental Jewish song publisher who is certain that his *Crocodile Crawl* will be a huge hit ('We don't care for false modesty here in Denmark Street'). The satirical targets of the film are not as clearly defined as they had been in *As Long As They're Happy*, but they can be broadly described as the banalities of popular taste and their commercial exploitation. Sam Coslow's songs, such as *Crocodile Crawl*, effortlessly represent Tin-Pan Alley's vacuity, and the business empire of Sir James Colebrook ('three newspapers, hundreds of cinemas and thousands of mobile fried fish shops') neatly references the growing commodification of leisure and consumption: 'You buy one of his newspapers in the morning. You go to one of his cinemas in the afternoon. You buy fish and chips at night wrapped in one of his own newspapers.' As a rapacious capitalist, Sir James is a more formidable predator than an alligator like Daisy, an idea symbolised by the animal trophies stuffed and mounted in his palatial home. His daughter, though considerably more charming, has inherited his expectations of control. She dominates Peter, driving him around in her luxurious blue Cadillac, and her disdainful attitude to Daisy contrasts markedly with Moira's loving concern. The alligator wins the support of the warm-blooded characters in the film (Peter and Moira) and incurs the opposition of the more cold-blooded (the Colebrooks). Warmth and compassion are seen to emanate from a woman who lives in modest surroundings and is close to the natural world rather than from a wealthy family which lives for acquisition and dominance. Thus, in finally rejecting Vanessa for Moira and Daisy, Peter is placing the natural before the artificial and love before money.

An Alligator Named Daisy was the pre-Christmas attraction at the Odeon, Marble Arch. The critics gave it a mixed reception. With the exception of Dilys Powell,[13] reviewers from the heavyweight broadsheets remained stoney-faced before Daisy's charms. The *Manchester Guardian*'s critic (3 December 1955) believed that a single joke had been stretched beyond toleration, while *The Times* (5 December 1955) thought the film's recourse to farce to be as dated as the Keystone Cops. Caroline Lejeune (*Observer*, 4 December 1955) called it a 'damp romp' and voiced the sentiments of other reviewers when she wondered 'why they chose to make a film about an alligator when they have Miss Carson'.[14] The popular newspapers were kinder, although by no means unanimously so. Harry Deans (*Sunday Dispatch*, 4 December 1955) thought it gave 'the public what it wants', by which he meant 'wholesome laughter'. Fred Majdalany (*Daily Mail*, 2 December 1955) found it 'a funny film', at least 'within its simple limits'. Milton Shulman

(*Sunday Express*, 4 December 1955) also had his reservations, but was finally won over by the 'sheer energy of everybody'. The critics of the *News Chronicle* and the *Star* (2 December 1955) both considered Carson's musical numbers out of place; and it was really left to Lee Thompson's faithful supporter Peter Burnup of the *News of the World* (4 December 1955) to express unreserved pleasure in 'the most diverting bit of nonsense we've encountered in months'.

With three high-profile and box-office-friendly films in eighteen months, J. Lee Thompson had proved that he was more than just a director of low-budget thrillers. His versatility could extend to comedy, but it was clearly a stretch. His real talents lay in more serious subject matter, and particularly in the sort of tense suspense movie (*Yield to the Night*) he turned to as soon as *Daisy* was in the can. Strangely, there is a thread that connects the whimsical fantasy of *Daisy* with the stark melodrama of *Yield to the Night*, and it is one that runs through many of Lee Thompson's British films up to, and including, *The Passage*. What *Daisy* tries to do is to engage empathically with a protagonist for whom we might have little natural sympathy. In this case it is a dangerous reptile. In *Yield to the Night* it is a premeditated murderer. In *Ice Cold in Alex* the anti-heroes are a drunken officer and a German spy. In *Tiger Bay* they are a murderer and a compulsive liar. In *I Aim at the Stars*, the protagonist is a Nazi rocket scientist. The list could go on, but the challenge to find compassion and under-standing for the unappealing remains the same.

The Good Companions (1957)

Having demonstrated his proficiency with musical comedy, winning critical plaudits for his direction of Jean Carson's song-and-dance numbers, J. Lee Thompson was offered the chance to make that rarity among British films of the 1940s and 1950s, a musical. When Jessie Matthews and Jack Buchanan had been in their prime in the 1930s, musicals had been a familiar and popular part of British film culture.[15] The musical film allowed full exploitation of the new technology of synchronised sound, and while in Hollywood Busby Berkeley choreographed his erotic fantasies and Fred and Ginger danced gracefully through their romantic comedies, British studios were mounting rival spectaculars. Indeed, Fred Astaire originally agreed to partner Jessie Matthews in Victor Saville's *Evergreen* (1934) but was refused permission by RKO (Sellar et al. 1987: 22). Astaire's absence, however, did nothing to dent the box office performance of the film, and Matthews went on to star in a string of art deco extravaganzas, usually choreographed by Buddy Bradley and directed by Saville or Jessie's husband and dancing partner Sonnie Hale.[16]

The brash confidence of these movies evaporated under the heat generated by a new national cinema of social realism during the Second World War. When it condensed again, it found its way, not into popular musicals, but into the lush costume melodramas from Gainsborough Studios and the Technicolor fantasies of Powell and Pressburger. Even an injection of American know-how – in the form of director–producer Wesley Ruggles – could not revive the flagging musical genre, and his attempt to create an international hit with *London Town* (1947, USA: *My Heart Goes Crazy*) was an embarrassing failure. By the 1950s, British musicals were a very poor relation to their rich American counterparts, and were restricted to one or two per year.[17] Neither Rank nor ABPC, however, had totally forgotten the power of a genuine musical comedy star to generate revenue. Rank revived an old stager (Buchanan) and tested a new talent (Jean Carson) in *As Long As They're Happy* and *Daisy*, two comedies with music, but were reluctant to gamble on a fully fledged musical. Earl St John, the head of production at Rank, commented soon after the release of the two films: 'We couldn't emulate Hollywood. We haven't the talent for choreography, the high-powered dancers or the same knack with a popular tune' (*Picturegoer*, 14 April 1956).[18] ABPC were less easily deterred. As early as 1954 they were planning to remake Jessie Matthews's huge success of 1933, *The Good Companions* (Victor Saville).[19] In an article in *Picturegoer* (20 November 1954) Dick Richards, a journalist with an ear for studio gossip, noted the trend towards rehashing films of the 1930s and asked his readers: 'How'd you like Jean Carson as a "Good Companion"?' Carson was quickly snapped up by Rank. Audrey Hepburn, who would have fitted the bill, had already departed to Hollywood. ABPC were left with the fast-maturing Janette Scott. Her dancing and singing skills were modest, but ABPC was determined to push ahead with the project, and wanted Lee Thompson to direct. Although it was not his preferred career trajectory, Lee Thompson realised that he would have to take on the project to placate his studio head and to facilitate his move to more agreeable work:

> 'Robert Clark asked me to make *The Good Companions* and I turned it down for a very long time, and eventually Clark said: "I allowed you to make *Yield to the Night*. We all knew it wouldn't be successful. It lost us money, yet it did your career a lot of good." I said: "That's enough, Robert, I'll do *The Good Companions*."[20] I enjoyed making the film. We had a lot of fun with the musical numbers. I don't think it was very successful.'

Perhaps Lee Thompson should have stalled Robert Clark for a little longer. Another few months and he might have realised his mistake in trying to spruce up J. B. Priestley's tired old nag and turn it into a joy ride for teenagers. Not that the idea of a wide-screen colour musical for the emergent teenage market was a bad one. With commercial television slicing heavily into the adult audience segments, youth was emerging as the most cinema-friendly consumer group by far.[21] In particular, there was an increasingly significant market segment of young, predominantly male, lower-middle-class cinemagoers who were characterised by their selectivity about the films they watched (Harper and Porter 1999: 67). When *The Good Companions* was conceived, the impact which commercial television and the new youth culture would have on audience tastes was not yet fully understood. No one was too sure what a youth movie should look like, and there was nervousness about the sort of young-people-as-social-problem-pictures coming over from America.[22] The sullen and confrontational adolescents of *Rebel Without a Cause* (Nicholas Ray, 1955) and *The Blackbord Jungle* (Richard Brooks, 1955) had their British equivalents in a few films of the early-to-mid-1950s, but most British studios thought them too dangerous as objects of identification.[23] Transgression was consciously limited to the petty petulance of Sylvia Syms in *My Teenage Daughter* (Herbert Wilcox, 1956, USA: *Teenage Bad Girl*) or the righteous protest against the loss of their music master by the grammar-school boys and girls in *It's Great to Be Young* (Cyril Frankel, 1956). Films like these kept rebellion a genteel affair, safely confined to the socially advantaged, and maintained the interest of older filmgoers who were still thought to be vital to profitability.[24]

By October 1956, however, the power of rock and roll to galvanise an altogether less wholesome culture of youthful defiance was becoming clear. Elvis Presley and Bill Haley dominated the music charts, and Britain's own home-grown rocker Tommy Steele was proving an instant sensation. Seeing the success of Columbia's *Rock Around the Clock* (Fred Sears, 1956) in which Haley sent audiences wild, Anglo-Amalgamated, always open to an exploitation angle, rushed *The Tommy Steele Story* (Gerald Bryant, 1957, USA: *Rock Around the World*) into production. ABPC was committed to *The Good Companions*, a piece about the struggles of a concert party, The Dinky Doos, on the declining variety circuit in the midlands and the north of England. Admittedly, it tells the story of two young people's attempts to break out of a mundane and oppressive environment, but its message, made explicit in its title song – 'Good Companions, That's What People Ought to Be' – effaces all suggestion of a generation gap. Susie Dean (Janette Scott), the starry-eyed pearl in the concert party's oyster, may be striving for glamour and fame, but she is as near as the film comes to challenging a homely, cardigan-and-slippers, view of social organisation and responsibility. The film's values, like its style, remain more rocking-chair than rock and roll. The uncomfortable fit between *The Good Companions*' ethos and musical style and the rock and roll convulsions shaking its target audience are now clear to Lee Thompson: 'Yes, it was too old-fashioned. After all, this was a story about an old-fashioned group of people who got together to do a sort of concert on the pier; but it should have been made differently.'

Misgivings about the film's contemporary relevance are in evidence in its first few minutes. In what may be a late re-drafting of T. J. Morrison's script, self-reflexive doubts surface when a contemptuous theatre manager dismisses the concert party's performance:

> 'The original Dinky-Doos, first performance 1923 and still doing the same old-fashioned routines you did thirty years ago. Well, we're not in 1923 now, although that's where you ought to be, or the mortuary. Have you ever heard of striptease, rock and roll, television, talking pictures? You dated lot of hacks!'

Having set up a devastating line of criticism of the film itself Lee Thompson then gambles that the freshness of his treatment will be as convincing as the modernisation of The Dinky Doos under their new producer Miss Trant (Celia Johnson). Lee Thompson's confident direction, Gilbert Taylor's slick cinematography and Robert Jones' precision designs do rejuvenate the British musical in much the same way as the recruiting of composer Inigo Jollifant (John Fraser) breathes life into The Dinky Doos.[25] Shot in Technicolor and Cinemascope, the look of the film bears comparison with the Hollywood product, and the choreography was state of the art. As most reviewers agreed, the final production number *Around the World in Eighty Minutes* comes closer to the genuine Hollywood or Broadway article than any British attempt since Jessie Matthews and Jack Whiting danced their way across two huge sound stages in *Sailing Along*, nearly two decades earlier. However, *The Good Companions* could not successfully negotiate the tensions between its modernising impulses and its sense of nostalgia.

The contradictions were not missed by the shrewder critics. 'The old style and the new don't mix', wrote Caroline Lejeune (*Observer*, 10 March 1957), noting the picture's lack of 'character and unity' and concluding that, 'it is not a bad film, but it is not a good one'. Philip Oakes in the *Evening Standard* (7 March 1957) acknowledged some good dance routines, but suggested: 'By bringing the action up-to-date, director J. Lee Thompson has put his players in a no-man's-land.' Even Leonard Mosley, one of the director's most sympathetic critics, had to admit that, beyond one good production number, 'this film is a mess' because 'it can't make up its mind what it wants to be' (*Daily Express*, 7 March 1957). The updating of Priestley's text, Mosley felt, was 'as incongruous and embarrassing as if Lady Godiva were to ride through Coventry in a bikini'. Lee Thompson is really faced with an unenviable task. How can he enlist our sympathy for a group of performers who, even if they exhibited real talent, are performing in a style which is thoroughly superannuated? How can he do this when the whole purpose of the film is to demonstrate to a young audience the enhanced professionalism and superiority of modern metropolitan showbiz? As a great admirer of Priestley's work, Lee Thompson wants to retain some of the romanticising of theatrical life, even the lives of mediocre performers in unglamorous venues. He tries to preserve the notion of the touring troupe as a liberating alternative for men to the constraints of matriarchal marriage;[26] but this idea of the theatre as a liminal space for free expression sits uneasily with Susie's desire to break away from the stultifying effects of the variety circuit ('the same old stick-in-the-mud business going on and on').

Ultimately, the film looks back rather than forward – back to the dozens of backstage musicals that had preceded it, back to a golden age of the variety theatre, and back to an ideal of collective endeavour and mutual support which was fast losing ground in the 1950s' gallop towards individualism. 'There isn't too much good companionship left these days, is there?' Inigo complains. When he adds 'Most people are just out for a good time', he seems to be inviting the famous response from *Saturday Night and Sunday Morning*'s Arthur Seaton: 'All the rest is propaganda.'[27] Susie wants more than 'a good time': she wants stardom and riches. A true 'Golddigger of 1957', she dreams of being 'discovered' and acquiring a chauffeur-driven Rolls, giving clichéd expression to the frustrated yearnings of her generation. The irreconcilable tensions between individual ambition and the spiritual benefits of mutuality are largely glossed over, and so too is the problem for comradeship in a theatrical world where success is dependent on the patronage of powerful impresarios and music publishers. The problems posed by these contradictions are displaced onto apathetic audiences and protection racketeers. The attempts by the gangsters to disrupt the Good Companions' performance on the day it is being scrutinised by a West End impresario (John le Mesurier) in fact provide a rare moment of drama in the film. The moment, however, is liberally laced with humour, and eventually deteriorates into a free-for-all fight in the theatre. The slapstick-style fracas is energetically directed, but ultimately serves only to underline the unreality of the proceedings. Real drama and pathos are lacking in a narrative which is hackneyed and characterisations which are half-hearted. It needs an exceptional and dynamic star presence to bring it to life, and, for all *Films and Filming*'s (April 1957) comparisons of her to the young Judy Garland, Janette Scott does not have the necessary charisma. Without the natural talent as a singer and dancer that the role demands, she is obliged to act the part and, spiritedly as she performs, she remains an impersonator.[28] The dancing honours belong decidedly to Paddy Stone who also choreographed the routines with Irving Davies.[29] He moves elegantly and athletically, but his lithe-limbed balletic style does little to dispel the aura of campness that surrounds The Dinky Doos. Imaginative choreography, design and widescreen cinematography make the dance sequences visually memorable but, unfortunately, the musical contributions of Paddy Roberts, Alberto Rossi and Geoffrey Parsons are undistinguished.

On release in the early spring of 1957, *The Good Companions* struggled to appeal to a young audience which had already begun to taste the fruits of rock culture and New Wave theatre. *The Girl Can't Help It*, released just prior to *The Good Companions*, offered a fresh template for the musical film. *And Woman ...Was Created* (Roger Vadim, 1957), with its uninhibited dancing by Brigitte Bardot, made the routines in *The Good Companions* look staid and sexless. On the stage, John Osborne was articulating a new sensibility towards the frustrations of provincial life and, with *The Entertainer* (April 1957), a more incisive view of the decline of the variety theatre than a re-vamped Priestley novel could provide. Finally, the charisma of Fred Astaire and Audrey Hepburn in *Funny Face* (Stanley Donen, 1957) showed that, even in terms of a conventional musical, Hollywood could still supply more wit, charm and inventiveness. In comparison, *The Good Companions* was shown up as merely competent. It crept quickly from the West End and performed disappointingly on general release (*Kinematograph Weekly*, 28 March and 2 May 1957). More humiliatingly, it failed to secure a distribution deal for release in America.

Although his mid-1950s involvement with music and comedy is best thought of as a deviation from J. Lee Thompson's main creative trajectory, at least in terms of style and genre, the films do share some of the characteristic thematic concerns of his thrillers. Most obviously, one can detect the theme of entrapment and confinement. The protagonists in these films are all locked in constraining situations – whether it be living in a tiny one-roomed flat and dependent on parents for support (*For Better, For Worse*), or being governed by the time-tabled routine of suburban commuting (*As Long As They're Happy*), or encumbered with an unwanted reptile, and committed to a loveless engagement (*An Alligator Named Daisy*), or performing on a closed circuit of tatty variety theatres (*The Good Companions*). They all experience the existential role of escape from these situations. Liberation is a route to self-discovery and self-respect – whether it be the dignity inherent in financial independence (*For Better, For Worse*), or the psychological benefits of embracing the carnivalesque (*As Long As They're Happy*), or the unlocking of emotion involved in the acceptance of life's 'wild side' (*An Alligator Named Daisy*), or the self-affirmation granted by the approval of powerful others (*The Good Companions*).

In spite of the diverse source material of these films, the familiar discourses of confinement and liberation emerge from J. Lee Thompson's comedies and musicals almost as readily as they do from his more distinguished dramas. The lighter genre pieces may lack the dramatic elaboration provided by key moral dilemmas in Lee Thompson's melodramas and thrillers, but they do incorporate their own, more modest, ethical issues. *For Better, For Worse* explores the pressure to compromise principles created by economic stringencies. *As Long As They're Happy* deals humorously with the challenge to familial fidelity posed by celebrity charisma. *An Alligator Named Daisy* and *The Good Companions* both spotlight the clash between self-interest and responsibility to others. Not surprisingly, in all but *The Good Companions*, the role of these strains and dilemmas changes from the promotion of dramatic tension in the melodramas and thrillers to the facilitation of comic situations in these lighter genre offerings. The trans-formation of role is accompanied also by a change of tone to one which is more appropriate to comedy, but the essential mechanisms of Lee Thompson's cinema remain recognisable. The themes of confinement and liberation, elaborated by a discourse of moral dilemma, are worked through the contemporary preoccupations of British social life, just as they are in his more serious films. In particular, they are mapped onto anxieties about the challenges posed to established beliefs, conventions and modes of expression by new cultural developments: post-war housing problems and the spread of new social mores (*For Better, For Worse*); the impact of foreign cultural forms on the British way of life (*As Long As They're Happy*); the megalomania of media tycoons and the dangers of materialism (*An Alligator Named Daisy*); and the erosion of small-scale modes of entertainment and the sense of community they engender (*The Good Companions*).

Broadly speaking, then, these films index an anxiety about social change for which their generic styles offer reassurance. This is perfectly in line with the often-noted function of comedy in giving relief from tension by simultaneously evoking and dispelling anxiety. Beyond a certain sentimentality about young love and a distrust of materialism, however, they fail to exhibit a coherent cultural view or system of values. With their bourgeois protagonists' parochial concerns, and occasional xenophobia, they seem at times irredeemably conservative. But, at others, their zest for the carnivalesque, their support of youth and their opposition to the hegemonic power of wealth give them a progressive power and oppositional appearance.[30] As popular works designed for a heterogeneous audience they resist the closure of meaning, but they do offer broad populist resolutions to the problems experienced by their protagonists. These problems and their resolutions are summarised in Table 1:

Table 1. Problems and their resolutions in the comedies and musicals of J. Lee Thompson

	For Better, For Worse	*As Long As They're Happy*	*An Alligator Named Daisy*	*Good Companions*
Protagonists	Young married couple	Middle-aged stockbroker	Young unmarried couple	Young unmarried couple
Antagonists	Bourgeois parents and service providers	Family and foreigners	Bourgeois family	Spivs and impresarios
Problem	Independence	Cultural change	Responsibility	Ambition
Symbol	The flat	The crooner	The alligator	The West End
Resolution	Assertion of independence	Acceptance of change	Love before money	Communally supported success

Notes

1 The remark was attributed to Hitchcock by Desmond Knight, one of the stars of *Waltzes*, and has been quoted a number of times, most recently in Barr (1999: 127).
2 For a discussion of competing models of femininity in the film, see Landy (1991: 381–2).
3 *For Better, For Worse* was to mark the start of a firm friendship and productive partnership between Lee Thompson and Harper which would quickly lead to *Yield to the Night*.
4 Unlike Hitchcock's *The 39 Steps* which promotes a jaundiced view of marriage before redeeming the institution in its closure (Barr 1999: 150–60), Lee Thompson's film begins with a rosy view and moves to a more realistic understanding.
5 'New Realm', appropriately, is the name of the removal company employed by Tony and Anne.
6 Quoted in Everett (1986: 14).
7 Raymond Stross had wanted Dors to play one of Bentley's daughters but her commitments to Carol Reed's *A Kid For Two Farthings* had precluded any more than one day's filming. Rank's advertising still made the most of her brief appearance, featuring her prominently on the film's posters in her basque or a dramatically slashed cerise evening gown smothered in (as the campaign book boasted) 257,000 sequins. The publicists were convinced

that her changes of attire would 'create the biggest sensation since Chataway ran thataway against Russia's Vladimir Kuc'.

8 Wisdom's is one of a number of cameo appearances, which include Gilbert Harding as a stern-faced critic at Bobby Denver's concert. When asked by one of Denver's more mature female fans 'Do you dig him?', Harding replies witheringly 'Dig him? I'd bury him!'

9 Connoisseurs of Mr Derek Hill's critical appraisals will be relieved to know that he did not go easy on *As Long As They're Happy*. Calling it a 'shambles of a film' and 'the most slap-dash production in years', he suggested that 'only the credit titles prove that there was either script or direction', and that 'the few amusing moments seem to be either freaks or flukes' (*Films and Filming*, May 1955).

10 In *Picturegoer* (2 April 1955) journalists Tom Hutchinson and Derek Walker had a 'row' over the appropriateness of Carson's role in *As Long As They're Happy*. Hutchinson argued that Jean's talent was so significant that she deserved a glamorous starring role especially written for her.

11 The style was too much for the *Financial Times* (14 March 1955) which described it as an 'exhausting and noisy tumult'.

12 Old cars with lots of character were almost obligatory in British comedies after *Genevieve*. *For Better, For Worse* also has its own 'old crock', named 'Albertina'.

13 Powell's review in the *Sunday Times* (4 December 1955) described the film as 'boisterous fun' with 'patches of satire and a notably engaging alligator'.

14 A. Critlow (*Daily Herald*, 2 December 1955), for instance, also preferred Miss Carson to Daisy, while Harold Conway (*Daily Sketch*, 1 December 1955) voted for Miss Dors.

15 In 1932 alone twenty-one musicals were filmed in British studios (Richards 1984: 253). Ironically, although Matthews and Buchanan were often paired together in shows, they thoroughly disliked each other (Sellar et al. 1987: 22).

16 The films included *It's Love Again* (Saville, 1936), *Gangway* (Hale, 1937), *Head Over Heels* (Hale, 1937) and *Sailing Along* (Hale, 1938).

17 In 1955 American studios made no less than nineteen musicals. US production companies also made three musicals in England in the 1950s: *Where's Charley?*, by Warner Bros at Elstree, and *Invitation to the Dance* (Gene Kelly, 1954) and *Tom Thumb* (George Pal, 1958), by MGM.

18 Earl St John was no doubt mindful of comments like Laurie Henshaw's in the same issue: 'I have felt like reaching for the safety-catch of my gun whenever I've seen the sign: "A New British Musical".'

19 Based on the novel by J. B. Priestley (1929), the film was adapted from a musical version that premiered in the West End at Her Majesty's Theatre in 1931 (songs by Richard Addinsell).

20 The gist of this statement – that in making *The Good Companions* Lee Thompson was paying back his studio for the opportunity to make *Yield to the Night* – is correct, but the use of the past tense ('It lost us money', etc.) is not strictly accurate. Lee Thompson had actually agreed to direct and co-produce *The Good Companions* by early May 1956, prior to the London

premiere of *Yield to the Night*. His comments on adaptation and casting were reported by Dick Richards in *Picturegoer* (19 May 1956).

21 Harper and Porter (1999: 79) compare audience surveys to conclude that the proportion of the cinema audience constituted by 16–24-year-olds, rose from 23 per cent in 1946 to 44 per cent in 1960.

22 Lazlo Benedek's disaffected biker film *The Wild One* (1953) had been refused a certificate by the BBFC.

23 Roy Walsh (James Kenney) in *Cosh Boy* and the slightly older Jordie (Lawrence Harvey) in *I Believe in You* (Basil Dearden, 1952) are examples of delinquents in British cinema of the period.

24 For a contemporary discussion of the dilemma posed by the relative growth of the teenage audience, see Ernie Player, 'Should filmland ignore the teenagers?', *Picturegoer*, 25 January 1958.

25 Inigo had been played by John Gielgud in the original film, and Lee Thompson had initially hoped that Ian Carmichael would play the role in his remake (*Picturegoer*, 19 May 1956).

26 In the attempts of Jess Oakroyd (Eric Portman) and Jimmy Nunn (Bobby Howes) to distance themselves from their wives (Thora Hird and Beatrice Varley), we can perhaps see a refraction of Lee Thompson's own struggle to leave his wife and family – a theme which would be more marked in his next film, *Woman in a Dressing Gown*.

27 The final draft of Alan Silitoe's novel was completed only a few months after the release of *The Good Companions*, in August 1957 (Laing 1986: 63).

28 While many journalists praised Janette Scott's singing, the *Daily Mirror* (8 March 1957) revealed that her voice had been dubbed by 'a popular recording star'. Scott, herself, was frustrated by the dramatic limitations which the part of a charming ingénue like Susie Dean placed upon her. Concerned about being typecast as 'a nice typical teenager', she complained to *Picturegoer* (29 March 1958): 'I don't think I've been an *interesting* enough person on screen. I want to have some *character*, some *guts*. Gentle romance just is not enough. To make a lasting impact on screen a girl needs drama, excitement, something as real as life.'

29 The two had been Jean Carson's dancing partners in *As Long As They're Happy*.

30 This Janus-faced aspect of British post-war comedy has been noted in other studies of the genre, notably Ian Green's 1983 work on Ealing.

Prisons without bars

6

The most powerful physical image created in the period of major naturalistic drama is the living room as a trap. (Raymond Williams 1979: 203)

Without talking about it much, they both began to think of the house as a trap, and they no more enjoyed refurbishing it than a prisoner would delight in shining up the bars of his cell ... 'I don't know what's the matter with us,' Betsy said one night. 'Your job is plenty good enough. We've got three nice kids, and lots of people would be glad to have a house like this. We shouldn't be so *discontented* all the time.' 'Of course we shouldn't!' Tom said. Their words sounded hollow. It was curious to believe that that house ... was probably the end of their personal road. It was impossible to believe. Something would have to happen. (Sloan Wilson, *The Man in the Grey Flannel Suit*, 1956)

Yield to the Night was a watershed film for J. Lee Thompson. It marked a moment of revelation which would profoundly influence his career trajectory. Although it had not been a moneymaker for his studio, its quality, and the intensity of its vision, had been too great for critics to ignore. Its success at Cannes had demonstrated to ABPC that it had in Lee Thompson a director of international class who was prepared to extend himself beyond the boundaries of emotionality usually imposed on British genre cinema and on into new territory. Above all, he had shown an all-round directorial ability which had not been seen in British studios since Carol Reed came to film-making maturity in the late 1940s. Not only could Lee Thompson coax a more inspired performance from an actress of apparently limited range like Diana Dors than the declining powers of Reed had managed (in *A Kid For Two Farthings*), but he was capable of developing the distinctive pictorial style that was so rare among British directors. *Yield to the Night* also demonstrated that he had no fears in dedicating his talents to serious adult subjects at the leading edge of social controversy.

For ABPC, the problem was how to retain this talent and harness it profitably to appropriate subject matter. For Lee Thompson the problem was how to free himself from the constraints of cautious studio managers and accountants. Ten years earlier, in the more confident period of post-war expansion, a misfit such as J. Lee Thompson, kicking his heels around fortress Elstree like some cricket-sweatered POW in Colditz, would have been given no opportunity to tunnel to freedom. By 1956, however, as ticket sales continued their decline and television licences continued to proliferate, confidence was at a premium in the film industry. The hedging of bets was the order of the day. Film production had ceased at Highbury, Islington, Lime Grove, Teddington, Isleworth, Welwyn, Denham, Ealing, Riverside and Wembley; and Associated British itself had already diversified into commercial television with contracts for weekend programmes in the midland and northern regions. The film production schedule at Elstree was obliged to accommodate the making of television programmes, and new film scripts were increasingly assessed according to their potential in European rather than just home or American markets (Warren 1983: 111–22). ABPC still liked to think of Elstree as the English answer to Hollywood, and clung to the ideal of a studio with a roster of contracted artists, but as financial belts were tightened in what was already a thrifty organisation, the independent production system was welcomed as a canny way to cut costs and maximise cash flow. ABPC would offer studio space and financial backing to independent producers who, in return, would defer half their fees until a situation of net profit was reached. At such time the independents would be entitled to one-third of worldwide profits. The system reduced the economic cost to the studio and gave an opportunity to frustrated film-makers on their own payroll – like J. Lee Thompson – to give expression to their wilder creative urges.

At the end of 1956, having given this studio its due pound of flesh by delivering *The Good Companions*, Lee Thompson took a page in *Kinematograph Weekly* (13 December 1956) to sing the praises of the trend towards independent production, and to announce to the trade that the time had come for 'courage and experiment'. Commenting that this film-making trend was as inevitable as 'the rain on location', he informed readers: 'In February next year I shall begin work on my first independent production. I shall join the ever-increasing number of British producers and directors who have successfully negotiated their emancipation from the restrictions of the front office.' On the face of it, this might indicate a desire (to use the terminology of *Cahiers du cinema*) to move from *metteur en scène* to full-blown *auteur*. However, Lee Thompson's aims were more modest than the unbridled expression of an individual vision. His article in *Kinematograph Weekly* ridiculed the image of the art film-maker who has lost touch with the mass audience, decrying 'long-haired high-brows [who] run amok with experimental projects which satisfy their own peculiar tastes while making the average picturegoer sick'. The advantages of independence were, for him, the opportunity to take risks and the freedom to innovate in the interests of producing films that the paying public would want to see. He wanted, in short, the chance to be more commercially effective than the studio system, but in a way that rejected the element of cynical exploitation that characterised much of the system's products. The established studios, he felt, had a role in making both spectaculars and 'the standard bread-and-butter picture with popular stars in popular roles in popular subjects'; but the independents could enrich the diversity of film culture with the sort of modest but 'sincere' production 'which has been made because someone really wanted to make it and devoted time and talent and salty sweat to its conception'. The independent production would be marked by the integrity of its purpose in offering the audience an alternative to the usual formulaic diet. Independence from 'the front office' would also, Lee Thompson believed, free up the mechanisms of production. Producers would be able to set their own timetables and look beyond studio-contracted actors in their casting of roles and studio-contracted writers for their scripts. New talent would be given every chance to emerge.

Lee Thompson had formed a partnership with Frank Godwin and Ted Willis. Godwin was an experienced accountant who had been working in the Rank Organisation since 1943, part of the time as assistant to the head of production, Earl St John. In 1955 he had tried his hand at freelance producing with *Portrait of Alison* (Guy Green). Ted Willis had a long pedigree as a writer. He had been in the left-wing political struggles of the late 1930s and had begun writing plays for the radical Unity Theatre during the war.[1] When producer Gabriel Pascal and director Brian Desmond Hurst had decided to film one of his plays, he had embarked on a screenwriting career (Willis 1991: Chapter 2) in which he had become a founder member and chairman of the Writer's Guild of Great Britain. A pioneer of broadcast soap opera (*The Robinsons* and *Mrs Dale's Diary*) for the BBC, Willis was perhaps most famous as the creator of *Dixon of Dock Green*, the television police series which was the BBC's populist baulkhead against the waves of commercial television programmes of the late 1950s.[2]

The partnership was formed to make entertainment films with box-office appeal, but given the political sympathies of Willis and Lee Thompson, it was also an opportunity to explore subjects which would, like *Yield to the Night*, challenge the complacency and conservatism of British film culture. The intent was to make socially aware films about the lives of ordinary people. Willis had been particularly impressed by the work of Paddy Chayefsky, whose teleplays had, as he put it, 'kicked open a door' for him (Willis 1991: 137). Chayefsky conceived of the television play as 'a theatre, not for the middle class but for the masses' (137), which would deal with the problems of unexceptional people in situations which would be easily identifiable by the audience. This 'marvellous world of the ordinary' (Chayefsky, quoted by Willis), in which characters were caught in a moment of crisis, would give viewers new insights about their own lives.[3] Inspired by his approach, Willis had written a one-hour teleplay about a middle-aged working-class woman coping with her husband's infidelity. It had originally been titled *Amy* after its central character, but Willis had quickly changed it to *Woman in a Dressing Gown*, emphasising its wider relevance to people in Amy's class and domestic situation. Despite an initial rejection from Associated Rediffusion's drama editor, its cause had been taken up by the director Peter Cotes,[4] who had cast his wife Joan Miller in the role of Amy. Broadcast in 1956 to the London area only, the play had been a massive popular and critical success (139). As a proven success with a strong social realist theme, Lee Thompson was happy to make the adaptation of *Woman in a Dressing Gown* his first independent production, stressing at once its serious intent, its popular appeal and its class consciousness by describing it as 'a *Brief Encounter* on a lower social scale'[5] (*Kinematograph Weekly*, 13 December 1956).

The film's themes – infidelity, divided loyalties and marital break up – had clear resonances with Lee Thompson's own life. His divorce was still a fresh memory:

> 'The marriage break-up had occurred, I think, during *The Weak and the Wicked*. I was already divorced from my first wife and living with Joan Henry ... At the time, you know, I was riddled with guilt because I was living with Joan Henry and my wife and children were just around the corner, so to speak, and it was a time of great inward turmoil for me. But somehow that seemed to spark me to some of my best work.'

The trauma of leaving his family and the excitement of his new relationship did indeed seem to intensify Lee Thompson's desire for independence and experiment in his professional life. The nervous energy released is evident in *Woman in a Dressing Gown*'s restless camerawork, insistent directorial style and, most of all, in the high-octane performance which he encouraged from *Dressing Gown*'s star Yvonne Mitchell.

Woman in a Dressing Gown (1957)

> My own greatest desire is for realism. Therefore I employ what is
> called melodrama – but which might as well be called ultra-realism
> –for all my thinking has led me to the conclusion that it is the only
> road to screen realism that will still be entertainment. (Alfred
> Hitchcock 1936)

The film's plot is a straightforward one. Middle-aged Jim Preston
(Anthony Quayle) is a clerk at a timber yard who is having an affair
with a young female colleague, Georgie (Sylvia Syms). He agrees
that it is time to seek a divorce from his scatterbrained and untidy
wife Amy (Yvonne Mitchell), and to leave her and his teenage son
(Andrew Ray). When Amy receives the news, she blames her own
inadequacies and makes a pathetic, and ultimately futile, attempt
to smarten herself and tidy her home before confronting her rival.
When her struggles to control her image finally break down she
tries a direct emotional appeal to the lovers, but when that seems
to have failed she regains her dignity by ordering her husband out
of their flat. Jim leaves, but instantly realises that he cannot part
from Amy and his son, and the final shot shows the family united
again.

It is an unremarkable story, with an apparently conventional
closure, that demonstrates the resilience of the family as a social
institution. In Lee Thompson's hands, however, this prosaic 'slice
of life' is turned into a full-blown melodrama, replete with ironic
counterpoint, elaborate cinematography and bravura performances.
At the end, the family emerges not as an idyllic cocoon of serenity
and Christian fidelity but as something, if not more akin to Mary
Hilton's condemned cell then at least resembling penal servitude.
When the camera pulls away from Jim and Amy's home it leaves a
place of frustrated desires, disillusioned love and stifling contain-
ment in which two people have been forced to confront the
realisation that they are, for better, for worse, largely what the other
has made them. Whereas Tony and Anne in Lee Thompson's
earlier comedy *For Better, For Worse* could look forward optimis-
tically to independence from parents and the more spacious
accommodation that increased salary would bring, here there is

no escape from the mutual entrapment of matrimony and the claustrophobic closeness of working-class housing. However one shifts one's sympathies between Jim's longings for sexual adventure and fulfilment and Amy's limited horizons and naïve faith in domesticity, the muffled sound of an existential scream can still be heard, although not, it seems, by Jean Luc Godard. In an extraordinarily vitriolic review in *Arts* (30 July 1958), Godard used the film as an occasion to launch a stream of abuse at the whole notion of a British national cinema. *Woman in a Dressing Gown*, he felt, had once again demonstrated the utterly abject state of a cinema whose incompetent film-makers had completely betrayed the talent of its actors:

> How have the descendants of Daniel Defoe, Thomas Hardy and George Meredith reached such a degree of incompetence in matters of art? Why, for instance, do English actors who are the best in the world (cf. Charles Laughton, Cary Grant) become absolutely commonplace as soon as they start work at Elstree or Pinewood?

Any virtues that *Dressing Gown*'s scenario might have had, he believed, were lost in Lee Thompson's 'lunatic' and 'pretentious' direction, 'an incredible debauch of camera movements as complex as they are silly and meaningless'. The result was merely ugly, unfunny and in the worst of taste, with a central perform-ance dramatically lacking in 'sensitivity and discretion' by Yvonne Mitchell as 'a virago half-way between an ostrich and Donald Duck'.

Putting aside, for a moment, the hysterical tone and rampant misogyny of Godard's review, it is significant in raising two key issues in assessing the value of *Woman in a Dressing Gown*: the suitability of Lee Thompson's treatment of his social-realist subject matter, and Mitchell's high-profile performance. Both directorial treatment and performance are aspects of a film's style and are sometimes given scant consideration in critical works whose interrogation of texts is motivated principally by sociological or political, rather than aesthetic, interest. The stylistic elements in *Dressing Gown*, however, are so prominent that commentators like Marcia Landy and John Hill are obliged to interpret them. While Landy (1991: 235) largely ignores the performative aspects of the text, she draws our attention to the film's obtrusive camerawork: 'Repeatedly, the camera moves through a window (often with bars) in order to violate private space. Moreover, characters are frequently shot with objects – tables, shelves, bottles, laundry – intervening between spectator and character.'

This mediated style of filming, which so annoyed Godard, would have been familiar to anyone who had seen *Yield to the Night*. Landy reads it as an effective way of calling attention to 'the constraining world inhabited by all the characters, but especially Amy', and indeed the view from behind the clutter of crockery, ironing and bric-a-brac emphasises not only Amy's lack of house-keeping skills but the constricted horizons of domestic life and relationships. Objects accumulated over years of marriage, and which are symbolic of family life, crowd in on Jim and Amy, demanding attention and denying their owners psychic as well as physical space. The camera searches for a clear view just as the characters themselves struggle to get a perspective on each other. They are too close to see clearly. 'You see the same person every day – you don't see them at all', Jim admits to Georgie. Part of the problem, perhaps, is that the attention is distracted by the objects that surround them and come, mentonymically, to stand for them.

Melanie Williams (1999a) has pointed out that, in the way it echoes the claustrophobic perspectives of *Yield to the Night*, *Dressing Gown*'s *mise-en-scène* implies the idea of housewife as domestic prisoner. Quoting from a 1957 BBC broadcast by a clinical psychiatrist and child-care expert, she shows how Amy's situation contrasts ironically with contemporary notions of the freedom and self-fulfilment to be found in housework.[6] Lee Thompson's film, she argues, is offering what amounts to a feminist critique of the circumscribed life and arrested personal development associated with the housewife's role a full six years before Betty Friedman's account of 'women's discontent in contemporary times' *The Feminine Mystique* (1963). *Dressing Gown* dramatises the discrepancy between the myth of domestic serenity and fulfilment (the patriarchally-endorsed 'feminine mystique') and the reality of most women's lives.[7] Williams notes that Amy's inability to finish her housework, no matter how early she rises or how much effort she expends, corresponds precisely with Friedman's argument that 'the more a woman is deprived of function in society ... the more she will resist finishing her housework or mother-work, and being without any function at all' (Friedman 1963: 239). Denied wider social participation, Amy's emphasis on housework as a Sisyphean task becomes 'a strategy for covering up the emptiness of her life' (Williams 1999a: 12).[8]

A further strategy, Friedman suggests, is to bolster self-esteem by stressing the creative and innovative approaches which the individual can bring to domestic labour. There is a perfect example of this, as Williams points out, when Amy distractedly announces to Jim: 'I tried a new way with the chips. Cook 'em for a minute or so, then take 'em out, leave 'em for another minute, then put 'em back. It makes 'em crisp.' This demoralised search for pride in the brittleness of fried potatoes wonderfully expresses the pathos of her situation and her need for self-deception – to believe in her competence in manipulating the feminine mystique. We have previously had the charred results of Amy's frying techniques shown to us in gruesome close up. They are part of the domestic jungle of steaming kettles, hot irons and drying laundry that Gil Taylor's camera sniffs around like an inquisitive predator.[9] Taylor would go on to photograph Polanski's *Repulsion*, a film in which a woman's worsening mental state is expressed in the camera's obsessive concern with the deteriorating condition of her apartment and the skinned rabbit she has neglected to cook. In *Dressing Gown*, his literal foregrounding of the ordinary also mirrors Amy's state of mind. The cooker, the ironing board and the radio loom large in her consciousness, just as they do on the screen. Lee Thompson confronts us with the distorted perspectives of Amy's world, obliging us to notice elements of the *mise-en-scène* which we might normally take for granted. What in another film might be inconsequential props and set dressing, in this become potent signifiers of disturbed perception.[10]

These everyday objects that the camera forces us to register are as significant to Jim as they are to his wife. They are the small irritants whose continuous presence drives him away from the home and into infidelity. It is not Amy from whom Jim wants to escape so much as the noisy and unkempt compound she presides over. 'I feel I'm living in a blind alley', he tells his wife as if he were the fall-guy in a film noir, but the walls of his alley are lined with tables crowded with bottles and draws crammed with unfolded linen. They are synecdoches of his despair as much as of Amy's inability to manage her world. Andrew Sarris (1968: 89) observed of Hitchcock that objects are 'never mere props of a basically theatrical *mise-en-scène*, but rather the very substance of his cinema', and if Lee Thompson tends to use them in a more passive way, they still 'embody the feelings and fears of the characters'.

For John Hill, it is *Dressing Gown*'s peculiar style that saves the film from being 'a dour little morality play, counselling compromise and acceptance, and beset by a condescension so characteristic of writers who self-consciously attempt to write about "ordinary people" and their "ordinary lives"' (Hill 1986: 98). He notes the alarming contradiction between Ted Willis's notion of the cinematic style appropriate to social realism and Lee Thompson's flamboyant directorial signature. According to *Dressing Gown*'s writer, a director serves the script best when he avoids 'tricks and devices which draw attention to his own contribution' (Willis 1959: 17).[11] Far from being unobtrusive, however, Lee Thompson's direction challenges the conventions of realism by rejecting naturalism and creating a 'dissonance between subject-matter and style' and a distanciated viewing position (Hill 1986: 98). Not surprisingly, this dissonance and distanciation in the filming of a melodrama leads Hill to relate Lee Thompson's work on *Dressing Gown* to that of Douglas Sirk on movies that were being produced in Hollywood in the same period.

The 1950s' melodramas of Sirk, Nicholas Ray, Vincente Minelli and Otto Preminger were cautious attempts to air some of the hidden problems of the American bourgeois family. Unlike some of the literary contributions to the exposure of suburban mores (Grace Metalious' *Peyton Place*, for example, created a sensation in 1956) they generally tread softly on patriarchal sensibilities. Sanitised accounts they may have been, but in the early 1970s they began to be championed by a new generation of film analysts as essays in the emotional alienation characteristic of much bourgeois family life. In particular, the approach of Douglas Sirk was singled out by film theorists like Willeman (1971; 1972), Elsaesser (1972) and Halliday (1972) as being particularly subversive.[12] Sirk, it was argued, adapted his knowledge of German expressionism and Brechtian theories of performance to undermine Hollywood conventions and the dominant understandings of the family on which they were based. The key to Sirk's subversiveness was not in his scripts but in his manipulation of *mise-en-scène* pathos and irony. Both the techniques and the effects attributed to Sirk are apparent in *Woman in a Dressing Gown*, but their setting is transposed down the social scale to the upper-working-class/ lower-middle-class family living in an English council flat. Elsaesser (1972: 10), discussing the melodramas of Sirk, Ray and Minnelli, refers to 'an intensified symbolisation of everyday actions, the heightening of the ordinary gesture and the use of setting and decors so as to reflect the characters' fetishist fixations'. This use of hyperbole and the externalisation of feeling into the *mise-en-scène* are accompanied, in Sirk's cinema, by visual distancing devices, dynamic camera movements and ironic musical counterpoint which interfere with melodrama's 'normal' processes of identification. The result is to set up what Hill (1986: 98) terms 'a dialectic of involvement and alienation, of drawing an audience into identification with characters while maintaining a critical distance'.

Woman in a Dressing Gown is a textbook example of the distanciated style and its dialectic of involvement and alienation. Scenes often begin with a shot from behind a structure which breaks up the frame into vertical or horizontal planes and emphasises the camera's presence before panning or tracking right to take a closer view of the action. Our angle of view is constantly shifted and obscured. We find that we are positioned disconcertingly behind fixtures or fittings, and then suddenly obliged to study some sublimely banal object like a tea cosy. Just when we are relaxing into more conventional medium shots our complacency is challenged by an uncomfortable close-up before the camera dollies away to position the viewer outside a window. Point-of-view shots are used sparingly and carry surprise value, especially when they are given a distorted expressionist feel – when a distraught Amy watches a plate fall from her hands, for example. But, always, the active camera is moving our viewing position around, urging the spectator to concentrate but discouraging the simple identification with one character. Although the camera often observes Amy, sometimes alone in her flat, it is frequently Jim's perception of Amy that we are offered. Those irritating mannerisms and habits, which strangers might miss but which cause over-reactions in familiars, are picked out and emphasised – the way Amy tweaks Jim's cheek, or pours his beer, or steals the bedclothes, and, of course, her ever-present dressing gown. This critical examination of Amy militates against her easy representation as a woman wronged and gives us insight into the reasons for Jim's dissatisfaction, but it avoids totally siding with her husband. His faults are evident, too, from his taciturn withdrawal from marital conversation to his tendency to patronise his wife and undermine her confidence.[13] Wife and husband are seen to be, in large measure, what each has made the other, or as Jim puts it: 'Perhaps she's what she is because I am what I am.'[14]

Although the dialogue confirms and underlines the ways in which these two characters have become locked into a closed circuit of emotional malnutrition, the most compelling evidence of their relational failure is contained in Lee Thompson's *mise-en-scène*. Sound plays a vital role here, just as it had in *Yield to the Night*. The domestic interior is turned into a sonic battleground. The banality of Amy's world is expressed in the ceaseless stream of light-and-cheerful music from her radio, while Jim searches vainly for the silence that will allow him peace and introspection. Lee Thompson insists that Amy's music is loud so that we can share Jim's irritation and wince with him as she shrieks over the radio. As jazz, calypso and light orchestral music compete for attention, we become aware that the Prestons' aural environment is as confused and cluttered as their domestic space. Their temperamental incompatibility is symbolised by Jim's loathing of the noise which Amy innocently inflicts upon his ears. For Jim, the radio is the sound of marital discord, but for his wife it offers contact with a world beyond the home, an indispensable aid in the maintenance of morale, and a key to more profound mental states.

Lee Thompson uses this diegetic music in a distinctly Sirkian fashion to provide ironic counterpoint to the action of the film. Knowingly, the (unidentified) piece by Tchaikovsky that moves Amy to sudden sadness, is the *Pathétique* symphony, whose title implies both the extremes of emotion which are a feature of the melodramatic form, and the pathetic naivety of Amy's trust in her husband.[15] A little later, when Amy is struggling to come to terms with her husband's infidelity, her distress is juxtaposed with the tirelessly jolly jazz of her son's Chris Barber disc. Amy's depth of feeling, already anticipated by her reaction to the Tchaikovsky piece, is now thrown into relief by the shallow bonhomie of the more ephemeral tune. Diegetic music again mocks the complacent assumptions of monogamy when *Cosi Fan Tutte*, Mozart's comedy of temptation and infidelity, accompanies Amy's attempts to rekindle the flames of her marriage. The irony, here, is that Mozart's opera rhetorically proposes the ubiquity of female unfaithfulness just when Amy is enduring the pain of male adultery.[16] Like the camera, music is used to probe beneath the surface of Amy and Jim's relationship to draw out its hidden dimensions, just as the film itself exposes the concealed realities of family life. This is made explicit in the moment when Amy catches herself singing *Oh, Oh Antonio*, a melody which she had previously valued for its jaunty good spirits. The irony of its lyrics about an unfaithful lover who has abandoned his sweetheart may already be evident to the audience, but Amy suddenly appreciates their relevance. This realisation registers the totally anomic state in which Amy now finds herself. Like her marriage, the song has presented only the illusion of happiness. The disintegration of her trust in aural signifiers mirrors the dissolution of her faith in the security of her marriage and is expressed visually in the collapse of a gate-legged table loaded with bottles as Amy succumbs to alcohol and depression. The emotional prop provided by popular music has been summarily removed.[17]

Whereas Amy needs the stimulus and reassurance of the radio (here represented as the housewife's friend, as it had been in *For Better, For Worse*), her husband favours a quiet home. His comfort with radio-free silence complements his anxieties about articulating his dissatisfactions with his marriage. In his childhood, feelings 'were things you just didn't talk about', he tells the talkative Amy whose radio constantly claims the domestic space as her own. Aurally as well as emotionally alienated, Jim can only break the news of his infidelity to his wife when she has switched off the blare of the radio.

In contrast, Jim's desire to be free from the relentless soundtrack of his marriage is realised in the tranquillity of his lover's apartment. Georgie – cool, elegant and professional – is the complete antithesis of Amy. The two women symbolise the two worlds in which Jim moves. If Amy is a product of the pressures created in the domestic sphere, Georgie epitomises the values of the workplace. She is smart, efficient and economically ambitious, and although she is capable of genuine tenderness and emotional nourishment she can see beyond Jim's romanticism and sentimentality. She sympathises with his humanist belief that 'it ought to be possible to be happy without trampling on people', but she knows that 'it isn't'. While Amy emphasises her maternal role by addressing Jim by the infantilising diminuitive 'Jimbo', Georgie stresses his adulthood by using his surname 'Preston'. She relates to him not only in the intimate private sphere as a lover, but in the public sphere as a colleague and equal, sharing an office and buying him a drink after work. To Jim, Georgie represents a free will he can no longer exercise in his domestic life. She is the choice of a man whose horizons have expanded, who longs for more than the suffocating domesticity which Amy offers.[18] The film expresses the difference between the freedom and constraint represented by the two women in a variety of ways. Georgie's apartment is not only quiet, but tidy. Its surfaces are clear of the clutter of Amy's home, just as Georgie's mind is free of the jumble and confusion that disrupt Amy's thoughts and shackle her imagination.

It is in the semiotics of dress, however, that the distinctions between the two women are most evident. The immaculate Georgie is always impeccably attired. As with 'the other woman' in *Yield to the Night* we are first shown her well-manicured hands and her feet in sleek court shoes, the synecdoches of feminine neatness, before being given the full picture. That, unlike Amy, she is a woman in full control of her femininity is further evidenced in her carefully pinned coiffure and her spotless white blouse. A mistress she may be, but she is no Jezebel. Her sex appeal is muted by a demureness of dress and adornment. Amy, on the other hand, is seen to have 'let herself go'. Her lack of concern for her appearance indexes her complacent attitude to her marriage. Her hair refuses to accept a style, her feet are cocooned in carpet slippers and her everyday attire has become the ubiquitous crumpled silk dressing gown that defines Amy in the film's title. Whereas Georgie is always dressed for a life lived in public, Amy's dress is strictly private. The dressing gown is a symbol of her housebound existence, singing her favourite songs like a caged bird in 23, Nightingale House. As the characteristic dress of the invalid it also suggests that Amy is suffering from some malaise, but she is physically quite healthy. The pathology, of which the dressing gown is a sign, is located not in herself but in her situation.[19]

When Jim confesses his infidelity, however, Amy's reaction is to identify her own appearance as partial cause and potential cure. Pawning a ring and pressurising her son for a loan, Amy gets her hair professionally styled in an attempt to compete with her rival. Her efforts are in vain, however, as rain washes out her perm.[20] Typically for a melodrama in which 'the characters' behaviour is often pathetically at variance with the real objectives they want to achieve' (Elsaesser 1972: 10), Amy's worst of all possible 'bad-hair-days' continues when she rips her favourite dress trying to squeeze into it, and then imbibes too much whisky in an attempt to fortify her courage to confront Georgie. When the two women finally meet, it is in their accustomed costumes: a hung-over and ungroomed Amy rises from her bed to see off the challenge of her husband's dapper mistress in the same robe in which she fries his chips. The scene is the film's pivotal moment and Lee Thompson marks its tension by largely eschewing the distanciating devices which have kept the audience's emotional responses in check. By reducing the frequency of camera movement and dispensing with the meditated view, Lee Thompson allows the audience to share the characters' suffering and the full emotional impact of the sequence.[21] He intensifies things further by careful attention to lighting and composition. This strategic change of style makes it one of the film's most memorable moments for its editor Dick Best:

> 'If you analyse the angles on that, when they have the showdown, the way Lee's planned it is that she [Georgie] sits like an iceberg, the mother jumps around and Anthony Quayle is pacing in the background. That is a good example of how Lee creates the emotional truth of a scene. It's not just shoot a medium shot, shoot a long shot, two close-ups. It's not like that, it's planned.'

The characters are arranged in the frame in ways which express their unease and disconcertedness, and each is given a key close shot so that the pain which they are mutually experiencing can be registered on their faces. Towards the end of the scene, when the Prestons' son returns and blames Georgie for the destruction of his family, she tells him that 'people can't help their feelings'. It is the film's emblematic statement, not only because it justifies the promiscuous approach to identification which the film's visual style has fostered and the full empathic response it now invites, but because it points to a divorce between morality and emotion, for so long the matrimonial pairing of British film culture. *Dressing Gown* continues the evangelical work of *Yield to the Night*: the promotion of an empathic understanding unclouded by moral censure. In its desire to expel the notion of sin from the inter- pretation of sexual relationships between consenting adults, the film looks forward to the liberalisation of censorship and a coming cinema of permissiveness in which characters and audiences will no longer be obliged to be ashamed of feelings which they cannot 'help'.

For all its technical virtuosity and arch deployment of irony, it is probably in the simple eschewal of both guilt and emotional repression that *Woman in a Dressing Gown* makes its most significant contribution to 1950s' British cinema. Ultimately, it is this that prevents it from being the '*Brief Encounter* of the council houses' (Durgnat 1970: 58). Like most contemporary reviewers, Raymond Durgnat admired the film's sincerity and uncompromising approach, but (again like *Yield to the Night*) it is remembered principally for the remarkable performance of its female lead. Jean Luc Godard may have thought Yvonne Mitchell resembled a creature halfway between an ostrich and Donald Duck, and Lindsay Anderson (*New Statesman*, 12 October 1957) may have been reminded of 'Hermione Baddeley in one of her turns in an Ambassador's revue', but most critics on both sides of the Atlantic thought Mitchell's performance to be one of extraordinary quality. C. A. Lejeune (*Observer*, 6 October 1957) thought it perhaps 'the finest performance on the screen ever given by an English actress', and described it as 'so poignant, so convincing, so utterly true to life down to the smallest detail'. In the *Financial Times* (7 October 1957) Peter Forster credited Mitchell with a 'sheer dramatic power rare among younger actresses' while *The Times* (7 October 1957) praised the 'perfection' of her creation of Amy, adding that Mitchell, Willis and Lee Thompson had, between them, 'accomplished one of the rarest of all achievements in the cinema, the true, complete and wholly convincing portrait of a woman'.[22]

What critics found particularly compelling was to see an actress with a reputation for being cultured and intelligent playing so prosaic and muddleheaded a character. Isabel Quigly (*Spectator*, 11 October 1957) expressed their fascination when she wrote that 'it is interesting – at times it seems almost incredible – to see someone so almost intimidatingly civilised, playing a woman of endearing, exuberant vulgarity'. The contradiction is beautifully caught in her reference to 'the oafishness of gesture over the exquisite bone structure'. To critics on the Left, like Lindsay Anderson and the indefatigable Derek Hill, who called Mitchell's performance 'heartless', the disjuncture between the actor's persona and her character's background and personality militates against authenticity in the portrayal. 'The part is obviously outside Miss Mitchell's own experience', Hill argued, 'with the result that her playing is based on technique instead of observation' (*Tribune*, 18 October 1957). 'Every gesture, every intonation', he suggested, 'comes from an actress's handbook.' And, the final twist of the knife: 'The real trouble is that she is clearly incapable of feeling any sympathy for the character she is portraying.' This last comment is gratuitously insulting, but Hill was justified in pointing to the theatricality of Yvonne Mitchell's playing. What C. A. Lejeune liked so much about it was the way in which it approached the finest of stage acting ('the wonder is that such a mood of understanding could have been sustained through the necessarily broken process of film production').

The debate around Mitchell's portrayal of Amy comes just at that moment when the codes of realism in British theatrical presentation started to be reprogrammed by the New Wave. The arrival of authentic working-class actors who had not had their regional accents drama-schooled out of them, and the sort of documentary style that would find favour in 'The Wednesday Play' on television, would provoke a discussion of performativity that is still current.[23] In 1957 the debate hung on the appropriateness of naturalism and understatement. Much of Yvonne Mitchell's performance, particularly in the first hour of the film, does have a histrionic quality which is controlled only by the sureness of her technique. John Curtis (*Films and Filming*, October 1957) was critical of the lack of subtlety and variation of pace in her acting, complaining that she was 'blazing away all the time'. Dilys Powell, a critic always more comfortable with restraint and control, used the simile of 'a wasp in a bottle' to make the same point. In delivering such a 'full-on' performance, however, Mitchell was doing no more than following her director's instructions. Lee Thompson wanted his debut in independent production to take risks, to challenge the conventional, and his direction of his leading lady was a key part of his strategy. Supported by Joan Henry, he encouraged Mitchell to go 'over the top' in a way which would distinguish her performance from Joan Miller's more reserved portrayal on television and which would complement the excess in the film's visual techniques:

'Looking back, maybe I did go a little over the top, but it was a bravura performance and I encouraged her. Perhaps, if I had to do it over again, I would reduce it slightly, but I really felt at the time that this rather drab subject matter needed a performance that was a little *crazy*, and so I encouraged Yvonne to pull out all the stops ... I don't think I would change very much today. I think it was the right way to approach this particular subject.'

Clearly, commercial considerations were involved in Lee Thompson's decision to go for flamboyance – the fear of the box office reaction to drabness – but there was also a need to find the emotional truth in the character of Amy. This conception of the rightness or authenticity of a performance is significantly different from the more sociological or naturalistic idea held by Lindsay Anderson and Derek Hill. They are interested primarily in the way Amy represents the life and problems of a particular social class, but Lee Thompson, for all his left-wing sentiments, wants to probe beyond the generalities of class to the specificities of family relationships and the irresolvable contradictions implicit even in the association of individuals. For him, the art of film making works best in the interrogation of social psychology rather than sociology and must always be driven by the search for emotional honesty and the dramatisation of subjective responses to moral conflicts. Because Amy buzzes like a 'wasp in a bottle' in the first half of the film, it makes her slow yet desperate attempts to find the oxygen left in her marriage all the more touching when the time comes to moderate the performance. Lee Thompson sought actors who could achieve this kind of range, and Yvonne Mitchell and Sylvia Syms were ideal for his purposes. Both were prepared to throw themselves into their parts with a minimum of self-consciousness, as Syms explained to Peter Haigh a few years later (*ABC Film Review*, June 1960):

'Yvonne and I work well together for one reason in particular: we're both emotional actresses as opposed to technical ones. An emotional actress *lives* her part – gets inside it. It's more than just speaking lines – it's re-living life ... Being the emotional type enables you to do your scenes oblivious to cameras and lights.'[24]

The emotional power of Yvonne Mitchell's performance clearly communicated itself to the jurors at the Berlin Film Festival where she was awarded the Silver Bear for Best Actress. Brought to the July Festival in unseemly haste, *Woman in a Dressing Gown* also secured the International Critics Prize. Leonard Mosley gave British readers of the *Daily Express* (19 July 1957) advance warning that 'a wonderful' ground-breaking picture was on its way: 'A film with the tang of *truth!*' that would at last deliver to cinemagoers a sensitive drama about ordinary people. 'The snobs in the film industry', he wrote, 'who usually make films about so-called "little people" almost always manage to patronise them – and make them seem unreal and dull at the same time. But not this time.' When the film had its British premiere at London's Warner Theatre in October 1957 a large majority of critics shared Mosley's view and Lee Thompson was widely praised for his directorial work, described by one reviewer as 'a masterpiece of atmospheric detail' (Harold Conway, *Daily Sketch*, 4 October 1957) and by another as 'flawless' (*Kinematograph Weekly*, 26 September 1957). However, *Dressing Gown* had to struggle for attention with the fiercest of competition from David Lean's widescreen epic *The Bridge on the River Kwai*. A week into its run, *Kinematograph Weekly* (17 October 1957) was delighted to report that Lee Thompson's film was managing 'to keep its head above water', and a strong effort was put into its marketing when it went on general release.[25] The result, according to Willis 1991:141) was that *Dressing Gown* grossed £450,000 in Britain on a £99,000 investment, and went on to earn close to £1 million in all.[26]

In his seminal article on melodrama, Thomas Elsaesser (1972) suggests that it is a more accessible medium for communicating truths about human relationships than art cinema, and asserts its ability to offer a critique of dominant ideology and prevailing social conditions. In his discussion of the subversive potential of melodrama's *mise-en-scène* he stresses the importance of 'an aesthetics of the domestic' in which 'the pressure generated by things crowding in on the characters ... by the claustrophobic atmosphere of the bourgeois home', and by 'a sense of hysteria bubbling all the time just below the surface', contribute to a feeling that there is always 'more to tell than can be said'. These characteristics have rarely been more clearly illustrated than in *Woman in a Dressing Gown*, even if the home portrayed is less than bourgeois. There are moments – like the one when the Prestons' son removes the third cup from the tea tray and symbolically represents the departure of his father – when our support seems to be enlisted for the family unit. That support, however, is never unqualified and unequivocal. The tension noted in melodrama by Jean-Loup Bourget (1978) between a moralistic championing of the family and a whimsical attachment to romance and escape is never resolved and we are asked to experience the pain of desire unfulfilled, as much as the relief of security regained. The alienating properties of the institution of marriage are never concealed or projected away. The few glimpses we have of Jim's work are insufficient to support the Chuck Kleinhaus (1978) line that it is the essential, or 'real', site of alienation. Although they do supply a context for the psycho-drama of family life, the contradictions of work under capitalism are not simply shifted into the private sphere. Similarly, the inadequacies the film depicts cannot be simply written off as those of its protagonists alone. Their problems are undeniably their own, but there is nothing to suggest they are unique, and the vividness and irony with which they are presented does little to relieve anxiety about the institution they reflect. Ultimately, *Dressing Gown*'s refusal to make moral judgements and ascribe blame to individuals leaves the structures of patriarchal marriage exposed.

No Trees in the Street (1959)

> Look at your working classes now. Haven't they got it all? But they're not exactly a testament to the highest achievements of the human race, are they? (Edgar in David Mercer's *Where the Difference Begins*, BBC Television, 15 December 1961)

No Trees in the Street began life as a controversial play written by Ted Willis almost ten years before its release as a film, when he was still involved with Unity Theatre. The play was based on people he had known during his childhood in north London. 'I think I wrote it to exorcise certain ghosts', recalled Willis:

> The central characters are a mother and daughter – the mother an evil, foul-mouthed woman without a decent motive to her name, the daughter a young woman who is struggling to escape the lower depths of poverty. The mother mocks her efforts and, in the end, creates the circumstances in which she can sell her daughter to the local bookmaker for a cash payment. I had seen this happen as a teenager and I had been a little in love with the real-life girl. (1991: 75)

A hit in the provinces, the play challenged the bourgeois sensibilities of West End theatre critics who effectively drove it out to the prestigious St James Theatre into lower status venues (1991: 83–92).

Notwithstanding the play's reputation as a people's favourite, to revive a stage drama written in the late 1940s and set in the late 1930s was hardly a progressive step for a film production company dedicated to exploring the problems of contemporary society. One consideration in its favour as a project may have been the thought that the slow relaxation of censorship now made the play potentially filmable. A more progressive regime at the BBFC had made it clear that it was prepared to consider the sort of images and subject matter at which it would have blanched in the past.[27] Indeed, BBFC secretary John Nichols was quoted as positively welcoming 'provocative films that air our social problems' (*Kinematograph Weekly*, 14 March 1957).[28] Even the cautious and conservative Rank organisation had allowed Basil Dearden and Michael Relph to film a daring study of teenage delinquency in Liverpool – *Violent Playground* (1958). The film had offered nothing more radical than environmental theories of crime and a (qualified) endorsement of liberal approaches to the punishment of offenders, but it had shown considerable sympathy towards Johnny (David McCallum), its young antagonist (Hill 1986: 79–83; Chibnall 1997). Moreover, James Kennaway's screenplay seems to owe a not insignificant debt to *No Trees in the Street*. Both plots have a plain-clothes policeman becoming romantically attached to the older sister of a delinquent youth, and both climax with a young gunman resisting arrest in a police siege.[29] Its similarities to *Violent Playground* (which have, strangely, passed unnoticed or at least without comment), however, failed to deter Lee Thompson from pressing ahead with *No Trees* when he finished *Ice Cold in Alex* early in 1958.[30] Associated British had already agreed to finance the film on condition that the profits from *Woman in a Dressing Gown* were held back to offset any potential loss on the new project (Willis 1991: 141).

Ted Willis' work was much in demand on both small and large screen. Between *Dressing Gown* and *No Trees* he adapted another of his teleplays, *The Young and the Guilty* (1958) for Peter Cotes's debut as a film director.[31] Willis's style, combining, as it did, class consciousness and social concern with a distaste for overt expressions of sexual desire and a stress on individual responsibility (Hill 1986: 100), supplied something of a model for the social-problem melodramas of the late 1950s and early 1960s. His approach to the submerged problems of urban society was ideal in uncovering these issues for cinematic exploitation and, at the same time, pacifying the censor with its 'responsible' attitude to reform on the part of benevolent authority figures.[32] It is to Lee Thompson's credit that he managed to curb Willis' tendencies towards moralising (particularly in the context of unregulated sexual desire) in *Woman in a Dressing Gown*, and to resist the writer's inclination to condemn irresponsible behaviour in individuals. In *No Trees in the Street*, the checks and balances, which in their previous collaboration had moderated and ironised the melodrama, are largely abandoned, and with them goes any subtlety the film might have had.

The cast of *No Trees* is a familiar one. Sylvia Syms stars as Hetty, the young woman fighting against the morally corrosive effects of slum conditions and feckless parents. Her mother Jess, a woman whose moral sense has long since been corrupted by her environment, is played by Joan Miller, who had been the original Amy in the teleplay of *Woman in a Dressing Gown*. Herbert Lom, an actor Lee Thompson came to think of as 'like a mascot' because he cast him so frequently, plays Wilkie, the local wideboy who has successfully built a criminal career as a way out of poverty. Carole Lesley, another of the *Dressing Gown* cast, returns as Wilkie's moll Lova. Even Melvyn Hayes, who plays Hetty's tearaway younger brother Tommy, had appeared in *Dressing Gown*, admittedly in a bit part as a news vendor.[33]

Most of the film's action takes place in Kennedy Street, an area of slum tenements in London's East End just before the Second World War. Bucking the developing trend towards location shooting, the street was meticulously created at Elstree to the design of Robert Jones. The set is impressive, but its artificiality only adds to an overall ambience of theatricality which no amount of authentic detail can quite dispel. In fact the attempt to evoke the atmosphere of the late years of the Depression and convince the audience of the reality of what they are viewing becomes clichéd and slightly desperate. A choir of unemployed Welsh miners sings in the street, graffiti about Oswald Mosley defaces the walls and the news hoardings announce Hutton's record-breaking cricket score against Australia. If Jones had worked wonders in making tangible Mary Hilton's environmental deprivation and Amy Preston's slatternly lifestyle, his best intentions simply add to the sense of excess which weighs down *No Trees*. The film goes beyond a strong sense of period into a heritage theme park recreation, replete with barrel organs, pawnbrokers, Jewish delis, musichall songs, cockroaches, cloth caps, mufflers, bread and dripping and armies of brown ale bottles on the kitchen table. Clichés abound, but at least it is not the romanticised vision of a lost community which is so evident in contemporary writing on the working class like Richard Hoggart's *The Uses of Literacy* (1957). Kennedy Street is no Paradise Lost where doors were always unlocked and the homing pidgeon was a man's best friend. There is no attempt to advance Hoggart's fashionable thesis that, for the working class, the price of material improvement is cultural and spiritual loss, a surrender to the 'shiny barbarism' of Americanised commercial mass culture. Instead of a shared commitment to mutual support and respectable values, the community of *No Trees* is poisoned by its conditions of life. 'People don't live here, they exist like animals', Hetty remarks bitterly in a statement that encapsulates the film's less than rosy view of the past. Survival seems to depend on petty criminality and is made bearable by a ready supply of bottled beer and stew with dumplings. Collective action offers no solution to Kennedy Street's inhabitants who regard their neighbourhood mainly as a brick cage. It is clear that when the Blitz comes the Luftwaffe will be doing the residents a favour: Come friendly bombs and fall on Kennedy Street (to adapt Betjeman). Hetty would like to do the job herself: 'I'd like to burn it down', she declares, 'the whole street, every rotten house. I'd like to stand a mile away and hear it crackling.' Even the most successful man in the street, Wilkie the bookie, who has overcome the twin handicaps of class and race ('my folks were nothing; nothing with an accent'), still cannot leave. He presides over his territory from his first-floor offices as an *éminence grise*, feared, respected, affluent but still unable to remove 'the smell of the street' from his skin.

At a time when a new American president would shortly make the name Kennedy a byword for optimism, *No Trees* makes it a sign of no hope. The street is a metaphor for dead-end lives, a cul-de-sac of opportunity. The sense of hopeless fatalism that pervades the place is personified in the figure of Bill (Liam Redmond), a blind man who, when he is not making a little on the side by fencing stolen goods, sits in Jess's garret twisting wreaths for those unfortunate residents who have proved that 'there's only one way to get out' of Kennedy Street. This place is a 'death trap', he intones, 'get out quick'.

It is not difficult to see why J. Lee Thompson would have been attracted to a scenario which so clearly foregrounds his obsessional themes of entrapment and the yearning for escape –here symbolised by the picture of Cornwall that Hetty has torn from a magazine and pinned up. The only chance of getting to Cornwall (the 'chance of a lifetime', as her mother terms it), however, is to accept the advances of Wilkie, to use and be used. It is the sort of stark moral conflict on which Lee Thompson thrives, and it is the type which confronts all those who live in Kennedy Street. In Willis' original play, Jess sells her daughter to Wilkie, as in Graham Greene's *Brighton Rock* Rose's parents sell their permission for her to marry the gangster Pinkie.[34] The film removes the financial transaction but retains the sense of exploitation, the idea that a mother would be prepared to use her daughter's body as a passport out of poverty. Jess's son, Tommy, must also be ready to exploit and injure others in his attempt to be a somebody. Prostitution and gangsterism are the only chances for those Tommy calls 'people like us'. The lesson his upbringing has taught him is that 'you've got to be tough'. He also lacks the coolness of Wilkie's temperament. Like Frankie in *The Yellow Balloon* and Gillie in *Tiger Bay* his eyes betray his fear, just as Wilkie's ice-cold stare betrays the deadening effects of childhood deprivation. Tommy simply cannot 'hack it' as a hoodlum. In panic, he kills a shop owner and seeks sanctuary in the family garret. When the police come for him, he panics again and this time a struggle with his sister for possession of his gun ends in his own death. The pressures of Kennedy Street have ensured another recipient for Bill's wreaths.

Like so many of Lee Thompson's killers, Tommy is more victim than victimiser. As Wilkie remarks bitterly, 'his life went wrong the day he was born' – but unlike Mary Hilton or *Tiger Bay*'s Korchinsky, he never really earns our sympathy or the film's redemptive absolution. This may have a lot to do with a perform-ance by Melvyn Hayes that makes Yvonne Mitchell's in *Dressing Gown* seem like a model of theatrical restraint. Both Frank Godwin and Lee Thompson had been seduced by a screen test in which Hayes had demonstrated extraordinary emotional commit-ment to the role of Tommy in a performance which Lee Thompson described, rather perversely, as 'excitingly wrong' (*ABC Film Review*, September 1958).[35] Unfortunately, instead of toning down Hayes's manic acting, his director allowed him his head. The intention was probably to contrast Tommy's hysteria with Wilkie's control and to suggest that an environment such as Kennedy Street is dehumanising in the way it can turn a boy into a fright-ened animal. The result, however, was to lose the depth of character and affecting pathos that led the viewer to identify so strongly with the plight of Hilton and Korchinsky.[36] The failure to construct Tommy as a sympathetic character unbalances the film's dialectic between free will and determinism. Because Tommy is a hysteric with 'no backbone', he gives in to his environment, whereas the more personally resourceful Wilkie turns the privations of Kennedy Street to his own advantage. However, the character of Frank Collins (Ronald Howard), the young detective, demonstrates that, given sufficient moral fibre, there is a third alternative to surrender and exploitation. With effort, a slum background may be transcended. Thus, as John Hill (1986: 101) notes, the film's 'logic of environmentalism is radically undercut by an emphasis on individual responsibility'. A trope associated with American gangster films, that of having a criminal and a guardian of morality come from the same deprived neighbourhood (McArthur 1972: 39), is used in *No Trees* to suggest that moral judgements need not be subservient to environmental pressures.[37] In spite of their shared origins, Frank embodies optimism and decency while Wilkie represents pessimism and depravity. The two men's battle for Hetty's soul provides a more effective dynamo for drama than Tommy's ill-fated criminal career and histrionic posturing.[38] Although it is the virtuous but bland Frank who eventually wins Hetty, her relationship with Wilkie is the most interesting of the film. In Willis' play Wilkie rapes Hetty with the collusion of her mother, but so sordid a plot line would, if passed at all, have guaranteed the film a commercially disastrous 'X' certificate.[39] Instead, Hetty falls for Wilkie because he refrains from raping her when given every opportunity.

This accommodation to the censor actually does no harm as far as the film's characterisations are concerned. Hetty and Wilkie are given additional dimensions, bringing them much closer to the type of psychologically complex and contradictory character that Lee Thompson usually favoured. The director is able to explore the ambivalence involved in the way Hetty is both drawn to and repelled by the Godfather of Kennedy Street. She is attracted by his strength, authority and confidence but deplores his cynical exploitation of others. His cynicism is evident in his categorisation of Hetty as the 'last item' on his mental list of achievements, but, in passing up the easy choice of rape when she lays half-dressed and inebriated on her bed in front of him, he shows (not least to Hetty) that he has retained some sense of decency and compassion.[40] When Hetty wakes, Wilkie, in apologising for his attempted seduction, displays an unexpected thoughtfulness and vulnerability which she finds irresistible.[41] In the end, it is her desire which precipitates their sexual union. Such uncoupling of desire from moral restraint is a motif characteristic of Lee Thompson, rather than of Ted Willis, and here it gives *No Trees* not just a relational complexity which it otherwise lacks, but an emotional core which rests uneasily with Willis' more conventional and predictable moral order. Shot in noir style, this sequence in Hetty's bedroom has a dark intensity and an ambiguity which contrasts with the formulaic situations and responses that dominate this melodrama.[42]

When Hetty at last chooses life with Wilkie she believes she has reached the escape velocity which will propel her from the street of her birth. She packs a suitcase to accompany him to Cornwall, the Shangri-La of her imaginings. It is the second time she has packed it but, like Jim Preston's case in *Dressing Gown*, it never leaves the flat. Wilkie is suspicious of her relationship with her police suitor and proceeds to humiliate her in front of Frank and her family by ordering her around and suggesting that Lova (Carole Lesley), his regular 'moll', will accompany them to Cornwall. Conventional morality and sentiment reassert themselves. Hetty is shaken out of her infatuation with Wilkie, who is exposed as the bullying spiv we first thought he was. In spite of suggestions that Wilkie may be covering his jealousy and hurt with a show of machismo and that he continues to care for Hetty, there is no way that J. Lee Thompson can restore any audience sympathy for the character. Wilkie's criminality may be (partly) explained by a theory of environmentalism but Ted Willis' commitment to respectability will not allow his antagonist's behaviour to be excused. In the end, Wilkie must be condemned by Hetty, not only as a personification of the corrupting effects of his neighbourhood, but as a parasite on its people. As he struggles to diffuse the responsibility for Tommy's death ('No one is to blame – we're all to blame'), Hetty is more judgemental. 'I used to blame the street,' she tells him, 'but it's you and people like you, who are the real killers.' In the final analysis, then, the deprivation and discrimination in Wilkie's past count for little once he has joined the oppressive class of criminal parasites who, in Willis' view, debilitate the working class and retard collective action. Rather than the 'toffs', who Tommy pictures 'sitting round their posh radiograms', it is apparently villains like Wilkie who are directly responsible for Kennedy Street's kids' lack of a square meal since 'the Coronation tea party'.

This inclination to install criminality as cause rather than effect of Kennedy Street's malaise threatens to completely muddy the waters of the film's political rhetoric. Perhaps the police inspector who doubts that the street's residents 'would be any better if they lived in decent houses' is right. Perhaps there is something to his assertions that 'these people are here because they haven't got the guts to be anywhere else' and that 'they don't deserve any better'. By 1958 Willis' belief in the beneficial effects of 'decent housing' and 'air that doesn't stink' was still strong, but his optimism was constantly dented by the persistence of delinquency in areas of new housing. Indeed, his *raison d'être* for *No Trees* seems to have been to persuade the increasingly youthful cinema audience that, in the MacMillan age of high-rise plenty, the pretext for crime had disappeared. Willis' preoccupation with mapping the effects of the 'social revolution', evidenced in slum clearance and post-war proletarian affluence, was clearly expressed in his contribution to a discussion on 'Vital theatre' for *Encore* magazine (March 1959: 42):

> 'I live on the fringe of a big LCC estate full of ordinary working-class people. Before the war, one in every three houses would have an unemployed man, an unemployed son. Now they are all working, and there's quite a bit of money coming into the house. A working-class woman who lives near us has a husband who is a steel erector, and they have just bought a car. Well I can't tell you the difference this has made.'

The contrast between the life choices available in the late 1930s and those in the late 1950s is stressed in *No Trees* by a framing device, added after initial press screenings of the film.[43] The titles come up over an aerial view of contemporary London to the accompaniment of Laurie Johnson's jazz score.[44] One almost expects a narrator to announce that there are 8 million stories in the Naked City, but instead we see a boy running over a bomb site, just as we had in *The Yellow Balloon*. The youth (a fresh-faced David Hemmings) is apprehended by Frank Collins who proceeds to lecture him about carrying a flick knife. He learns that the boy lives in the new development where Kennedy Street once stood, and, in an effort to show him how much easier life is now on the model council estate, he relates the tale of the old street. At the end of the long flash-back, when the boy is taken to Frank's home to have a wound tended, we learn that the policeman has kept Hetty on the 'straight and narrow' by marrying her.[45] Bombs and rebuilding have not solved all the problems of Kennedy Street because human behaviour is ultimately not reducible to environ-mental influence alone. But the fragile tree that now grows where the slums once festered is a sign of progress and hope.[46]

Because it fits so closely with his published views, it is tempting to attribute the film's attempt to dramatise the social progress made over the previous twenty years, and to challenge environmental explanations of contemporary crime, primarily to Ted Willis. But Lee Thompson, somewhat surprisingly for a film-maker who could present the social outsider so sensitively, endorsed the Willis thesis with enthusiasm: 'It was an answer to the angry young men set', he was quoted as saying (*Daily Herald*, 6 March 1959): 'The story maintains that, though perhaps small, social progress has been made in the past 20 years.' He did not want to make a film about modern youth 'going wrong because of poor social conditions', because 'We ain't making excuses for the Teddy Boys. We've had enough of those films. We are saying, in effect, stop your silly whining, look at what it used to be like' (*Kinematograph Weekly*, 10 April 1958).

For staunchly socialist critics, it was not difficult to see this emphasis on individual responsibility and the potential achieve-ments of Tory housing policies as serious ideological backsliding on the part of Willis and Lee Thompson. Derek Hill (*Tribune*, 13 March 1959) was not slow to ask: 'What do these proud friends of the Left imagine they're doing with a production which tells a story of a pre-war East End environment corrupting its inhabitants' lives and then ends with a complacent glance at today's living standards

and a sharp word to the young that they've never had it so good?'
But this apparently reactionary message failed to satisfy in more
politically conservative circles. In the *Daily Telegraph* (7 March
1959) Campbell Dixon questioned the narrow materialism of
Willis' approach, challenging him to explain why, 'in the Welfare
State, adolescents receiving high wages, and living in comfortable
State-subsidised homes, are smashing old people's heads in, and
stabbing people in the back with a callousness almost unknown in
1938'.[47] Like most of J. Lee Thompson's pictures, this was clearly
not a film about which viewers could easily agree. In spite of his
ideological reservations, Campbell Dixon actually thought that *No
Trees* had been 'skilfully directed' with characters 'drawn with
sympathy and (you feel) first hand knowledge' and, among a
number of fine performances, the one from Sylvia Syms was
'worth an Oscar'. He had significant support from sections of the
Sunday press review corps, including the *News of the World*'s Peter
Burnup who called it 'a lovely film' (8 March 1959) and the
People's Ernest Betts who thought it 'great stuff', enthusing that
'scene after scene knocks you out with a blast of dramatic
dynamite' (8 March 1959). The majority opinion, however, was
that a potentially serious film about social conditions has been de-
railed by crude characterisation, over-dramatic acting and an
inconsistent message. The result according to Anthony Carthew
(*Daily Herald*, 6 March 1959) 'hopelessly mixes good dramatic
moments with crude travesty, passages of sincerity with sociological tracts'. The *Monthly Film Bulletin* (March 1959) was in no
doubt that Lee Thompson should shoulder the responsibility for
the 'crude sensationalism' of the film, describing his direction as
'hysterical' and the acting as 'pitched throughout on a level of
pathetic desperation'.[48] The performance most often exempted
from criticism was that of Sylvia Syms. Such a refined voice and
flawless complexion on a slum-bound shop girl might have strained
credulity but the comparatively restrained emotionalism of her
portrayal brought for Frank Jackson (*Reynold's News*, 8 March 1959)
'a quiet, honest truth I did not find in the rest of this noisy film'.

By the time of the film's release, however, J. Lee Thompson
had earned enough critical respect for most reviews (Derek Hill's

apart) to dispense knocking notices with a heavy heart. Fred Majdalany (*Daily Mail*, 6 March 1959), for example, could almost be seen shaking his head when he wrote, 'Why does a talented film-maker like J. Lee Thompson make *No Trees in the Street?*' *Picturegoer*, which had so liked *Dressing Gown*, was forced to conclude that its 'consistently strident' tone made *No Trees* a failure but insisted that it was a 'gallant' one and a film that although 'faulty' was still 'important' (21 March 1959). Like so many other commentators, *Picturegoer* admired Lee Thompson's sincerity and willingness to tackle unglamorous subjects in innovative ways. 'Of all the producers and directors operating in British films', it felt, 'Frank Godwin and J. Lee Thompson are two of the rare ones who attempt to present British life with some resemblance to truth.' The same sentiment seemed to be endorsed by C. A. Lejeune (*Observer*, 8 March 1959) when, acknowledging *No Trees*' deficiencies, she praised it for being 'in there trying'.

Notes

1 Unity's Outside Show Group performed drama in air-raid shelters, Underground stations and on street corners. See Willis (1970) for his recollections of his early career in political activism and drama.

2 Willis' film-writing credits included *Holiday Camp* (Ken Annakin, 1947), *The Huggets Abroad* (Ken Annakin, 1949), *Good Time Girl* (David MacDonald, 1948), *Trouble in Store* (John Paddy Corstairs, 1953), *Burnt Evidence* (Daniel Birt, 1954) and *It's Great to Be Young* (Cyril Frankel, 1956).

3 Chayefsky's best-known play is *Marty*. Originally broadcast on American television, this story of a New York butcher's discovery of love was adapted for the cinema in 1955, directed by Delbert Mann and starring Ernest Borgnine.

4 Cotes exemplified the interconnections between London's stage, television and film communities. A half-brother of the Boultings (with whom Lee Thompson's editor and cinematographer had established their careers), Cotes was a leading West End theatre director and a senior producer for both the BBC and Associated Rediffusion. He was married to the actress and television personality Joan Miller, who had played one of the prison officers in *Yield to the Night*.

5 Filming took place at Elstree in March and April 1957. Lee Thompson had formed a second independent production company, Kenwood Films, with *Yield to the Night*'s producer Ken Harper, and they had tentatively scheduled a production of the suspense thriller *The Snorkel* for early

summer. However, Kenwood Films was still-born and *The Snorkel* was made by Hammer later in the year.

6 One is reminded of the touching faith in the efficacy of radio advice shown by another of Lee Thompson's housewives: Anne in *For Better, For Worse*.

7 It was not only full-time housewives who were subject to the 'Feminine Mystique'. Working wives like Sylvia Syms were rarely able to escape fully from its influence. As she told Brian McFarlane (1997: 549), Yvonne Mitchell's role as Amy was 'very close to me, because one of my problems was that, as well as being a gifted actress, I thought it was my bounden duty to be a gifted housewife – to the detriment of my work, because I was always in conflict'.

8 From this perspective, *Dressing Gown* conforms to Laura Mulvey's conception of a melodrama 'coloured by a female protagonist's dominating point-of-view' (1977: 54) which offers a female audience the pleasure of recognising those contradictions of patriarchy which are routinely hidden from inspection. Lee Thompson, however, is still disinclined to consider it a film targeted at one sex or dealing only with a female point of view: 'I didn't think of it as a "woman's film". I just thought of it as a damn good part for a woman. I was hoping for a wider audience than it got, but it is still one of my favourite films.'

9 Gil Taylor proudly told *Kinematograph Weekly* (14 March 1957): 'In one take alone we had fourteen different [camera] movements.' When he recalled his work on the film more than forty years later, however, it was not the ostentatious camera movements he remembered but the lighting of one sequence in particular: the scene in which Jim reveals his affair with Georgie to his wife. The problem, as he and Lee Thompson saw it, was to create a dramatic atmosphere without losing the reality of a room lit by a single ceiling-light:

> 'Lee said: "How can I play this scene? It runs two or three minutes with this bloody council house light." He said: "What can you do? Is it possible you can take the light down until we're almost against black velvet?" I said: "Yes, I think so", which I did; and I had to bring it up again slowly because the boy [Andrew Ray] makes an entrance at the end. But the fact is that the drama in [that sequence] from my point of view was unique because you do this and it works so well. You know what I mean – a little part of the moon.'

10 This process of scrutinising mundane aspects of the environment had been explicitly commented on in *Yield to the Night* when Mary Hilton talks about knowing her cell 'better than any room I've ever lived in', while the camera shows us 'every crack in the walls, the scratches on the wooden chairs', etc.

11 Willis' recommendations are solidly in line with the Italian neo-realists and Andre Bazin's advocacy of a cinematic naturalism which passively records real life.

12 A special issue of the journal *Screen* (vol. 12, no. 2, Winter 1977–78), for example, was devoted to Sirk's work. See also Stern (1979).

13 As Melanie Williams (1999a: 7) notes, the film rejects the conventional fit between morality and identification. Rather than offering us identification with a moral character and refusing us identification with less moral ones, 'the film problematises identification with any of the characters, thus suggesting the difficulty of being able to know anybody from the position of observer'.

14 The line is almost identical to one in *The Fallen Idol* when Baines says of his wife: 'Perhaps she was what she was because I'm what I am.' Willis did not write all of *Dressing Gown*'s dialogue. Joan Henry certainly contributed some lines: 'I'm supposed to be rather good at dialogue and love scenes so I was always having to do these. Lee said: "My God, look at what Ted Willis has written! His idea of a love scene is sitting down by the kitchen sink having *Green Grow the Rushes-O* playing. You'll have to change this." So I did a lot of that.'

15 Williams (1999a: 15) interprets this moment as part of the film's proto-feminist critique of patriarchal marriage:

> This consciously quiet moment in an otherwise hectic film, together with the bathetic juxtaposition of Tchaikovsky and chips, high art and household drudgery, suggests a strong feeling of human potential gone to waste, creative energy channelled entirely into the trivialities of housework ... and the sadness of that waste is evoked by Amy's wistful comment on the music and most of all, by the music itself, which suggests the depth of feeling that cannot be expressed by the emotionally inarticulate characters.

16 The Prestons' neighbour Hilda (Carole Lesley) neatly reverses the sexist rhetoric of Mozart's librettist when, recalling her father's infidelity, she complains to Amy: 'Men are all the same. When they want you, they can't do enough, but when they've got you –it's like the never-never – they think they've paid after the first instalment.' *Cosi Fan Tutti!*

17 Paradoxically, the lament about the philandering 'Antonio' who has left his lover 'all alone-io' also contains the seeds of feminist defiance:

> I'd like to see him with his new sweetheart,
> Then up would go Antonio and his ice-cream cart.

These seeds may be seen to sprout in Amy's later declaration: 'I don't need you anymore, Jimbo. I can work. I can find a job ... Maybe this is the best thing that can happen to me. For years I haven't thought of myself, only of you. Now it's changed ...'.

18 Clearly, to Jim, Georgie represents freedom and progress, but Lee Thompson is careful to indicate that there is no easy solution to his condition. He is cooped up in an office with Georgie just as he is trapped in his council flat with Amy. The liberty represented by Georgie's apartment is also qualified by the same visual rhetoric of barred windows, and the unwelcoming social climate for marital infidelity is signalled by the rain that falls continually outside.

19 Ironically enough, the film's press book offered six stills of Yvonne

Mitchell modelling 'a range of modern dressing gowns which give wide scope for fashion tie-ups around the title of the film'. In contrast, only a single still of Sylvia Syms showing 'how a smart business girl should be dressed' was available.

20 Typically, Lee Thompson chooses to emphasise her dishevelled state by filming her sodden feet squelching along the pavement in a pair of old lace-ups.

21 The impact of these later scenes on critics used to the pulling of emotional punches is indicated in Harold Conway's description (*Daily Sketch*, 4 October 1957) of the way they 'set my nerves jangling in acute emotional embarrassment'. The phrase is echoed in Raymond Durgnat's assessment of the film as having 'the considerable and un-British merit of being embarrassingly moving' (1970: 181).

22 The popular press reacted to the performance with near unanimous enthusiasm: Ivan Adams in the *Star* (3 October 1957) thought it 'the best of its kind since that of Anna Magnani in *Rose Tattoo*'. The *Sketch*'s Harold Conway (4 October 1957) and the *News of the World*'s P.L. Mannock (6 October 1957) both nominated it as performance of the year. Jympson Harman (*Evening News*, 3 October 1957) considered it 'the finest' of Yvonne Mitchell's many 'moving performances', as did Ross Shepherd in The *People* (6 October 1957). There were similar plaudits in papers as culturally and politically diverse as the *Daily Worker* (5 October 1957) , the *Daily Mirror* (4 October 1957), the *Evening Standard* (3 October 1957) and the *Sunday Express* (6 October 1957) where Milton Shulman was dazzled by Mitchell's 'display of baffled, pathetic femininity'. Only Frank Jackson in *Reynold's News* (5 October 1957) was prepared to label the performance as 'overdone'.

23 For a discussion of the ways in which the films of Mike Leigh and Ken Loach represent different paradigms of realist performance in recent British cinema, see Hill (1999: 192–204).

24 Raymond Durgnat (1970: 181) felt their performances managed to illuminate some important insights to the cultural responses of their characters: 'Yvonne Mitchell's oven-heat hysteria brings out the frenzy so often a regular part of an apparently mediocre existence, while Sylvia Syms notes the vehement brittleness within middle-class blandness.'

25 Although Lee Thompson was busy filming *Ice Cold in Alex*, Frank Godwin and Ted Willis made personal appearances at a number of provincial trade and press shows (*Kinematograph Weekly*, 24 October 1957).

26 Janet Thumin (1991) lists *Dressing Gown* as one of the twelve most popular films and one of the six most popular British films at the British box office in 1957.

27 Hammer's colour shocker *The Curse of Frankenstein* (Terence Fisher, 1957) is commonly thought to mark the beginning of the new climate of censorship, the liberality of which is most evident in the certificating of the prostitution melodrama *The Flesh Is Weak* (Don Chaffey, 1957) and the naturist drama-doc *Nudist Paradise* (Charles Saunders, 1958).

28 Nichols resigned in June 1958 shortly after the completion of *No Trees*.

29 Whatever the inspiration for *Violent Playground*, Lee Thompson is a great

admirer of the work of James Kennaway who came from the same part of Scotland (Perthshire) as the director's family. Lee Thompson bought the rights to Kennaway's second novel *Household Ghosts* nine years before he eventually filmed it as *Country Dance* (1971, USA: *Brotherly Love*).

30 He was even prepared to cast Melvyn Hayes in a role similar to that of the delinquent he played in *Violent Playground*.

31 Cotes' 'mission statement' was virtually identical to that of the Lee Thompson–Willis–Godwin partnership: 'I want to make a film about real people experiencing real problems – the type which audiences of all sorts recognise as similar to their own problems' (*Films and Filming*, March 1958: 9).

32 Landy (1991: 482) effectively summarises the significance of Willis' texts when she comments more generally on the social-problem films of the period as follows: 'While offering an index to social and ideological transformations concerning youth, race, sex, and social class that will surface in more direct fashion in the popular culture of the late 1960s and 1970s, the films remain committed to traditional institutional structures.'

33 Frank Godwin had noticed Hayes in late 1955 when he appeared in *The Unloved*, a television play set in an approved school. By the time he was offered a small part in *Dressing Gown* he had played the young Victor Frankenstein in *The Curse of Frankenstein*. Some critical remarks he made to Godwin (not realising he was the film's producer) nearly lost him the chance of a role in *No Trees*, but Godwin was sufficiently impressed by Hayes' performance in the television series *The Silver Sword* to give him a screen test (*ABC Film Review*, September 1958: 15).

34 Greene's novel was published in 1938, the year in which *No Trees* is set.

35 In the same article in *ABC Film Review*, Frank Godwin commented: 'It didn't seem possible that a boy could act the way Melvyn Hayes did at that test. He really looked as if he had lived among cockroaches, that he really was half-starved.'

36 Fred Majdalany noted the problem in his review of the film in the *Daily Mail* (6 March 1959): 'At no point does the particular thuglet under examination become moving, pitiable or even moderately interesting.' While a number of critics were impressed with the commitment that Hayes put into his role, Caroline Lejeune (*Observer*, 8 March 1959) was disappointed that he had been 'allowed to over-act hysterically'.

37 The same trope reappears in the following year's *Hell Is a City* (Val Guest, 1960) in which both Inspector Martineau (Stanley Baker) and the killer Starling (John Crawford) are old boys of the same school.

38 Whether there is any significance to the fact that the names of the two antagonists make 'Wilkie Collins' remains a mystery.

39 The certification of *No Trees in the Street* remains a matter of some dispute. The *Monthly Film Bulletin* (March 1959) records the film's certificate as 'X', and Tony Aldgate (1995: 40), working with BBFC records, maintains: 'On completion, it was [given] an 'X' certificate, largely because the censor's reservations about a key scene involving a young man ("the boy must not be young, he must be about 18") and a gun ("there must be no emphasis

on the power of weapons") had clearly not been resolved to the BBFC's satisfaction.' On the film's London release, however, newspaper reviews state that *No Trees* is an 'A' certificate picture, as do the advertisements for the film's general release. The discrepancy suggests that late changes may have been made in order to please the censor, and it may well be significant that the *MFB*'s plot summary makes no mention of the framing device which throws the film into historical relief (see below). Furthermore, John Trevelyan, the new secretary of the Board, may have been inclined to make a peace offering to Lee Thompson, the BBFC's most vocal critic.

40 Alternatively, we might interpret Wilkie's reticence as a sign that his ego requires Hetty's seduction and willing consent. Charles Hatton's novelisation of the screenplay certainly suggests this reading: 'But he didn't want her on these terms. She had to come to him knowingly and willingly; otherwise it would be a dead loss' (Hatton 1958: 109).

41 As Hatton (1958: 111) expresses it: 'She no longer feared him; he was in many ways just a lost man on Kennedy Street, as helpless as any of the others, looking for consolation from a woman.'

42 After similar sequences featuring Sylvia Syms in *Dressing Gown* and *Ice Cold*, Lee Thompson was developing a reputation for erotic love scenes. Isabel Quigly (*Spectator*, 13 March 1959) commented that he was 'one of the few British directors who can make a love scene seem at once tender and credibly passionate'. For Lee Thompson's account of directing Sylvia Syms in these sequences, see Lee Thompson (1959).

43 This is referred to as 'a revised version' of the film in *Films and Filming*'s March 1959 review.

44 The overhead view of a residential area recalls the opening of *Dressing Gown*.

45 Although Willis undoubted sees the marriage as a desirable outcome for Hetty, feminists might deplore the loss of her feistiness and independence. In the pre-feminist 1950s one might be surprised to find this sentiment expressed, particularly by a man, but Frank Jackson of *Reynold's News* (8 March 1959) provides a surprise when he describes the fate of Hetty: 'There in the kitchen ... we find a sadder, wiser, mouse-like Sylvia Syms, all the revolt crushed out of her, washing up dishes for a dull, honest policeman.' Pretty soon she may start spending her days in a dressing gown.

46 Rather cynically, the film's campaign book suggested that, as a publicity 'stunt', cinema managers present a tree to their local council for planting on a housing estate.

47 On the other hand, the reviewer in *Films and Filming* (March 1959) could identify no coherent message, 'no moral' and 'no solution' offered, and wondered why the film-makers developed such a project.

48 Although Melvyn Hayes is the worst offender, the far more experienced Joan Miller and Stanley Holloway also turned in performances which were too ripe for many critics. Holloway, in particular, as Miller's boyfriend (an ageing music hall performer down on his luck) gives his cheerful cockney character about as much depth as his nickname, 'Kipper'.

13 A bad-hair-day: a dishevelled Amy (Yvonne Mitchell) confronts the immaculate Georgie (Sylvia Syms), while Anthony Quayle plays the man in the middle in *Woman in a Dressing Gown* (1957)

14 On the set 3: J. Lee Thompson (right) discusses one of *Woman in a Dressing Gown*'s pub scenes with Yvonne Mitchell, while Anthony Quayle studies his script

15 What KATY did: Harry Andrews, Sylvia Syms and John Mills on their long, long journey to Alexandria in *Ice Cold in Alex* (1958)

16 Ironing out their differences: Hetty (Sylvia Syms) keeps Wilkie (Herbert Lom) at bay in *No Trees in the Street* (1959)

17 Gender confusion: wide-eyed Gillie (Hayley Mills) appropriates a symbol of masculine empowerment in *Tiger Bay* (1959)

18 Following in father's footsteps: on board the *Paloma*, John Mills tries to persuade his daughter to denounce Horst Buchholz (centre) as the *Paloma* drifts beyond the three-mile limit

19 The empire and its enemies: Capt. Scott (Kenneth More) maintains a stiff upper lip while Van Leyden (Herbert Lom) gets hot under the collar at the scene of the massacre in *North West Frontier* (1959)

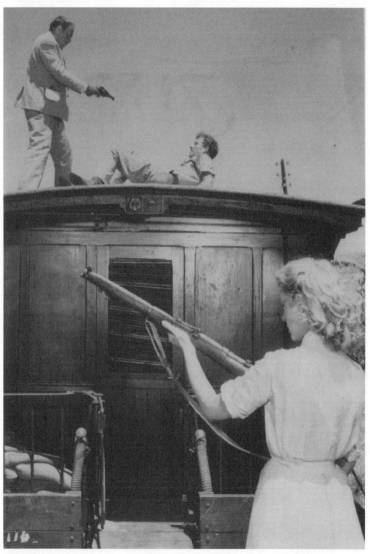

20 The ethics of lifetaking 1: Lauren Bacall makes a decisive intervention in the struggle between Herbert Lom and Kenneth More on board *Empress of India*

21 Spaceman: an American lobby card advertising *I Aim at the Stars* (1960), the film that affronted British critics

22 The ethics of lifetaking 2: incriminated by the absence of scars on her back, Anna (Gia Scala) awaits execution as a spy in *The Guns of Navarone* (1961). Disguised as German soldiers are (left to right) Stanley Baker, Gregory Peck, David Niven and Bobby Darren

Picture-making is often sheer misery. Planning them is great fun. Making them is rather like riding on a switchback at a fair; you hardly dare imagine what is coming next. (Carol Reed, quoted in Wapshott 1990: 239)

For the first twenty-three years of his career, J. Lee Thompson's film-making activities were confined to England. The nearest he came to an overseas location was visiting J. B. Priestley on the Isle of Wight. When, as a director, he occasionally took his crew out of the studio, it was never further than a couple of hours' travel from Elstree or Pinewood. Films like *Balloon, Yield to the Night, Dressing Gown* and *No Trees* begin expansively with exterior (sometimes aerial) shots of London, but quickly move inside the studio to build their claustrophobic tension. By the time *No Trees* was made, however, Lee Thompson had enjoyed his first taste of location shooting abroad. If it was not for the extreme desiccation of the environment he encountered, one might say he plunged in at the deep end, because the Libyan desert is one of the most unfriendly settings for film making imaginable. But Lee Thompson, now realising his full potential as a director, was not to be deterred by difficulty, and positively thrived on risk taking. He knew, too, that if he was to break free from the confines of low-budget film making in England and develop his career as an international director, he would need to demonstrate his ability to handle film units in far-flung locations. The Libyan adventure of *Ice Cold in Alex* would soon be followed by a much larger scale visit to the arid plains of northern India to make *North West Frontier*. These would both be pictures about dangerous journeys in which the protagonists break out from encircling forces and, in unreliable transport, cross hostile terrain to reach a place of liberation. In the process they would learn much about themselves, and this would bring them to new states of awareness by the conclusion of their expeditions. It is not difficult to see these films as allegories of Lee Thompson's own journey from the closed arena of Welwyn Studios to the open vistas of Hollywood. The challenges that his protagonists have to overcome reflect his own struggles to realise his vision of what film making should be, and the dangers they face are paralleled in the hazards and privations of his chosen locations.[1]

Ice Cold in Alex (1958)

> The Chief Principal Matron of the Middle East, Miss P. Woster said 'We are very proud of the work our Sisters have done ... One Matron wrote and told me that they were machine-gunned by German planes and had to burrow in the sand just after leaving Tobruk. Luckily we were not hit', the letter continued, 'but what an awful job it was getting sand out of our hair.' (*Egyptian Mail*, 9 February 1943, quoted in Taylor 1997: 48).

> Do you know the next drink I'm going to have? A beer, Tom. A bloody great tall, ice-cold glass of Rheingold in that little bar off Mahomet Ali Square in Alex. (Landon 1957: 78)

Given the popularity of the genre during the 1950s, it is surprising that it took until 1957 for J. Lee Thompson to make a war film. Encouraged by the box office returns of British Lion's *The Wooden Horse* (Jack Lee, 1950) and *Odette* (Herbert Wilcox, 1950), Associated British had scored a hit with their first attempt at a wartime retrospective, *Angels One Five* (George More O'Ferrall, 1952). Strangely, three years passed before they tried another RAF film, *The Dam Busters* (Michael Anderson, 1955). It turned out to be the top grossing film of the year. Michael Anderson followed up his blockbuster with the more modestly profitable *Yangtse*

Incident (1957), before Lee Thompson was called up to tackle one of the more unusual successes of the war-novel explosion of the mid-1950s. *Ice Cold in Alex*, Christopher Landon's account of an ambulance crew's nightmare journey through the desert after the fall of Tobruk,[2] was conspicuously lacking in the jingoism and *Boys' Own* heroics of other war-story bestsellers. Rather than the splendours of victory, it presented the war in microcosm as a struggle for survival which tested human resolve and endurance to the limits.

Generically, Christopher Landon's book is a war story, recounting the experiences of allied service personnel on a mission to return two stranded nurses to Alexandria. The story begins with some bombing and shelling, there are two encounters with German troops during the ambulance's 600-mile drive, and a wealth of authentic detail about the military lifestyle,[3] but this is as far as the conventions of the combat narrative are taken. The mission is a non-violent one and there is not a single exchange of fire in the whole book. The death of one of the nurses is an avoidable accident for which the British and Germans share the blame, and the conduct of the Afrika Korps is generally courteous and considerate. Nor is the story told only from one point of view. All the main participants (including, eccentrically, KATY the ambulance) are given turns as narrator. Rather than the tag 'war story', it might be more accurate to describe *Ice Cold in Alex* as a story of human strength in adversity, in which war supplies the context. Its sub-textual concerns might more easily be found in accounts of mountaineering or polar exploration than in narratives of warfare.

Much of Landon's book describes the developing emotions within the claustrophobic confines of the isolated ambulance as it navigates the desert wastes: the mutual respect earned by each member of the group's displays of courage and fortitude; the growing feelings of suspicion that Zimmermann, the South African captain, might be a German spy; and the special bonds of affection that link Mechanist Sergeant-Major Tom Pugh paternally to Captain Anson and romantically to Nursing Sister Diana Murdoch. All these feelings are intensified by the pressure cooker of the desert and the additional fears generated by the war. The journey they complete in their crumbling ambulance is cerebral as much as physical. Anson overcomes his stress-induced dependence on alcohol; Pugh puts the death of his wife behind him and finds a new woman to love; Diana supresses the memories of her broken home and discovers both the depth of her physical resilience and the strength of her new love; and Zimmermann transcends his Nazi indoctrination to reach a new understanding of his adversaries. Each also comes to realise that there are more profound and intractable enemies than their human foes: fear, loneliness, addiction and the unalterable forces of the natural world.[4] From being 'only a grain of the mass' (Landon 1957: 22) in a disintegrating military formation, the 'hardened sweats' Anson and Pugh re-establish their individuality and sense of worth through their own successful completion of an impossible trek. The chilled lager with which they reward themselves at journey's end is the symbol of their salvation.

Although the idea of filming Landon's book came from ABPC's writing department rather than from Lee Thompson himself, its themes meshed perfectly with the preoccupations of his work. First, the narrative placed its subjects in a highly constrained situation, in which they were under severe pressure. As Lee Thompson explains: 'It was a concentrated film. You see, I'm by far best at small, concentrated subjects. This was four people in an ambulance ... I feel that's very dramatic, to put people in confined spaces and have their characters examined in what I call "confinement".' As we have seen, his prison, domestic and crime dramas all share a feeling of entrapment. Second, the narrative describes the sort of hazardous journey which would become a feature of Lee Thompson's cinema after this film.

Once the rights to Landon's book had been secured, W. A. Whittaker was given the task of producing and Lee Thompson was brought in to direct.[5] Whittaker was not a producer who concerned himself much with the creative aspects of film making. As Lee Thompson recalls: 'He was more on the business side. He was a very straightforward character, very anxious to keep on budget, and what I call a company man. He was a very nice fellow and I got on well with him, but I wouldn't call him a very imaginative producer.'

Lee Thompson was able to bring together his favourite creative team of Taylor, Jones and Best to realise a script which Christopher Landon had adapted from his novel with the assistance of T. J. Morrison, one of ABPC's most experienced scenarists, and with further advice from Walter Mycroft, the former head of production at Elstree who had 'discovered' Lee Thompson. The studio clearly had high expectations of the film and to demonstrate further just how much talent they were prepared to lavish on it John Mills was added to the cast. Even the presence of Mills, however, could not persuade the notoriously tight studio to allow Gil Taylor to shoot with colour stock.[6] Lee Thompson was able to retain Sylvia Syms and Anthony Quayle from *Woman in a Dressing Gown*. Quayle, a big and muscular man, was ideal for the part of the German spy (renamed Captain Van der Pool for the film) and Syms was given a wonderful opportunity to extend her acting range in the role of the nurse Diana Murdoch. *Picturegoer*'s Donovan Pedelty described it as 'the fattest, juiciest role for a young romantic actress in British films since Madeline Carroll roamed the Trossachs handcuffed to Robert Donat for *The 39 Steps*' (*Picturegoer*, 21 September 1957). For the smaller part of the shell-shocked nurse who is killed when the Afrika Korps fires on the ambulance, Lee Thompson wanted Carole Lesley, the young blonde actress with whom he had become infatuated. He remembers:

> 'I took her to the desert and I had to remove her from the role because I wanted her to play as a brunette. I got a black wig for her. I wanted her to look different from the parts she'd played, but she virtually refused to wear it and, to my regret, I asked her to quit the picture ... I should have persevered with her and dispensed with the black wig because I think she had a great ability to be a serious actress and it would have been great fun playing her in this role.'

Gil Taylor, however, did not share his director's enthusiasm for Lesley: 'She wasn't good enough, but he had this terrible crush on her and wanted to use her for parts, but the company said no ... this girl had her mirror out every second, she was quite pretty – very frail – but she just couldn't act.'

Lesley was replaced in the role by Diane Clare, but if she felt any bitterness over the black wig fiasco, it was not apparent when she told *Picturegoer* (29 March 1958) that she owed it to Lee Thompson to make a success of her career because of the faith he had shown in her.

The principal casting was completed when Harry Andrews was given the part of Sergeant Major Tom Pugh. Andrews was a character actor who had already put his army experience to good use in previous war films.[7] His casting, coupled with that of John Mills, was not without its problems for the book's adaptation. In Landon's text, Pugh's paternal attitude towards his captain implies that he is the older man, and in the screenplay written before casting, Pugh is described as being 'about 40' while Anson is 'in his late 20s' (*Master Scene Screenplay*, 20 April 1956). John Mills, however, was close to 50, a few years older than Andrews, and hardly suitable to play a young officer. Moreover, if the book has a central character, it is Pugh, to whom it is dedicated. It is Pugh, too, who attracts the romantic attentions of Nurse Diana in her quest for a strong, dependable father-substitute. Diana is jealous of Pugh's affection for Captain Anson, whom she regards as the type of officer 'she had danced with, dined with, and fought off with good-natured firmness in the backs of staff car or taxi' (Landon 1957: 79). In the adaptation, however, John Mills' star status demanded that Anson be the film's main protagonist and the principal recipient of Diana's affections. Even though Mills was more than twice the age of Sylvia Syms and much the puniest of the male cast, his claim to be the romantic lead pressed itself well above that of a craggy middle-aged supporting actor like Andrews. So, in the film, it was to be Anson who 'got the girl', even if a controversial sequence in which Diana seduces him with a kiss seemed unexpected and largely unmotivated by the film's narrative twists.[8] Anson, after all, is not only looking forward to an ice cold beer in Alex but also to a hot date with Ariadne, the woman he had shared with a fellow officer who had been obliged to remain in Tobruk. Transferring his affections to Diana might ease the guilt he feels at taking advantage of his comrade's enforced absence but he dismisses their liaison as a desert fling:

'It wouldn't work out. I would like to think it could, but it wouldn't. It would only make you unhappy.' Diana does not 'give up so easily', but it seems she will still have Ariadne to contend with.

In the end, it is probably to the film's credit that it eschews the book's more conventional romanticism and stays true to the pattern of ambivalent and contradictory alliances which develop between the protagonists under the extreme conditions of their ordeal. The desert obliges the breaking of rules, and antagonistic types are required to shelve their differences. Compromise is the order of the day when the only glory is survival.

The conditions under which the film was made were barely less arduous than the ones it depicts. The unit spent seven weeks, some of the time under canvas, in the Libyan desert. The work was physically demanding for men well into their 40s and, even for those used to service life conditions were uncomfortable. For a London girl fresh from RADA like Sylvia Syms it must have been a shock to the system. 'The biggest discomfort was the flies – thousands of them', she told Peter Haigh (*ABC Film Review*, June 1960).[9] Thirty years later, when she spoke to Brian McFarlane (1997: 550), the memories were still vivid:

> 'It was very arduous ... We were in Tripoli for a while and used to travel to the location each day, moved by the British Army. The men were under canvas and the women were in stone sheds inside a ruined Italian fort. It was very difficult for me, being so young, it would have been impossible without the men in the cast being like Dutch uncles to me. We didn't have time to do much 'acting' – we were cranking the engine and driving that thing in the most appalling conditions, so that we just became those people. We were either very hot or very cold; when the wind blew at night it was bitterly cold.'[10]

Cinematographer Gil Taylor recalls 'a very difficult shoot' which involved moving 'five generators with a Brute light on each one' by means of 'Italian Range Rovers with Italian technicians and my own English people who helped to cart the stuff about'. The problems, however, lay not only in moving equipment 'up hill and down hill' but in the clash of egos between four complicated actors:

'When I say "complicated", they were all charming, but they used to get the microscope out each day because this always happens when you get four or five actors in a long piece. They think one's saying a bit too much. They get a bit jealous and want to knock some dialogue out, you know. So Lee always had difficulties there, but he was a wonderful man and he overcame them because he was a tough man and insisted on it being done, and he was able to do it with persuasion rather than argument.'

Lee Thompson remembers some tension between John Mills and Anthony Quayle, which was hardly surprising given the gruelling schedule and 100° temperatures. In those days Sylvia Syms had a reputation for abrasiveness and a tendency to be socially withdrawn which ABPC publicity attributed to her off-screen nervousness. During the shoot, Lee Thompson counselled her that being a screen personality involved more than giving a good performance in front of the camera, and the change in her attitude was noticed on her return to England by at least one journalist.[11] She was, however, lucky to get back from the desert without serious injury as she revealed in the television documentary *A Very British War Movie* (Channel 4, 28 August 1999). In one highly dramatic scene, she is leaning against the front of the ambulance when it begins to roll rapidly downhill, causing her to dive away in fear of her life. Her fear was real enough because no safety precautions were taken:

> 'Tony and Johnny and Harry said, "You're going to have it on a hauser aren't you?" and "Oh, yes", Lee said. And when he came to shoot it, of course, he shot it for live and the thing hurtled past me. And I remember, and I wonder if *Lee* remembers, that the three men went up and threatened to thump him. You can see how close I was on the actual shot, and it rolled fast and it was heavy.'

Messrs Mills, Quayle and Andrews might have expected conditions to ease once they returned to Elstree at the end of November 1957. Peter Evans of *Kinematograph Weekly* certainly reported that he had 'never met a unit so pleased to be back from location – location allowances or not' (5 December 1957). But they reckoned without three days in 'the bog' – a tank of peat, Fuller's earth and a plastic compound, mixed together to simulate a marshy salt flat in the desert. Anthony Quayle as Van der Pool is rescued from this 'quicksand' by Mills and Andrews in an exceptional suspense sequence. *Picturegoer* (29 March 1957) called it 'probably one of the most unpleasant sequences ever staged in a British studio', and reported the distressed response of Quayle who, 'like Sylvia Syms, experienced the dissolution of the barriers between acting and being: 'I wasn't acting all the time. I really was fending for myself in that awful stuff. Still, it was worth it for the sake of realism.'[12] Lee Thompson admitted: 'I wasn't the most popular man around towards the end of the third day's shooting. But I had to have it right' (*Picturegoer*, 29 March 1957). The director's insistence on realism was also in evidence in the filming of the final scene – the bar in Alexandria – where the four survivors of the epic trek toast each other with cool beers in glasses prominently labelled 'Carlsberg'.[13] This, however, was a more pleasant experience for all, but especially for John Mills:

> We shot the famous scene at the bar in the studio on our return to Elstree. The property master mixed everything he could think of to look like lager. Nothing worked. Lee decided I would have to drink the real thing. At 8.30 one morning on the set I took a deep breath and downed, without pausing, a pint of continental lager. Six takes and six pints later I was completely plastered; shooting was postponed until after lunch to give the gallant captain time to sober up. I still reckon that to be the happiest and most enjoyable morning I have ever spent in any film studio. (Mills 1981: 341)

By the time shooting on the film 'wrapped' in time for Christmas, its rigours were legendary, but its director's vision and insistence on authenticity had produced a piece of cinema which, in Gil Taylor's words, 'will live forever, because it is so very exciting to look at'. 'Exciting' is the operative word, because Lee Thompson had given an extra dimension to a literary work which is engaging in its study of characters, provocative in its presentation of issues and inspiring in its celebration of survival. The elements of suspense, which are muted in the book, are given the full treatment in its adaptation, producing a sustained tension from the delicate navigation of a minefield, through the rescue from the quicksand to the climactic cranking of the ambulance up the sand hill to deliverance. The transformation of *Ice Cold in Alex* from a story of endurance into a full-blown thriller may be attributed largely to Lee Thompson, who stretched its moments of tension well beyond their descriptions in the script. As John Mills recalled (McFarlane 1997: 416): 'Lee Thompson was a wonderful director; he could make a scene out of nothing. For instance, the minefield sequence was two lines in the script, yet it took four days to shoot and was one of the best sequences in the film; most of it was put in on the spur of the moment by Lee Thompson.'

The suspense scenes are expertly put together. Taylor's camera focuses in on small details: the beads of sweat on blackened skin; the tongue that sweeps the bottom lip in anxiety; the sinister shape beneath Quayle's boot as Mills dusts away the sand in the minefield sequence. Dick Best's cutting uses these close-ups to give a sense of immediacy, a feeling of being there, of sharing the danger – and the relief, when Leighton Lucas' musical score registers the all-clear. By the time we reach the final and back-breaking task of getting KATY up the slippery incline we are almost feeling every turn of her starting handle. The action of winching, which was dismissed in Landon's text as 'not seem[ing] to take any effort' (Landon 1957: 175), is given Herculean propor-tions by the shots of the straining upper body, shot low-angle against the sky, in the heroic style of Soviet statuary. When Diana absentmindedly lets go of the starting handle and all their hard work is undone as KATY careers downhill we share the despair and abjection at achievement squandered.[14]

Suspense is the scaffolding which gives shape and depth to what might otherwise appear a turgidly linear narrative, but the story is given a timelessness and resonance by its incorporation of mythic elements. Like Argonauts in search of the Golden Fleece or knights pursuing the Holy Grail, the members of KATY's crew face a succession of trials of strength and ingenuity before they can grasp the 'amber nectar' of their quest. It is faith in the restorative power of the ice-cold prize that sustains Captain Anson as he battles the privations of the environment, the demons of his addiction and the dilemma posed by the knowledge that the man on whose physical strength he depends is an enemy agent. Above all, his faith gives him the will to survive and the power to lead. Tom and Diana draw their own inspiration from their deep attachments to their visionary captain, providing him with the know-how and compassionate support to complete the journey. The 'labours' performed by KATY's crew also have a timeless, mythic quality to them, as if the Gods of War were using them as sport: a test of courage in a dangerous wilderness (the minefield); a trial of physical strength (Van der Pool taking the weight of the ambulance on his back when the jacking stones crumble); a test of navigation skill (the route through the Qattar Depression); a rescue (the quicksand) and the final labour of Sisyphus (rolling the ambulance uphill only for it to slide back).[15]

It makes considerably more sense to think of *Ice Cold in Alex* as a mythic journey or hero's quest narrative than to fit it into the genre of the 'combat film'. The generic elements of the combat film have changed little since 1944, when Raoul Walsh's *Objective Burma* showed a platoon, led gallantly by Errol Flynn, surviving against incredible odds to complete its mission. The message that war is hell but enobling of survivors and its dead may still be found in Steven Spielberg's epic *Saving Private Ryan* (1998). Colin McArthur (1980: 882) has summarised the characteristics of the genre with specific reference to the way it developed in the fifteen years after the Second World War:

> Whether the origins were American, British or Soviet, the classic combat-movie tended to be characterised by the following features: the inclusion of several scenes in which large-scale combat is presented; a focus in the narrative on the platoon as the central group, with half a dozen figures prominent within it; concentration on a single or small series of specifically military engagements ... the absence of any critique of the war *per se* – although individual soldiers may have problems of fear or breakdown; and the almost total absence of the enemy except as a faceless amorphous opposing force – something 'foreign' that we are not permitted to 'know' in the film.

MacArthur cites two British films, made shortly before *Ice Cold in Alex*, as genre exemplars: *Cockleshell Heroes* (Jose Ferrer, 1955) and *The Dam Busters*. We might also point to *Sea of Sand* (Guy Green,

1958) a film released in the same year as *Ice Cold* and also set in the North African desert after the fall of Tobruk. *Sea of Sand* has a small platoon with a mission, feuding officers, battle scenes, a largely unquestioning commitment to the war, and a faceless enemy interested only in the destruction of the film's protagonists. *Ice Cold in Alex* has none of these. *Sea of Sand*'s tight military unit in armoured vehicles is replaced by an almost random assortment of auxiliaries from the nursing and ambulance corps and a hitch-hiker of ambiguous affiliation. Their transport is a non-combatant vehicle and they have no brief to engage the enemy. Their 'mission' is not military but humanitarian, and they offer little or no resistance when challenged by German troops. Rather than being a faceless enemy bent on killing, the German soldiers behave like stern-but-concerned policemen. They respect humanitarian needs, regret the fatal injury to one of the nurses, advise against bringing women into a war zone, provide field dressings and even allow safe passage to KATY (admittedly to advance Van der Pool's undercover mission).[16] Van der Pool is presented sympathetically as a man of strength, dignity and courage who experiences divided loyalties.

If *Ice Cold in Alex* carries any propaganda message, it is not about the tyranny of Nazism or the benefits of heroic sacrifice, but about the ways in which the common confrontation of adversity can promote understanding and forge affectionate relationships between individuals. The key sequence is the bar scene in Alex when Anson, Tom and Diana conspire to save Van der Pool from a firing squad by concealing his identity as a spy and presenting him as a German soldier who has voluntarily surrendered. 'Here's to you, Otto', says Anson, offering him a toast, 'we all know we damned well wouldn't be here if it hadn't been for you.' His incriminating name-tags are discreetly pulled off and they all shake hands. In reply, the Nazi agent registers his ideological change: 'It has been an experience. All against the desert, the greater enemy. I've learnt a lot about the English – so different from all I've been taught.' In spite of its nationalistic undertones, Van der Pool's brief farewell articulates the broadly socialist sentiments of the film in which the group's only salvation is seen to be the implementation of the adage: 'From each according to his [or her] abilities, to each according to his needs.' An unstinting mutual effort brings to all the undifferentiated rewards of survival and iced beer. All, in Anson's words 'deserve it', because they have all contributed as much as they are able to the common cause. This sense of equality between the principal protagonists, which cuts across divisions of rank, gender and national allegiance, is subtly emphasised by the framing and compositional strategies adopted by Gil Taylor's camera. What one commentator has criticised as 'poor' compositions which too often leave the actors 'just standing in a line' (Tanitch 1993: 96) may be understood alternatively, as a device to encode their equality. This egaliatarian aspect of comradeship is reported in Eric Taylor's study of nursing in the Second World War. One of his informants, Norma White-head, a nurse in Tobruk during Rommel's siege recalls (Taylor 1997: 41):

> 'Being together in the desert all working for a common aim, men and women alike irrespective of rank, forged bonds between us. Discipline such as we had formerly known, disappeared. In its place came a companionship. The custom of officers to address men as "Driver" or "Corporal" ceased. Everyone was known by his name, usually his first name. We were all part of a team. And no one took advantage of the new relationship. We were all a long way from home and a kind of affinity grew – a feeling that in our shared plight we had something that people who have never been in similar situations will never be able to understand. We all respected one another.'

Of course, equality and mutuality are not uncontested in *Ice Cold*. KATY's crew constitute an *ersatz* family in which Van der Pool is the black sheep and Anson the vulnerable patriarch. The tensions, suspicions and attractions which flow among the family members give *Ice Cold* a continuous emotional under-swell, which again sets it apart from most other 1950s' war films. The most developed analysis of gender in these texts is Christine Geraghty's, and it is worth examining the play of masculinities in Lee Thompson's film in the light of her discussion.

Geraghty (1984: 63) argues that war films, unlike most other 'male genres' which tend to be dominated by individual heroes, are characterised by the ideological and formal importance of the male group, which stands as a metonym for the nation. In films made during the Second World War the propaganda function of group and nation building is crucial: 'It is important that the group is something which has to be worked for and created in the same way as the population as a whole is asked to agree to work together as one nation.' This group building is something which frequently entails, and facilitates, the overcoming of individuals' fears, allowing 'otherwise ordinary men to behave courageously' (64). However, the cultural project of unifying the nation lessens in importance in the post-war films, with a consequential change in the representation of the male group. The active service unit's connections to life at home become less explicit and class divisions become more evident. Typically, there is a new emphasis on the heroes, individuals who are 'set apart from the rest by their exceptional courage and commitment' (65). Here Geraghty's argument dovetails with that of other writers, such as Neil Rattigan (1994) and Robert Murphy (1997), emphasising the reconfiguring of the Second World War in the 1950s. However, the structure of relationships in *Ice Cold in Alex* is too fragile to bear the full weight of these readings. First, *Ice Cold* resembles war-time accounts of the building of comradeship within a group. Although Anson and Pugh already share a close professional and personal relationship, the other two surviving members require careful incorporation into a unit which functions effectively by virtue of its members' recognition of their mutual dependence. Anson is its acknowledged leader, and it is his determination that finally ensures its survival, but this does not mean that the film is an unqualified celebration of the indomitable spirit of the officer class. As a hero, Anson is deeply flawed, struggling against the alcohol dependence that allows him to be bribed with gin to accept Van der Pool onto the ambulance. Subject to bouts of panic, he has to be constantly nurtured by Tom and Diana. He is a small man battling bravely with forces that threaten to overwhelm him, and at one point he collapses from exhaustion and is carried like a child in the arms of the more robust Tom Pugh. His motivation for reaching Alex is as much self-centred as it is altruistic. He wants to prove to himself that he can do it, and he wants to reward himself with alcohol.[17] As he shouts to the others as they struggle to get the ambulance up the hill: 'I'm going to get KATY to Alex. Understand? I'm going to. It's a personal thing.' John Mills, in fact, was attracted to the part because it would destroy forever 'that ridiculous stiff upper lip image I had been stuck with' (Mills 1981: 341). So if Anson is a hero, he is a highly revisionist one.[18] Of course, the fact that an officer rather than his NCO is selected as the object of Nurse Diana's affections is symptomatic of the trend towards the celebration of middle-classness that Rattigan notes (particularly in the way her romantic inclinations in the book are redirected). But there is no attempt to minimise the contribution of Sergeant Major Tom Pugh. Rather there is a suggestion of the 'natural alliance' between the classes, which Rattigan recognises as characteristic of wartime, as opposed to post-war, films.[19]

Ice Cold in Alex also bucks the trends in 1950s' war films in its treatment of sexual relations. Geraghty describes these movies as emotionally repressed zones in which sexual love 'becomes marginal', and is overshadowed by the fear of impotence: 'Unable to admit to feeling, the heroes of the war films can scarcely articulate emotion, let alone act on it, and what pleasure they have seems to come from their skill with and control over machines' (Geraghty 1984: 66). Andy Medhurst (1984: 38) agrees that the denial of sexuality in these texts is so marked that they become 'films about repression' in which any brief heterosexual scenes are intrusive and unsatisfying because the films are driven by a genuine but largely unacknowledged, 'non-sexual love between people of the same sex' (37). While there is support for his thesis in the examples he selects – *The Dam Busters* and *The Cruel Sea* (Charles Frend, 1953) – erotic currents are much closer to the surface in *Ice Cold in Alex*.[20] In Landon's 1957 book and the film's initial script (20 April 1956: scene 40), Tom Pugh seems to have coped with the death of his wife by shifting his affections to Captain Anson before finally centering on Diana. As they watch Anson negotiating the minefield she is already aware that she is jealous of his place in the sergeant major's heart and asks Tom,

'You love that man, don't you?' To which he replies, 'I wish I had a son like him' (Landon 1957: 74). This exchange, with its scarcely veiled suggestion of homosexual desire, is missing from *Ice Cold*'s script, but so too is the suggestion that Diana has 'saved' Tom from his gay self by reawakening his heterosexual impulses. The film, however, retains Tom's nurturing behaviour towards Anson – adjusting his blanket, protecting him from gin, carrying him in his arms – and contrasts it with Van der Pool's more robust and muscular performance of masculinity which acts as a challenging counterpoint to the other men's introversion. There is support for Medhurst's thesis, too, in *Ice Cold*'s cinematography which, in its selection of low angles to photograph glistening male torsos, borders on the homoerotic. However, the alluring presence of Sylvia Syms' Diana diffuses what might otherwise develop as a tense masculine triangle.

Never less than demurely clad, Syms nonetheless exudes a magnetic sexuality, as if the contradictions of her persona are working to generate an erotic charge that crackles around KATY's metal walls. As nurses do in so many British films, she doubles as both madonna and siren. On viewing Syms in *Woman in a Dressing Gown*, an American studio executive had called her 'the sexiest English girl we've seen' (*Picturegoer*, 21 September 1957), and in *Ice Cold* her Englishness is effectively juxtaposed against the alienness of her environment. Surrounded by 'hardened sweats', robbed of privacy, sand-blasted and sun-beaten, she retains a cool and untarnished grace, like a well-watered Surrey lawn among desert scrub. This does not mean, however, that she fails to register emotion. Leonard Mosley (*Daily Express*, 27 June 1958) referred to 'the turbulent feelings struggling beneath her khaki shirt', and the subtlety of her performance lies in the evident tensions in concealing both the fear and the desire of her character. Placed in the most vulnerable and demanding of situations, Diana must become 'one of the lads', submerging her femininity in order to convince her male companions that she can do her share. But that femininity is never far below the surface of her matter-of-fact manner or her coarse cotton uniform, and both she and her companions remain constantly aware of its presence and potential.

'Never mind your ruddy make-up, get up!' Anson bellows at her as her attempt to push KATY sends her sprawling on the sand. But Diana has no make-up to apply. Her lipstick, the scarlet emblem of her femininity, has been worn to a stub writing the details of her dead nursing colleague on the cross that marks her grave.[21] But, however she is 'knocked', like Madeline Carroll in *The 39 Steps*, she never quite loses her 'ladylikeness'.

Although the suppression of desire is not hard to sense in the course of the narrative, its eventual expression still comes as something of a surprise.[22] Advance publicity featuring Mills and Syms in a clinch had prepared audiences (particularly those familiar with Landon's book) extra-textually, but Lee Thompson makes little attempt to signal the direction of Diana's desire in the film itself. Her tender seduction of Anson is brief and the consummation of their desire (the proof of Anson's potency) is quickly faded out, but it proved to be the film's most controversial passage. Two months before *Ice Cold*'s release, the *Daily Express* (23 April 1958) ran a story reporting the censor's call for cuts to the love scene and Mills' 'unrepentant' attitude. As he put it in his autobiography:

> I had never ... had a chance to play a full-blooded love scene ... Sylvia and I rolled around in the sands of the desert in the moonlight with no holds barred. Lee Thompson was very happy with the scene and I personally enjoyed every minute of it. I found it a refreshing change from 'Up periscope' ... When I saw the film the scene had totally disappeared. Lee fought for it, but it ended up at the censor's request on the cutting room floor. (Mills 1981: 340–1)

Lee Thompson dismissed the BBFC's demands as 'absurd', given that the scene was 'very tame',[23] and he is supported by Sylvia Syms who does not recall the scene as being 'particularly daring': 'I think they had to cut one close-up of what looked like an exposed bosom. In fact, all John did was to undo some buttons and I knew I still had a bra on.'[24] The man who edited the sequence, Dick Best, blames the stills photographer and the ABPC publicity department which had decided to 'hype it up' by taking a misleading still of the scene depicting Sylvia Syms 'with her blouse nearly off at the top':

'It was never, ever, shot like that in the film. One button got undone, I think ... But I don't remember having to make a cut there. I mean, if it was as bad as the press were making out I'm sure I would remember. No, I mean it was nothing, absolutely nothing. Maybe we had a take where a bit more was undone. I don't remember.'[25]

Its love scene was not the only problem *Ice Cold* encountered with the BBFC. Lee Thompson (1958) claimed that, when the script was submitted before production, over ninety cuts were demanded if the picture was to receive an 'A' certificate, commenting: 'If we had paid heed to all of them, characterisation would have been negligible.' Many of these cuts involved the expletive 'bloody', but the censor also requested visual and ideological caution. No blood was to be seen when the nurse is shot and, more sinisterly, Van der Pool, the German agent, was not to be presented in a favourable light. When interviewed for BBC2's *Empire of the Censors* in 1994, J. Lee Thompson said: 'They [the BBFC] felt perhaps it was wrong to whitewash the enemy ... they felt that the villain had to have his comeuppance and so forth, and we had endless and absurd arguments about it'. Creditably, the director resisted these attempts to alter the meaning of his film, and maintained its distance from the conventional combat movie in the way it softens distinctions between heroes and villains.[26] Not only is Anthony Quayle's character given a sympathetic treatment, inviting admiration for his strength, courage and team-spiritedness, but John Mills is given a disquietingly Aryan look. The dark hair which Anson sports in the book was deliberately changed to blonde for the film as part of Lee Thompson's policy of transforming star personas. In its ambiguous representations and ambivalent attitudes, *Ice Cold* can be viewed as a transitional film from celebrations of heroism and national achievement like *The Dam Busters* and *Reach For the Sky* (Lewis Gilbert, 1956) to the more cynical critiques of the Second World War like *Orders to Kill* (Anthony Asquith, 1958) and *Yesterday's Enemy* (Val Guest, 1959) which set the tone for the 1960s.[27] Lee Thompson regards it as an 'anti-war film' in its depiction of togetherness between the English and

German characters, but it lacks the explicit critiques of war evident three years later in *The Guns of Navarone*.

Members of the creative team behind *Ice Cold in Alex* knew they had made a fine film, and hindsight has not tarnished their opinion. Lee Thompson is happy to assert that he 'loved making *Ice Cold in Alex*' and still loves to watch it occasionally: 'I must say, I think it was a damned good film, though I say it myself.' Dick Best regards it proudly as his top picture:

> 'It's the favourite film I've ever done, including *The Dam Busters*, which I'd place second ... It's very human, and that's my preference for films, not special effects and blockbusters, but films about people and caring about the people in the film. And one cared about all those people. It's got some very telling moments, some very exciting sequences without bravado, and it's got excellent performances.'

And its cinematographer, Gil Taylor, agrees that *Ice Cold* 'will live forever'. Its high placing – sixth in *Empire* magazine's list (October 1998) of great war films – indicates its enduring popularity and its appeal to a new generation of (male) film buffs; and in 1999 Channel 4 television selected it as the 'ultimate' British war movie, screening it at peak viewing time on a Sunday evening.

Even before its British premiere, *Ice Cold* had won the International Film Critics Prize at the Berlin Film Festival by a unanimous vote.[28] The support of the London critics was almost as overwhelming. In the fan press, *Picturegoer* (26 July 1958) led the chorus of approval, praising Lee Thompson as 'the busiest experimenter in British films'. 'This time', the review continued, 'he takes a formal British screen subject, the war film, strips it of its worst cliches and triumphantly makes the characters live in your mind longer than the action.' *Films and Filming* (August 1958) was barely less enthusiastic, calling *Ice Cold* a worthy contender in any international festival, comparing its 'hotted-up' brand of film making with Henri Clouzot's *Wages of Fear* (1953) and enthusing about the ability of its actors to deliver impressive performances in spite of a 'rather hackneyed' script. But the magazine's plaudits went primarily to J. Lee Thompson, 'who here achieves his best directorial work to date': 'He has a clear, penetrating eye, and every time goes right to the heart of a scene. Above all, he knows *when* to shock.'

In the trade press, Josh Billings, impressed by *Ice Cold*'s lucrative West End run, called it 'a great war film' (*Kinematograph Weekly*, 28 August 1958); and the popular press was unanimous in its recommendation, praising the movie's exciting suspense sequences, effective photography and quality of performances:

> It is an exciting and agonising story, admirably told and splendidly acted (Elizabeth Frank, *News Chronicle*, 27 June 1958).

> The suspense is terrific (Jympson Harman, *Evening News*, 26 June 1958).

> Chair edge suspense [with] very solid performances from all (*Sunday Graphic*, 9 June 1958).

> [A] splendid film – pure cinema – shatteringly exciting (Wayland Young, *Evening Standard*, 26 June 1958).

> I would say this is the best picture we have made this year ... so brilliantly realistic that you half expect to find sand in your shoes when you come out of the cinema (Anthony Carthew, *Daily Herald*, 27 June 1958).

In the *Daily Express* (27 June 1958), Leonard Mosley, a veteran of the Western Desert who had known both spies and hardened sweats, toasted J. Lee Thompson with a cold lager for his faultless authenticity and the way he had 'milked the cream of good drama and suspense' from the story. Fred Majdalany in the *Daily Mail* (27 June 1958) agreed that the director's 'skill in making the most of every suspense sequence is matched by his impressive photographic use of the desert backgrounds'.

Complaints were also few among the reviews in the 'heavyweight' press. While considering *Ice Cold* a little too long and not quite in *The Wages of Fear* class, the *Daily Telegraph*'s Campbell Dixon praised its 'suspense, good performances and fine photography', and *The Times* (30 June 1958) agreed that the performances were convincing and the characters, although familiar, 'well conceived' in a story that 'never flags'. Even the *Sunday Times*' Dilys Powell (29 June 1958) was captivated by Gilbert Taylor's 'unsensational but imaginative photography' which so evoked the mood of the desert locale, and by characters who were 'unusually alive', adding that direction and editing had made the film 'constantly exciting'. Matthew Norgate in the *Manchester Guardian* (28 June 1958) congratulated Lee Thompson on directing 'with a certainty of touch and a careful eye for detail', concluding: 'All concerned should be proud of a war film which in most respects stands comparison to *Bridge on the River Kwai.*' There were really only three dissenters from the critical consensus. The *Observer*'s C. A. Lejeune (29 June 1958) remained unmoved by a film she found 'worthy but snail-paced', as did the *New Statesman*'s William Whitebait (19 July 1958), no lover of the war genre, who found *Ice Cold* 'as flat and barren as its landscape'. The film's third detractor was, predictably enough, Derek Hill, who used his review in *Tribune* (4 July 1958) to continue his vendetta against Lee Thompson, attacking him as an arrogant charlatan enthusiastically peddling establishment ideas and paving the way for German rearmament. It was a strange charge to level against a pacifist socialist like Lee Thompson, but no more ironic than the alliance forged between ABPC's exploitation department and the War Office to promote *Ice Cold* as a potential tool for army recruitment as National Service came to an end and the Aldermaston marches began. As a story of resilience in adversity in North-East Africa, the film could be viewed without too much imagination as a post-Suez fillip to morale.[29] With Cyprus on the verge of conflagration and violence breaking out in the Middle East in the summer of 1958, the British Army must have been grateful for any promotional material, even the equivocal messages of *Ice Cold in Alex*. The film's exhibitors were advised to link up with their local Army Recruiting Office to establish a centre in the cinema foyer with 'displays by local units, parades, demonstrations and a foyer exhibition of interesting Army relics', and to try to arrange for an old army ambulance to be stationed on the cinema car park. The Associated British–Pathe campaign book also suggested that the film's opening might be made 'a Gala occasion' with invited army officers, a guard of honour composed of veterans of the Western Desert campaign, and a regimental band playing on stage. It is curious, to say the least, that such a strident display of militarism was considered appropriate to a film in which the depiction of combat and soldierly heroics are so low-key that one reviewer could claim that its 'magic' was 'that you forget the war and are aware only of men and women reacting to fraught circumstances.'[30]

After *Ice Cold*, Lee Thompson made two more monochrome dramas of men and women in 'fraught' circumstances' – *No Trees in the Street* (see Chapter 6) and *Tiger Bay* (Chapter 8), postponing his planned starring vehicle for Carole Lesley, *Cinderella Nightingale*. Robert Muller's book about the exploitation of feminine beauty in the film world was published in 1958 and would have made a fascinating exercise in self-reflexivity both for Lesley and for Lee Thompson. When it was published in paperback by Pan in 1962 the advertising blurb called it a 'sizzling, up-to-the-minute close-up of the amoral machine that turns a beautiful body into big business'. Its story of Iris Littlewood, an ambitious shop-girl who becomes 'the darling of the photographers, the prey of the columnists, the favourite "pin-up" of a fickle public' has resonances in the careers of both Diana Dors and the more tragic Carole Lesley. The growing demands for Lee Thompson's services meant that the film was never made, and Lesley was obliged to make *Operation Bullshine* (Gilbert Gunn, 1959) instead. A similar story by Muller was filmed by Val Guest in 1964 as *The Beauty Jungle*. Ironically, it starred Janette Scott, who had played the ambitious ingénue in Lee Thompson's *The Good Companions*.

North West Frontier (1959, USA: *Flame Over India*)

I hate to admit it, but I think I can understand how her Daddy must have felt when he came back from India, all those years away. The old Edwardian brigade do make their brief little world look pretty tempting. All home-made cakes and croquet, bright ideas and bright uniforms. Always the same picture: high summer, the long days in the sun, slim volumes of verse, crisp linen, the smell of starch. What a romantic picture. Phoney, too, of course. It must

have rained sometimes. Still, even I regret it somehow, phoney or
not. If you've no world of your own, it's rather pleasant to regret
the passing of someone else's. I must be getting sentimental.
(Jimmy Porter in John Osborne's *Look Back in Anger*, 1956)

Our little train trundling across the desert is like our little world
trundling through space. Mr Peters here will sell us guns and we
can fight each other. (Van Leyden, *North West Frontier*)

With the completion of *Tiger Bay* at the end of 1958 J. Lee
Thompson decided to take an opportunity to broaden his canvas
beyond the intimate dramas he has become so accomplished at
filming. Over at Rank, producer Marcel Hellmann, a veteran of
both the German and British film industries, who had produced a
number of Associated British films during the 1950s,[31] was
planning to spend a staggering £500,000 on a fully fledged epic
of empire. Guaranteed American distribution, and the presence of
a genuine Hollywood star in Lauren Bacall, gave him the luxury of
a budget three times bigger than normal for Rank, although still
relatively modest by the standards of Tinseltown spectaculars.
Associated British was happy to take its share of the considerable
director's fee this budget allowed by lending out the director now
thought by many to be the most accomplished to emerge from the
British studio system in the post-war years.

Imperial adventure films had been a prominent genre within
British cinema since the days of silent film, but they had enjoyed a
particular vogue in the years immediately before the Second
World War. Early Technicolor epics like *The Drum* (Zoltan Korda,
1938, USA: *Drums*) and *The Four Feathers* (Zoltan Korda, 1939)
had spearheaded Alexander Korda's assaults on international
markets, spreading the myths of empire as they went. Jeffrey
Richards (1973) has shown how these and many similar films
produced in America as well as Britain drew on the popular fiction
of Victorian juvenile periodicals like *Young England, Union Jack*
and *Boys' Own Paper* to celebrate the codes and archetypes of
imperial rule. The mission of conquest, 'civilisation', and the just
maintenance of order evinced in these texts has much the same
mythic status in the collective consciousness of the English (rather
than the British, perhaps) as the struggles to push the frontier

westward have in American culture. In the first seventy years of the twentieth century films of this type were central to the understanding of national identity, containing as they did, powerful legitimating ideas for expansionist policies and providing potent sources of patriotic pride. As Marcia Landy (1991: 98) points out, the western and the empire film share the same dichotomy between savagery and civilisation and a strong male protagonist. However, whereas in the western this figure successfully represents relatively uncontested national values – the rugged individualism of the self-made man – the empire film attempts to elevate the values and mores of a dominant class to universal status. The protagonist is rarely an unattached loner, but more usually the legitimate representative of a colonial bureaucracy or army, charged with a strong sense of duty, an unshakeable belief in the rightness of his mission and a keen awareness of 'the white man's burden'. He is typically represented as a peacekeeper who is required to give paternal protection to a simple and childlike indigenous people who are threatened by power-hungry revolutionaries with only their own self-interest at heart.

With the steady dissolution of the British Empire after the Second World War, imperialist films like those produced by Korda largely disappeared, their ideological power passing to the genre dealing with the fight against the Nazi threat. When they reemerged in the 1950s, they offered, to one degree or another, revisionist interpretations of the imperial project, appropriate to changing circumstances.[32] Although in the mid-1950s the revisionism of films such as Zoltan Korda's *Storm Over the Nile* (1955), a remake of his *The Four Feathers*, was tempered by the need to rekindle national pride, this need would become more acute in the aftermath of the Suez disaster of 1956.

The revival of films dealing with the British Raj in India began with *Bhowani Junction* (1956), George Cukor's steamy saga of passion and violence in the final days before Indian independence. From that point, the films begin to look further back to the long history of religious tensions and military action in India's north-west region. Inspired by Hollywood's recent treatment of the theme in *King of the Khyber Rifles* (Henry King, 1954), Warwick

Productions released *Zarak* (Terence Young, 1956) a widescreen Technicolor yarn of banditry on the Afghan frontier. The film emphasised the respect and affection created by the sporting contest between a rebel chieftain (Victor Mature) and a British officer (Michael Wilding). It probably owed a good deal of its box office success to the presence in the cast of the voluptuous Anita Ekberg, but the enthusiasm was sufficient for Victor Mature to be reincarnated in *The Bandit of Zhobe* (John Gilling, 1959), a thinly disguised clone of the earlier film in which antipathy to the Raj is the product of dastardly deceit on the part of a rival tribal leader. Jeffrey Richards (1973: 206) has noted that both films share the assumption that 'the Indians do not have any real grievances against the British and that basically conflict between them was a game which when real danger threatened (Afghan invasion in this case) would be abandoned in favour of co-operation against the enemy'.

This, then, is the context in which we must situate Marcel Hellman's decision to make *North West Frontier*, a story of Moslem revolt and anti-Hindu pogrom set at the turn of the century. The script had originally been developed by Frank Nugent from a magazine story by Patrick Ford and Will Price, but Lee Thompson was keen to give the screenplay more intellectual substance and asked Hellman to bring in Robin Estridge, one of Rank's most talented screenwriters.[33] Estridge and Lee Thompson were determined to see if they could make a standard tale of adventure compatible with the type of cinema of ideas which so interested them. 'The whole original story', insists Lee Thompson, 'was rewritten by Robin Estridge with my help as director.' In this sense, *North West Frontier* was direct preparation for the director's collaboration on *The Guns of Navarone*, with Carl Foreman, a writer with a similar desire to marry an issue-based cinema to the action film.

It was just as well that the filming of *Ice Cold in Alex* had prepared Lee Thompson for the rigours of location work in inhospitable environments, because in India the flies, the heat and the trackless terrain were back with a vengeance. His principal stars, too, were accustomed to roughing it. Kenneth

More (a natural casting for the capable English officer Captain Scott) had served in the navy and just completed *A Night to Remember* (Roy Baker, 1958) in which he endured the freezing waters of Ruislip Lido. Lauren Bacall, as the feisty American governess of the young Hindu prince, had spent weeks accompanying her husband Humphrey Bogart on one of the most insanitary locations in movie history during the making of *The African Queen* (John Huston, 1951).[34] Cast and crew were based at Jaipur in a hotel which was formerly the Maharaja's palace, but most days they had to drive out into the Sind Desert in temperatures up to 120 degrees fahrenheit.[35] Kenneth More (1978: 174) remembered that 'the crew dropped like flies with dysentery and fever and malaria'. These casualties, which included his own stand-in, must have reminded More that his great-grandfather, an officer in the Indian Army just like More's character, had died of cholera in Jaipur almost exactly 100 years before.[36]

Keeping a cast focused in these conditions was made all the more difficult by the frictions which almost inevitably develop on a film set. Although Bacall developed a friendly relationship with More (in spite of his unrequited desire for an affair), she was immensely irritated by producer Marcel Hellman. 'There were always tremendous rows between them', remembers Lee Thompson. 'I didn't know what it was about, but she couldn't stand him on the set anywhere near her.' Apparently she was not the only one to be aggravated by Hellman, as Kenneth More revealed in his autobiography:

> When, in his view, things were going a bit slowly, Marcel would stand behind the camera, take out his watch, and shake his head. This used to worry me, but not as much as it annoyed Lee Thompson. One day we had been filming since sun-up in the heat of the Sind Desert, and finally finished a big scene where the rebels had tried to attack a fort. ... Everyone was tired and edgy, the prospect of a bath and an iced beer seemed infinitely attractive.
>
> At last the sun was too far down the sky for any more work. We climbed thankfully in our cars to drive twenty miles over the dusty desert to our hotel. Lee and I were already in the back of the car when we saw Marcel running towards us, unfortunately for him

with his watch in his hand. Lee had taken a lot of watch-pulling that day and this was too much. As Marcel pushed his head through the car window to speak to Lee, Lee deliberately wound up the glass. Marcel's head was trapped between the window and the top of the car. Lee tapped the driver on the shoulder. 'Drive on', he ordered, and poor Marcel had to do a side-step for about ten yards by the side of the car. They weren't on speaking terms that night. All ambassadors were withdrawn, but the next day, of course, things got better again. They had to. We all had to carry on working together. (175)

Despite the occasional flaring of tensions, Lee Thompson insists that 'it was a very happy company except for this miserable situation between the producer and Lauren Bacall. Lauren was absolutely marvellous on location. She loved the roughness of the location.' Unlike Sylvia Syms she never complained about the flies and remained 'a real sport', as did Kenneth More. But 'sport' or not, there were times, particularly in the ambitious crowd scenes, when things were in danger of getting out of hand. In the days when the empire still flourished the makers of films had always been wary of using indigenous people as extras in scenes of mob violence or rebellion. The fear was that they would identify too closely with their roles and the situation might get out of hand. Ten years after independence, however, the makers of *North West Frontier* felt that the risk was past and that it was now possible to use Indian extras to film spectacular crowd scenes at a fraction of the cost of using European actors. The production was able to assemble crowds of 5,000 at two rupees (three shillings) per head.[37] The standard rate would have been £3. 5s a day in Britain. But even such modest wages represented a substantial windfall for the families of impoverished rural Indians who flocked to join the production. In fact, their joy at this unexpected good fortune itself caused problems in creating an impression that these were despairing refugees, as the director explained:

'Here was a tragic scene. Hordes of inhabitants of a disturbed, rebellious countryside, fleeing in danger of their lives. But what do we get? A lot of grinning, laughing, joking Indians who look upon the affair much as a band of Cockneys would look during August

Bank Holiday on Hampstead Heath.' (*Flame Over India* campaign manual, Twentieth Century Fox Film Corporation, 1959)

With only two days to film the scenes and Hellmann constantly consulting his watch, Lee Thompson had eight bilingual Indian assistant directors bellowing through loud speakers in a desperate attempt to persuade the crowd to look frightened. Once motivated, however, the crowd became such an awesome force that the director feared for the safety of his principal actors, especially Lauren Bacall. As he told the *People*'s reporter Ernest Betts (11 October 1959):

'Betty [Bacall] fainted twice while we were taking those scenes. She just went down in the dust in the middle of the crowd. She's a strong personality and doesn't mind what she's asked to do. She'd hate you to know what happened. But I can tell you, she was really frightened, and so was I. I watched those scenes and said to myself, "Good Lord, she's lost".'[38]

The film also required extensive set-construction work on location: 700 workmen were engaged to build the walls of a city, 400 feet long, 28 feet high and 8 feet thick. The stone had to be hauled seven miles from a quarry and water had to be piped from ever further afield. The production unit had to arrange for the feeding and accommodation of this huge workforce for two months before the five-day shoot of the attack on Haserabad could take place. This was film making on a scale beyond the experience of almost any British director, and there must have been a certain degree of relief when Marcel Hellman decided that the necessary footage in India had been secured and took the unit off to Spain to complete the exteriors.[39] Interiors were shot in the sanctuary of Pinewood Studios.

Twelve years after the Indian independence campaign might now seem a relatively safe distance from which to begin a reassessment of the 165 years of British imperial presence on the sub-continent. At the time, Marcel Hellman and the Rank executives may have believed that British and international audiences would be ripe for Raj nostalgia, and they may well have been correct; but the world into which *North West Frontier* was released in the autumn of 1959 was far from fully post-colonial. Indeed, 1959 had proved to be a particularly bloody year in the struggle against imperialism. The increasingly violent suppression of resistance to the Chinese domination of Tibet had forced the flight of the Dalai Lama to India, giving a contemporary resonance to the evacuation of a young spiritual leader in Lee Thompson's film. In Rhodesia [Zimbabwe] a state of emergency had been declared in February. Black African nationalists had been arrested and their independence parties dissolved. The repressive nature of British colonial rule had been further exposed in the summer when fifty Africans were killed in anti-imperial riots in Nyasaland and eleven more were murdered in an attempt to break the spirit of disobedience at a Kenyan concentration camp for suspected Mau-Mau sympathisers. In Parliament there were accusations of a cover-up. Even as *North West Frontier* made its way on to general release in November 1959, the news carried reports of the crisis in the Belgium-controlled Congo where seventy had died in anti-imperial violence in Stanleyville. This was not a peaceful post-colonial world in which old differences could be easily put aside and the beneficial aspects of imperial rule and its codes of honour revalued. The wounds of empire were not simply refusing to heal, they were still being inflicted. If J. Lee Thompson needed any further reminder that the Indian struggle for independence had not yet been consigned to history he had only to refer to his leading Indian actor I. S. Johar, a film writer, director and producer in his own right who in this picture was playing a humble engine driver. After graduating with a Master's degree in economics, political science and law he had been gaoled by the British during the campaign of civil disobedience after the Second World War.[40]

We should not be surprised, then, if *North West Frontier* is an equivocal film, a picture which, to some extent, wants to have its Imperial cake as well as to eat it. An entertainment film playing to international audiences in such an ideologically sensitive climate must inevitably make compromises, tempering didactic impulses with discursive discretion. While radical voices may have clamoured for a frontal assault on the crumbling citadel of empire, what we are given is a more cautious and allegorical fable in which the critics and apologists of empire contribute to a discourse that links Lee Thompson's dazzling suspense set pieces. Along the way, there is an undeniable nostalgia for the spirit, style and commitment to duty of the empire-builders, and a rather-too-rosy interpretation of their benevolent intent, but ultimately they are viewed as a breed whose time has passed. Their unwanted intervention in the internal affairs of a distant nation is no longer tenable. Like 'Victoria', the ancient railway engine on which the film's protagonists journey to safety, British rule has reached the end of the line, it has simply run out of steam.

The opening narration of *North West Frontier* sets the tone of resigned exasperation which the soldier Captain Scott (More), a self-styled peace-keeper, adopts in the face of the evident inability of those he polices to live peacefully with each other:[41]

> 'Men find many reasons for killing each other, greed, revenge, jealousy, or perhaps because they worship God by different names. Rebel fanatics are gathering in the hills. Their objective: to kill a six-year-old boy because he is a prince and future leader of his people. His father, the Maharaja, has appealed to us, the British, asking us to take his son to the garrison town, Haserabad, and then to send him from there to safety in Delhi.'

Thus, it is clear from the outset that Captain Scott (a name redolent of British heroism and self-sacrifice) is conscious that his duty is to shoulder 'the white man's burden', an encumbrance familiar from a century of imperial fiction.[42] The 'paternal' role of the British in India is directly invoked by the need to protect a child from the threat of violent fanatics. The imminent danger, graphically evident in Lee Thompson's footage of the Maharaja's murder and the torching of his palace, elides ideological consid-erations and invites the viewer to accept Scott's viewpoint that his mission is humanitarian rather than military.

There follows ten minutes of sumptuous cinema, with hardly a word of dialogue, in which Lee Thompson allows Geoffrey Unsworth's widescreen Eastman colour photography to carry the narrative. From the stunning shot of a scarlet turban symbolically unwinding down a flight of palace steps strewn with corpses to the scenes of panic in Haserabad, Unsworth's camera keeps panning and tracking its way across vistas of natural beauty and human misery. The restless camera manages to give the impression that even the generous dimensions of Cinemascope are insufficient to capture the full enormity of the tragedy that is unfolding before us. And at the centre of the bustling crowd activity we find the last train out of Haserabad festooned with white-robed refugees clinging to carriage roofs and sides like some bizarre floral decoration.

Lee Thompson picks out Scott ushering the young prince (Govind Raja Ross) and his governess Catherine Wyatt (Bacall) through the panic as Hindu refugees still push through the city gates already being closed against the advancing Moslem forces. Previously, the only British film to realise the full potential of Cinemascope in creating vistas like these had been *Bridge on the River Kwai*, but although Lean and Jack Hildyard used the breathtaking beauty of Ceylon's jungle to memorable effect, even *Kwai* had no crowd scenes to rival those of *North West Frontier*.[43] Ivan Adams in the *Star* (8 October 1959) described the spectacular opening sequences as 'possibly the loudest, liveliest, high-wide-and-handsomest beginnings to a film yet contrived', and they were a calling-card Hollywood would find hard to ignore.

The second 'movement' of *North West Frontier* is a relatively slow one set in the haven of tranquillity that is the governor's mansion. While all about are losing theirs, Sir John Windham (Ian Hunter) and his staff are keeping their heads with typically English cool while the rebels lay siege to Haserabad. Crisply attired in the whitest of crumple-free suits, the pukka sahibs assess the situation, formulate tactics and look forward to the arrival of the inevitable relief column. It is an opportunity for the rostering of what will effectively become the film's entire *dramatis personae* for the remainder of its duration. As in *Bhowani Junction*, the characters who are assembled around an Indian railway track are emblematic of the British Raj and the forces that will eventually bring about its demise.

The empire-builders are represented by Captain Scott, the governor's wife Lady Windham (Ursula Jeans) and his secretary

Mr Bridie (Wilfrid Hyde White). While Scott represents a virile young military strain of what Sapper termed 'the breed', Bridie and the governor's Lady embody the established virtues of the British imperial regime. Both have dedicated their lives to the service of the Raj and neither is phased by the danger that confronts them. Their Englishness gives them an imperturbable confidence, a grace under fire, and their experience of colonial conditions allows them to adapt and improvise as necessary. Lady Windham is quite prepared to die by her husband's side and remains impervious to criticism of the Raj: 'Half the world mocks us', she declares, 'and half the world is only civilised because we have made it so.' Bridie is the typical eccentric ageing English bureaucrat whom Wilfrid Hyde White could play in his sleep (and, judging by the super-relaxed style of performances like this one, probably did). His amiable and slightly bumbling manner suggest he is ready for retirement, and he speaks wistfully of his memories of England.

The empire's subordinates are represented by two soldiers, a railwayman and the young Prince Kishan. The two Indian soldiers (S. M. Asgaralli and S. S. Chowdhary) are under the command of Scott and are as steadfast and unflappable as the Brits. Their discipline is impeccable, but, like good Victorian children, they are seen but not heard.[44] Engine driver Gupta is another of the empire's loyal servants in the mould of Kipling's Gunga Din. Played with comic exaggeration by I. S. Johar, who inflected his dialogue with 'babu' patois, Gupta represents the civil population as the imperial administrators would like it to be. He is a model of tolerant uncomplaining pacifism who is driven to desperation by his countrymen's inability to live peacefully together. His hope for a tranquil future lies in Prince Kishan, the vulnerable hereditary leader who stands both for India's long cultural traditions and their fragility in the face of religious fanaticism.

The critics and enemies of the empire are represented by the dissident American governess Catherine Wyatt, the amoral arms dealer Mr Peters (Eugene Deckers) and the cynical Dutch-Indonesian journalist Van Leyden (Herbert Lom). Both Catherine and Peters are ambivalently related to Britain and its imperial

project. Peters boasts a British passport but has failed to internal-
ise the behavioural and attitudinal code which distinguishes the
pukka patriot. Being British in India entails more than simply
carrying the right passport, and Peters affects a professional
'impartiality' in the business of arms' dealing which identities
him with the destructive forces of *laissez-faire* capitalism. His self-
interested rejection of imperial ideology and his Hobbesian belief
in the natural savagery of man is made evident in this exchange
with Captain Scott:

> PETERS Why do fighting men pretend to despise those that make
> and sell them their tools?
> SCOTT A soldier's job, Mr Peters, is not primarily to kill. We have to
> keep order and stop your customers from tearing themselves to
> pieces.
> PETERS You really believe that?
> SCOTT What I dislike about you chaps is that you sell your stuff
> without discrimination.
> PETERS To the other side, you mean? You think we should be like
> God, only on the side of the British, but the Germans and the
> Japanese and the Hottentots, they all think God's on their
> side ...
> SCOTT You may feel different about it when you get one of your
> own bullets in the stomach.
> PETERS If you think I'm ashamed that these are my merchandise
> you're wrong. Men make wars, not guns. Before there were
> guns men used swords, spears, blocks of wood, anything they
> could lay their hands on.

Clearly, Peters embodies both the contradictions of capitalist
enterprise and the commercial logic of free trade which will
undermine the protectionism of empire. His speech about 'swords'
and 'spears' however, exposes the atavistic impulses underlying
his discourse of professionalism and modernity. Peters' impatience
with British paternalism and its assumptions of natural superiority are shared by Catherine who, as an American, represents an
imperial power-in-waiting, and as an emancipated woman she
offers resistance to the chauvinism of the Edwardian male. She
has a contempt for the empire's favourite beverage which symbol-

ises the complacency and ethno-centrism of its drinkers. 'The British never seem to do anything until they've had a cup of tea, by which time it is too late', she comments, later responding to Scott's request for a cuppa by sardonically suggesting he might have coffee, 'or would that bring the empire crashing down around us?'. Catherine is also prickly in the defence of proto-feminist principles, rejecting Lady Windham's credo of dutiful support for her husband in favour of a more independent approach. Unafraid to speak her mind – 'I believe that's what it's for' – she is a challenge to Scott's unexamined assumptions about women's relationship to men. When he discusses her late husband, the Maharaja's doctor, for instance, he assumes that it is 'impossible to be married to a man like that without living up to his ideals'. But Catherine unexpectedly replies: 'I didn't live up to them. I think I hated them. I hated the squalor and the dirt, the places we had to go and live. I hated his being a doctor at all. I even left him once and went back to the States.' These are attitudes usually associated with flighty and feckless youth rather than with the mature heroine of an empire film, but they serve to give her character depth and to demonstrate her capacity to learn and to change, qualities she transfers to Scott. Theirs is a classic case of opposites attracting, because for much of the film their verbal exchanges are argumentative. Catherine is the first American woman Scott has met and he is shocked by her radicalness:

> SCOTT Are you one of those emancipated women we're having so
> much trouble with at home?'
> CATHERINE I might be, what's wrong with that?
> SCOTT Oh, they're just a lot of cranks.
> CATHERINE A woman who has a mind of her own is a crank! Well, I
> think men who spend their lives obeying orders are cranks!
> SCOTT Look, you just can't go around doing what you like in life.
> My job is to obey orders...
> CATHERINE Like an animal in blinkers.

Although both gender and nationality inform the philosophical differences between Catherine Wyatt and Captain Scott, they are differences between allies dedicated to the same cause. Their disagreements with the surly journalist Van Leyden are much more fundamental. Van Leyden is separated by race, religion and ideological allegiance. His identity as a mixed-race Moslem and active supporter of the rebel cause is revealed only after he has boarded the train, but he had already been marked out as untrustworthy by the British establishment in Haserabad by virtue of his profession and his foreignness. He is only granted a place on the train by threatening to reveal the whereabouts of the prince. His fellow passengers agree with Lady Windham's assessment that he is 'a very ill-natured fellow', with the exception of Bridie whose hyperbolic Englishness obliges him to adopt Van Leyden as an underdog in need of support.[45] As we might expect of a man who carries around a copy of Gibbon's *Decline and Fall of the Roman Empire*, Van Leyden articulates a clear anti-imperialist argument. He rejects Scott's rhetoric of peace keeping and his condescending view of rebels as children: 'They're not children. They're grown men. Uneducated men, I grant you, but fighting for freedom, for the freedom of *their* country.' The British presence in India is not, he suggests, an altruistic gesture to keep order in a fractious country, but a self-interested exercise in power and exploitation which encourages social antagonisms: 'You set Moslem against Hindu, you divide in order to rule.' His recommendation is that the British should 'go home and keep order at home and stay there for good'. He realises, however, that the imperial power, like a virus on the host body, will not depart of its own accord: 'The cure for some diseases is often violent or painful. War is like that, but sometimes it's the only cure.'

Evidently, these are not simply characters, but mouthpieces for particular points of view; but if the status of the film as a discussion of the idea of empire, rather than merely a story of empire, is still in doubt one has only to refer to the name of the steam train on which theses characters embark: the *Empress of India* or, as her driver affectionately calls her, 'Victoria'. Jeffrey Richards (1973: 149) has pointed to the significance of the railway engine in the building of the Empire and to its place within imperial mythology:

> The incorporeal god of the Empire was steam. One of the cult
> mysteries of the Imperial age was the growth of the railways and

an interesting sub-genre of the cinema of Empire is provided by the Imperial railway film. The nineteenth century was pre-eminently the age of the railways. They were the symbol of the industrial might and technological development of Victorian England. There was something strangely romantic about them. They seemed to be instruments provided by Providence to link up the Empire.

The unifying function of the railways and the romance of steam travel are prominent in *North West Frontier*, but the age of 'Victoria' (a relic of the nineteenth century in the Edwardian age) and her condition offer allegorical comment on the state of imperial rule. 'Victoria' is an aged shunting engine, accustomed to pushing things around but now in a condition of near decrepitude.[46] She has trouble maintaining her pressure and blows off steam without warning. Only the dedicated ministrations of driver Gupta keep her on the rails at all. However, 'Victoria' is the only transport available to try to break through the stranglehold which the rebels are applying to Haserabad. Her dramatic dash for freedom, covertly building up speed and smashing through the rebel-controlled gates at the perimeter of the city, gives Lee Thompson another opportunity to demonstrate his prowess as a director of suspense sequences. He does not waste it. But as the train emerges into the open desert pursued by mounted tribesmen the familiarity of the image from a dozen westerns becomes over-whelming.[47] As a number of contemporary reviewers noted, *North West Frontier* is an Eastern western but none commented on the efficacy of using an American generic form to examine the validity of a British social construction. The iconography of the 'cowboys-and-indians' film works perfectly in its Eastern setting. The tiny 'wagon train' winds its way across arid plains and through mountain passes. It is dwarfed by the awesome scale of its environment. Indians watch and signal from the hills, mounting surprise attacks and being repulsed by a Maxim gun. The American-coded visual perspective that this gives is re-enforced by Hollywood-identified Lauren Bacall's verbal sniping at the excesses of British militarism and cultural conceitedness. The consequence is a distanciation from the familiar messages and understandings of the imperial epic, and, to some extent, an internationalising of its significance.

One might expect that the mediated viewing position that results from these presentational devices would interfere with the audience involvement so necessary to a successful thriller. Indeed, Lee Thompson's refusal to tell his stories 'straight', in a style unmediated by ideological concerns and cinematographic flourishes, was a constant provocation to the critics. *North West Frontier*, however, is one of the best examples of the ability to integrate narrative tension with symbolism and ideas on which his importance as a film-maker largely rests. The use of the railway track in the film is a key example: its thin fragile rails offer the only lifeline in a hostile environment. The line may have been built in a pioneering spirit, but it no longer extends the power of its builders. Instead it is a vulnerable escape route for a regime in retreat. The broken and twisted condition of the track (coupled with the dilapidated engine 'Victoria') may be read as a metaphor for the distressed and superannuated state of the empire, but the film also uses it as the basis of two major suspense sequences. In the first, Victoria's fractious passengers have to work together to replace a damaged rail in front of the engine with good track from behind, leaving the company completely vulnerable to attack from the rebels mustering in the hills.[48] In the second sequence, set on a railway bridge like the one over the Kwai, Victoria's passengers have to walk a rail above a vertiginous ravine, before the engine itself is forced to negotiate the bent and inadequately supported track. The high-wire style of the walk is made even more heart-stopping by Van Leyden's covert attempts to send the boy prince plummeting to his death. Lee Thompson creates a tour de force of swaying bodies, crumbling railway sleepers crashing to ground and spinning train wheels searching for traction, but, at a more symbolic level, it also encapsulates much of the film's repre-sentation of the imperial condition. Balanced precariously on a structure liable to collapse, our *Boys' Own* empire hero needs the physical support of an armaments' dealer (arms around his waist) to prevent him from falling as he tries to ensure the safety of Hindu India's future, in spite of the clandestine attempts of an

Islamic nationalist to disrupt his task. The imperial high-wire act works equally well as metaphor and as breath-robbing suspense.[49]

With the benefit of hindsight, Lee Thompson and Estridge knew exactly how bloody the path to, and the consequences of, national self-determination would be, and they convey this in the most graphic way in depicting the aftermath of the massacre on the refugee train. The scene of slaughter which Victoria's passengers discover along their route is a harrowing reminder to audiences of the pogroms which followed Indian partition.[50] The scale of the disaster is revealed in high-angle long shot with bodies scattered all around the abandoned train. What had been a vehicle literally overflowing with life when last we saw it is now a silent tomb. The camera tracks across the bloodied corpses as Scott picks his way among them, looking for meaning as much as concealed terrorists. 'You call this keeping order?' Van Leyden taunts him, but the Raj's enemy is as sickened by the slaughter as is its defender. While the two men bicker unproductively, Catherine searches among the dead to find signs of life. Miraculously, she discovers an unharmed baby, a symbol of hope who they name 'India'. Van Leyden dismisses their find with a cynical 'One life saved, thousands lost', but Scott is genuinely moved and, for the first time, admits he was wrong in discouraging Catherine's search ('When those devils do a job, they do it properly'). The British help the American to nurture the child, making a cot while Prince Kishan looks on. Lee Thompson takes the opportunity to contrast the adaptation of a glove as an improvised teat-and-bottle for the baby with the jammed mechanisms of the Maxim gun. Both are 'ingenious' devices but, as Van Leyden points out, one is a 'life saver' rather than a 'life destroyer'. Few activities on Victoria's journey are without metaphorical meaning. Sometimes it is underlined with dialogue, as in the scene in which the young prince expresses his desire to drive the train himself and Scott gives him guidance. 'When I grow up I will buy my own engine', he tells Scott, who will only accede to his request to become the engine driver 'presently, when I say so'.[51] At other times the symbolism is silent and unemphasised, as when the prince watches Lady Windham struggling to build a house of playing cards on the rattling train. Empire building, like nation building, is a patient enterprise whose structures are susceptible to the rhythms of change.

There are, of course, considerable continuities of form and theme between *North West Frontier* and J. Lee Thompson's previous work. The integration of ideas and action and the prominence of suspense have already been noted, but thematically there is also a concern for the vulnerable evident throughout his cinema, though it is particularly marked in the earlier children-at-risk films, *No Place For Jennifer*, *The Yellow Balloon* and *Tiger Bay*. *North West Frontier* is another story of confinement in which the protagonists interact in claustrophobic proximity, isolated from the environment. Formally, however, the film is closest to *Ice Cold in Alex* with which it shares a narrative structure based around a hazardous journey. Much else in the two films is also remarkably similar: the inhospitable desert terrain; the ramshackle 'feminised' vehicle on which the passengers depend for survival; the enemy agent who must be unmasked; the trials of courage and ingenuity; the independent young woman who is attracted to the officer in charge; the ill-assorted collection of individuals who shelve their differences to combat adversity; and the idea that the physical journey is one which also brings mental enlightenment. One might also point to the degree of whimsy and sentimentality evident in *Ice Cold* in the anthropomorphising of the ambulance and in the drinking scene, but which is taken further in *North West Frontier*. The devotion of Gupta to his engine ('Victoria talks to me. I understand her language'), and the questionable importation of a level of whimsical Englishness usually reserved for Ealing comedies, at times draw the film dangerously close to full-blown parody. Its critics particularly deplored the use of the Eton Boating Song, which is initially part of the film's diegesis but is then incorporated into the score where its role becomes less ironic. Scott originally sings the offending song in an attempt to communicate the flavour of Henley Regatta, a part of the British ruling class's 'season' and 'one of those things' Scott says he joined the Army 'to get away from'. The song, however, is a powerful invocation of both genteel English life and the public-school spirit with which empire-builders like Scott are imbued. While Bridie and Lady Windham beam nostalgically and the others listen in a spirit of amused indulgence, the tune casts a spell on the proceedings, floating out over the empty plains like a magical mist. As the ancient engine rolls along, Gupta perched with a parasol on its tender, the refrain 'All swing together' effectively sums up the Imperial dream while simultaneously emphasising the bizarreness of its presence in this setting. It is an extraordinary moment in which meaning and counter-meaning swirl around the notes with only the infectious quality of the melody as resolution. As a moment which captures the grand *folie* of empire, it has rarely been surpassed. To adapt the famous comment on the charge of the Light Brigade: 'C'est magnifique, mais est-ce-que c'est juste?'[52]

Scenes like these also draw much of their emotional effectiveness from a peculiarly British sentimentality about steam locomotion which may have its origin in the role of the railways as a symbol of national power and industrial success. In a film like *Brief Encounter* (David Lean, 1945) engine steam seems to intensify the passions and its dramatic release almost compensates for the emotional continence of the characters. From Ealing's *Titfield Thunderbolt* (Charles Crichton, 1952) onwards the old steam engine becomes (particularly, perhaps, for men) a potent symbol of a nostalgic attachment to the past, a lost 'age of steam' now replaced by characterless transport, petty bureaucracy, and bogus notions of efficiency. In fact, *The Titfield Thunderbolt* had already fused the romance of the railways with the sporting bonhomie connoted by the Eton Boating Song in a sequence in which a hand car is bowled along to the melody. By the time the *Empress of India* was given the chance to prove that she could still cut the mustard, the steam locomotive was threatened with imminent replacement by the diesel engine and the elaborate British railway network was about to be 'rationalised' by Dr Beeching.[53] *North West Frontier* uses the old engine to mobilise a broad nostalgia for a vanishing way of life just as it uses the 'weight' and solidity of Kenneth More's star persona to create empathy with the dependable, dutiful 'breed' of imperial policemen. But these are very knowing tropes used to counterbalance the film's support of the modernism exemplified by Bacall's character and the *fait accompli* of the empire's demise. Characters like Gupta and Bridie are deliberately over-drawn, and Scott is given an ironising self-reflexivity which allows him to poke fun at the gross stereotypes of imperial mythology and the code of military honour, as if he has already seen Korda's empire epics. Even when he quotes Kipling at the end of the film we know that this is pastiche, in the way we know that Indiana Jones is pastiche.

Fortunately, *North West Frontier*'s archness does not prevent the film from being exciting, any more than the knowing postmodernity of Indiana Jones keeps viewers off the edge of their seats. In the last reel, Lee Thompson strings three suspense and action sequences together in a style that is now a staple of the action film, but which, in 1959, could still produce breathlessness in some reviewers – 'Phew, the sheer excitement of it!' gasped *Picturegoer*'s headline (31 October 1959), without a trace of irony. In the first sequence, Van Leyden seizes control of the Maxim gun and waits to assassinate the boy prince when he comes through the carriage door. Catherine asks him what the killing will prove, to which he responds: 'It proves that I'm a true Moslem, that I care enough to fight and maybe to die for my faith, for a country that will be all Moslem, a free country, and I will belong there.' They are the words of a fanatic, but the passionate honesty with which they are delivered commands respect, especially when Peters, the arms' dealer, tries to tell Van Leyden that he is simply a criminal who belongs in gaol. 'I find the moral indignation of an armaments' peddler rather touching', he replies with an effective sarcasm that suggests that Lee Thompson and Estridge have more sympathy with a violent man who acts out of conviction than one who is interested only in financial gain.

Van Leyden is a zealot whose religious nationalism has overwhelmed his feelings of compassion, but he is still reluctant to take life unnecessarily. Even as he peers down the sights of the Maxim gun at Victoria's other passengers, Lee Thompson is not content to abandon him as one of Scott's 'devils', alien and unfathomable. Catherine poses him the key philosophical dilemma of the film: 'Isn't killing always useless? Has the taking of a human life ever solved any problems?' This question of the emotional and intellectual defence of deadly force is at the root of so much of Lee Thompson's cinema, from *Yield to the Night* to *10 to Midnight* and the revenge movies he made with Charles Bronson in the 1980s. Here, Van Leyden offers a defence in terms of both expediency and humanitarianism: 'I like children as much as you do', he tells Catherine, 'but that boy ... is a symbol of an outworn tradition that stands between my country and freedom ... I must kill him, in order to save the lives of thousands. One life will be lost, but thousands will be saved.' It is Bridie who relieves the tension by kicking the barrel of the gun to the side and setting up a struggle on the carriage roof between the gallant Scott and the determined Van Leyden. This scene, although thrillingly staged by Lee Thompson, was already a cliché of the adventure film by 1959, but that has not stopped the situation being used by directors (with varying degrees of irony) over the decades since.[54] In *North West Frontier*, however, its conclusion carries a message. As he is about to finish off Scott with his revolver, Van Leyden is shot dead by Catherine, as if answering her own question about the justification for killing. She takes a life to save others in a moment that sums up the film's concerned but ambivalent attitude to violence. As Van Leyden's body lies in the dust by the railway track it is dismissed with a disdainful look by one of the rebels who are now riding to attack the train in the final part of the sequence. This is the closest we come to the people Van Leyden has been championing and suggests that his passion was misplaced and that, beyond the imperial pale, there are indeed bloodthirsty and unknowable barbarians. This is, of course, a cornerstone of empire mythology and it is too heavy for this film to shift. It would take another twenty years or so to finally clear it away and allow film making that more adequately reflects, as John M. MacKenzie (1992: 22) puts it, 'the cultural frameworks of the indigenous peoples of empires'.[55]

The rebel attack is finally repulsed by Victoria's entry into a two-mile-long tunnel, and Prince Kishan is delivered safely to Kalapur. There is no reassurance, however, that this is the end of the troubles for the Raj. The British officials are more interested in buying a new machine gun from Peters than in the welfare of the prince. It is clear that they will continue to store up trouble for themselves. The inevitability of further conflict is made clear when Prince Kishan, thanking Scott for saving his life and professing his friendship, nevertheless asks him: 'But you are British, will I have to fight you?' Scott dismisses the idea, but Kishan knows what his father has told him, that he will 'have to fight the British to make them go away'. There is no other way he will be allowed to 'drive the engine'. Catherine is shocked by his ingratitude, but Scott knows the score. 'That's all the thanks we ever get', he tells her philosophically.

Although Scott's mission may have done little to alter the long-term prospects of the Raj, it has helped him to see beyond the military conditioning he has received since childhood. He begins to see soldiering as 'a mug's game', and as a gesture to Catherine offers to put the tin soldiers back in the box; but she, too, has modified her opinions and has no desire to rob him of the job that gives his life meaning. As Scott jokes: 'They all fall for the uniform in the end.' Their selves, and the reactionary and modernising forces they represent, have been drawn towards the compatibility signified by their embrace. They have both 'learned a couple of things on this journey'. As they depart together to find a home for baby India the camera pulls away to settle on the *Empress of India*, still steaming like an old war horse after battle, proud but no longer needed.

North West Frontier opened at Rank's flagship Odeon in Leicester Square, London, to a chorus of approval from the popular press which saw it as a worthy successor to *The Bridge on the River Kwai*. 'At last we have beaten Hollywood at its own game,' enthused Anthony Carthew in the *Daily Herald* (9 October 1959), a sentiment echoed by the *News of the World*'s Peter Burnup (11 October 1959) who called *North West Frontier* 'the greatest British picture of its kind in many a year'. Lee Thompson had given these critics exactly the kind of film they were looking for to take the British film industry more effectively into international markets in just the way that Korda had before the war. They were quick to recognise and celebrate the director's role. Giving 'Top marks plus' to the film, George Sterling (*Sunday Dispatch*, 11 October 1959) praised Lee Thompson's skill in creating a 'magnificent adventure' and his ability to communicate his own enthusiasm to his stars who 'add lustre to themselves and to British film'. In the *Daily Express* and the *Daily Mail* (9 October 1959), experienced critics Leonard Mosley and Fred Majdalany, respectively, recognised this as a significant advance for J. Lee Thompson. Majdalany unreservedly called him 'the best of our younger generation of directors'. He had shown 'that he can tackle the big outdoor picture as confidently as the more intimate urban subjects in which he has previously specialised'. Mosley felt this placed Lee Thompson in an 'exclusive club' with Carol Reed and David Lean by adding 'one of the most exciting and colourful adventure films which we have seen on our screens from any country this year' to a recent string of 'brilliant' smaller scale dramas.

While there were a few quibbles about the believability of the film's dialogue and the pulp fiction quality of its plot, there was near unanimous praise for its handling of suspense and spectacle, the grandeur of its cinematography, and the precision of its casting and performances. Many of the reviewers of the 'quality' papers were also in step with this critical consensus, notably Dilys Powell and C. A. Lejeune. Powell found the tension 'well sustained' and 'the spectacular stuff' to be 'handled with a confidence none too common in the British cinema' (*Sunday Times*, 11 October 1959); while the often curmudgeonly Lejeune admitted not only the overall 'excitement' of the spectacle, but to being gripped by the 'quiet' acting of the film's 'inner story' (*Observer*, 11 October 1959). What debate there was centred on the politics of the film rather than the acknowledged accomplishment of its direction. Predictably enough, those who questioned the progressiveness of Lee Thompson's text were led by Derek Hill, whose *Tribune* piece (16 October 1959) pulled few punches in calling *North West Frontier* 'an appalling film':

> Appearing at this time it can only be interpreted as a defence – and an encouragement – of the Suez mentality ... The Indians come in two varieties – the comic coon – ... and with less emphasis, the noble

savage. The treatment of the two villains is equally significant. An armament manufacturer who sells weapons to both sides is considered an amiable rogue and gets off, almost literally, with a nod and a wink. But a half-caste Moslem, the only character with any kind of ideals, has to be killed.

Hill had some support from David Robinson whose mixed review in the *Financial Times* (12 October 1959) suggested that 'the jingoism of this film would have been reactionary even in 1905', and from the *Daily Worker*'s Nina Hibbin (10 October 1959). Always the Feste to Hill's Malvolio in the *Twelfth Night* of socialist film criticism, Hibbin's wry review admits to finding much of the film 'wildly exciting' and an entertaining debate on empire ('I put my shirt on Herbert Lom who seemed to be talking sense'), but expresses shock at an 'absolutely flabbergasting burst of bare-faced jingoism'. It is, of course, the use of Eton's anthem to which she takes exception. Writing in the radical press's third journal *New Statesman* (17 October 1959), David Sylvester discerned Lee Thompson's intentions a little more clearly:

> This is a film that tries to do with the theme of Empire-builders versus rebellious natives what the modern Western does with that of cowboys versus Indians, not to treat the moral conflict in terms of white against black but to show that our side is not altogether good and the other side not altogether bad.

Considering that *North West Frontier* arrived on the very day that the Tory Party was returned to power with an increased majority, it is little wonder that critics of the Left searched the film for evidence of reactionary thinking. But David Sylvester is right to regard it as a revisionist epic of empire which continually stresses the complexities of moral debate. In the homespun phrase of the *Manchester Guardian* (10 October 1959), the film gives '"fair do's" all round' in the classic liberal manner, while acknowledging the untenable nature of imperialism. Although it was made by a director who describes himself as 'very left-wing in those days', it is not a didactic movie. Within the commercial and ideological constraints of British studio production and international distribution, it could never hope to deliver the kind of radical polemic which might have satisfied Derek Hill. It can be legitimately criticised for ignoring the most repressive aspects of British rule in India and allowing its light satire of the Raj to shade into an equivocal celebration of British indomitability and sang-froid, but it stops well short of being an apologia for empire without quite being an apology to its subject people.

Notes

1 The danger of the location should not be dismissed. Tom Hutchinson, the *Picturegoer* journalist who visited the unit in Libya and had to be stretchered out, reported: 'It was the toughest, toughest film location I've ever encountered. I had lost seven pounds in weight and a lot of sleep. I had gained five thousand flies, experience and a disease that was to confine me to the British Military Hospital in Tripoli for five days' (*Picturegoer*, 7 December 1957).

2 First published in book form by William Heinemann in 1957, but previously serialised in America's *Saturday Evening Post*.

3 Landon apparently served in the 1st South African Division in the Western Desert. His book appears to be based on a true story and is dedicated to Tom Pugh, one of the book's main characters, 'remembering many years friendship'. Landon was born in West Byfleet, Surrey, in 1911, and was educated at Lancing College and Cambridge University before working as a freelance writer on magazines and newspapers. He lived in Sussex and died in 1961, leaving a wife and three children.

4 As one passage in *Ice Cold In Alex* put it: 'It was one of those times when it didn't matter much whether you had the red desert rat or the broken palm painted on the front of your truck, because ahead of you were hundreds of miles of loneliness and soft sand and rock, the doubt of thirst, the danger of error in navigation or the chance of a stray mine' (Landon 1957: 89). The page number is from the 1959 Pan Books edition.

5 Well before shooting was competed, the readers of *Picturegoer* (30 November 1957) were being made a 'preview' offer of Landon's book by Odham's Popular Book Club at less than a third of its published price. 'So good, it's being filmed' ran the advertising copy which also featured production photographs.

6 This was surprising as Taylor had filmed John Mills' last outing for ABPC *It's Great to Be Young* (Cyril Frankel, 1956), in colour. It seems that the studio preferred to reserve colour for musicals, comedies and subjects likely to appeal predominantly to a female audience. Black and white is a cooler medium and therefore less appropriate, as *The Times* (30 June 1958) pointed out, to suggest desert heat.

7 Including *The Red Beret* (Terence Young, 1953) and *A Hill in Korea* (Julian Amyes, 1956).

8 Sylvia Syms explained her character's motivation thus: 'I decide that he's the type who'll never speak unless I make him, what with the danger and the other two men there. So I seduce him' (*Picturegoer*, 21 September 1957). In the earlier screenplay, romance blossoms between Diana and Tom Pugh. In scene 96 they go to sleep in the back of the ambulance holding hands and by scene 138 they are kissing. Anson flirts with her, but any open competition between the two men is nipped in the bud by Diana's assertion that she always knows what she wants. Pugh's anxieties about incompatibilities in their status are finally banished in scene 173 by a night of passion before they set off on the last leg to Alex. As they approach the city, Anson offers his congratulations (scene 184):

> ANSON Another good man gone!
> PUGH We're counting on you as best man, sir.
> ANSON Hell, Tom, I started the job and I'm going to finish it properly. Give the girl away.

9 Her words echo those of one of the real-life nurses in the Western Desert in the early 1940s, Marjorie Doyle, who told Eric Taylor (1997: 36–7): 'We learnt how to live with flies, bugs, beetles, rats and mice. We soon got into eating with a fork and spoon and using the other hand to waft away the flies as we lifted food to our mouths.'

10 Lee Thompson prefers to emphasise the grandeur of the desert rather than its irritants: 'Oh, yes, well, the flies were everywhere. She complained about the flies a lot, dear Sylvia. [But] I have very fond memories of the desert ... It was fascinating, and at night sound carries for miles, and we were living in an old fort miles into the desert. It was a wonderful experience.'

11 Margaret Hinxman, 'She's learning to be a star', *Picturegoer*, 29 March 1958. Some of the anger which one or two of her co-workers noticed might also be attributed, in part, to her knowledge that she was easily the lowest paid of *Ice Cold*'s stars. The contract she had signed with ABPC kept her on a miserly £30 per week, in spite of her status as the country's fastest rising young female star (McFarlane 1997: 549)

12 Sylvia Syms recalled his ordeal when she was interviewed for *A Very British War Movie* (Channel 4 Television, 28 August 1999):

> 'They made this huge tank and they filled it with all sorts of crud ... Now I imagine that on the first day it was probably quite warm but, of course, it was the middle of winter when we got back so it got colder and colder, and I'm absolutely certain that, by the time Tony was immersed in it, it was very, very cold and he was very brave about it because what you see is what you get. I mean, he went *right underneath* ... He had to have his nose and ears and everything cleaned out afterwards ... it was a very hard sequence.'

13 This scene has become one of the most famous examples of product placement in British cinema. In the book, the lager brand is the American-manufactured Rhinegold, a name with interesting national and mythic connections, but ABPC's exploitation manager arranged a tie-up with the

distributors of the Danish product as well as with Austin Motors, the manufacturers of KATY the ambulance. Carlsberg Lager was advertised with a still from the bar scene and, later, footage from the scene was used in the company's television commercials.

14 KATY's downhill roll, which so wonderfully pulls the 'sand mat' from under the feet of the audience, is another of J. Lee Thompson's late innovations to the script. It is present in neither Landon's original text, nor in its initial adaptation (dated 20 April 1956).

15 There is a further reference to Greek mythology in the name of the woman Anson is going to see in Alex. 'Ariadne' led Theseus out of the labyrinth, and in *Ice Cold* she acts as a kind of homing beacon, helping Anson to navigate through the desert maze. His apparent rejection of Diana as a long-term partner suggests Ariadne continues to be his guiding spirit.

16 There is evidence that the Afrika Corps did show considerable courtesy towards ambulances in reports given to Ernie Pyle (1945), a war correspondent with the British Army.

17 One is tempted to read Anson as a distorted projection of the director himself, and Pugh as resembling his cinematographer.

18 The character of the flawed and brittle commanding officer with an alcohol or narcotic problem had previously been largely confined to American films. See, for instance, *Halls of Montezuma* (Lewis Milestone, 1950) and *Attack!* (Robert Aldrich, 1956).

19 In the earlier script (20 April 1956), Pugh is so conscious of the class difference between himself and Diana that he tries to end their relationship (scene 138).

20 James Chapman (1998: 66) singles out Lee Thompson's film to challenge the prevailing critical construction of the 1950s' war film as 'grey and insipid', asking rhetorically how that construction might possibly account for 'the psychological intensity and latent eroticism of a film such as the much-underrated *Ice Cold in Alex?*'

21 In an unpublished paper on aspects of gender in *Ice Cold*, Melanie Williams (1999b) has also noted the duality in the representation of Diana, noting that Sylvia Syms' portrayal resembles the fluctuating hot and cold polarities typical of 'the Hitchcock blonde'. Suggesting that, for most of its course, the film offers us the idea that a woman can be a sensible, pragmatic and capable team member, she is perturbed that it becomes 'afraid of the logic of its own argument'. In what might be seen as retribution for her sexual forwardness with Anson, Diana's positive representation is undermined by her carelessness with KATY's starting handle: 'Diana is a site of struggle and debate over feminine identity: her capability and sexual agency suggesting one form of new womanhood, but compromised and brought back to the inevitability of her inferiority by a feminine moment of weakness.'

22 Particularly as the major erotic indicator, previously, has been Diana's sensuous lighting of a cigarette for Tom.

23 In an interview for Channel 4's *Empire of the Censors* in 1995, Lee Thompson recalled: 'There was no nudity in that love scene, it was only

passionate kissing. And I remember saying: "What exactly is it that you object to? People kiss and they kiss passionately." And the censor said: "Yes, but they're rolling about in the sand." Apparently, making love in the sand was, er, a no-no.'

24 Quoted in McFarlane (1997: 550).

25 The rushes of the scene were also viewed by the *Picturegoer* journalist Tom Hutchinson. Although Lee Thompson now regards the sequence as 'tame', at the time of the film's release he quoted Hutchinson's description of it as 'one of the most provocative love scenes ever shot in Britain' (Lee Thompson 1958). There was certainly plenty to interest the censor in the initial script (20 April 1956) where the love scene was, of course, between Diana and Pugh. Again, buttons are important in this sequence (scene 172). Diana toys seductively with the second button of her blouse as Pugh tells her that they must part but he will never forget her.

> DIANA (*tauntingly*) Why don't you look at me?

He turns his head very slowly and looks at her. From his angle, we see her fingers suddenly pause in idly playing with the button. Then her other hand comes up to her shirt front and together both hands suddenly clench on the material. Pugh's eyes suddenly widen as he watches her. Then, with a long sigh, he half closes his eyes and leans forward to take her in his arms. She has now turned towards him (*away from camera*), and we see his arms come round her now bare shoulders, as he pulls her towards him almost roughly as their lips meet (*slow dissolve*).

26 Derek Hill, Lee Thompson's most hostile critic, found 'the gentlemanly presentation of every German in the film' particularly galling:

> Personally I can't help seeing it as part of the policy of selling us the last war as a cleanly conducted exchange of differences ... [I]t's easy to be internationally-minded over past, beaten enemies, especially if the powers that be want to soften public hostility to re-arming them. *Ice Cold in Alex* is little more than part of the big white-wash, directed by a man who seems happy to jump at the crack of any whip. (*Tribune*, 4 July 1958)

27 David Lean's *Bridge on the River Kwai* (1957) and Roy Baker's *The One that Got Away* (1957) also occupy this transitional category.

28 The Golden Bear was awarded to Ingmar Bergman's *The End of the Day*. *Kinematograph Weekly* (10 July) reported that, apart from some reservations about *Ice Cold*'s length, 'the critics were unanimous in praising individual performances, the pictorial beauty of Lee Thompson's work, and its uplifting spirit of human fellowship'.

29 *Ice Cold* was released only eighteen months after Anthony Eden had, humiliatingly, been forced to withdraw British troops from Egypt after an attempt to gain control of the Suez Canal.

30 Ivor Adams, *Star*, 26 June 1958.

31 Notably the musicals *Happy Go Lovely* (Bruce Humberstone, 1950) and *Let's Be Happy* (Henry Levin, 1957).

32 *Men of Two Worlds* (Thorold Dickinson, 1946) was a precursor to films like Harry Watt's *Where No Vultures Fly* (1951) and *West of Zanzibar* (1954) which reconfigure the colonial project in Africa as one concerned not so much with law and order, as with modernisation and ecological conservation.

33 Estridge had, for example, scripted *A Day to Remember* (Ralph Thomas, 1953) and *Above Us the Waves* (Ralph Thomas, 1955).

34 The privations of filming *A Night to Remember* are recalled in More's biography (More 1978: 172–3) and those of *The African Queen* by its cinematographer Cardiff (1996: 148–62).

35 For some of the more remote locations, such as a deserted railway station, they had to abandon vehicular transport altogether (*People*, 11 October 1959).

36 Anon., *Kenneth More, Fans' Star Library*, 44, Fleetway 1959.

37 The rate doubled for the massacre at the railway station where 'corpses' were given a further bonus for having fake blood squirted over them. The *People* (11 October 1959) reported that Lee Thompson was happy to do most of the bloodying himself.

38 Bacall's problems were increased by worries about her young son in London who was ill with measles.

39 Although this was not without its problems, because it was too expensive to ship the old shunting engine they had been using for so many scenes in India and a replica had to be found in Spain (*Flame Over India* campaign manual).

40 Unsurprisingly, Derek Hill (*Tribune*, 16 October 1959) thought he 'should be ashamed of himself', playing 'the comic coon' in an imperial epic.

41 Richards (1973: 123) observes that, unlike empire films set in Africa in which the hero is usually the district officer, those set in India 'almost invariably' have a military man as their protagonist.

42 The idea of 'the white man's burden' is discussed at length by Richards (1973: Chapter 8) who suggests that in imperial ideology 'the relationship between ruler and ruled was idealised as that of a father and his children'. In this paternal role of defending 'the oppressed against the oppressor', the British hoped to be 'loved rather than feared'.

43 Rank recognised the special quality of *North West*'s cinematography by offering promotional stills in 14"35" Cinemascope format 'chosen to illustrate the breadth and spectacular nature of the film' (*North West Frontier*, showman's guide, Rank Film Distributors, 1959.)

44 Lee Thompson's desire for historical fidelity is evidenced in his employment of Hara Sen, a retired major from the 11th Sikh Regiment as technical adviser on army matters.

45 Van Leyden sardonically parodies this English trait when he assures the others: 'I merely sympathise with small minorities fighting the aggression of big nations.'

46 The old round-barrelled steam engine used in the film was rescued from a scrap yard by Marcel Hellmann. The engine had begun service as a troop transporter in 1887 and had travelled the railways of India for over sixty years (*Flame Over India* campaign manual)

47 Imagine a change of transport and you have John Ford's classic *Stagecoach* (1939).
48 The attack, when it comes, anticipates a similar one in David Lean's *Lawrence of Arabia* (1962). It is also interesting to note that while his tutor in suspense, Hitchcock, mostly used the interior of the train as the venue for tension, Lee Thompson shifts his focus to the rails.
49 Although the suspense is beautifully handled the sequence is let down by a rather obvious use of back projection and a crude model shot.
50 Viewers familiar with the history of the Raj might also recall the Amritsar massacre of 1919 in which more than 300 Indian civilians died when troops opened fire on a protest meeting. This infamous moment in imperial history was later depicted in Richard Attenborough's *Gandhi* (1982).
51 A critique of the expansionism inherent in empire building is encoded into a conversation between Gupta and the prince about engines. Gupta wonders why people become dissatisfied with small engines but then, when they acquire a bigger one, are no more satisfied because they want a bigger one still. The solution for Gupta is to be happy with the small engine.
52 To tie in with the film, the 'Eton Boating Song' was rearranged as 'a catchy beat ballad guaranteed to delight teenagers everywhere – even if it may also knock some Etonian top-hats sideways', and recorded by the Knightsbridge Chorale. The tune was also renamed the '*North West Frontier* March' for its publication as sheet music (*North West Frontier* showman's guide).
53 The number of steam locomotives operating on British railways dropped by almost two-thirds between 1955 and 1963. The last went into service less than six months after the release of *North West Frontier*. In 1963 the Committee of Inquiry chaired by Dr Beeching recommended the closure of 5,000 miles of unprofitable railway line.
54 The scene was a dangerous one to film, as Lee Thompson told the *People*'s reporter Ernest Betts (11 October 1959) 'The train was doing 15 miles an hour ... To have faked that scene would have destroyed the character and all the tension I'd been building up.' The train-top fight was reprised in *Octopussy* (1983) where pukka Britisher James Bond (Roger Moore) battles an Indian villain (Kabir Bedi).
55 Yorke (1996) provides a useful account of the increasing adoption of these cultural frameworks in films about the British empire from *Exodus* (Otto Preminger, 1960) to *Gandhi*; although he too easily dismisses *North West Frontier* as a perpetuator of heroic myths.

Deutsche stars

By 1958 British production houses were becoming increasingly conscious of the importance of continental as well as American markets. *Woman in a Dressing Gown* and *Ice Cold in Alex* had both been premiered with striking success at the Berlin Film Festival, and Rank had begun to use German stars to ease its product into European cinemas. *The One that Got Away*, with Hardy Krueger playing the Luftwaffe pilot Franz Werra who escaped from imprisonment in Canada, had done spectacular business in Germany and Austria, reputedly being seen by 72,000 people in only three weeks at one Viennese film house (*Kinematograph Weekly*, 6 November 1958). The film's producer, Julian Wintle, quickly went into partnership with another of Rank's producers, Leslie Parkyn, founding Independent Artists to capitalise on the markets opened up by *The One that Got Away*. Their first production at their own Beaconsfield Studios teamed Hardy Krüger with Sylvia Syms (already known in Germany from *Woman in a Dressing Gown*) in a story of Anglo-German romance at Cambridge University, *Bachelor of Hearts* (Wolf Rilla, 1958).[1]

Impressed with his success in Germany, Wintle and Parkyn next approached Lee Thompson to direct a vehicle for another 'Deutscher Star', Horst Buchholz, the 24-year-old heart-throb from Berlin who had been featured in twelve continental films over the previous four years. The picture was to be based on a French short story by Noel Calef entitled 'Rudolphe et le revolver', but its dockland's locale was to be shifted to Cardiff's Tiger Bay, a multi-racial community with a long-established reputation for toughness and, more recently, well-known as the birthplace of popular singer Shirley Bassey.

Tiger Bay (1959)

> When the stars threw down their spears,
> And watered heaven with their tears,
> Did he smile his work to see?
> Did he who made the lamb make thee?
> (*The Tyger*, William Blake, 1794)

'The first two days of rushes, when I saw that wonderful face, those wonderful eyes on the screen, I knew that we had something very special.' (J. Lee Thompson on Hayley Mills)

By the time Lee Thompson joined the *Tiger Bay* project in August 1958 filming was due to begin in less than a month. Producer John Hawkesworth, who had made his name as an art director on such films as Carol Reed's *The Third Man* and David Lean's *The Sound Barrier* (1952), had completed a script with Shelley Smith, and most of the casting had been done. Lee Thompson's impact on the production, however, was immediate and dramatic. He recruited his friend John Mills to play the part of the police Superintendent who, unusually for 1950s' British films, becomes the film's antagonist. Mills was expected to play opposite a young Australian boy who had already been cast as the child who witnesses a seaman's murder of his lover. However, when Lee Thompson visited John Mills' home, he was inspired to make a last-minute change, which would ensure *Tiger Bay*'s fame by launching the career of an unsuspecting child actress. John Mills recalled the occasion in his autobiography (Mills 1981: 342–3):

> I was more than anxious after *Ice Cold* to work with Lee again, whom I thought brilliant. Our friend seemed slightly distraught during lunch. He didn't really talk about the film. Most of his conversation seemed to be with Hayley [Mills's 12-year-old daughter] .... After lunch Lee suggested a walk round the farm. There was

something important he wanted to discuss. 'Listen, this may seem quite mad to you, but I've got a terrific hunch. I want to make a switch and change the little boy into a little girl. I know it's right. The whole story will be much more touching and moving in every way.' – 'Well, I can see that's possible', I said, 'but isn't it a bit late for a major change? It's a difficult part. A star part really. The picture will stand or fall on that character, and it could take weeks to find the right girl.' – 'It won't, you know', said Lee, 'I've already found her.' He stopped and looked at me. 'It's Hayley.' I stared at him 'Hayley? But listen, Lee, she's never been in front of a camera in her life. She might be ghastly. And then how do you think I should feel?' – 'Johnnie, I told you I've got a terrific hunch, I think she'll be sensational.'

John Mills had misgivings about his younger daughter entering the acting profession, but Hayley jumped at the chance offered to her and her parents agreed to the experiment. They were amazed when Lee Thompson dispensed with a screen test, confident in his eye for photogeneity. 'I could photograph her myself with a No. 2 Brownie Kodak box-camera with my eyes shut, and she'd still look good,' he told an incredulous John Mills, adding that he did not even want Hayley to read the script. Lee Thompson also remembers that afternoon well:

'I saw Hayley playing in the garden. She had a little caravan in the field below and she came out of this caravan wearing the little trousers and shirt that eventually she wore in the film, and suddenly I thought My God! How much better it would be if the part was played by a girl. It suddenly all came to me, I could see it before my eyes with this charming little girl who had never acted in her life before. So I happened to ask John, would he ever allow her to make a film. He said yes and very nicely said, you know, if she would be in your hands.'

John Hawkesworth and Rank's studio head John Davis both agreed to the change, as did Horst Buchholz when he was introduced to Hayley. 'He thought she was a delightful child', says Lee Thompson, 'and I remember him saying to me: "I shouldn't be doing this because she is obviously going to steal the picture from me, but go ahead and sign her."'

From the very first morning on the set at Beaconsfield Studios, Hayley Mills was a revelation. In her first studio scene she was being interrogated by her father in the role of the police superintendent. He was amazed at her memory for lines and her composure on the set:

> I simply couldn't believe what was happening. She looked as if she'd been born in front of the camera. All the other children I had suffered with in films had to be told continually not to look into the lens. Lee shot close-ups with the camera two feet away from her face. She looked left, right, over it, below it, but never at it. I am usually very secure on my lines, but that morning I was so astonished at what was going on that I dried up at least three times. (Mills 1981: 344–5)

Lee Thompson was equally amazed and, breaking unusually early for lunch he took John Mills to the local pub for a champagne celebration:

> Lee stood fiddling with one of the paper darts he made daily from a copy of *The Times* throughout all his films ... He raised his glass. 'Well, Johnnie,' he said, 'I've made a lot of films, but I'm going to drink to the most exciting and magical morning I've ever spent in any studio. That child is going to be a bloody sensation. Here's to her. Cheers!' ... I knew without any shadow of doubt that J. Lee Thompson was right.' (345)

Lee Thompson knew that his gamble in casting an untried performer would pay off and, forty years later, his memory of filming those scenes with Hayley Mills is still vivid:

> '*Tiger Bay* is one of my all-time favourite films that I made. I still can't get over the thrill I got when I first saw Hayley on the screen, with those wonderful big eyes ... She was an ideal little person to work with because you knew ... when you just looked through the lens at her that the camera loved her ... You just knew that she had such a rapport with that camera and that's what film making is about – the rapport between the camera and the artist. It's that magic you cannot explain. You either have it or you don't. The very best actor or actress in the world, if the camera doesn't love her, half the performance has gone.'

The director's strategy was to treat his young star as an adult, and to avoid talking down to her.[2] He also tried to keep her relaxed and unselfconscious, not letting her see any rushes until the time arrived for her to re-enact the murder which her character had viewed through a letterbox. Lee Thompson ran the appropriate footage and asked Hayley to simply act out what she had seen. As her father recalled (1981: 346): 'With no rehearsal she just did it. One second she was Horst Buchholz with a gun and the next second the girl. At the end of it, she did a grotesque fall ending up flat on her back. It was one of the best pieces of mime I've ever seen.' One take was all she needed. Perhaps the most extraordinary aspect of her performance was that she rarely appeared to be listening to the advice from her director, humming quietly to herself as scenes and motivations were explained. The results, however, were so accomplished that Lee Thompson come to accept the humming as a good omen for the next scene. He readily accepted, too, the pranks she liked to get up to on set:

'I remember once when she was in the church loft and she was carrying a candle and one of the studio technicians had to put her mark down on the floor. He knelt down to hammer in the mark where she would stand and she couldn't help it – the candle was dripping over with grease and she dropped a bit of grease on the carpenter's head. It was just that she never saw me watching her and she never looked up to see that she'd been caught (*laughs*). But it's a picture I remember of her so vividly, just tipping the candle slightly over so a blob of grease fell on his head. She was a delightful child to work with and there were no problems from either John or Mary Mills. If I wanted them to come and watch a scene they would, but otherwise they left her entirely in my hands. It was one of the best experiences I've ever had in film making because I knew I was working with real gold with Hayley.'

In fact, the six weeks of shooting at Beaconsfield Studios had been preceded by four weeks on location in Cardiff. Hayley Mills has a good recollection of her first day before the cameras in Cardiff's docklands.[3] As she told Brian McFarlane (1997:409):

'I wasn't anxious, but I was a little bit unsure of myself, slightly lost ... because it was the first day, and the first day was a scene on the ramp at the beginning of the movie. All I had to do was watch some boys fighting with guns, playing Cowboys and Indians, and stare at them through the railings. It was outside, there were other kids there and there was so much to take in, so much going on. My parents were there and it was reassuring and very normal to have my father in the film also, because I'd been on so many film sets with him. The only difference now was that the camera was pointing at me. I had to have a fight with one of the oldest boys because he snatched a packet of sausages from me; I remember finding it terribly difficult to pound this boy on the chest. I can see now that I was inhibited in doing that because it *was* the first day; if we'd shot that scene a week later I wouldn't have had any trouble at all! I was well into it by that time. When you start acting young, it is an extension of your own imaginative games.'

Her memories of Lee Thompson's direction are as happy as are his recollections of her performance:

'He was very gentle, very kind, he never made me feel nervous or worried about what I had to do. In a very gentle way he explained what he wanted and said things that I could understand about Gillie [her character] and what she was feeling, and he appreciated what I did, which made me feel reassured.' (1997: 409)

From working with a regular team of actors and ABPC technicians in accustomed surroundings, J. Lee Thompson was faced, on *Tiger Bay*, with a largely unfamiliar cast and crew. John Mills, of course, was a known quantity and, remarkably for an actress of her stature, Yvonne Mitchell had agreed to take a small part as the film's murder victim, but the capabilities of the rest remained to be discovered. Fortunately, the key positions of producer, cinematographer and film editor were occupied by men of outstanding ability. Lee Thompson happily names John Hawkesworth as 'one of the best producers I ever worked with, because he made everybody feel comfortable'. Lighting cameraman Eric Cross could draw on thirty years' experience in the film business, and his familiarity with documentary techniques gave *Tiger Bay*'s location footage an intimate and informal quality. His skill with light and camera placement also enabled him to replicate, in interior shots, the angled and mediated style of camerawork that Gil Taylor had developed with Lee Thompson on earlier pictures.[4]

'He'd seen my films and he knew what I was wanting', says Lee Thompson, 'but he did a marvellous job; he made Hayley look gorgeous, just out of this world.' His skill was matched by editor Sidney Hayers who had cut *A Town Like Alice* (Jack Lee, 1956), *The One that Got Away* and *A Night to Remember*, and was about to launch his own directing career with *Violent Moment* (1958). His work on *Tiger Bay* is sometimes stunning (in the murder sequence, for example) and always keeps the film pacey, complementing the vitality of the performances.

Although *Tiger Bay* begins with a killing it is not a murder mystery, nor is it even primarily a psychological portrait of a fugitive. It is more a study of loyalty, betrayal and belonging. There are certainly echoes of Reed's *Odd Man Out* in its sea port setting, flight from justice and attempted escape by boat. There are also parallels with Reed's haunting film in *Tiger Bay*'s mobilisation of sympathy for a killer, romantic construction of the outsider and themes of loyalty and sacrifice; but Lee Thompson never really strives for *Odd Man Out*'s allegorical pretension or sense of tragedy. His focus is firmly on the attractions and conflicts within dyadic human relationships and the way in which these are intensified by social exclusion. At a deeper subtextual level one can also detect Freudian discourses on child development and reflections of some of the social and international tensions which occupied the news headlines during the period of *Tiger Bay*'s creation.

Tiger Bay began filming only a few days after white youths in London's Notting Hill had mounted well-publicised attacks on the area's black residents. A larger scale riot in the same area occurred towards the end of the film's location shooting (25 September 1958). In these circumstances, *Tiger Bay*'s opening scenes may be seen as establishing a more inclusive definition of Britishness without identifying the presence of black people as problematic. We begin with a ship – a carrier of foreign influences, if you like – arriving in port and we follow the disembarkation of a Polish seaman, Korchinsky (Horst Buchholz), as he rides out the good-natured taunts of his shipmates about the failure of his girlfriend to meet him at the quayside.[5] As he searches her out, Eric Cross' camera surveys the vistas of the city docks just as Robert Krasker's had in *Odd Man Out* and Gordon Dines's had in *Pool of London* (Basil Dearden, 1950). As Korchinsky moves through these docklands, however, it becomes evident that this is not white Belfast but a multi-racial community like Notting Hill. Korchinsky ruffles the hair of a black child as he crosses a playground where the swings and roundabout are shared by mixed racial groups. West Indian and white men are gambling in the street in front of his girlfriend's lodgings, which are owned by an Indian doctor. But, instead of his girlfriend Anya, he discovers the room occupied by Christine (Shari), a prostitute of mixed race.[6] Lee Thompson's intention was to depict racial togetherness in a matter-of-fact way, implying that ethnic diversity was not in itself a problem. 'There was no patronage in it', he insists, 'it was shown as it was.'[7]

Agitated by fears of sexual betrayal, Korchinsky obtains a new address for his lover and leaves with the doctor's warning ringing in his ears: 'Don't let your emotions run your life.' On his way to the new address, he seeks directions from 10-year-old Gillie (Hayley Mills), a girl from London who has been sent to stay with her Welsh aunt, and discovers that she lives in the rooms beneath Anya's. We have already encountered Gillie in the context of a multi-ethnic game of cowboys-and-indians. In an unmistakable quotation of Carol Reed's first shot of Bobby Henry in *The Fallen Idol*, we first see her staring wistfully at the game through the bars of some chained railings, a symbol of captivity and isolation which Lee Thompson had used to good effect in the opening of *Yield to the Night*. Gillie's sorrowful eyes evidence her exclusion from the game, a boys' pastime for which girls must pay a heavy entrance fee. Participants must have a gun, and Gillie, as a girl, does not have the required equipment. She is not content, however, with girlish games, and her masculine attire of black slacks and T-shirt and her angry refusal to be classed as 'a lady' emphasises her gender dissatisfaction. This odd girl out is a 'tomboy' with a pretty obvious case of penis envy. The nearest she can get to a gun is to spend the change from the purchase of her aunt's sausages on a toy cap-bomb, but this is insufficiently phallic to gain the respect of her male peers. Her dressmaker aunt (Megs Jenkins) regards this kind of gender confusion as a symptom of society in decadent decline ('Sure don't know what next, little girls wanting to play with guns and bombs and dressing up like gangsters') and is convinced that her niece will 'end up in gaol'.

This is clearly psycholigically rich territory, but beyond hints of a broken home and evident exclusion by the local community, *Tiger Bay*'s script misses the opportunity to explore the reasons for Gillie's disaffected state more fully. Instead Lee Thompson keeps the action moving with the confrontation between Korchinsky and Anya (Yvonne Mitchell). He discovers that he is being shut out of Anya's game just as Gillie is being excluded from the boys'. Anya, in fact, is a woman who does have a gun, given to her by her new lover Barclay (Anthony Dawson), a 'respectable' radio broadcaster, 'not a dirty sailor'. Assured of her security by the weapon and resentful of Korchinsky's possessiveness, she rejects his desire to keep her as his plaything: 'I'm not an animal for a little boy to keep in a cage,' she rages at him. 'I'm a woman, a woman with a heart and a body which is my own to give how I like, when I like.' As she continues to berate him in Polish, scorning his offer and taunting him with the prowess of her new lover, he is reduced to bellowing 'Bitch!' at her until, provoked beyond endurance, he seizes the gun and shoots her.[8] As in *The Window*, the killing is witnessed by a child, Gillie in this instance, who watches through the letterbox. Shots of the feuding couple are intercut with reaction shots of Gillie's widening eyes, framed in the aperture. The tempo of Hayers' cutting increases steadily as the gunshots send Gillie blinking and stumbling back to a stairwell where she drops her toy bomb in fright, replicating the sound of the gun shots. With Anya's fatal collapse framed by the letterbox, Gillie conceals herself in a meter cupboard, the light falling dramatically on her terrified eyes. From here she observes Korchinsky hiding the gun and, as he waits to make his escape, she steals it to cure her 'lack' and improve her social acceptability. It is a thrilling sequence and one of Lee Thompson's finest. Camera angles are never less than inventive and impeccably chosen. The symbolism is powerful, the editing precise, and the *mise-en-scène* is as satisfyingly seedy as is Pinkie's boarding house in *Brighton Rock* (John Boulting, 1948).

Keeping possession of her gun now becomes Gillie's priority.

She gives misleading information to Superintendent Graham (John Mills) who is investigating the murder upstairs, allowing suspicion to fall on Barclay whose affluence she despises ('that horrid man with a car'). When her aunt, still hoping to convert her 'little devil' into a little angel, packs her off to sing in the church choir, Gillie packs her pistol. Clad in an angelical white surplice, she proudly displays her gendered status symbol to one of the boys in the choir. The sequence challenges contemporary codes of censorship as directly as the use of 'bitch' had in the earlier scene. The iconography of innocence and spirituality presented by the church setting and the virginal choristers contrasts perversely with the violence and sexuality suggested by Gillie's gun. In the context of the African–Caribbean wedding at which she is sing-ing, Gillie's phallic display to a smaller boy and her offer of a bullet indicates that she is beginning to discover her sexuality and is already aware of its inchoate power. As a child, Gillie may be excluded from the boys' games, but as a woman, a confident and demanding sexuality will ensure that playmates will not be hard to find. Subtextually, the scene is steering close to the wind in its exploration of pre-pubescent sexuality, but Hayley Mills plays it with such charm and impish innocence that the full implications of the scene remain below the surface.

Just as Gillie is enjoying her new position of control, her voice soaring to the rafters on her solo – 'The Lord is my Shepherd' – she spots Korchinsky in the congregation and her confidence drains away. Like a choirboy robbed of his top notes by the onset of puberty, Gillie's voice is broken by her awareness of Korchinsky. She can no longer sing for the wedding because, although she does not realise it, she is experiencing a nuptial moment of her own. At the end of the service he chases her through the shadowy church before she confronts him with the gun, ordering him to 'stick 'em up', as if incorporating him into her world of play.[9]

It quickly becomes apparent that Korchinsky is not a cold-blooded criminal like Len in *The Yellow Balloon*, but is as fright-ened and friendless as Gillie. She sees in his social isolation a reflection of her own and, as happens with the child and the killer in *Hunted*, a bond of affection begins to grow between them.[10]

Reclaiming the gun, Korchinsky repositions Gillie in both the gender and the moral order. Her precocious and presumptuous appropriation of adult male power is turned into the subordination of a female child but, in the process, she acquires a spiritual ascendancy granted to her by her religious environment and the nurturing, feminine role which Korchinsky expects her to play.[11] While Korchinsky becomes a substitute for the father Gillie has lost and an anticipation of the lovers she has yet to meet, she is cast by him as both daughter and guardian angel. As she again sings the words of Psalm 23, 'Though I walk in death's dark veil, yet will I fear no ill', her attachment to him seems to offer the possibility of redemption as well as the escape to the sea which they both crave. To each the ocean represents a place beyond the law, where Gillie can transcend the circumstances of gender, age and locality and Korchinsky can evade the punishment for his crime. For the sailor, however, the ocean can be only a temporary refuge because, rather than a solution, it is at the heart of his problem of rootlessness and lack of belonging. 'All my life I have been at sea', he confesses to Gillie, 'and all my life I've been trying to get away from the sea.'

How many of the symbolic meanings I have been merrily decoding were consciously encoded by the creators of his drama is open to question. It is possible that they considered it no more than an unassuming little thriller; but from the moment J. Lee Thompson decided to change the sex of his child star, he released a stream of serendipitous possibilities to enrich the semantics of the text. Gender reversal enables him to ring the changes on most previous child-meets-criminal dramas. This type of story has its prototypes in the single-sex Dickensian dyads of Oliver and Fagin (*Oliver Twist*) and Pip and Magwitch (*Great Expectations*) where the adult is either loathsome exploiter or loathsome benefactor. Lee Thompson's own *Yellow Balloon* traded on the loathsome exploiter stereotype, while Charles Crichton's *Hunted* offers a variation on the criminal-as-protector theme. *Tiger Bay* briefly suggests that Gillie may be in danger in the noir sequence where she goes on the run with Korchinsky, who contemplates disposing of her in the inky water of the dock. He may be a killer, but the danger to him that Gillie as a witness represents is outweighed by his paternal concern and emotional need. They are two outsiders joined in a strange non-carnal union, sanctified in the church where they first exchange words and socially endorsed by the wedding revellers who shower them with confetti.[12] As Korchinsky picks a confetti horseshoe from Gillie's hair it is clear that here is a more multi-faceted relationship than that between *Hunted*'s Chris and little Robbie.

Rather than the sinister subterranean world to which Len lures Frankie in *The Yellow Balloon*, Gillie leads Korchinsky out of the city to a place of purity, a country retreat where their relationship can blossom, where the Tyger can lie down with the lamb. The impression of a honeymoon is reinforced by Laurie Johnson's romantic score, and Lee Thompson shows remarkable confidence that any implications of illicit desire can be kept at bay. But his assured direction makes it clear that Korchinsky is no Humbert Humbert and Gillie is no Lolita. Freed from the pressures and demands of the city, sailor and child can briefly relax into a more playful state.[13] Korchinsky, however, knows that Gillie is being sought by the police and that his own arrest is only a matter of time. Leaving Gillie in the valleys he returns to Tiger Bay to collect his belongings and to secure a passage on the next cargo boat to sail. His flight is aided by both the mulatto prostitute whom he had encountered earlier at Anya's old address, and by Gillie who, having been discovered in her rural hideaway, does all she can to hamper the police investigation.

Despite her best intentions, she lets slip information which incriminates her sailor boy, but by the time Superintendent Graham finally gets on Korchinsky's trail, his ship is already steaming out of port. Gillie is taken along on the pursuit as an identification witness, and she again tries various strategies to slow things down, feigning illness and injury but failing to convince the resolute Graham. Boarding a motor launch, the pursuers manage to stop Korchinsky's ship, *Paloma*, on the edge of the three-mile limit, the boundary of police jurisdiction. In the boarding of the merchant vessel and the disputes over national boundaries that follow, contemporary audiences would have been clearly reminded of the

fishing war with Iceland, over the attempt to extend territorial limits, which was raging at the time *Tiger Bay* was made.[14] Lee Thompson performs another mischievous reversal, turning an Icelandic gunboat into a British police launch and commenting wryly on the arbitrariness of international boundaries.

On board the *Paloma*, Graham brings Gillie face to face with Korchinsky and asks her to identify him as Anya's killer. When she refuses to do so, an exasperated Graham tries a lecture on the importance of truthfulness, but Gillie is bound by a loyalty more powerful than abstract concepts like honesty and wickedness. Korchinsky clenches and unclenches his fist in anxiety as he listens to the policeman's impassioned appeal to Gillie's conscience and we share his relief when she decisively refuses to incriminate him.[15] As he did in *Yield to the Night*, Lee Thompson has managed to create in the audience an extraordinary level of empathy with a character we have seen commit murder. It is a tribute to the emotional power of his direction and the compelling performances he coaxes from his actors. Here, Horst Buchholz, an actor hitherto better known for his sultry good looks than the proficiency of his performances, generates an intensity of feeling that one would never have expected him to achieve (any more than one would have expected Diana Dors to distinguish herself quite so remarkably as Mary Hilton). But as effectively as Buchholz plays his part, it is ultimately the extraordinary magnetism of Hayley Mills' performance that ensures our sympathy for his character. Anyone of whom Gillie is so fond cannot be bad. We may not fully understand her love for Korchinsky (just as she may not), but we are made to feel its strength and to condone its transcendence of legal moralities. It is Korchinsky's ability to attract Gillie's love and to reciprocate it that redeems him in our eyes.

Finally abandoning the attempt to change Gillie's mind, Graham decides that he will go ahead and arrest Korchinsky without her testimony, but he is stopped by the *Paloma*'s captain who tells him that the ship has drifted outside the three-mile limit. It seems that Korchinsky is safe, but Gillie unwittingly prolongs his ordeal by trying to stow away on the *Paloma*. Graham stalls the ensuing search, hoping that his own navigator can place the ship's

position within British territorial waters. Here, for the first time, Lee Thompson's direction falters, allowing some of the tension which he has so carefully built to be dissipated by Laurie Johnson's jaunty incidental music and a generally too light-hearted treatment of the search for Gillie. Dramatic tension is reinstated when Gillie's plea to sail with him is rejected by the frightened Korchinsky, who instantly regrets offending her. Seconds later, however, his loyalty to the girl is put to the sternest of tests as a sudden roll of the ship pitches Gillie into the sea. With no one else close enough to rescue her, Korchinsky's choice is clear: jump into the water and save her or stay on board and save himself. Doing nothing might preserve his life but his moral redemption depends on his continued commitment to the girl who has pledged her loyalty to him. His long dive into the waves confirms that the sea does indeed hold the key to his destiny ('All my life I've been trying to get away from the sea'), and as he shepherds Gillie to the safety of the police boat, the waters cleanse him spiritually. The tarnished angel he met in church and the power of love she has liberated have finally led the sinner to absolution. Even his adversary, Graham, recognises Korchinsky's moral transformation once he has manhandled the fugitive onto the launch. As his hopes of freedom disappear into the distance with the *Paloma*, Korchinsky paternally embraces the rescued child, kissing her head, and telling his nemesis contemptuously that he has got his man. 'Yes I have', replies Graham unjoyously, 'and a very brave man.' It is a moment of great poignancy, guaranteed to bring a lump to most viewers' throats, but frustratingly its impact is cushioned by the swelling strings of Johnson's theme music which banish a sense of tragedy and moral ambiguity with the sounds of optimism and lush romance. The happy resolution the score suggests overlays the truth implicit in the ending, that Korchinsky will be separated from Gillie by a long prison sentence or by the hangman's rope. Lee Thompson certainly realised what Korchinsky's likely fate would be, as he wrote (Lee Thompson 1963): 'If that really happened, I think the murderer would have been hanged. There have been many crimes like the one he committed. It was a loose woman who was killed by a Polish sailor

in a tawdry lodging house, so he wouldn't have stood a chance in English law.' But although an opportunity is missed to remind us that mercy was not a quality much exhibited by the British penal system of the 1950s, the slight fudging of *Tiger Bay*'s ending does not undermine the emotional construction of the film as a whole. Like *Yield to the Night*, it remains a shining example in British cinema of a film which is prepared to immerse its audience in the depths and complexities of human emotional response without allowing genuine sentiment to degenerate into false sentimentality. *Tiger Bay* might be criticised (as it was by Raymond Durgnat [1970: 66]) for eliding the politics of race by situating its story in a multi-racial community and then making its misfit protagonists white, but this would be a harsh judgement. Its commitment to the outsider is unwavering and, if the agents of exclusion and their society are represented as largely unmalicious, the experience of exclusion is sensitively and beautifully conveyed.

Rank must have realised that it had a winner when the audience at *Tiger Bay*'s preview screening in Cardiff became so enraptured with Hayley Mills' performance that it broke into spontaneous applause after her re-enactment of the murder scene. If the executives of the company were in any doubt, the notices which followed must have restored certainty. The critics sang the praises of the film with a unanimity which few of J. Lee Thompson's previous films had enjoyed. Not surprisingly, most reviews heralded the arrival of a new child star. 'This Babe is a Honey', proclaimed the *Daily Mirror*'s Dick Richards (28 March 1959): 'she steals the film from right under the nose of her talented father'. Harold Conway in the *Daily Sketch* (26 March 1958) agreed that 'she has made everything else I have seen in the cinema this week seem unimportant ... she is the most exciting, most heart-warming eruption in British films for years'. In the *Evening Standard* (26 March 1958) John Waterman was able to overcome his aversion to 'cinemoppets' and acclaim an 'astonishing performance' in which, 'with a range of facial expression and a way of speaking dialogue as if she means it, Hayley Mills makes older starlets look more like China figures than actresses'. The response was not restricted to the dew-eyed uncles of the tabloids.

The hawk-eyed aunties of the broadsheets were equally captivated by Hayley's big-eyed debut. Caroline Lejeune (*Observer*, 29 March 1959) reserved her highest praise for Hayley's performance and her sister in the Sunday press, Dilys Powell (*Sunday Times*, 29 March 1959), described 'young Miss Mills' as 'a gift to the screen, ... a child player who responds without self-consciousness to direction, who succeds not by mere cuteness but by a feeling for timing which enables her to stand up to an established player'.

While the reviewers were completely enchanted by Hayley Mills, they certainly did not lose sight of the film itself and the contribution of J. Lee Thompson as director. 'Be sure of this', emphasised David Marlowe in *Picturegoer* (16 May 1959), 'it was his patience, his perception, his moulding that resulted in this fine screen portrayal.' Dilys Powell rated *Tiger Bay* Lee Thompson's 'best film so far', and the reviewer of *Films and Filming* (May 1959) was in full accord, insisting that Lee Thompson should take the lion's share of the credit 'for the imaginative way this fast-moving piece of melodrama is projected (almost flung) into life'. The director 'displays a masterly sense of character and suspense. Details suddenly invest stock situations with a flash of honesty that is both true and dramatic.' Margaret Hinxman (*Picturegoer*, 25 April 1959) described the direction of this 'crackerjack thriller' as 'firm, pointed and absolutely true to the story', while Josh Billings of *Kinematograph Weekly* called it 'sensitive and showmanlike' and 'a beautifully balanced job' in which 'a surging undercurrent of suspense subtly prevents sentiment from cloying'. Critics of all persuasions were impressed by the sense of honesty and truth with which J. Lee Thompson had invested the film. *The Times* (30 March 1959) noted that the director had 'a keen eye, a highly dramatic sense and an individual way of expressing what he sees', and the *Manchester Guardian* (28 March 1959) believed that *Tiger Bay* had been made 'an outstandingly good British film' by its director's 'attention to significant detail' and 'really fine judgement as to pace and tension'. Some critics felt that Lee Thompson was at last getting over the ostentatiousness which they had seen as a blight on his earlier work. David Robinson in the *Financial Times* (3 April 1959) grudgingly admitted that *Tiger Bay* was 'at

least good enough to show that J. Lee Thompson, given more efficient and less pretentious scripts than he has worked on recently
... can be a very workmanlike, if not exactly inspired, director';
while Paul Dehn, later to be the director's scriptwriter on his
Planet of the Apes films, was rather more generous: '*Tiger Bay* sees
J. Lee Thompson hitting his stride with a polished, compelling
and, for once, unmannered thriller' (*News Chronicle*, 26 March
1959).[16] If *Tiger Bay* was not J. Lee Thompson's finest film, these
were certainly the best reviews he would gather in his career.

I Aim at the Stars (1960)

> It horrifies me. In my view this is a film which ought never to have
> been made for the purpose of public entertainment (C. A. Lejeune,
> *Observer*, 27 November 1960)

> Like a true clown, J. Lee Thompson has wound up the perform-
> ance with the whitewash bucket on his own head. (Derek Hill,
> *Tribune*, 2 December 1960)

With Horst Buchholz in a leading role, *Tiger Bay* was naturally
given a prominent release in Germany, promoted as an example
of Rank's '*Frischer Wind*' (a breath of fresh air). Lee Thompson
followed in its wake not so much to promote *Tiger Bay* but to
spend three months making a film in Munich for Columbia. *I
Aim at the Stars* was his first foreign commission and a highly
controversial one because it was a bio-pic of Wernher von Braun,
the German rocket scientist who had designed the deadly V-2
missiles which had plagued London in the last months of the
Second World War. Von Braun was recruited onto the USA's post-
war rocket programme where he was eventually responsible for
developing and launching Explorer I, America's first earth satellite. By the late 1950s, von Braun was a national hero with his own
television show.

The US Army saw the celebration of von Braun's achievement
as a useful promotional and recruiting tool, and producer Charles
H. Schneer spent two years researching the project and developing a script with Jay Dratler. Lee Thompson was offered the

chance to direct the picture because Schneer wanted an independent view on his subject, especially one which might wish to emphasis von Braun's failings. Having been impressed with some of Lee Thompson's films, Schneer thought he was an appropriate choice to give 'a correct balance' to the story (Lee Thompson 1960). As an ex-RAF flyer, Lee Thompson's sympathies were with the victims of the V-2 rather than its creator, but as he explained when the picture was released in Britain:

> I have always been interested in controversial subjects and I was happy to accept the challenge of making this one for it provided me with the opportunity of posing four questions of international importance:
> 1 What constitutes a War criminal?
> 2 If a country at war captures a 'brilliant enemy scientist', who is guilty of inventing and using atrocity weapons – should that scientist be punished or should his brains be utilised for further scientific progress?
> 3 Should a Scientist be burdened with a Conscience?
> 4 Should a Scientist be 'Nationalistic'? (Lee Thompson 1960)

These questions constitute more than a subtext: they are the central concerns of the film and are carefully woven into its discourses, giving Lee Thompson ample opportunity to explore the kind of taxing moral quandries which are typical of his film making. What emerges is a study of obsession and its corrosive effect on moral values in a man who, while often in conflict with the Nazi Party, shared its belief in the justification of the means in terms of the end. It is also an examination of the powerful attraction to others of the drive and determination that obsession brings.[17] Lee Thompson was intrigued by the continuing charisma of a man who might easily be considered both a war criminal and a traitor to his country, given his defection to the Americans before the fall of Berlin. He described his meetings with von Braun as 'colourful', and wrote that 'We disliked each other on sight' (1960). He still recalls 'terrible arguments', particularly over 'the bunker scene' in which von Braun, faced with the inevitable defeat of Germany, discusses defection to the enemy with his colleagues as the best way to continue space research: 'I said: "You were really a

traitor. Your country was in dire straits and you decided to surrender to the Americans. ... You have to write this scene because
you played it in real life."' With the help of the British playwright
John Whiting, von Braun wrote his own defence, justifying his
decision to surrender to the Americans rather than the Russians.

The case against von Braun is represented initially by his
fiancée Maria (Victoria Shaw) who is jealous of his commitment
to space exploration and questions his humanitarianism. Later in
the film, his chief critic is an American officer Taggert (James
Daley) who has lost his wife and child in a V-2 attack. This character,
according to Lee Thompson (1960), is 'a "composite" of many influential people in America who still hold the view that von Braun
should never have been brought to the States – let alone decorated
by Eisenhower'. The character also voices many of the director's
critical thoughts about scientists' lack of social responsibility:

> TAGGERT Who the hell do these scientists think they are? They've
> got us all in the palms of their hands. You, me, Joe Doakes, the
> President. What they do dominates the entire world and they
> don't accept responsibility. Men and women don't mean any
> more to them than guinea pigs they tie up under their atom
> bombs, or the monkeys they shoot up from here in their
> precious rockets. They change sides without batting an eye-lid.
> They've no loyalties to anything except their own research. And
> when they've destroyed the whole damn world and everything
> in it they'll still be saying 'Oh sure, we made the bomb that did
> it, but it's not our responsibility'.

But while Lee Thompson might have continued to agree with
Taggert that, '[t]he conquest of our own human problems is more
important than the conquest of space', like his character he was
drawn by the magnetism of von Braun. At the end of the film
Taggert tells von Braun, 'You know, I've almost grown to like you',
to which von Braun replies: 'Suppose I could say the same about
you, except one never really likes one's conscience.' Lee Thompson confessed that he too 'almost grew to like von Braun' (1960),
admiring his 'brilliance and tenacity of purpose' but still not being
able to accept his worldview.

I Aim at the Stars gave Lee Thompson the opportunity to work with another 'Deutscher Star', Curt Jurgens, who played von Braun with what *Variety* (7 September 1960) described as a 'quiet, persuasive intensity'. Continuity with the director's British pictures was maintained in part by the casting of Herbert Lom as a colleague of von Braun who falls in love with an Allied spy (Gia Scala, who would play another spy in *The Guns of Navarone*), and by Laurie Johnson's score, but mainly by the film's visual enthusiasm. Even a detractor like Philip Riley (*Films and Filming*, January 1961) had to admit that 'the direction and photography had considerable style', and *Variety*, less inhibited in its praise, admired 'the whirlwind pace' which Lee Thompson had instilled in the 'exciting, artfully constructed picture'.[18]

The film enhanced Lee Thompson's reputation in Germany and established his name in America, where some of his best films like *Yield to the Night* and *Ice Cold in Alex* had been butchered beyond recognition by distributors. *I Aim at the Stars* was given a blaze of publicity in the USA with enthusiastic backing from the US Army, senators and congressmen, and a sympathetic reception from science clubs, educationalists, and a general population caught up in the excitement of the 'space race'. Columbia's press book described the picture as 'one of the most important films of our times' and recommended the full ballyhoo in its promotion. In Washington, the film was given an unprecedented senate preview, hosted by Senators Hill and Sparkman of Alabama, home of von Braun's Redstone Missile project, and in Colorado it played to 'the largest single audience ever to watch a motion picture' – 22,000 boy-scouts from all over the world at their jamboree. The US Army, which had offered every assistance to the filming of the picture, made it a feature of a special recruitment campaign. Such unqualified support for von Braun's achievements was not perhaps quite what Lee Thompson would have wished, but in Britain he encountered a diametrically opposite reaction.

Scandalised by the fêting of von Braun in America, anti-fascist action groups in Britain were determined to give *I Aim at the Stars* a rough reception when it opened in London eight weeks after the American premiere. Reviewers were invited to a screening of a documentary on the Warsaw ghetto to which the BBFC had refused a certificate because of its scenes of shocking inhumanity. At the preview of Lee Thompson's film at the Leicester Square Theatre, protesters showered invited guests with leaflets suggesting that showing the picture made 'mockery of the tributes to our fallen dead'. Some activists managed to walk on stage with a banner proclaiming 'Nazi Braun's V-2 rockets killed and maimed 9,000 Londoners' (*The Times*, 25 November 1960). Lee Thompson had anticipated that the film would be controversial and had a statement about why he agreed to make the film posted in cinemas. It failed to impress the critics, who were unanimous in their condemnation of the film as a tasteless lionisation of a murderer.

The reviewers in the London evening papers set the tone. Felix Barker in the *Evening News* (24 November 1960) adopted an attitude of conspicuous ennui, finding the film 'superficial' and 'flat', and claming to have had 'more excitement from a 4d [four-penny] rocket in my back garden'. Alexander Walker in the *Standard* (24 November 1960) was more vitriolic. He was concerned that the film failed to show the devastation caused to London by the V-2. He 'loathed' the 'sly way that this film glamorises von Braun' and deplored 'a specious and slippery ending which seems to suggest that saving America's face when Russia pipped her in the satellite race somehow justifies von Braun's work on the V-2'. The following day, the rest of the critics began to pile in to the film. Considerations of the cinematic merits of *I Aim at the Stars* were completely overshadowed by its politics. Whatever his personal beliefs or scientific principles, von Braun's expertise was thought to have helped to maintain the Nazi regime by enhancing its war machine.[19]

Like Peter Burnup, an admirer of Lee Thompson's cinema, reviewers found the film 'hard to take' (*News of the World*, 27 November 1960). Caroline Lejeune, who knew a victim of the V-2, went so far as to say that general exhibition, especially in London was 'ill advised' (*Observer*, 27 November 1960). In a passionate denunciation of 'this stupid, immoral, elephantinely tactless film' in the *Spectator* (2 December 1960), Isabel Quigly wondered how so 'skilful' a director as J. Lee Thompson could lend his powers of 'visual excitement' to so 'offensive' a subject.[20] Leonard Mosley, another supporter of the director, felt that he had made a disastrous error of judgement in taking on the film. Having discussed it with Lee Thompson he knew that the 'skilled craftsmen' had 'many qualms about making it' and could see that 'he has tried to inject into it many of the doubts which he painfully felt about von Braun's attitude', but he had failed to avoid completely 'the hero-worshipping element' (*Daily Express*, 25 November 1960). Von Braun might be looking at the stars, but London critics judged that Lee Thompson was definitely standing in the gutter. Known as a British film-maker of integrity, he had suddenly allowed himself to be used to make 'an American apologia for expediency' (*Sunday Express*, 27 November 1960). He remains unrepentant, however: 'I knew that the British press would accuse me of making a hero out of Wernher von Braun, but what I did was, really, I told the true story, which is a fascinating story, and *I Aim at the Stars* is for me one of my better films.'

Quite what long-term damage was done to Lee Thompson's reputation in England by his bio-pic of von Braun is unclear, but it is unlikely that the success of *The Guns of Navarone* the following year fully erased the memories of critics and members of London film community. *Guns* was snubbed by the British Academy in spite of its Oscar nominations, and no other J. Lee Thompson film ever attracted the attention of BAFTA. Lee Thompson would return periodically to direct in Britain, but, from the close of 1960, his future was as an international film-maker based in Hollywood.

Notes

1 Syms went straight on to star with another German actor, Curt Jurgens, in Rank's *Ferry to Hong Kong* (Lewis Gilbert, 1959). Rank was also exploring southern European markets with films set in Italy, like *Danger Within* (Don Chaffey, 1959), and in southern France, like *Seven Thunders* (Hugo Fregonese, 1958)

2 He told *Kinematograph Weekly* (6 November 1958) that child actors responded to this approach: 'If in my own mind I reach the stage where I feel I should be coaxing them with sweets, then I fight down the impulse very quickly.'

3 Hayley also remembers doing a screen test with Buchholz and 'falling instantly in love with Horst' (McFarlane 1997: 409). But this may have been the informal meeting, which Lee Thompson arranged.

4 Cross was chief cinematographer on the documentary series *This Modern Age*. His feature-film work included *Song of Freedom* (J. Elder Wills, 1936), *First of the Few* (Leslie Howard, 1942), *Tawny Pipit* (Bernard Miles, 1944), *Chance of a Lifetime* (Bernard Miles, 1950) and *Private's Progress* (John Boulting, 1956).

5 There are echoes here of the less good-natured goading which railwayman Heal (Michael Laurence) receives before murdering his lover in *For Them that Trespass*.

6 In an interview in *Picturegoer* (10 January 1959) Shirley Bassey claims that she was promised a role (presumably either Anya or Christine) in the film. 'Who better to play the part than me?' she complained. 'Why, I was born there.' She attributed the loss of the role to her agent demanding too high fees.

7 Not all the black residents of Tiger Bay agreed that the film's intentions were progressive. One was quoted in the *Spectator* (31 October 1958): 'When people see the story of this film they are going to think that Bute Road and Loudoun Square, what they call Tiger Bay, is where a man can pick up a girl easily. They'll think all coloured people have loose morals. Think we play dice down here all day.' His views were echoed by Cardiff City Council, which complained that the area was being 'grossly misrepresented ... merely for the depraved tastes of people who like sensationalism in pictures' (*Manchester Guardian*, 4 March 1959). Local MP L. J. Callaghan, acting on the Council's behalf, unsuccessfully attempted to persuade Rank to change *Tiger Bay*'s title (*Sunday Times*, 21 December 1958).

8 In isolation, the sequence might be interpreted as a xenophobic warning about the un-British intemperance of foreigners, but little in the rest of the film supports this reading.

9 There is a reminder here of Lance Comfort's cruelly neglected *Bang! You're Dead* (1954: USA: *Game of Danger*) which also depicts a child with a gun making faltering steps into the adult world in what Brian McFarlane (1999: 137) describes as a 'frightening conflation of play and reality'. A child with a loaded gun is also featured in *A Cry From the Streets* (Lewis Gilbert), another film released in 1959. This recurrent motif perhaps indexes both concern about the corruption of innocence and the fear of the threat posed by the rising generation.

10 *Hunted* had also been photographed by Eric Cross.

11 Having surrendered her symbol of phallic power, the pistol, Gillie immediately replaces it with a white altar candle, an object whose sexual symbolism is overlaid with spiritual authority.

12 The un-British exuberance of these Caribbean street celebrations supplies an appropriate endorsement of the unconventional nature of Korchinsky and Gillie's relationship.

13 If not quite a place of corruption, the docks are tainted by the morally corrosive effects of the cash economy. The first sequence in the film is the counting out of money on a docked ship, and Korchinsky offers a bribe to facilitate his selection as a crew member.

14 The scenes aboard the *Oswestrey Grange* (renamed *Paloma* in the film) were

shot in worsening weather at the beginning of October 1958. High seas forced actors and crew to disembark by rope ladder and a tragedy was narrowly averted when John Mills' wife Mary lost consciousness on the descent to the launch and had to be rescued (*News of the World*, 5 October 1958).

15 For J. Lee Thompson, Gillie's dilemma constituted the ethical core of the film. As he told Bill Edwards of *Kinematograph Weekly* (6 November 1958), 'The little girl is confronted with the problem "How far can loyalty go? Does personal loyalty excuse telling lies?" We have answered that in certain circumstances it is permissible ... but the child is punished for the action she takes by her own conscience, and by physical danger.' The earlier characterisation of Gillie as an inveterate liar, however, undermines the suitability here of the notion of a moral dilemma, suggesting that untruthfulness is unlikely to worry her conscience.

16 Most critics in the popular papers found Lee Thompson's direction very much to their taste. For example: 'The wise and lively eye of director, J. Lee Thompson makes it a thriller out of the ordinary' (Derek Adams, *Star*, 26 March 1959); and 'Admirably directed' (Jympson Harman, *Evening News*, 26 March 1959).

17 These concerns would be replayed in much of Lee Thompson's later cinema, particularly in *Cape Fear* and the series of revenge movies he made with Charles Bronson.

18 The typical Lee Thompson cinematography did not endear itself to the *Monthly Film Bulletin* (December 1960): 'In an effort to keep the ramshackle structure intact, J. Lee Thompson here reverts to his former fragmented, agitated camera style. Mannered panning shots and crafty cutting abound, leading to a kind of stylistic St Vitus dance. The newsreel shots of crashing rockets are quite impressive.'

19 The general attitude to von Braun was summed up by Dee Wells' comment in the *Sunday Express* (27 November 1960): 'All I can say is he can't get in that rocket and buzz off soon enough to please me.'

20 Quigly was particularly disturbed by the way in which the visualisation of the narrative inevitably enlisted the audience on the side of von Braun's V-2 project: 'after innumerable failures, we are bound – physically, visually bound – to feel a sort of elation when his first successful rocket goes whirling off across the screen (at London, of course)' (*Spectator*, 2 December 1960).

The Guns of Navarone (1961)

> 'I try to get a "peace message" into the film. Maybe somebody will tap me on the shoulder and say "You're fooling yourself, it's just a big spectacle with 800 horses", but for me it isn't.' (J. Lee Thompson on making *Taras Bulba*, 1963, *Films and Filming*, April 1963)

> 'I wanted to take what was essentially a typical, action-packed wartime melodrama and give it some pretentious overtones.' (Alexander Mackendrick, the original director of *The Guns of Navarone*, quoted in Webster 1991: 104)

Although Carl Foreman is rightly considered the driving force behind *The Guns of Navarone*, he inititally required some convincing that Alistair MacLean's tale of a desperate mission to destroy German cannon on a Greek island was filmable. Foreman, a Hollywood exile since the McCarthy witch-hunts, was encouraged by Mike Frankovich, the head of Columbia Pictures, to think about the book's adaptation. Frankovich thought it an ideal project for the screenwriter of *Bridge on the River Kwai* (even if his work had been rejected by director David Lean)[1] and *The Key* (Carol Reed, 1958). The pressure from Frankovich was sufficient to overcome Foreman's fears about being typecast as a writer of war stories and his desire to work on a more intimate, social realist film, and to persuade him to commit himself wholeheartedly to a project which would be the most ambitious in British screen history (Webster 1991: 102). It would take over three years and more than $5 million to bring *The Guns of Navarone* to the screen.

Speculation about the casting of the film began in the autumn of 1958, when William Holden, Marlon Brando, Alec Guinness, Cary Grant and Jack Hawkins were being touted as its stars (*Daily Express*, 30 September 1958). Four months later the *Daily Herald* (30 January 1959) revealed that only one actor had actually signed on for the film – Trevor Howard. This was immediately denied by Foreman[2] who told the press that he had sent letters to every top agent in London, New York and Hollywood, asking them to 'stop pestering' him until he was ready to cast. Uncertainty continued for another year. Just days before filming began in February 1960 it was expected that Britain's most bankable star, Kenneth More, would have a leading role as Sergeant Miller, the explosives expert in the Special Forces sabotage team. More regarded it as his 'big chance' to become a truly international star, and his place was booked on a plane to Greece. Unfortunately he managed drunkenly to insult Rank's chairman John Davis at a dinner just before he departed. A vindictive Davis immediately withdrew permission for More to work, giving as his reason a violation of the Film Producers' Code by Danny Angel, an independent producer with whom More also had a contract (More 1978: 182–3).[3] Luckily, Foreman was able to replace More with one of his initial choices for the role, David Niven, although many critics would regard his casting as a mistake when the film was eventually previewed.

Niven was not the only person to be recruited to the project at the eleventh hour. A couple of weeks before filming began, J. Lee Thompson had no idea he would be in the director's chair. Columbia's first choice had been Alexander Mackendrick who had attended the same Glasgow school as Alistair MacLean. Mackendrick had been closely involved in the planning of the film, scouting Greek locations with production designer Geoff Drake, and trying to add depth to Foreman's 'action' script with classical allusions (Webster 1991: 104). As the first day of shooting approached, however, it became increasingly clear that the artistic differences between Foreman and Mackendrick were irreconcilable and the director was summarily paid off. Lee Thompson's name was put forward by Gregory Peck who, together with Anthony Quinn and Anthony Quayle, had secured a leading role in the film. Peck had been impressed by *North West Frontier*. Carl Foreman had the film flown out to Rhodes where he was waiting to begin work on the picture and agreed to hiring its director. For Lee Thompson it was a daunting prospect:

'I had one week to prepare the film. Geoffrey Drake was a great help to me, but, you know, Carl Foreman was a very complex, interesting and strange fellow. He did not really want you to be successful. To begin with, he wanted to direct it himself, and when it was decided to get rid of Mackendrick he thought it would allow him to do that, but they eventually chose me, I arrived on location to find a very embittered Carl Foreman. He didn't want me really, he wanted himself, and that's very understandable. He'd been writing it, and then he'd got rid of Mackendrick who I would think was not his first choice anyway. So now he was faced with having to get another director when he very naturally wanted to direct it himself ... Remember he used to have the company with Stanley Kramer, and Kramer, of course, went on to become a number one director and now Carl was very anxious to follow in Kramer's footsteps ... he was hoping he would step in and have his life's dream.'[4]

When Lee Thompson arrived in Greece he was confronted not only by a disgruntled producer but by an array of actors who had yet to establish a pecking order. As the new boy in this particular constellation, David Niven was the most insecure about his position. Describing his first day on the set, Lee Thompson told Sheridan Morley (1986: 290):

'David was very cheery but a little anxious that, with all those other stars around, he was just going to be left standing about a lot. He felt that his character wasn't as well developed as some of the others, and he wanted to be convinced that I'd look after him and try and bring out the comedy in the role, which he knew he was good at. He felt, maybe rightly, that all the characters had been written as supermen without much depth. But you have to remember also that he'd just won an Oscar, and so there was a certain amount of rivalry on the set between him and Peck and Quinn, all eyeing each other warily and wondering which of them was going to come out ahead.'

One way in which this friendly rivalry was expressed was in attempts to make alterations to the script, but Lee Thompson was determined to establish his control of the situation: 'I had carefully worked out every shot in my own mind and I knew that, on this occasion, I couldn't be flexible. I had to be firm and simply say, "No, let's do it my way"' (Webster 1991: 106). His uncompromising approach won the respect of the cast and most of the rivalry they felt towards each other was channelled into the games of chess which Anthony Quinn had introduced on the set. No doubt the presence of the actors' families on location also helped to defuse tension.[5]

For J. Lee Thompson, the most difficult person to handle on the set continued to be Carl Foreman, who took every opportunity to exert a directorial influence on proceedings. The result was a relationship which combined both admiration and annoyance:

> 'I was very fond of Carl, although we had bitter rows. I was fascinated with him, and he was such a good writer, but a very lazy writer. He didn't want to discuss scenes too deeply. That was because he wanted to discuss them deeply on the set in front of actors (*laughs*). I mean, overnight I'd say, "What do you mean by this, Carl? What are you getting at in this scene?" And he'd give me some mumbo jumbo, and then when I was coming to shoot the scene the next morning he'd sit with the actors and me and say exactly what he had in mind which he could have told me the night before, but he wanted to reserve it for the actors. A very complex person, and very desirous of directing himself.'

The production benefited from unprecedented co-operation on the part of the Greek State. Anxious to buff-up a reputation it felt might have been tarnished by the troubles in Cyprus over the previous few years, and keen to develop its tourist industry, the Greek Government put much of its army, navy and airforce at the disposal of Carl Foreman, including six navy destroyers, several air-sea rescue boats, launches, scout planes, helicopters, tanks, armoured cars, jeeps, army trucks, howitzers, mortars and machine guns. In addition, it supplied 2,000 extras from the ranks of the Greek military forces and the National Gendarmerie. The Ministry of Commerce helped by waiving all regulations on work permits and customs duties, and the Department of Archaeology even arranged for scaffolding around the Parthenon in Athens to be removed (for the first time in living memory) so that filming might take place. Most extraordinary of all, an agreement was reached with the Foreign Ministers of Italy and Turkey to allow military equipment and personnel onto Rhodes, one of a group of islands which had been formally demilitarised under a treaty signed at the end of the Second World War.[6]

The production unit completely took over Rhodes' newest hotel, The Miramar, for several months, leaving each morning at dawn in a convoy of twenty-one buses, trucks and cars, but often being forced to complete the journey to inaccessible cliffs by foot or donkey ride. The old city of Rhodes doubled for Navarone, while a German wartime fuel depot with a vast chamber excavated in a cliffside was used as the entrance to the gun cave. In spite of an accident which blew a huge hole in one of the Royal Hellenic Navy's patrol boats, Carl Foreman was ceremoniously made an honorary citizen of the island and the set was visited by the Greek Prime Minister and by the royal family who later hosted a party for the film unit aboard a navy destroyer. The potential for megalomania in all this was recognised by Foreman who told Leslie Mallory, one of the corps of journalists haunting the location:

'There are times when this thing I've started overwhelms me. Here I am hobnobbing with Ministers and Archbishops with whole flotillas of destroyers cavorting up and down at my say-so. So that I don't get too cosy, I remind myself that with this bunch of actors I'm dealing with wild beasts.'[7] (*News Chronicle*, 14 April 1960)

While cast and crew toiled on location for five months, losing three weeks to the island's worst weather in thirty years, Shepperton Studios were being prepared for their return. The cave housing the two massive guns was constructed at a record cost of £100,000 and Geoff Drake also designed the largest marine set ever built in a European studio so that the wreck of *Maria*, the saboteur's boat, could be filmed under controlled conditions. 'Control' over the high-pressure water jets and the simulated waves in the 250,000-gallon tank, however, did not prevent injuries to all of *Guns* stars when the sequence was filmed.[8] Bizarrely, the most serious turned out to be David Niven's split lip, which became infected and forced his hospitalisation with general septicaemia. Not only was Niven close to death, but the whole production was jeopardised because the actor was essential to the shooting of the key scene in the gun cave. Foreman and Lee Thompson had emergency meetings with studio executives and representatives of the banks and insurance companies who were covering the picture. In his autobiography *The Moon's a Balloon,* Niven reported what he was told had been the comment of one of the Columbia executives ('the Big Brass'): 'We all love him – but wadda we do if the sonofabitch dies?' (Niven 1972: 300). Fortunately, the 'sonofabitch' returned to the set (against doctor's orders) and completed the crucial scenes before relapsing for the next seven weeks.

Niven's was not the only collapse suffered by the production. A few months before, the gun cave itself had come crashing down, adding another £20,000 to an over-budget already swollen by huge delays in the shooting schedule. Lee Thompson remembers what might have been a fatal catastrophe, had the set builders been working overtime that evening as usual:

> 'Oh yes, that was dreadful. It was built outside on the lot at Shepperton and it had been raining, and I was actually there when it happened. There was suddenly this awful sound and I looked across the field and this whole set was collapsing. And that took quite a long time to repair. [The film] was running behind schedule because there were all sorts of other shots we had to do on the back lot, and the weather was getting worse and worse at this time. It was well over budget, I know that, but Carl wanted the best, so we just stuck at it until we got it. He was not a man who would sacrifice what he thought was essential to a film by cutting down the length of time.'

Carl Foreman had hoped to get *The Guns of Navarone* onto cinema screens by Christmas 1960, but shooting had taken nine months and was completed only in November at a cost of £2.5 million. It may have almost broken the bank at Columbia but it had certainly broken the mould of British film making. It proved that British production with American backing could offer more than cosy comedies and modest thrillers. *Guns* opened the door to lavish epics like *Lawrence of Arabia* (David Lean, 1962) and *Cleopatra* (Joseph L. Mankiewicz, 1963), and helped to give US studios the confidence to invest in British productions over the following seven or eight years. When David Niven confides in Gregory Peck at the end of the film, 'To tell you the truth, I didn't think we could do it', and Peck replies, 'Neither did I', they were speaking the thoughts of their producer and director. So what of the film itself?

Carl Foreman's adaptation of Alistair MacLean's novel turns a relatively straightforward tale of daring-do into what Raymond Durgnat (1970: 88) termed 'an ironic epic of heroism'. The two texts share a narrative structure, plot details and a celebration of the human capacity for dogged perseverance in the face of apparently impossible odds. But beyond these common characteristics there are substantial divergences, particularly in characterisation and meaning construction.

On a cursory inspection, MacLean's book might be classified as a typical *Boys' Own* adventure story of the 'commandoes-give-the-Bosch-a-bloody-nose' variety that so proliferated in the 1950s. Look more closely and one finds a work of greater subtlety, with a distaste for violence and a compassion for the enemy soldier which casts him as a victim almost as often as an aggressor. Although it trades unashamedly in the excitement of combat, and while it leaves us in no doubt about whose side we should be on, it tries hard not to celebrate warfare or to engage in jingoism. The book certainly offers us heroes, but they are not, by and large, English heroes. The principal protagonists are a New Zealander, a Scot, a Greek and an Irish American, along with a young Englishman who is a disabled (if courageous) passenger for most of the mission; but they are not heroes by virtue of their nationality. It is their strength of character that makes them heroic, and their courage is not of the reckless, dare-devil, variety but necessitates a resolute overcoming of fear. They are the best of men in the worst of situations, but, in the great scheme of things, they are only pawns in a profligate game of life and death played by remote military commanders. Frequently, they express a greater respect for, and empathy with, the German pawns than their own High Command.[9]

MacLean, however, is not a writer primarily interested in characterisation. His gift is to keep the reader turning the page, and the kind of suspense he deals in leaves little time for developing the personalities of his protagonists or examining their weaknesses. They exist in a condition of hyper-performance – super-fit, keenly intelligent, mega-talented and endlessly supportive of other team members. Foreman could readily see that, from a dramatic point of view, he needed to introduce some tension and conflict within the saboteur group, and to highlight temperamental differences between its members. His principal change was to reverse the relationship between the leader of the saboteurs, the New Zealand mountaineer Captain Keith Mallory (Gregory Peck), and the Greek 'fighting machine', Andrea (Anthony Quinn). In MacLean's text, Andrea, in spite of his senior rank in the Greek Army, is Mallory's faithful servant, his 'alter ego, his Doppelganger' (MacLean 1957: 25). He calls Mallory 'my Keith' or 'my Captain' suggesting an attitude which verges on worship. The relationship resembles that of Pugh to Anson in *Ice Cold*, but Foreman turns Andrea into a man 'who hated only two things in life – Germans and Keith Mallory' (souvenir brochure). In the film Andrea holds Mallory responsible for the earlier death of his wife and children, killed by Germans to whom Mallory had shown compassion. 'I still had some romantic notions, in those days, of fighting a civilized war', Mallory confesses cynically, 'me and my stupid Anglo-Saxon decency.' Foreman also makes significant changes to the character of the explosives expert, Corporal Dusty Miller (Niven). In the book he is a hard-boiled Irish American with 'no illusions left' (MacLean 1957: 24). In the film, he is re-drawn as a professor of chemistry, a reluctant soldier with a sardonic attitude which allows him to cope with his complete distaste for war. He is transformed from MacLean's 'tough' cookie' who addresses Mallory as 'boss' into an English gentleman who prefers 'old bean' to 'boss' and who acts as the moral conscience of the team. Just as with Andrea, the supportive attitude he shows to Mallory in the book is changed to one of hostility. Little wonder, then, that in the film's trailer Gregory Peck's voice announced: 'Some of us hate each other even more than we do the enemy.'[10]

Much of Miller's antipathy to Mallory is a product of Miller's attachment to a new character introduced by Foreman. Major Ron Franklin (Anthony Quayle) does not appear in MacLean's text, but in the film, he commands the expedition until he sustains a broken leg during the cliff climb. Thus, he carries the narrative function of the book's Andrew Stevens, the boyish navigator who has to be stretchered around the island of Navarone. Franklin is a gung-ho enthusiast for combat – 'a man who still has to prove himself a hero' – who believes that the ends justify the means. But, in spite of this, he has earned the unswerving loyalty of the more feminine-coded Miller, who is willing to shoot Mallory if he acts on Andrea's suggestion that the injured Franklin be dispensed with for the good of the mission. Miller and Franklin have 'been together a long time' and there are discernible undertones of homosexual love in Miller's devotion to the senior officer he addresses as 'Lucky'. When he is reluctantly forced to leave the disabled major to the attentions of the enemy, he lights a cigarette and puts it between Franklin's lips, telling him: 'I shall miss you ... When this is over we'll meet at Simpson's. You can buy me lunch – roast beef, Yorkshire pudding, a nice little red wine ...'.

Foreman's internally combustible team of saboteurs is completed by two 'born killers', Pappadimos (James Darren), the baby-faced native of Navarone who has received 'the wrong kind of education' in America and revels in killing; and Brown (Stanley Baker), 'the Butcher of Barcelona', a specialist with the knife who has been killing Germans since the Spanish Civil War, but who is now sick of the slaughter.[11] Clearly, within the restrictions of an action movie, there is a genuine attempt to give substance to the trailer's assertion that 'is this a story of human beings, each with his own intense personal fears, his deep personal conflicts ...'. The homogenous emotional terrain of MacLean's book is given further variety by changing the gender of the two Greek resistance fighters who give aid to Mallory's team. However, few concessions are made to gender stereotyping in introducing women into MacLean's masculinist scenario.[12] Maria (Irene Pappas), the sister of Pappadimos, is a tough and capable guerrilla warrior, a passion-ate partisan who is not afraid to take the lead sexually.[13] She describes her compatriot Anna (Gia Scala) as 'a good fighter, as good as any of you', adding that, 'she kills without mercy'. Apparently struck dumb by the traumas she has suffered at the hands of the Nazis, her silent quest for revenge in fact turns out to be a charade to cover her activities as a German agent.

Foreman's screenplay, then, attempts to develop psychological complexity and dramatic tension in its reconstruction of Mac-Lean's band of saboteurs. Similarly, it seeks to widen and intensify the discursive elements of MacLean's text, sharpening its moral issues and underlining its allusions to classical mythology. The press statement Foreman issued at the time of the film's release makes it clear that he saw the mission on Navarone as an heroic quest with a symbolic goal:

> It seems to me more than literary coincidence that Alistair Maclean's novel is set on the same stage as the *Odyssey* and the *Iliad* and the legends of Jason and the Argonauts and Theseus and the Minotaur, for, like so many of these epic tales of adventure born on the blue waters of the Aegean, the story tells of men who dare even the Gods as they struggle towards their goal. (Souvenir brochure)

Consequently, *Guns'* prologue is set on the Acropolis where this story's connection to classical myth is emphasised with a voice-over which refers to 'the legend of Navarone'.

Not only does the setting carry heavy symbolic weight, but the object of the quest – to locate and spike the mighty guns – has barely concealed allegorical power. Even in MacLean's largely prosaic text, the image of the guns evokes the myths of ancient Greece. First there is the Minotaur, the dark presence in the cave 'crouched massively above like some nightmare monsters from an ancient and other world, the evil, the sinister silhouette of the two great guns of Navarone' (MacLean 1957: 235). And then, in the obvious phallic symbolism of the huge gun, there is the impli-cation of Oedipus's challenge to the phallic power of his Father: 'twelve-inch bore if an inch, that gun was the biggest thing he had ever seen. Big? Heavens above, it was gigantic!' (236).

The film further mines this rich symbolic vein through the associations of phallic power not only with the rule of the father –

in the sense of the Führer and his military machine – but with its ultimate expression war itself. The act of emasculation – the disabling of the guns – is carried out not so much in the strategic pursuit of military victory but as an act of humanitarianism which will allow the evacuation of British forces on a neighbouring island. Although the 2,000 servicemen trapped on Kheros will clearly be useful in the future prosecution of the war, their function in the film is primarily symbolic, to stand in opposition to the guns as representatives of life. Their passive condition –waiting for rescue – contrasts diametrically with the active threat of aggression posed by the guns. Anti-war sentiments are thus strongly encoded into the film: the culture of death, represented metonymically by the guns, must be emasculated so that the culture of life may flourish. Those warriors who remain most closely in touch with vitality survive the mission while those who have been largely absorbed by the culture of war and for whom the promotion of violence has become an end in itself (Pappadimos, Brown, Anna) perish with the destruction of the guns.[14]

That *The Guns of Navarone* was intended by its makers to be an anti-war film was clearly stated by Carl Foreman in his preface to the film's souvenir brochure: 'The effort required for the production of this film will be more than justified if, in addition to providing entertainment on its own level, it will cause people to wonder when such nobility of purpose, such dedicated courage, will cease to be wasted on the senselessness of war.'[15] His sentiments were perfectly in line with those of J. Lee Thompson who, not long after *Guns'* release, wrote in *Films and Filming* (April 1963): 'I am a pacifist. If there was another war, I don't think I would go.' The ethics of war and the moral dilemmas encountered in combat, supply a sub-text to *Guns* whenever a lull in the action provides space for its development. Mallory offers the key statement when he tells Franklin: 'The only way to win a war is to be just as nasty as the enemy. One thing that worries me is that I'm going to wake up one morning and find that I'm even nastier.' This notion of war as a powerful moral corrupter sets up a sub-textual problem which parallels the behavioural problem posed by the diegesis of the narrative. The issue is not only 'will they be able to destroy the guns?', but 'will they be able to do so without fatally compromising the moral code which grants them their heroic status?' Thus, there are two concomitant struggles going on in the film. One is behavioural, the other ethical. The former may be of primary interest to most of the audience, but the latter is of greater concern to the producer and director.

While the source of moral corruption may be the destructive drive energised by Nazi ideology, its victims are certainly not confined to one side in the military conflict. *Guns* draws distinctions between evil ideologues like the SS officer Sessler (George Mikell), who tortures without compunction, and German men of honour like Oberleutnant Muesel (Walter Gotell) who refuses to 'make war on wounded soldiers'. The Allied side, too, has its butchers like Pappadimos and Brown, as well as its gallant intellectuals like Miller and its tarnished knights like Mallory (a name with direct associations to chivalric myth). War is the great moral leveller, 'using up and wasting the good and valuable'.[16] Two narrative events in particular bring these subtextual concerns to the surface, centering the ethical problems of war on the values of expediency, loyalty and responsibility.

First, there is Mallory's decision to use the injured Major Roy Franklin for disinformation purposes by leaving him, convinced of the truth of false information, to be interrogated by the enemy. Mallory sees this as the least damaging solution to the severe moral dilemma posed by the deteriorating health of Franklin. Although it has involved lying to his superior officer and exposing him to possible torture, he regards it as the only viable solution if he is 'to get the job done.' He is challenged, however, by Miller who refuses to accept that the expediency demanded by war must necessarily over-ride the primacy of friendship and humanity. For Miller, one's first duty is to one's own, to those who are closest emotionally and physically:

> MILLER There have been a thousand wars and there'll be a thousand more until we all kill each other off completely. I don't care about the war anymore. I care about Roy.
>
> MALLORY And if Turkey comes into the war on the wrong side?
>
> MILLER So what. Let the whole bloody world come in and blow

    itself to pieces. That's what it deserves.

MALLORY And what about the 2,000 men on Kheros?

MILLER I don't know the men on Kheros, but I know the men on Navarone.

Shaken by the intensity of Miller's reaction, Mallory seeks confirmation that his treatment of Franklin was 'civilised' from Anna, the resistance fighter. Unable to speak, she signifies her support by tearfully kissing him.[17] At the time it seems to express the preferred ethics of the film's makers, but its legitimacy is thrown into doubt by the unmasking of Anna as a traitor whose morality has been corrupted by her fear of physical pain. Ultimately, the success of the mission, the destruction of the death guns and the rescue of the men on Kheros, seems to justify Mallory's tactics, but Foreman's script refuses to provide total resolution. This is hardly surprising, because the issues of loyalty to friends and fortitude under interrogation loomed large in his biography as a victim of the MacCarthy witch-hunts in Hollywood.

The treachery and cowardice of Anna also provide the occasion for the film's discourse on responsibility. After he strips Anna's back to reveal no trace of the whipping scars she was supposed to have received from her Nazi captors, Miller sardonically points out that, if the mission is to be accomplished, she will have to be executed. Mallory rounds on him, contemptuous of the vengeful pleasure he is taking in challenging his superior officer to shoot a woman in cold blood: 'You really want your pound of flesh, don't you?' The exchange that follows reveals the way in which war both robs the individual of volition and turns human responsibility into the duty associated with rank:

MILLER I'm not anxious to kill her. I'm not anxious to kill anyone. You see, I'm not a born soldier. I got trapped. You may find me facetious from time to time, but if I didn't make some rather bad jokes every now and then, I'd go out of my mind. No, I prefer to leave the killing to someone like you [Mallory], an officer, a gentleman and a leader of men. A hero.

MALLORY You think that I enjoy this, any of it? You're out of your mind. I never wanted it, I was trapped into it, just like you, just like anybody else in a uniform.

MILLER Of course you wanted it. You're an officer, aren't you? I never let them make me an officer. I didn't want the responsibility for anything.

MALLORY Then you had a free ride. All this time. Someone's got to take the responsibility if the job's going to get done. Do you think that's easy?

MILLER I didn't know. You begin to wonder who really is responsible when it comes to the dirty work, who really is guilty: the man who gives the order or the one who has to do it with his bare hands?[18]

Mallory's response to his taunting is to acknowledge the duty of his rank and accept the responsibility of executing Anna himself. He levels his revolver at her but the need to pull the trigger is alleviated when she is shot by her compatriot, Maria, who assumes a personal responsibility unmediated by military discipline. It is not difficult to read this liquidation of a character whose mute masquerade conceals a garrulous informer as Foreman's symbolic act of revenge on the moral cowards who covertly supplied names to the House UnAmerican Activities Committee. When he told Leslie Mallory (*News Chronicle*, 14 April 1960) that 'I want to show how people become informers and betray their own kind, and how they feel about it afterwards towards themselves and those they have betrayed', he clearly had in mind traitors who were closer to him than the wretched Anna.

Ethical discourses and moral dilemmas may proliferate in *The Guns of Navarone* – as they do in most of the films made by Lee Thompson and by Foreman – but their consideration is overwhelmed by the irresistible narrative drive of the movie. This is what Raymond Durgnat (1970: 88) meant when he argued that 'an ironic epic of heroism was turned back into an ordinary epic by J. Lee Thompson's emphasis on energy'. This emphasis on energy was already present in the film's literary source, and there is no evidence that Foreman was less than fully aware of its importance. The reason he had 'enjoyed the book' was that 'MacLean has the story-teller's gift for keeping his audience constantly enthralled by maintaining the pace and drive of his tale'. As far as its potential for filming was concerned, 'this was one big thing in the book's favour. It moved.'[19] Foreman's intention was not to lose this movement, but to supplement it with a discursive content which would make the film more intellectually stimulating. Lee Thompson was sympathetic to this aim, and although he thinks that by 'today's standards' the film would be thought 'much too talky' he considers he got the balance about right for the period in which it was made: 'I thought the scenes had something to say politically, and I thought they played in a good way.'[20]

As usual, Lee Thompson excels in the creation of suspense – from the beautifully-paced sequence aboard the *Maria* in which Mallory's team obliterate the crew of a German patrol boat that has intercepted their vessel to the white-knuckle moments inside the gun cave as the garrison steadily dismantles the lock on the giant gates – the tension remains bow-string taut. Although the style and scale of such stretched-screen thrills would become commonplace in the James Bond films and the caper movies of the following two decades, audiences in 1961 had seen nothing quite like it. Nor had they experienced the sheer immediacy of the film's celebrated shipwreck scene in which the sound was cranked up to seat-shaking levels as mountainous waves menaced the audience from the screen. In sequences like these, Lee Thompson introduced audiences to what cinema would become in the age of the multiplex. He was aided by some immaculate cinemascope photography from Oswald Morris, who had learnt how to shoot seas when he worked with Huston on *Moby Dick* (1956), and a rousing score by Dimitri Tiomkin which may have flirted with nationalistic cliché at times, but provided a memorable theme.

It is fair to say that none among the distinguished cast produced the acting performance of his or her life. The ensemble nature of the piece meant that even some of the leading parts (especially those played by James Darren, Gia Scala and Stanley Baker) had few lines, and even the more developed roles offered only limited opportunities for the sort of stagecraft with which British screen actors were familiar. Most commentators agreed that Niven, the quintessential officer, was miscast as a corporal, and that Anthony Quinn stole the acting honours, but the performances are impressive chiefly in their physicality rather than in their delivery of dialogue. Audiences, in any case, were given little time to dwell on the niceties of acting technique as they were swept from one perilous situation to the next. Thus it was mainly Lee Thompson's ability to visualise MacLean's thrill-a-minute literary style that caught the attention of audiences and reviewers. As the critic of *The Times* (27 April 1961) put it: 'The main credit for the success of *The Guns of Navarone* must go to Mr Lee Thompson who has handled his many scenes of violent-action magnificently. He has been given too much material to work upon and has found some of it indigestible, but his flair for action never deserts him.'

'Action' was what critics, and probably audiences too, wanted from the long-awaited movie. Where they found action and excitement, as they did in *Guns'* shipwreck scene, they were prepared to offer the highest praise, but they were often harsh on any deviations from their template of the British adventure film. For *The Times*, sequences like the shipwreck were 'tremendous and, at moments, even overwhelming' and were evidence that 'not for a long time has the screen been so charged with terrifying excitement, nor has suspense been so continuously sustained'. But Foreman's attempt to deepen characterisation and develop a pacifist philosophy were dismissed as inappropriate to the genre. The lesson to be learnt, *The Times* believed, was that 'a well-told and exciting story does not require too many characters, nor does it need psychological undertones' (27 April 1961).

Other critics also strongly resisted the idea of introducing any intellectualising into what Leonard Mosley (*Daily Express*, 27 April 1961) called 'a phoney-baloney war adventure, magnificently done' and 'a film for the masses'. The *Guardian* (29 April 1961) thought the film 'tremendous stuff – an almost uninterrupted purple passage of some two and a half hours', recognising Lee Thompson's 'high achievement' in maintaining tension and excitement, but criticising the plot as preposterous, some of the characters as absurd, and the philosophy as 'dreadful tosh'. David Robinson in the *Financial Times* (27 April 1961) found the film 'beautifully designed and majestically photographed' but felt that Lee Thompson, although 'a crack commercial director, was 'inclined to lean exceptionally on his script'. Again, as far as he was concerned, Foreman was guilty of wanting 'to lay upon the story a burden of meaning that it will not exactly bear'.

These reviewers had rightly identified a source of tension in the film. To develop philosophical discourses in a film that depends for its appeal on fast-moving action is difficult enough; but to promote convincingly a pacifist theme in a stirring tale of heroism in which intrepid men achieve their goals against almost incredible odds makes destroying the guns look easy by comparison. What is interesting about the reviews is that they gave no credit to Foreman for his gallant attempt. For 'high-brow' and 'low-brow' critics alike, philosophy was properly the preserve of the art film. Attempts to turn the entertainment of the masses into a cinema of ideas only served to scramble the categories which ordered critical practice. For the most part, the 'high-brow' critics felt obliged to confront this issue.[21] The reviewers in the popular press simply ignored the talk and enthused about the action:

[a] great picture in the class of *Bridge on the River Kwai* ... a picture of unexampled grandeur and excitement. (Ernest Betts, *The People*, 30 April 1961)

Make no mistake this is a really impressive piece of cinema full of great moments and superb technique. It bursts with suspense and excitement. (Felix Barker, *Evening News*, 27 April 1961)

[h]ere, for once, is a film which majestically fulfils, and even surpasses, the blaring promise of its own publicity. (Paul Dehn, *Daily Herald*, 27 April 1961)

The great moments of action are screen-fare at its best, but infinitely deeper is the film's probing into the hearts and minds of the men engaged in this fantastic enterprise. This is indeed a movie of magnificence. (Peter Burnup, *News of the World*, 30 April 1961)

Surprisingly, the credit for the film's accomplishments went not to the producer, who had nursed the project for three years, but to the director who was called in at the eleventh hour. Lee Thompson, according to Harold Conway (*Sunday Dispatch*, 30 April 1961), had done 'a wonderful job', and Paul Dehn (*Daily Herald*, 27 April

1961) declared him 'the film's true hero' because he 'here achieves total mastery of his craft'. Some reviewers even thought this achievement was in spite of Foreman's script: 'I have nothing but admiration for the director J. Lee Thompson, whose handling of a script full of absurdity and brash melodrama is marvellous. He has camouflaged the nonsense in thrills, deployed his huge forces with a breath-taking impertinence, made a mountain of a film out of a molehill bit of juvenile story telling' (Derek Monsey, *Sunday Express*, 30 April 1961). Only Peter Lewis of the *Daily Mail* failed to be persuaded by the compelling rhetoric of Lee Thompson's action sequences, finding the film altogether too far-fetched to enjoy. What Lewis wanted in a war film was realism rather than myth making, and this remained a pertinent issue even for some of the film's supporters.[22] Unsurprisingly, Lee Thompson's arch opponent, Derek Hill, was not to be numbered among those supporters. His review in *Tribune* (12 May 1961) was vitriolic even by the standards of his previous notices, deploring the 'conspiracy' among his fellow-critics to praise 'the monstrous idiocies' of *Guns* and pouring scorn on the 'grotesquely incompetent' editing, Lee Thompson's infantile handling of his subject and cast, and the script's 'miserable medley of schoolboy heroics'. He concluded by suggesting that the only justification for *The Guns of Navarone* would be 'to fire Foreman from one and Lee Thompson from the other'. Cinemagoers took as much notice of Mr Hill as they usually did and quickly made *The Guns of Navarone* the highest-grossing British film yet produced. Honoured with a premiere at the Odeon, Leicester Square (27 April 1961), in the presence of Queen Elizabeth and Prince Philip,[23] the film was carefully offered to selected cinemas and took nearly a year to go on general release. Before the end of August 1961 it had taken nearly $1.5 million in Britain playing in only forty-five cinemas and had broken the box office record for British films in America. Columbia's Michael Frankovich was so impressed with its performance that he announced to the world's press that 'Britain will soon become the film-making centre of the world' (*Daily Express*, 22 August 1961).

Notes

1 Lean claimed that he rejected two drafts by Foreman and that the final adaptation of Pierre Boulle's novel was done by himself and Michael Wilson (Silverman 1989: 118–19).

2 As a favour to Foreman, Trevor Howard had apparently played opposite Annette Stroyberg in a screen test for the film. The screen test had found its way on to television.

3 The Film Producers' Code was an attempt to stop television eroding the audience for films. Members agreed to offer their back catalogues to a film industry consortium before selling them to TV.

4 This was confirmed by Carl Foreman himself when he told John Francis Lane of *Films and Filming* (August 1960): 'I'd like to direct. If I hadn't got involved with political troubles in America, I'd be a director by now. You know, I was going to direct *High Noon* myself?'

5 Of the star sextet of Niven, Peck, Quinn, Quayle, Stanley Baker and James Darren, David Niven remained the most difficult to pacify with games of chess. Lee Thompson recalls: 'David Niven was always very caustic. He always liked to mix it up, David. He would always be happy to have some feud going on the set. But I was very fond of David.' Carl Foreman confided to a journalist that Niven was 'always complaining about something', but that he experienced just as much trouble with Peck's aloofness and Quinn's volatility.

6 Considerable technical aid was also supplied by the US Coast Guard ship *Courier*, stationed at Rhodes. Much of this production information is contained in the souvenir brochure *The Guns of Navarone* (Columbia Pictures, 1961).

7 By April the scale of the production was already taking its toll on Carl Foreman. As he told Anthony Carthew of the *Daily Mail* (11 April 1960):

> When I stop to think about it, I realise how crazy it is. It's only a film, after all, and yet it's been the subject of a cabinet meeting. One thing is certain: I'll never do it again. One epic is enough in any man's lifetime. In the 18 months I have been working on this film, I have gone grey and I reckon I have aged 10 years. I came into this business as a writer but look at me now – a business man, a father figure, a politician. I have to play nursemaid to stars and spend all day juggling with their egos.

8 Peck gashed his head. Quinn hurt his back. Niven and Quayle opened old war wounds and James Darren almost drowned (*Daily Mail*, 23 September 1960). The only way to keep warm in the icy water was with copious amounts of brandy, leaving most of the cast, with the exception of Gregory Peck, 'paralytic' by the end of the day (Morley 1986: 291).

9 For example, when the young Englishman Andy Stevens breaks his leg scaling a cliff, the expedition's leader, Mallory, muses: 'Now he was a crippled liability, would be a drag on the whole party … For a High Command who pushed the counters around crippled pawns slowed up the whole game, made the board so damnably untidy. It was almost inconsiderate of

Stevens not to have killed himself ...' (MacLean 1957: 97). The page number refers to the 1959 edition from Fontana Books.

10 Interestingly, *The Times* (27 April 1961) saw this introduction of internecine conflict within the combat group as something of a betrayal of the best traditions of the British war film, regretting that 'Mr Foreman has submitted to some of the worst Hollywood influences'.

11 Pappadimos is given a psychological profile similar to that of Panayis, one of the book's Greek resistance fighters. Brown is based solidly on Casey Brown, the book's Scottish radio engineer, although there is some attempt to make the character more psychologically complex.

12 Although MacLean apparently had no objection to the introduction of women as partisans, it did draw out the chauvinism in one of the film's critics. Roger Manvell in *Films and Filming* (June 1961) thought that 'surely ... it would be male partisans this group would need, if they needed anyone to cope with the Germans'. *The Times* (27 April 1961) viewed the introduction of women (and, with them, romance) into the narrative as an example of the worst of Hollywood influences on the British war film.

13 As they sit with Mallory on the front seat of a truck (in a scene which strongly recalls *Ice Cold in Alex*), Maria first asks Andrea about his (dead) wife and then clearly indicates her own romantic and sexual availability. Less progressively, the film's souvenir brochure positions Maria as 'trapped in a job for a man'.

14 Those who are close to absorption by the death culture but who retain a commitment to the ideals of life and liberty (Franklin, Andrea) survive in a wounded or disabled condition.

15 A similar idea is expressed in the film itself when Group Captain Jensen (James Robertson Justice), the officer who briefs the saboteurs, suggests that, although in war people dig deep to discover amazing resources in themselves, it is a 'pity we can't meet the problems of peace in the same way'.

16 Group Captain Jensen describes the mission as 'a waste of six good men', adding cynically: 'I suppose that doesn't matter, considering how many have been wasted already.' Miller underlines this squandering of precious lives when he castigates Mallory for leaving Franklin to the mercy of SS torturers, telling him: 'You've used up an important human being.'

17 The location of the scene – in a monastery – caused problems for the American censor.

18 Ironically, it is Miller, albeit a very different character, who shoots the traitor in MacLean's book. Foreman's Miller, however, is quite closely identified with the producer himself, who evidently shared his character's aversion to responsibility and rank. 'There's too much responsibility in being a producer', Foreman told John Francis Lane (*Films and Filming*, August 1960), 'and I don't like being called Sir.'

19 *The Guns of Navarone* (Royal World Premiere press release, Open Road Productions, 13 April 1961).

20 In the *Monthly Film Bulletin* (January 1961), however, Penelope Huston detected a serious imbalance: 'The moral arguments cut into the action

without extending it; there is too much diffusion, too much talk, too many themes raised and dropped, so that the adventure story is not lifted to another plane but overstretched, robbed of the tight narrative concentration needed for a mounting tension.' John Gillett in *Sight and Sound* (Summer 1961) agreed: 'These bouts of introspection are neither clarified nor explored, their only effect is to inflate the narrative unreasonably.'

21 Bucking the trend, Dilys Powell (*Sunday Times*, 30 April 1961) was so won over by the majestic Greek locations, sumptuous photography and narrative excitement that all else seemed superfluous. The *Observer*'s Penelope Gilliat (30 April 1961) also admired a narrative that 'drives like a fist', and the beauty of the cinematography, but scoffed at the characterisations and was saddened by the talent and effort squandered on war films.

22 Derek Monsey, for example, was concerned that *Guns* presented 'a cheap, phoney, artificially glamorised picture of war to a generation which wants to know – and should be told – the truth' (*Sunday Express*, 30 April 1961).

23 Remarkably, Alistair MacLean was only persuaded to attend the premiere at the last minute on the agreement that his mother would be presented to the Queen (Webster 1991: 108).

Cape Fear (1962)

> He had killed this man. He had turned this elemental and merci-
> less force into clay, into dissolution. He searched through himself,
> looking for guilt, for a sense of savage satisfaction, a feeling of
> strong and primitive fulfilment. All the neat and careful layers of
> civilised instincts and behaviour were peeled back to reveal an
> intense exultation over the death of an enemy. (John D. Macdonald,
> *The Executioners*, 1957)

> 'Man was born of the ape and there's still an ape curled up inside
> every man. The beast that must be shackled in chains. You are that
> beast, Caesar. You taint us. You poison our guts. When we hate
> you, we're hating the dark side of ourselves.' (Governor Breck in
> *Conquest of the Planet of the Apes*, 1972, Director: J. Lee Thompson)

'Gregory Peck liked what I was doing on *The Guns of Navarone*, and one day he gave me a novel to read called *The Executioners*, and he said: "Would you like to make a film of it? It's going to be my next film in America." So I said, "Certainly I'd like to." And that was my first American film.' This is how J. Lee Thompson relates the genesis of *Cape Fear*, the film that would set his career in a whole new direction. Peck's sudden offer made it possible for Lee Thompson to realise his long-held ambition to be a Hollywood director. 'Ever since I was a child I dreamed of Hollywood', he admits. 'I wanted to be an *American* film director.' Many British film-makers had shared that ambition, but very few at that time had succeeded in making a career in Los Angeles. Victor Saville had crossed the Atlantic twenty years earlier and had enjoyed a decade of directing in Hollywood, sometimes being used to make British subjects like *Tonight and Every Night* (1944) before work ran out and he returned to England.[1] Roy Baker, a contemporary of Lee Thompson and a director with a similar flair for suspense and noir stylistics, had made a few films in America in the early 1950s, and had directed Marylin Monroe effectively in *Don't Bother to Knock* (1952), but he also had returned to Britain. More recently, Lee Thompson's colleague at ABPC, Michael Anderson, had been given the opportunity to direct the big budget *Around the World in Eighty Days* (1956) for Mike Todd and he and Ken Annakin were beginning to establish themselves as international directors. Carol Reed had made films for American producers but had never made the move to Hollywood. It was only really Alfred Hitchcock who had made a permanent transition to the US cinema. Now Lee Thompson had the chance to direct a thriller set in the American Deep South with a very Hitchcockian emphasis on suspense. He was even to have a Bernard Herrmann score.

Written by John D. MacDonald, one of that American breed of college-educated hardboiled writers, *The Executioners* is a thriller concerned almost as much with philosophy and evolutionary anthropology as it is with action and tension. Published by Ballantine in 1957, it examines the relationship between civilisation and the primitive. In particular it contrasts the codes and ethics of the legal system (emblematic of civilised society) with savage human instincts for violence, revenge and the protection of the family group. Its protagonist Sam Bowden is a New England attorney with a wife, Carol, and three children between 6 and 14. He is part of the professional backbone of his community and the embodiment of its normative regulation. His credo is: 'I can't operate outside the law. The law is my business. I believe in due process' (MacDonald 1957: 30).[2] Sam's well-ordered existence is plunged into turmoil by the arrival of Max Cady, as sadistic rapist whom Sam had helped to convict many years before. Released from gaol, Cady is bent on revenge and the destruction of the Bowden family.

At first, Sam believes that the threat can be dealt with within the legal framework provided for the regulation of disputes and the protection of citizens. 'This Cady thing has to be handled within the law', he tells Carol. 'If the law can't protect us, then I'm dedicated to a myth and I better wake up.' (1957: 11). But Cady demonstrates that criminals can understand and manipulate the law as well as attornies do and that, if he is to be deterred, extra-legal means will have to be used. As Sievers, the private detective Sam hires, puts is: 'A type like that is an animal. So you fight like an animal.' Soon, the champion of due process is hiring thugs to put Cady in hospital and, when this too fails, is thinking up ways he can, within the protection of the law, kill his tormentor.

Brian McFarlane (1996) in his analysis of MacDonald's text, discusses Cady's arrival in psychoanalytic terms as representing 'the return of the repressed', a creature of the id which is invading Sam Bowden's conscious mind. He also points to the way in which the disruptive threat that Cady poses relates to the alien invasion narratives which were common in the science fiction of the Cold War period (Jancovich 1997). Undoubtedly, *The Executioners* is a paranoid text which lends itself to allegorical and symptomatic readings, but the authorial intent seems to be to challenge cosy assumptions about the sophistication and irreversible progress of human society. Civilisation reckons without humanity's animal nature, and Cady is a timely reminder of the bundle of instincts, needs and desires which drives human behaviour. The law, it seems, can only lay a gloss over the tribal sanctions of an earlier and more simple social organisation. As Sam tells his wife:

> 'It would be a hell of a lot easier to handle Cady during more primitive times, or in a more primitive part of the world. I am a member of a social complex. He is an outsider. I would rally my gang and we would kill him. I would very much like to kill him. I might even be able to manage it. You are reacting on a primitive level. This is actually what your instinct tells you I should do.' (MacDonald 1957: 36)

Thus, an atavistic discourse is quite explicit in MacDonald's text. Cady comes out of Sam's past, but he is also a figure from a shared earlier stage of social evolution, a world we have apparently left but not forgotten.

As *The Executioners* progresses, Sam is obliged to call on his folk memory and to revert to the practices of the world we think we have lost. In the end he finds that the only way to deal with his predator is to turn predator himself, setting a baited trap for Cady and fatally wounding him as he flees into the woods. Surprisingly, Brian McFarlane accepts MacDonald's closing description of Sam and Carol – 'A handsome, mild and civilised couple, with no visible taint of violence, no lingering marks of a dreadful fear' (1957: 182) – at its face value. His comment, 'There is no suggestion of a re-examination of the nature of the way they live, only a sense of fear's having been dispelled' (McFarlane 1996: 174), seems to miss both the irony in MacDonald's prose and the way that the Cady episode has fundamentally changed the Bowdens' perception of their life. They have experienced a reversion to the primitive and they have come to understand their savage natures. With his 'brood threatened', Sam has become a hunter and has killed, and they have both woken up to the dangers that surround their privileged existence. As Carol puts it, she has lost 'an enormous and infantile trust that this world was made for me to be happy in'. She now realises that, there 'are black things loose in this world. Cady was one of them. A patch of ice on a curve can be one of them' (MacDonald 1957: 180).

In adapting *The Executioners*, James R. Webb remained faithful to the spirit of MacDonald's work, retaining much of the novel's characterisation and plot.[3] The changes he made, in reducing the size of the Bowden family and changing the location and outcome of the denouement, however, serve to intensify the action and provide a more exciting and symbolically powerful climax. In the novel, Cady is a more distant presence, wounding one of the Bowdens' boys with a sniper's bullet. The screenplay dispenses with both sons, reducing the Bowden children to just one daughter, Nancy, who becomes Cady's principal target. By concentrating on the threat of sexual violence to the weakest and most vulnerable of the Bowdens, Cady's carnal savagery is emphasised, and he is obliged to confront his intended victim, creating a situation ideal for depiction.

The book's action takes place (one presumes) in carefully ordered New England, MacDonald's home, the cradle of WASP civilisation , but the screenplay shifts events to the bayou country of America's south, a place in closer proximity to the wild and where, in the early 1960s, legal discrimination and inequality were commonplace. The film's final tense minutes were to be played out in the primordial swamplands of Carolina's Cape Fear river, a more evocatively primitive site than the well-appointed environs described in the novel. Moreover, Webb's screenplay brings Cady and Bowen together in mortal combat in a confrontation which is dramatically more satisfying than MacDonald's fleeting brush between the two men as Cady makes his escape from the Bowden home. As Nicholas Anez (1991) has noted, Webb's script is a substantial improvement on the novel and takes great care to tighten its plotting and provide convincing motivations for its characters, in spite of the fact that much of the explanation of Cady's nature provided in the book is stripped away in emphasising his representation as an elemental force.

Webb's script must have seemed tailor-made for Lee Thompson's strengths as a director: a taut story with a minimum of characters; a steamy atmospheric setting; a protagonist backed into a metaphorical corner with only one way out; set piece suspense sequences; and a theme of humanism v. savagery. In many ways, *Cape Fear* would distil the essence of Lee Thompson's cinema, and may therefore be regarded as the culmination of his British film-making trajectory rather than the beginning of his Hollywood career. Although Hitchcock had enjoyed a hit the year before with *Psycho* (1960), the black-and-white thriller was rapidly becoming outmoded in the American cinema. It was associated with the pre-McCarthy film noir and the Poverty Row B-movie. Hitchcock would make no more, and in the hedonistic 1960s, the thriller would quickly be challenged by the less intense caper movie and the exotic espionage spectacular. Mean streets would give way to international playgrounds. Just as *Cape Fear*'s bourgeois protagonist is forced to look back to his savage origins, so the film itself glanced back to an era of film making which was waning fast. It may be too fanciful to see its lonely houseboat on the swampland as a last enclave of a beleaguered genre, but there is an overwhelming sense at the end of *Cape Fear* of a threshold being crossed, of things never being quite the same again. The plot of the film certainly looked back to a series of crime thrillers in which criminals take revenge on the families of law officials. In *The Big Heat* (Fritz Lang, 1953), *The Killer Is Loose* (Budd Boetticher, 1956) and *The Case Against Brooklyn* (Paul Wendkos, 1958), policemen's wives are the targets of vengeful gangsters. *Cape Fear* supplements these murderous schemes with the threat of rape in a way which, in representing the crime as a cold-blooded but sexualised exercise of power and control, anticipates feminist criminology.

Once one has witnessed the extraordinary power of Robert Mitchum's performance as Max Cady, it is easy to assume that the casting of *Cape Fear* was constructed around this star 'fixture'. But, of course, as producer Sy Bartlett's partner in the film's production company, Gregory Peck was the first name on the call sheet. Mitchum was offered the Cady role only after Rod Steiger had been seriously considered and Telly Savalas screen tested. Savalas eventually accepted the supporting role of Sievers, the private detective hired by Sam Bowden (Peck) to keep an eye on Cady. The parts of Bowden's wife and his 13-year-old daughter went to Polly Bergen and Lori Martin, familiar faces on American Television. Although Lori Martin acquits herself well enough, Lee Thompson was unable to get quite the quality of performance from the young actor that he achieved with Hayley Mills.[4] 'I was always a little disappointed with Lori Martin and the performance I got out of her', he confesses, 'because she wasn't as childlike as I would have liked her to be. She always wanted to make herself more adult, even to the extent of putting tissue paper in her bra to make her have bigger breasts.' Mitchum, however, he praises as 'superb' while admitting that he was not the easiest actor to work with and noting that the charismatic quality of his performance created some jealousy from Gregory Peck. When it came to the editing, Peck was concerned to prevent the minimising of his own role in favour of Mitchum's:

'Dear Greg got a bit upset with me because he thought that I hadn't looked after him enough in the film, that it was entirely stolen by Mitchum. And I had to remind him, and I said: "When I first read this script that you gave me I told you that the main part of Cady was an absolute stealer of the film. So whoever's going to play him (we hadn't cast Mitchum at that time) is going to walk away with the picture." And Greg said, "That's OK." But when we came to shooting it, he was very unhappy at times [because he] felt that I was tipping the film towards Robert Mitchum ... There was a certain tension that grew up between me and him. He was torn between being a producer and being the star of the film ... I'd say "What do you want me to do, Greg? I've got to try and get the best performance from you and the best performance from Mitchum." But there were these little outbursts of Greg's when he was the actor and not the producer, but everything was OK in the end ... And also, you see, Mitchum played the part of a drunken ex-convict, and he lives his parts. So he was frequently quite drunk on the set, but he would always come up and play the scene marvel-lously. There was a lot of drinking going on.'[5]

The film's location, Savannah, Georgia, held a special significance for Robert Mitchum. As a 16-year-old hobo in the midst of the Depression, he had been picked up in Savannah for vagrancy. His encounter with the local police had suggested that their commit-ment to due process, expressed in *Cape Fear*, was far from solid. 'We don't like Yankee bums around here', he was warned. When Mitchum told the arresting officer he had $38 in his pocket, 'he just called me a so-and-so wise guy, belted me with his club and ran me in'. Escaping conviction for burglary only because he was in gaol when the crime was committed, his judge made it clear that the law in Savannah would not tolerate his kind. 'Well I guess we can't hold you on that charge [burglary]', he told the young Mitchum, 'but a nice little indeterminate sentence for vagrancy should put you right.' The future star spent a week on a chain gang repairing roads before grabbing an opportunity to escape. 'They fired a few shots after me and that was that. In those days they wouldn't spend ten cents to catch you if they missed with a rifle. They'd just go out and round up someone else.'[6]

Returning both as character and actor with a deep sense of injustice, Mitchum's overbearing presence is established in the opening shots as he strolls confidently through the streets of Savannah and into the courthouse. A woman drops a box file as he brushes past her. A man averts his gaze from Cady's stare. Cady's gait and body language are those of a man who is afraid of no one and craves the chance to dominate any meeting – a lazy ease overlaying a strong sense of menace. When he seizes Bowden's keys and traps him in his car he is clearly unintimidated by the attorney's status, and he is able to imply the darkest of threats with laconic pleasantries and chillingly false bonhomie: 'Give my love to the family, Counsellor. I'll be seeing you.' The words are delivered in a voice which Lesley Stern (1995: 204) has described eloquently as 'honeyed, drawling, full of mocking self-conscious irony, evoking a vague insolence, and above all an insistently sardonic quality'.

Although Cady is described in MacDonald's novel and in the film as 'an animal', Mitchum plays him as the shrewdest and most intelligent of predators, able to control his simmering anger, match his tactics to the occasion and release his power to maximum effect. His pride in the abilities and prowess he has honed during years in prison is evident in the sequence where he is picked up in a bar by the police and taken in for interrogation. First he nonchalantly seduces Diane Taylor (Barrie Chase), even as he is escorted from the bar, and then, when the police try to humiliate him with a strip search, he displays his vanity and muscular physique by pulling in his stomach and puffing out his chest. Mitchum was one of those swaggering masculine actors who, in Joseph Losey's memorable phrase, 'wear their cocks on their sleeve' (Ciment 1985: 78), and he transfers all of his phallocentric arrogance to the character of Cady. He is a man supremely at ease with his animal instincts, in contrast to Sam Bowden who has sublimated his anti-social drives and celebrates his sophistication. Cady remains untamed after years of caging, whereas Bowden appears thoroughly domesticated. The two antagonists are presented as polar opposites – the lone and disaffected drifter, prowling the streets; and the sanitised family man, head of a comfortable bourgeois household and networked into the local community.[7] The contrasts are as stark as those of *Woman in a Dressing Gown*. Lee Thompson gleefully depicts the Bowden family, with almost comic-book simplicity, as a sexless 'hi-honey-I'm-home' household, emphasising the banality of their lifestyle in their regular visits to the bowling centre.[8] But this is not depthless post-modern pastiche. The Bowdens will gradually have their veneer of banality stripped away and their full resources exposed. Cady will force them to examine the depths of their personalities and the strength of the ties that bind them together. At the bowling centre, when Bowden, conscious of Cady's gaze, misses a 'spare', his daughter tells him: 'Dad, you're slipping.' He is indeed beginning to slide towards Cady's level, and slipping, too, is the moral universe that has supplied him with his certainties. The legal apparatus which Bowden represents is revealed as what Cady contemptuously calls 'a nice tight little corporation' which is prepared to connive at extra-legal methods to protect its members. The politically correct term 'citizen', frequently used to describe Cady, becomes saturated in irony as the upholders of the rule of law increasingly come to accept Peggy Bowden's shameless assertion that 'a man like that doesn't deserve civil rights'. Police Chief Dutton (Martin Balsam) is vocal in his guarantees of constitutional rights – 'I couldn't arrest the man for something that might be in his mind, that's dictatorship' – but he is happy to recommend the services of a private eye who quickly hires thugs to beat up Cady.

As the legal functionaries slip deeper into vigilantism, Cady continues to position himself beyond the pale. He shows his predilection for sexual violence in his treatment of his 'pick-up', Diane Taylor. Diane is a well-educated woman, attracted to rough men with animal magnetism like Cady. Her low self-esteem and the film's preoccupation with basic instincts are expressed in her sexual responsiveness to Cady's degeneracy and the way she takes perverse comfort in the knowledge that she 'cannot sink any lower'.[9] However, she does not fully appreciate how low Cady can go. In a scene in a lodging-house bedroom, she lays expectantly on the bed while a bare-chested Cady stalks around her. The Lewton-esque *mise-en-scène* is saturated with noir shadows and dangerous eroticism. Lee Thompson cuts between point-of-view shots, capturing her increasing apprehension and her predator's pleasure at her discomfort. As apprehension crystalises into a *frisson* of fear Diana bolts for safety, but Cady springs on her like a panther on a gazelle.[10] We do not witness the assault, but the aftermath is chilling. Declining to give evidence against her attacker, she asks Sievers: 'Do you believe I could ever, ever in my whole life, step up and repeat to another living soul what that man ... what he did?' Unlike Martin Scorsese's more explicit remake of the film (1992) Lee Thompson's original employs Val Lewton's method, inviting us to imagine what took place in that room to so traumatise a woman accustomed to rough treatment from her sexual partners. The scene intensifies Cady's threat. If this is his effect on an 'experienced' woman, how devastating would be his attentions on the innocent Nancy?

Subsequent scenes dramatise the threat by bringing Cady into closer proximity to Nancy. In a sequence at the quay to which Cady has followed the Bowdens, he watches Nancy in her shorts painting the family boat. He manages to provoke Sam Bowden with lascivious comments about Nancy – 'She's getting to be almost as juicy as your wife, ain't she?' Then, when Peggy Bowden is late meeting her daughter from school, Nancy panics as Cady approaches her. Lee Thompson treats the moment as a classic Hitchcock suspense set piece, ironically shooting the ex-con through the bars of the school's railing and tricking the audience into believing that the man following the fleeing Nancy is Cady, but who turns out to be the school janitor. Cleverly, framing only the lower torso of the pursuing figure, Lee Thompson not only conceals the man's identity but suggests sexual intent by emphasising his crotch. A final Hitchcockian twist is supplied when, accompanied by Bernard Herrmann's portentous score, Nancy runs from the caretaker straight into the waiting Cady, escaping only to be knocked down by a passing car.

Before their final showdown, Sam Bowden makes a desperate attempt to end Cady's cat-and-mouse game by buying him off. They meet in a bar lined with prints of sailing ships, the vessels which brought both immigrants and slaves to the Americas, reminding us of the repression and exploitation which accompanied the mission to civilise the New World. Bowden, the product of 'pioneer stock', hopes that where the law has failed money may succeed, before deadly force will be necessary. But Cady's wrath is not for purchase. He reminds Bowden that one cannot put a price on the value of a family, whether it is the family he has lost during his years in gaol or the one he intends to destroy now he is free. The time he has had to brood has sharpened his sense of injustice and deepened his need of sadistic satisfaction:

> 'When I was in the bucket, all I could think about was busting out and killing somebody. I wanted to kill him with my bare hands, slow. Every single night for seven years I killed that man. And on the eighth year I said, "Oh no, that's too easy, that's too fast." You know the Chinese death of a thousand cuts? First they cut off a little toe; then a piece of your finger, your ear, your nose. I like that better.'

Bowden reacts with a show of moral rectitude, calling Cady a 'shocking degenerate' and adding: 'I've seen the worst, the dregs, but you are the lowest. It makes me sick to breathe the same air.' But, by the end of the film, Bowden has sunk to Cady's level. His final speech, as he points a gun at his vanquished opponent, is a deliberate echo of Cady's bitter prison reminiscence. When Cady invites him to shoot – because 'I just don't give a damn' – the attorney tells him:

> 'That would be letting you off too easy, too fast. Your words, do you remember? I do. No, we're gonna take good care of you. Gonna nurse you back to health. Make you strong, Cady. You're gonna live a long life – in a cage. That's where you belong and that's where you're going. And this time for life. Bang your head against the walls, count the years, the months, the hours until the day you rot.'

This last exchange follows the film's great suspense set-piece in the Cape Fear swamplands where Sam Bowden has sent his wife and daughter as bait in a trap to lure Cady to his death. With Peggy and Nancy waiting anxiously in a houseboat and its river-bank chalet, and with Bowden and his unofficial police escort hiding in the undergrowth, Cady slithers through the reeds and into the water with all the cold and silent cunning of an alligator. In a wilderness in which legal protections have become irrelevant, this is to be a primitive contest between predators: the patient hunters and the wild animalistic stalker. In this dark night of the hunter it is Cady who scores the first kill, noiselessly drowning Bowden's police minder and then releasing the houseboat from its moorings before terrorising Peggy on the drifting craft. By the time Bowden swims to the rescue, Cady, in a brutal parody of conventional seduction, has invited Peggy to trade her own body against the violation of her daughter. But as Bowden clambers on to the boat, Cady doubles back to confront Nancy in the isolated chalet. As in previous films, Lee Thompson uses the diegetic sounds of a radio to supply ironic counterpoint to the action. Nancy's terrified brandishing of a brass poker as she is frozen like a rabbit in the headlights of Cady's controlling gaze is accompanied by mellow jazz music. It is Herrmann's chilling score, however, that propels the final combat between Cady and Bowden. Jumped by the adrenalin-fuelled lawyer as he drags his prey into the jungle, Cady almost succeeds in killing him with his 'bare hands' in the waters of the swamp. But Bowden manages to stun his adversary with a rock as he fights with tooth and claw for survival. 'Suddenly you know how thin civilisation is', remarked Alexander Walker (*Evening Standard*, 10 January 1963), and, as the mud-streaked Cady moves in for the kill, shambling like a neanderthal, improvised pick-axe in hand, the scene is unmistakably primordial. As he swings his axe, Bowden reaches his gun and fires a disabling shot into Cady. Like another seductive face of evil, Harry Lime in *The Third Man*, Cady gives his permission for the *coup de grâce*, but Bowden holds off. Now driven, like Cady, by hate, contempt and the need for revenge, the once mild-mannered attorney wants only to prolong the suffering of his nemesis.

On the face of it, Cady has failed to exact his revenge, but in a more profound way he has succeeded in reducing the urbane Sam Bowden to his own level by stripping away his moral values and uncovering his basest desires. As Bowden relishes his description of Cady's death by 1,000 cuts and Herrmann's sonorous chords help the camera pull away from the antagonists, we know that we have witnessed what lies beneath the sophisticated organisation of American social life. Cady lies wounded, a spent force, his hooded eyes beseeching mercy, while Bowden crouches over him, hunched like an ape, his eyes exultant with triumph. We almost expect him to beat his breast and bellow to the forest. Instead the scene dissolves into the image of the Bowden family group, reunited and travelling home, each trying to come to terms with the revelations which Cady has brought them. As the camera pans away to the wild landscape, the apocalyptic sound of Herrmann's cadenza offers no hint of reassurance that a few centuries of 'civilisation' have eradicated millennia of primal savagery.

It is a closure almost as shattering as Mary Hilton's gallows walk in *Yield to the Night*. Dilys Powell, like other British critics, saw a version of the film trimmed of six minutes by the BBFC, but could still describe it as 'a savagely effective exercise in the shrieking nerve directed without quarter by J. Lee Thompson (*Sunday Times*, 13 January 1963). By confronting 'The Great Society' with the primitivism of its foundations and suggesting that evolution is a convenient illusion, *Cape Fear* presents a frightening idea which outlasts the shocks of its narrative. The politics of this idea are complex and contradictory, as is so much of the politics of Lee Thompson's cinema. Brian McFarlane (1996: 189) maintains that 'it is ideologically a very conservative film' which 'doesn't even begin to suggest the kinds of critique of middle-class family life offered by the 1950s' films of Douglas Sirk', and, viewed as he sees it – a simplistic victory of good (the wholesome family) over evil – one can understand why. Some credence is given to his reading by Lee Thompson's own (slightly ingenuous) assertion in 1962 that 'all we set out to make was a straight suspense melodrama' (*Daily Mail*, 3 May 1962), and by his later comment on Scorsese's muddying of the moral waters in his remake of *Cape Fear* that 'it has to have a good versus evil story' (*Guardian*, 27 February 1992). Even when its message about the brittle nature of civilised restraints is appreciated, *Cape Fear* might still be interpreted as a right-wing survivalist parable, advocating the right to bear arms and the necessity of each individual taking responsibility for his own protection. The term 'his' is used advisedly here because there is a strong suggestion of biological determinism in the film. Men, even gentle family men, are seen to have an inherent capacity for violence, and that violence is most easily mobilised by sexual competition.[11] But if this is an insight likely to find favour in feminist circles, it is accompanied by the less palatable suggestion that women are largely passive recipients of male desire and protection.[12]

Contrary to the film's review in *Variety* (7 March 1962), *Cape Fear* is not merely an 'exercise in cumulative terror' with 'no apparent intellectual purpose', but reading the movie is by no means straightforward and free from contradiction.[13] This difficulty in fixing the message of the film is what Raymond Durgnat referred to when he wrote of 'this curious prickliness of meaning' which is 'common in Lee Thompson films' (*Films and Filming*, February 1963). Bowden's decision not to take a life in cold blood is perfectly in line with the anti-capital-punishment views Lee Thompson expressed in *Yield to the Night*; but, conversely, Bowden's motivations are anything but humanitarian. Bowden seeks revenge for his own suffering in the prolonged humiliation of another. Just as in *Yield to the Night*, obsession has been transferred from one party to another, but this time it seems locked into an endless spiral of hatred with no obvious exit point.[14] Fear and violence have eaten away Bowden's humanity and it is the shock of what lies beneath that ultimately rescues *Cape Fear* from ideological conservatism. The knowledge that the tranquillity of suburbia, with its family pets, well-tended lawns and dads who take the kid bowling, is built on such shaky moral and emotional foundations is too disturbing to be labelled conservative. To say, as Lesley Stern (1995: 181) does, that there is 'no real sense that Cady infiltrates [the Bowdens'] world and their values' is to miss the wider revelation of the film. Taken within the broader scope of Lee Thompson's cinema, *Cape Fear* is concerned with the difficulties of acting in a humane way in a world which is frequently brutal and bestial. Although few seemed to notice at the time, its sense of overwhelming threat and mounting tension between implacable antagonists was entirely appropriate to a film produced during a period of noisy sabre-rattling between the super-powers of the USA and USSR,[15] and released in the year of the Cuban missile crisis. Like Bowden and Cady, the world survived – but only just.

The problems involved in getting *Cape Fear* past the BBFC without butchering the film have been carefully detailed by James

Robertson (2000). A recent highly publicised case of rape and murder in Bedfordshire[16] made the Board's examiners particularly sensitive to the idea that Mitchum's charismatic performance might 'stimulate morbid fantasy in the minds of the sexually unbalanced' (2000: 70). As well as insisting on an 'X' certificate, they demanded cuts to a number of scenes on the advice of a consultant psychologist. Dr Stephen Black recommended that, if possible, Cady's threat to rape, rather than simply abduct or even murder, Nancy should be removed, as should all suggestions of Cady' sexually deviant nature: 'Treated in this way the picture then becomes simply a threat, ill-defined, against which the fine father of a fine family is defending himself and his' (BBFC *Cape Fear* File: report by Black, 27 March 1962).

Horrified that his film was being simultaneously emasculated and given an 'X'-certificate, Lee Thompson flew to London at the end of April 1962 to negotiate the cuts. While reluctantly agreeing to dialogue cuts in the first two-thirds of the picture, he seems to have been particularly worried about the carefully orchestrated rhythm and balance of the film being upset by the shortening of scenes between Cady and Peggy on the houseboat, and Cady and Nancy in the chalet. (Robertson 2000: 72). *Cape Fear* had been assembled by Hitchcock's regular editor George Tomasini, who had kept the narrative moving at a brisk pace before drawing out the final swampland scenes into a slow and exhausting ordeal.[17]

Lee Thompson was also concerned about losing the scene he regarded as 'the kernel' of his movie, the sequence in which Sam and Peggy Bowden discuss the problem of young victims of rape being asked to give evidence. This problem of rapists escaping justice because their victims are reluctant to give evidence against them in open court was what 'enthralled' him about the film (Lee Thompson, 1963).

Lee Thompson returned to Los Angeles hoping that judicious re-editing and the inclusion of an additional scene giving more information about Diane Taylor's character would prove sufficient to allow his film to be released in Britain. The premiere had already been postponed from 10 May and the director had let it be known that censorship was to blame (*Daily Mail*, 3 May 1962). When the revised version was viewed by almost the entire BBFC team a few weeks later, however, substantial objections remained, particularly to the sequence in which Peggy is assaulted on the houseboat. New objections were also raised to some of the non-sexual violence in scenes involving Cady (Robertson 2000: 73).

Incensed by what he calculated to be a demand for 161 cuts, Lee Thompson railed against the Board and its president, Lord Morrison of Lambeth, to the *Daily Mail*'s Barry Norman (13 June 1962): 'I think the censors here have gone crazy. They are trying to make me a whipping boy. Lord Morrison is the nigger in the woodpile. This makes nonsense of the whole film. After 161 cuts even I won't know what the story is about.' John Trevelyan, the Board's secretary who was on good terms with Lee Thompson responded to this second attempt to pick a public fight with the BBFC by emphasising the need for the Board to 'exercise great care in dealing with brutality, sadism and rape' in a period when 'violence and sexual crimes are on the increase' (*Daily Mail*, 22 June 1962). By this time, however, the BBFC were already in receipt of a second revision of the film which again was considered unacceptable. Impasse was reached, with Lee Thompson refusing to cut any further and recommending to Gregory Peck that *Cape Fear* should be withdrawn from distribution in Britain. But Peck was reluctant to lose the British market for his film and took over negotiations with the BBFC. Lee Thompson was not impressed with the results:

> 'When Peck came to London and didn't support me on the fight I was making with the censor, naturally I felt upset about it ... I guess he saw that we weren't going to get anywhere and so he agreed the cuts (*laughs*). I do have to say that the cuts were 99 per cent Robert Mitchum, not Gregory Peck.' (Unpublished transcript of an interview for *Empire of the Censors*, BBC2, May 1995)

While remaining concerned about the houseboat scene, the BBFC got most of the cuts they had demanded and *Cape Fear* was reduced from 105 minutes to ninety-nine for its British release. The lost footage included the additional scene of Cady in his car with Diane Taylor which Lee Thompson had shot in response to earlier censorship demands (Robertson 2000: 74).[18]

The BBFC's efforts removed much of the frankness of the film, but left its mood of menace largely untouched. When it finally opened at the Odeon, Marble Arch, on 10 January 1963 it took more money than any Universal film previously released at the Odeon (*Kinematograph Weekly*, 7 February 1963). It continued to perform well on the Rank circuit, its quality highlighted by its supporting film, Butcher's flat and formulaic crime drama *Danger by My Side* (Charles Saunders, 1962). By and large, the critics deplored the concept of the film but paid its realisation grudging respect. As the *Sunday Telegraph*'s A. Dent put it, 'the film in its hateful way is spellbinding' (13 January 1963). In the *Daily Mail* Cecil Wilson called it 'a repellantly fascinating piece of Hitchcockery' (12 January 1963), while Margaret Hinxman (*Daily Herald*, 12 January 1963) though it 'not a pretty film, but a riveting one', with J. Lee Thompson telling 'his grim story with nerve-stretching excitement' and 'injecting a feeling of overpowering menace'. Alexander Walker (*Evening Standard*, 10 January 1963) found it 'a numbing little exercise in terror that works well', largely he felt because 'director J. Lee Thompson sets your alarm bells jangling so loudly you don't hear the little voice of doubt'. Some reviewers, however, simply could not stomach what the *Monthly Film Bulletin* (January 1963) described as 'an exercise in controlled sadism'. Left-wing critics were particularly disturbed by its Hobbesian view of social order. Nina Hibbin in the *Daily Worker* (12 January 1963), calling it 'home brewed poison', deplored its 'calculated wallowing in brutality'. The *New Statesman* (18 January 1963) considered *Cape Fear* 'an ugly construct', and the *Guardian* (12 January 1963) thought that 'it deserved to be cut' because, although 'a well-made film', it had 'no justifiable purpose'. As always, Derek Hill (*Financial Times*, 11 January 1963) was its most outspoken detractor. Finding unpalatable its 'enthusiasm for a hero who becomes steadily more brutal', he pronounced it 'an obnoxious work' in which 'the characters are stereotypes and the performances (apart from Barrie Chase and Martin Balsam) are wretched'. Its director, he believed, 'never makes Hollywood's interest in him ... in the least explicable'. But Hollywood had scant need for the understanding of Derek Hill. By the time *Cape Fear* had endured its near-death by

161 cuts in Britain, Lee Thompson had completed a big-budget epic with Tony Curtis and Yul Brynner – *Taras Bulba* (1963) – and was poised to make the extravagant *Kings of the Sun* (1964).

Welcome to the pleasure dome

When Lee Thompson went to Los Angeles to direct *Cape Fear*, he did not expect to make his home there. Having tasted Hollywood film making, however, he wanted more:

> 'Having got to Hollywood, I wanted to stay there. This perhaps was not the best career move, because I was offered *The Longest Day* and I didn't want to go back to England so I turned it down.[19] I was very anxious to stay in Hollywood so my choice was not of the best. I should have waited to get something very good which I was in line for but [was] too hasty in trying to set up my next film.'

Instead of letting Fox send him back to Britain he accepted United Artist's invitation to take a production unit to Argentina to make *Taras Bulba* with a budget of $7 million and a cast which included 10,000 gauchos and their horses.[20] The prospect of working with Harold Hecht, producer of *Marty* and *Birdman of Alcatraz* (John Frankenheimer, 1962), was a major inducement, but Lee Thompson still professed to be attracted by the story's exploration of the conflict between a father and a son, a theme which had fascinated him since seeing *Sorrell and Son* as a boy (Lee Thompson 1963). *Taras Bulba* gave him the opportunity to make a family tragedy on the grandest of scales. Now one of the highest-paid directors in the industry, he stuck with United Artists to make *Kings of the Sun*, another epic production, this time concerned with the Mayan civilisation in pre-Columbian Mexico and the decision to abandon the practice of human sacrifice. Again, it was the moral and political issues discussed in Elliot Arnold's original screenplay rather than the scope of its action that primarily attracted Lee Thompson: 'To me the cutting out of the heart is like the atom or hydrogen bomb – that was the awful evil in a world far better than ours. Eventually they realised "The only sacrifice the Gods need is that each day in our own life we do our best". Then came a dictator who wiped them all out' (Lee Thompson, 1963).

Kings of the Sun was his first collaboration with the spectacu-
larly successful Mirisch Corporation, an independent production
company which in the previous four years had notched up a series
of hits including Billy Wilder's *Some Like it Hot* (1959), *The
Apartment* (1960) and *Irma la Douce* (1963), Robert Wise's *West
Side Story* (1961) and John Sturges' *The Magnificent Seven* (1960).
Impressed with the latitude Mirisch afforded producer–directors
working with them, Lee Thompson signed a four-picture contract.

First, however, he completed two lavish comedies for Twentieth
Century-Fox. Both starred Shirley MacLaine. The first, *What a
Way to Go* (1964) assembled most of the biggest stars in Tinseltown under his direction – Paul Newman, Gene Kelly, Dean
Martin, Dick Van Dyke and (less than two years after *Cape Fear*)
Robert Mitchum – in a satire on Hollywood narrative and film-
making styles that is chiefly remembered for the seventy-two
outfits worn by Miss MacLaine (one of them too brief for the taste
of the British censor).[21] The second, *John Goldfarb, Please Come
Home* (1964), which Lee Thompson produced with MacLaine's
husband Steve Parker, featured a slightly less stellar cast. Peter
Ustinov as an Arab potentate with a sizeable harem provided the
main comic focus, and the giant set of his palace and the creation
of a lush American football field in the middle of the Mojave
desert took up most of the $4.5 million budget (*John Goldfarb*,
exhibitors' campaign manual, Twentieth Century-Fox, 1964).
Laughs? There were a few but, then again, one wonders if 'kookie'
comedy really requires this scale of expenditure. These were fast-
food movies at gourmet prices, expensive fripperies providing
ephemeral diversions but little of lasting substance for audiences.
Lee Thompson had been swept up into a decadent world of open
cheque books in which he could spend more on Shirley Mac-
Laine's costumes for one film than on the whole production of
Yield to the Night. The affluent Beverly Hills' life was becoming
increasingly attractive to a man who had spent twenty-five years in
the penny-pinching British studio system. 'I like Hollywood', he
wrote, 'and I don't like the people who smack it' (Lee Thompson
1963).

Notes

1 Charles Higham (1993: 268) has claimed that Saville's passage to America was sponsored by British Intelligence.

2 Page numbers refer to the 1997 edition published by Bloomsbury, London, as *Cape Fear*.

3 Webb, who subsequently won an Oscar for his script for *How the West Was Won* (John Ford, 1962) had twenty years' screenwriting experience behind him. He had worked with *Cape Fear*'s producer Sy Bartlett on the screenplay of *The Big Country* (William Wyler, 1958) and most recently had scripted *Pork Chop Hill* (Lewis Milestone, 1959) for Bartlett and Peck's Melville Productions.

4 Lee Thompson would have happily cast Hayley Mills in Lori Martin's role, but her success in *Tiger Bay* had brought her a lucrative Disney contract by this time.

5 In a contemporary interview Lee Thompson had described Mitchum as 'a real professional – he's never late on the set and he always knows his lines'. He acknowledged, though, that he had no fear of 'difficult' actors: 'Give me any of the so-called difficult stars to work with. I'd love it. Taylor, Brando – I'd work with them tomorrow if I had the opportunity ... I would look upon them as a challenge just as I would a difficult script' (Ferguson, 1962).

6 From an interview with Mitchum by Tony Wells: 'The truth about me', *Today* (16 February 1963).

7 In MacDonald's novel, Bowden's daughter characterises Cady as 'all bad' (MacDonald 1957: 58), and Lee Thompson stays true to that idea. 'I naturally didn't try to show any sympathy for the villain', he wrote in *Films and Filming* (April 1963). 'Here's a cut and dried black, no white, no shades at all.' But by dressing Mitchum in light-coloured clothing and avoiding the cliché of the bad man dressed in black, he allows the interpretation that Cady is a personification of the savagery that is in all of us, rather than some purely external evil.

8 Although in Britain in the early 1960s ten-pin bowling was an exotic and 'classless' new leisure pursuit, in America its mass popularity and accessibility meant that it had little value as a sport of social distinction. Now labelled as the banal recreation of the working man in texts like *The Simpsons*, bowling would perhaps be an unlikely pastime for a well-connected lawyer.

9 Sam Leavitt's camerawork expresses the idea of baseness visually by filming Diane and Cady in low angle from the footboards of Cady's car.

10 Nicholas Anez (1991), describing the scene as one of the most 'riveting' in the film, points to it as 'a stunning example of [Lee] Thompson's skill, conveying the extent of Cady's sadism without showing any actual violence'.

11 The ideas around atavism explored by the film are uncomfortably close to the fascist eugenics advocated by the American lawyer and historian T. L. Stoddard with his theory of the 'Underman': 'that primitive animality which is the heritage of our human, and even our pre-human past ... This primitive animality, potentially present in the noblest natures, continu-

ously dominates the lower social strata, especially the pauper, criminal and degenerate elements – civilisation's "inner barbarians"' (Stoddard 1922: 27). However, as Greene (1998: Chapter 3) indicates, Lee Thompson's rejection of the more pernicious elements of these ideas, as well as the policies recommended by Stoddard, is made clear in his film *Conquest of the Planet of the Apes*.

12 This suggestion is contested in Lee Thompson's 1986 film *Murphy's Law*, which ends in a similar confrontation between a desperate lawman and a psychopathic ex-con seeking revenge. The difference is that this time the ex-con is a tough and resourceful woman, as is the petty thief who aids Murphy.

13 In the *New York Times* (19 April 1962) Bosley Crowther also struggled with the film's meaning: 'There seems to be no reason for it but to agitate anguish and a violent vengeful urge that is offered some animal satisfaction by that murderous fight at the end.'

14 As (the significantly named?) MacDonald, the black liberal mediator in *Conquest of the Planet of the Apes*, expresses it: 'Violence prolongs hate, hate prolongs violence.'

15 The summer of 1961 saw President Kennedy agreeing to increased defence spending and the erection of the Berlin Wall by East German authorities.

16 The 'A6' murder for which James Hanratty was convicted, probably in error, and hanged.

17 Bosley Crowther in the *New York Times* (19 April 1962) described it as 'a cold-blooded, calculated build-up of sadistic menace and shivering dread ... accomplished with frightening adroitness'. He added: 'There is no waste motion, no fooling. Everything is sharp and direct like a sneaky electrical charge.'

18 This scene, together with the other cuts, has now been restored to television and video versions of the film.

19 Darryl F. Zanuck's star-studded $10 million recreation of the Normandy landings, *The Longest Day* (1962), eventually had three directors – Andrew Marton, Bernhard Wicki and Ken Annakin. It won Academy Awards for Cinematography and Visual Effects, and was nominated for Best Picture.

20 An account of the daunting logistics of making the film is provided in the British press book for *Taras Bulba*.

21 Designed by the legendary costumier Edith Head, Shirley MacLaine's costumes alone took up more than $0.5 million of the $7.5 million budget, making this the most expensive single wardrobe in movie history (*What a Way to Go* exhibitors' campaign manual, Twentieth Century-Fox, 1963).

23 Sex crime: Barrie Chase plays a victim of Cady's sadism in *Cape Fear* (1962) (American lobby card)

24 Establishing a pecking order: Sam Bowden (Gregory Peck) tries to warn off Max Cady (Robert Mitchum) in *Cape Fear*

25 Homage to Hitchcock: the promotion of *Return From the Ashes* (1965) owed a debt to *Psycho* (1960)

26 Candlelight and cowls: Sharon Tate presents a sacrificial dove in the occult thriller *Eye of the Devil* (1968)

27 Tempting fate: J. Lee Thompson pleads with David Niven to stay on his horse on location at a French chateau for *Eye of the Devil*

28 Act of betrayal: Janovic (Topol) is driven off to face a Russian execution squad in *Before Winter Comes* (1969)

29 The professor and the chairman: Dr Hathaway (Gregory Peck) almost has his mind blown as he talks with the Chinese Leader (Conrad Yama) in *The Most Dangerous Man in the World* (1969)

30 Brotherly love: siblings Hilary (Susannah York) and Pink (Peter O'Toole) reveal the foibles of the landed gentry in *Country Dance* (1970)

31 Caligula in jackboots: Malcolm McDowell goes over the top in *The Passage* (1979)

The prodigal's return

'I've been accused of selling out and when I look back, I really can't argue with that description of my career.' (J. Lee Thompson)

By the mid-1960s, J. Lee Thompson had established himself as a Hollywood director, enjoying big budgets and box office success. Ironically, it was precisely at this time that London came to be viewed internationally as the most exciting place to make movies. As the phenomenon of 'Swinging London' gathered momentum, the American studios were happy to channel finance toward their British operations. United Artists was the most enthusiastic investor in English film making and the Mirisch Corporation was United Artists' most prolific supplier of British-made product (Murphy 1992: 260). Mirisch's requirement of directors who were familiar with the working culture of the London studios coincided happily with Lee Thompson's need to take a break from Hollywood. All was not well in his private life. His marriage to Joan Henry was under strain from his taste for alcohol and amphetamine, his sometimes violent bouts of jealousy and his affair with the actress Susan Hampshire, then under contract at Twentieth Century-Fox.

As if sensing that he needed to purge himself of Hollywood indulgence, Lee Thompson returned to his Elstree roots to make a taut black-and-white thriller, steeped in irony and nihilism. He had been keen to film Arnold Wesker's 'kitchen-sink' drama *Chips With Everything* with United Artists, but the project proved too difficult to set up (*Kinematograph Weekly*, 11 July 1963). Instead, he chose *Return From the Ashes*, based on Hubert Monteilhet's novel *Phoenix From the Ashes*, first published in French in 1961 and in translation in 1963, having bought an option to the film rights from Henri Georges Clouzot. Mirisch had originally scheduled the filming for the early part of 1964, but it was postponed in favour of *John Goldfarb*.[1]

Return From the Ashes (1966)

Set in Paris, although filmed entirely in the studio and back lot at Borehamwood, *Return From the Ashes* is the story of Dr Michelle Pilgrin (Ingrid Thulin), a rich woman who is believed to have died during the war, but who returns from a concentration camp in 1945 to find her stepdaughter of a previous marriage having an affair with her husband, a selfish and calculating chess master. In a plot which strains credulity, Michelle, whose appearance has been altered by years of suffering, first chooses not to reveal her identity either to husband Stan (Maximilian Schell) or to her stepdaughter Fabi (Samantha Eggar). When the lovers notice her strong resemblance to the 'dead' woman, they offer Michelle money to impersonate 'herself' in order to get at her fortune (held in trust pending positive proof of her death). When her true identity is discovered, the unscrupulous and jealous Fabi plays out her Electra complex by hatching a plot to murder Michelle. But it is Fabi who is killed in her bath by the treacherous Stan who then tries to dispose of his wife as well. He believes he has got away with another perfect murder until, in the final twist, it is revealed that the indestructible Michelle has survived.[2]

Hammer had been turning out this sort of twisting psychological thriller, based on the Clouzot template, for the previous four years and had rendered it relatively conventional. One can see, however, its attractions to Lee Thompson. It offered the chance to return to an intimate subject with a small cast and to work intensively with actors, including Ingrid Thulin, known for her roles in Ingmar Bergman films like *Wild Strawberries* (1957) and *The Silence* (1963), and Samantha Eggar, a rising star who was under exclusive contract to a company Lee Thompson had formed with John Sutro and the celebrated novelist Graham Greene. The film's modest budget and appeal to the European market, through stars like Thulin, Herbert Lom and Maximilian Schell, allowed Lee Thompson to act as both producer and director, maintaining considerable artistic control over the production. The theme of the film – a woman who is twice wrongly believed to be dead – had definite continuities with the director's early works like *Double Error* and *Murder Without Crime*. Finally, the picture's convoluted plot allowed Lee Thompson to explore classic Hitchcock territory, just as he had with *Cape Fear*. A woman who is believed dead and who has assumed a new identity and who is then asked to impersonate her former self is a loud echo of Kim Novak's character in *Vertigo* (Alfred Hitchcock, 1958), while the murder of Fabi in her bath clearly recalls the death of Janet Leigh's character in the shower in *Psycho*. Tellingly, *Ashes* was promoted with the *Psycho*-style gimmick 'No one may enter the theatre after Fabi enters her bath!', the posters depicting the terminal ablution. 'I liked the result', says Lee Thompson, 'it was a fun thriller.' But he confesses that 'it wasn't very successful', partly, he feels, because he should . have insisted on some location work in Paris. Starting promisingly after its Gala premiere at the new Prince Charles Cinema in London's Leicester Square on 3 February 1966, unfavourable 'word-of-mouth' meant that it would struggle badly on its wider release with United Artists' *A Rage to Live* (Walter Grauman, 1966).

The critics were largely unmoved. Most thought the story far-fetched and the characters under-drawn, though there was praise for some of the acting and for Lee Thompson's reliable handling of suspense.[3] John Coleman in the *New Statesman* (4 February 1966) was representative when he wrote that 'in the prevailing absurdity a scene or two amuses through fitfully snappy dialogue or rococo directorial flourishes' but that 'it was all done a million times better in *Les Diaboliques*'. Dilys Powell thought the handling of the film 'skilful' but the result was 'sullen' and 'dislikeable' (*Sunday Times*, 6 February 1966) and Leonard Mosley seemed not to have forgiven Lee Thompson for *I Aim at the Stars* when he remarked of *Ashes*, 'I haven't seen a trashier piece of cinema for a long time' (*Daily Express*, 4 February 1966). But *The Times* felt that 'after a couple of disastrous incursions into would-be sophistication', Lee Thompson had retrieved at least 'something of his reputation with a return to the thriller' (3 February 1966).

Eye of the Devil (1968)

After completing *Return From the Ashes*, Lee Thompson was asked to stay on in Europe to make a supernatural thriller called *Thirteen* for Martin Ransohoff's Filmways production company, with the backing of MGM. It was to be based on Philip Loraine's recently published novel *Day of the Arrow* (1964), about a French aristocrat who, when the crops consistently fail on his land, is obliged by ancient tradition to offer himself, as the incumbant lord of the estate, as a human sacrifice. Ransohoff had assembled an extraordinary cast headed by David Niven, with whom Lee Thompson had of course worked on *The Guns of Navarone*, and Kim Novak, the seductive witch from *Bell, Book and Candle* (Richard Quine, 1958), this time on the receiving end of occult practices. In the supporting cast were the highly experienced Flora Robson, Emlyn Williams and, fresh from a role in Polanski's *Cul-de-Sac*, Donald Pleasence. However, it was the two young actors in the supporting cast who now make the film of particular interest. David Hemmings, who had played the role of the delinquent teenager in *No Trees*, was cast as the ironically named Christian, a pagan youth with uncanny archery skills. His career would soon shoot skyward, when Antonioni chose him over Terence Stamp for the lead in *Blow Up*. Sharon Tate was the protegée of producer Martin Ransohoff and would become the wife of Roman Polanski and the victim of Charles Manson. In Lee Thompson's film she plays Christian's bewitching sister Odile. With few lines, she manages to convey an extraordinary mysticism and perversity. Lee Thompson described her as 'a strange and haunting beauty. At once both very lovely and in an odd way also foreboding' (*Photoplay*, April 1966).

Robin Estridge, with whom Lee Thompson had collaborated so

effectively on *North West Frontier*, had radically redrafted Loraine's novel, eliminating its protagonist (an English artist named James Lindsay) and expanding the role of the nobleman's wife Catherine de Montfaucon. Characters had been simplified into a set of Gothic archetypes, giving the effect almost of Tarot cards brought to life. The strategy emphasises the historical continuity of the area of southern France in which the action is set. The family of Phillipe (David Niven) has controlled the region since feudal times, when it was a centre for the sort of heretical combining of paganism and Christianity practised by the Gnostics and Cathars. The suggestion is that the belief still persists that,when the vines are consistently blighted by lack of rainfall, the king must die to renew the earth. Thus, for Phillipe, self-sacrifice is the ancestral duty demanded in return for the privileges of his rank.

Many of the themes of Lee Thompson's cinema are woven into this scenario, notably the distaste for ritual murder (*Yield to the Night, Kings of the Sun*), the persistence of primitivism (*Cape Fear*), the heightened moral dilemma (in this case duty versus survival), the protagonist as victim, children under threat, and the ever-present sense of entrapment in an intolerable situation. The realisation of the project, however, became fraught with difficulties. It may have been tempting fate to title a movie *Thirteen*, and a jinx seems to have settled on the production. Lee Thompson recalls an atmosphere of tension within the production unit: 'It was fraught with intrigues between the cast. Sharon Tate, I remember, was the ex-girlfriend of Ransohoff, so there were always fireworks between her and the producer on the set. She went to live with Polanski during the film and Ransohoff was naturally furious about it and there were lots of worries and things going on.'

The biggest disaster was a riding accident to Kim Novak which prevented her from finishing the picture. Production was 80 per cent complete and the film's insurers had to pay out £600,000 for all Novak's scenes to be re-filmed with her replacement Deborah Kerr. 'I just groaned "Oh God, no"', Lee Thompson told the *Daily Mail*'s Harry Weaver at the time, 'I thought of all the wasted work' (3 January 1966). But he also regretted the loss of his Hitchcock-ian blonde, and now blames the atmosphere on set:

> 'Kim Novak was going to be excellent in the film, and it was a great
> tragedy when she fell off her horse and hurt herself like that. I
> think she wanted to get out of the film ... It was all to do with this
> triangle with Ransohoff and Sharon Tate and Roman Polanski ...
> David Niven didn't get on very well with Kim Novak, so he was
> delighted when his old friend Deborah Kerr took over.'

Shooting restarted in mid-December 1965 after a four-week pause,
the production sharing MGM's Borehamwood Studios with
Stanley Kubrick's *2001: A Space Odyssey*. The main location, the
impressive Chateau d'Hautfort in the Dordogne, had to be revisited
in the New Year when the defoliated condition of its environs
created continuity problems which are sometimes evident in the
finished film. Lee Thompson took the opportunity of re-shooting
to simplify the script and dispense with what he described as
'some self-indulgent, fussy camera angles and cinematic clever-
ness which didn't help the picture at all' (*Daily Mail*, 3 January
1966).[4]

The film's problems continued in post-production. MGM got
cold feet about some of Lee Thompson's unapproved modifications
to the script, afraid that Donald Pleasence's heretic priest would
cause protests from Catholic organisations. The studio delayed
the film's release for eighteen months as well as deciding to
change its title to *Eye of the Devil* to help suggest that the fertility
cult depicted owed its allegiance to Lucifer rather than Christ
(*Variety*, 13 December 1967). Eventually, the growing celebrity of
Sharon Tate and the meteoric fame of David Hemmings after
Blow Up obliged MGM to release the film. It opened at London's
Ritz Cinema in early March 1968 to gales of patronising laughter
from critics who scoffed at Niven's casting as a Frenchman and
derided the absurdity of the plot. Alexander Walker called *Eye of
the Devil* 'incredibly inept hokum' which had been 'groaningly
over-directed' (*Evening Standard*, 7 March 1968). Dilys Powell described it as 'hilariously bad' (*Sunday Times*, 10 March 1968); while
Ian Christie recovered from 'paroxysms of mirth' to recommend
that it 'should be buried deep in the vaults of MGM's graveyard'.
'The mystery is how so ludicrous a script ever came to be realised',
pondered David Robinson in the *Financial Times* (15 March 1968),

and Western Taylor (*News of the World*, 10 March 1968) recorded that 'the audience hooted'. These were Lee Thompson's worst reviews since *I Aim at the Stars*, even without a contribution from Derek Hill who had so angered the Rank Organisation that most publications feared loss of advertising revenue if they employed his services as a reviewer (Prothero 2000: 134).[5]

To use Penelope Houston's phrase (*Spectator*, 15 March 1968), *Eye of the Devil* may be something of 'an authentic folly', but it hardly merits the derision it received. Judged by the standards of 1960s horror films it is a little lacking in chills but is no more fantastical and considerably more stylish than Hammer's product – closer to Mario Bava than Terence Fisher. Like Bava, Lee Thompson piles on the Gothic clichés: hooded figures, candles, flag-stoned corridors, a mausoleum, a mysterious tower room, a closed rural community, a husband who is not what he seems, and a wife who does not understand what is going on. There is nothing very original in this imagery, nor in Robin Estridge's often camp dialogue ('These are not life-giving clouds'), but there is a vibrancy and riskiness about Erwin Hillier's cinematography which uses Lee Thompson's trademark restless camera, swaying and panning to induce what John Russell Taylor described nicely as 'a cheeringly consistent level of dementia' (*Times*, 7 March 1968). Too often the effect is muted by Ernest Walter's over-enthusiastic editing, but there are moments of haunting quality: the play of light on frightened eyes (another Lee Thompson motif), the procession out of the chateau, or the luminosity given to Sharon Tate's face.[6] Although *Eye of the Devil* may look old-fashioned beside *Rosemary's Baby*, Polanski's release of 1968, it made every effort to update the Gothic formula for 1965 and, as an exercise in campness, it runs *The Fearless Vampire Killers* (Roman Polanski, 1967) pretty close.

Lee Thompson returned to America in the spring of 1966 to renew his working partnership with Carl Foreman, this time on a western, *Mackenna's Gold* (1968). Like *The Guns of Navarone* it starred Gregory Peck – it even had Anthony Quayle among the cast – and much preparatory time was spent scouting the spectacular desert locations with *Guns*'s production designer, Geoffrey Drake. The uncivilised wilderness and frontier mentality alluded to in *Cape Fear* is explored on a much grander cinematic scale in *Mackenna's Gold*, which combines Foreman's critique of acquisitive capitalism – the lust for gold – with Lee Thompson's motifs of the desperate journey, the destructiveness of obsession and the need for revenge.

Leaving behind the pampered surroundings of a French chateau and the comfort of Borehamwood, this was back to endurance film making for Lee Thompson in temperatures reaching 120 degrees and locations subject to sandstorms and flash floods. But he still found time during the filming to marry for the third time. His relationship with Joan Henry had finally foundered when she could no longer cope with his violent outbursts. Robin Estridge had advised her to leave before she succumbed to a nervous breakdown. Lee Thompson's third marriage, however, has endured for more than thirty years, and his wife Penny has been successful in helping him to overcome a drinking problem that ultimately prevented him achieving his full creative potential.

Before Winter Comes (1969)

Soon after *Eye of the Devil* opened in London in March 1968, J. Lee Thompson took his new wife and their three large dogs to Austria to make a film for Robert Emmett Ginna and the British arm of Columbia Pictures, the backers of *The Guns of Navarone*. Technically, *Before Winter Comes*, based on a Frederick Keefe short story (*The Interpreter*) in the *New Yorker*, is a British film. It had a largely British production crew, including Gilbert Taylor making his first film with Lee Thompson since *No Trees*, and among the international cast were a number of British actors including *Guns'* David Niven and Anthony Quayle (making his fifth film with Lee Thompson). But its chief box office attraction was the Israeli entertainer Topol, making his first screen appearance following his huge success on stage in *Fiddler on the Roof*. One wag dubbed his role in *Before Winter Comes*, as a stateless gypsy with a taste for the black market, as 'fiddler on the hoof' (*Daily Sketch*, 2 May 1969).[7]

Like *The Third Man*, the film is set in occupied Austria at the end of the Second World War. In this instance the location is a displaced persons' camp on the border between the British and Russian zones. Major Burnside (Niven) is sent to get the ramshackle camp running efficiently, and to allocate refugees to the American and Soviet zones. He is aided in this task by an amiable and resourceful scallywag, Janovic (Topol), who acts as his interpreter while diverting a fair proportion of the camp's supplies in his own direction. The two men compete over Maria (Anna Karina) the owner of the local inn, but develop considerable respect for each other. In the end, Burnside is faced with a typically Lee Thompson moral dilemma when he is informed by the Russians that Janovic is a deserter from their army. The major wants to take the compassionate course and let Janovic go but cannot disobey the orders of the martinet Brigadier Bewley (Quayle) and reluctantly puts his interpreter in the truck to the Russian zone. Like *Yield to the Night* and *Tiger Bay*, the film ends with the character we have come to like so much facing execution.

Although very different in look and atmosphere, the film shares a number of themes with *The Third Man*: the imminent Cold War (the symbolic 'winter' of the film's title); the upheaval in moral values brought about by war; sexual competition between friends; an antagonist who is an attractive and plausible rogue; and a denouement involving disillusion and betrayal. But, whereas Carol Reed's film offers a dark and cynical version of human relationships in line with Graham Greene's pessimism and ambivalent moral code, *Before Winter Comes* is a more bitter–sweet story, treated in a lighter style. Its setting among the mountains south of Salzburg emphasises the life-enhancing properties of the natural world rather than the deadening effect of the ravaged Vienna seen in *The Third Man*. Both films are interested in the aftermath of war and the compromises and accommodations which human beings must make to survive,[8] but where Reed and Greene emphasise the pain, Lee Thompson and scriptwriter Andrew Sinclair more often see the humour. Sinclair's particular concern is the corrupting effect of militarism, and his script oscillates between light satire of army manners and culture (Bewley's inspection of the camp, for instance) and a more bitter condemnation of the military's involvement in civilian affairs. For example, Burnside, who desperately wants to return to proper soldiering, regards his role as an arbiter of people's destiny as 'trading in flesh', making his unit little better than 'a British Gestapo'. But, although he struggles to find his humanity, he is too steeped in military ideology and too committed to his faltering career to change. The frustrated hopes for a service which will put moral considerations before expediency, duty and submission to authority reside with his fresh-faced Lieutenant (John Hurt, in one of his first starring roles). His sense of bewilderment and indignation at the cowardly extinction of the life force that Janovic represents should be the film's emotional core. Unfortunately, however, the film never quite achieves this focus, and for this Lee Thompson must take responsibility. His direction is uncharacteristically loose and over-relaxed with little of the precision he brought to, for instance, *Cape Fear*. Although he draws some convincing performances from his actors (notably Niven, and Topol in his first screen role), he seems to adopt an almost *laissez-faire* attitude to Gil Taylor's camera, allowing it to zoom and pan at will.[9] Lee Thompson now says that he felt that his earlier, more prescriptive, style was beginning to hamper his creativity:

> 'As I grew more confident in walking on to the floor to direct a film, I would almost take a delight in not knowing what I was going to do because the spontaneity of the moment was better than something that you had preconceived, I felt – although it all depended. But I grew to love the feeling of "Well I'll go on the floor and I know that there are 100 ways to shoot this scene and that's a minimum", and I would rely on instinct rather than having everything "boarded out". But even when I was relying on instinct, I used to make out my little sketches for each shot because this was a safety net. If I started to get unsure, I would go back to my script, which would have these little drawings in it, and know that the scene could be played like that because I'd worked it out before. But, invariably one got something better if one just went along without a preconceived notion of everything.'

In this case, however, the triumph of spontaneity is at the expense of visual coherence and dramatic focus. Nevertheless, *Before Winter*

Comes is a thoughtful piece with a stunning setting, unusual story and strong acting. It did well in America, and won over a number of the tough London press corps, including Alexander Walker who thought it 'memorable' (*Evening Standard*, 2 May 1969) and Dilys Powell who was impressed with its actors' portrayal of the 'struggle between the ideal and the actual' (*Sunday Times*, 4 May 1969). There was widespread praise for the film's acting, but less consensus on Lee Thompson's direction, judgements varying from 'acute' (Cecil Wilson, *Daily Mail*, 30 April 1969) to 'flat-footed' (John Coleman, *New Statesman*, 2 May 1969). Patrick Gibbs in the *Daily Telegraph* (2 May 1969) perhaps got closest to the problem when he wrote that the film was too 'diffuse', lacking 'a drive in any one direction'. It was, he suggested, 'enjoyable in its parts', but 'unsatisfactory' in its whole.

The Most Dangerous Man in the World (1969, USA: The Chairman)

Lee Thompson was now almost alternating David Niven and Gregory Peck as his leading men, and soon after shooting *Before Winter Comes* with Niven he returned to London with Gregory Peck at the request of Arthur P. Jacobs, the producer of *What a Way to Go* and, most recently, the hugely successful *Planet of the Apes* (Franklin J. Schaffner, 1968). Jacobs had been developing a project based on *The Chairman*, Jay Richard Kennedy's novel about an academic involved in espionage inside Mao's China. The screenplay was by one of Hollywoods's most respected writers, Ben Maddow, responsible for the scripts of Clarence Brown's *Intruder in the Dust* (1949) and John Huston's *The Asphalt Jungle* (1950). Shooting was again bedevilled with problems. Elaborate sets were constructed at Pinewood, but recruiting sufficient numbers of Chinese extras to fill them was a headache. Unable to film in China at the height of the Cultural Revolution, the crew went to Hong Kong but was met with demonstrations and threats from Chinese communists who claimed that the film would be 'an insult to Chairman Mao'. Lee Thompson remembers that the crew members feared for their safety: 'In the end I had to secretly photograph some of the Hong

Kong scenes from cabs or private cars.' Official filming was can-
celled by the Hong Kong Government and had to be continued in
Taiwan. The final scenes, in which Gregory Peck flees pursuing
troops and struggles across the Chinese border, were actually shot
in Wales. Just prior to the film's release in Britain in July 1969,
the title was changed to *The Most Dangerous Man in the World*, an
ambiguous reference to both Chairman Mao and the explosive
device which secret service officers implant in the head of their
reluctant agent, Dr Hathaway (Peck).

The film capitalises on the international appeal of the James
Bond series, and uses a number of stock spy-genre situations, but
its protagonist John Hathaway is more typical of Lee Thompson's
films. As a pacifist scientist who is co-opted by the unscrupulous
security services in a joint NATO–USSR operation, he offers the
chance to revisit the ethical dilemmas posed in *I Aim at the Stars*.[10]
As in many post-war science fiction texts, science is seen as a
dangerous and unstable force which has the potential for life
enhancement (the enzyme growth-regulator which is the film's
Hitchcockian MacGuffin) or destruction (the bomb in Hathaway's
skull). Scientific laws and discoveries owe no national allegiances
– 'science has no nation', Hathaway maintains – but are constantly
exploited by partisan interests. The scientist is enslaved by two
masters: the state and his/her profession.[11]

Hathaway's knockabout verbal exchanges with Mao (Conrad
Yama) across a ping-pong table also allow the exploration of moral
differences between Eastern communism and Western liberalism
that are seen to centre on the value accorded to the individual.
Hathaway's belief in the uniqueness and preciousness of each
individual life leads to his (and Lee Thompson's) credo 'I'd rather
die than kill'. The director admits that he identified quite strongly
with Peck's character in the film, injecting some of his own sentiments into the script: 'I do have pacifist beliefs and I try to get them
into a picture that warrants it in any way.' Hathaway's idealism is
contrasted with the cynical expediency of his military controllers,
who conceal from him the fact that he is a human bomb and
debate the tactical consequences of using him to blow up Mao.
The scientist's belief in the value of the individual is further

316   J. LEE THOMPSON

contrasted with the mass hysteria of the storm troopers of the cultural revolution, the Red Guard, who, rather like the rebels in *North West Frontier*, are represented as unknowably 'other'. In their youth, fanaticism and lack of respect for established institutions they might be read as a projection of the fear and bewilderment provoked by the emergent political counter-culture in the West.

As in some of Lee Thompson's previous movies, the attempt to graft the film's discursive concerns onto a conventional action-genre narrative is sometimes strained, and the Bondian conventions threaten to trivialise the film's ideas.[12] As always, Lee Thompson keeps the film visually interesting with hand-held cameras and the dynamic whip pan he first explored in *Cape Fear*, but his experiments with convoluted time frames and complex editing techniques tend to complicate proceedings unnecessarily. After a break of ten years, Dick Best was once again editing Lee Thompson's rushes, and he found it a much more difficult task than in the old days at Elstree. He had to contend not only with the structural complexities of a narrative in which Hathaway is constantly broadcasting from China to a control room is the West (via an implanted transmitter), but with the extravagant practices of American film making and interference from Twentieth Century-Fox executives. His account is revealing of the clash between English and American film cultures which so characterised the dollar-dependent British cinema of the 1960s:

> '*The Chairman* was very, very hard for me – mostly because the action was taking place in at least two places at once. Lee, making the film for Twentieth Century-Fox, covered it endlessly in shots, which he couldn't do at ABC because they couldn't afford it. Although it was stuff you needed, this was enormous coverage. It wasn't like a straightforward story where you've got a complete sequence all at once. He started off shooting in the control room where they were listening to Gregory Peck, wherever he happened to be ... Everything in the control room was shot straight off, so I never had a complete sequence. I had nothing to cut away to ... And then he went on to all the other sequences, and gradually you could build them in. So it was really complicated. And he gave me copious notes, which he'd never done before, he'd changed his style. He dictated them to his secretary and sometimes I didn't get

them for days. The notes almost pinpointed every cut, which I found very difficult to follow and I didn't find that they always worked. But eventually we got it together.

He stayed around for a few weeks to supervise the cutting and then he went back, and we eventually sent the cutting copy over to Fox for the bosses, like Richard Zanuck, to see ... Within a few days I had a call. I had to go over for a week. No Richard Zanuck, he was in Tokyo. They made a few changes, Lee and the producer. A stand-by editor was lurking in the background, but did not contribute. When we'd done these little bits the producer said: "You can go home now and we'll send the cutting copy to you and you can get on with the dubbing." So I got back, and after three days I got a call at home saying: "You'd better come back to the studio. They've sent the film back with two boxes of deletions." They'd cut out several sequences and bits of sequences, about ten minutes or something. I imagine what had happened is that Richard Zanuck had got back and this editor had pushed his nose in. There was nobody here except the associate producer and myself to OK the dubbing, and we sent off each reel as we dubbed it with a magnetic track and a dupe of the picture to Hollywood, to the line producer Mort Abrahams. He viewed the dubbing on a projector in a caravan in the Mojave Desert and then we got little notes back to redub this and redub that. The man who played the chairman, his voice wasn't adequate and they hunted around and found an actor called, Lorne Greene, in America, and he came over and post-synched the whole of the part. We finally got a married print and we went back to Denham laboratories and got a second print, and we were viewing this print when we had a phone call from Twentieth Century-Fox in Soho Square to say: "You've got to change the title for England to *The Most Dangerous Man in the World*. In this country everyone will think that *The Chairman* is about business – boring." But they'd had the whole of the film to think of that, and they took till the second print! So all the titles had to be remade, and my heart really sank. It really was a nightmare.'

Best's account illustrates some of the difficulties of making films within the Hollywood studio system and the additional complications and frustrations involved in trying to co-ordinate post-production work in different continents. For Lee Thompson, the system of movie making by committee represented a considerable loss of artistic control compared with the freedom he had enjoyed at ABPC. The compromises that the system obliged directors to make explains the fragmentation of much of Lee Thompson's output after *Cape Fear*. Lee Thompson also recalls the post-production of *The Chairman* as 'a nightmare':

> 'When we showed the film at Fox, suddenly all these notes came from various people at the studio. They had a terrible system of inviting a lot of people to a screening and getting [them] to give their notes. And then the notes would be compiled and given to me and the editor. This was after I'd done my final cut. I remember [Dick Best] had to go back over to America and listen to all these suggestions. It was a nightmare because no longer did I control the film. So that was a time of great stress.'

The product of all this stress created little more than a rustle of interest among British reviewers. Some, like Cecil Wilson of the *Daily Mail* (1 July 1969), and Dilys Powell (*Sunday Times*, 6 July 1969) found it 'enjoyable' as a 'colourful if unbelievable' thriller, and the *Daily Sketch* (3 July 1969) even described it as 'great edge of the seat stuff', but most critics professed to being bored by a 'doggedly' directed film (*The Times*, 3 July 1969), one which the acidic Alexander Walker thought had about as much suspense as 'a tired skipping rope' (*Evening Standard*, 3 July 1969). At the British box office, *The Most Dangerous Man in the World* performed reasonably well considering it played during a heat wave and faced severe competition from *Oliver!* (Carol Reed, 1969), *Where Eagles Dare* (Brian Hutton, 1969), *The Italian Job* (Peter Collinson, 1969) and *Carry On Camping* (Gerald Thomas, 1969). It was Lee Thompson's third British release inside four months, *Mackenna's Gold* having opened in April. Although one dealt with China's Cultural Revolution, the others had little to say directly about the turbulent political world of the late 1960s.

Lee Thompson, however, had certainly not abdicated from engagement with current issues. He had, for example, been an enthusiastic supporter of Arthur Jacobs' desire to make *Planet of the Apes*, seeing its potential for the allegorical examination of American race relations.[13] The disturbances of the 'long hot summer' of 1964 and the riots in the Watts district of Los Angeles in 1965 (Sitkoff 1981) had made a deep impression on him, and he worked with

Jacobs to try to raise money for the project in the expectation that he would direct (Greene 1998: 82). When the film eventually came to be made, in 1967, his commitment to *Mackenna's Gold* ruled him out as director, but he eventually took over for the last two films in the *Apes'* series in the early 1970s, immediately foregrounding political themes which had been down-played in the previous film in the series: *Escape from the Planet of the Apes* (Don Taylor, 1971). Lee Thompson's interest in politically-aware film making is also evidenced in the full-page advertisement in *Kinematograph Weekly* (25 January 1969) that he took out to publicise a project in development with screenwriter Andrew Sinclair which would have confronted issues of violence, conspiracy and paranoia. From the description given, Sinclair's original screenplay for *You?* sounds a little like the Warren Commission meets William Castle. It was to be a mystery dealing with 'the assassination of leading political figures in the United States', and the audience was to determine responsibility: 'The guilt may lie in the national climate of violence, a conspiracy, or in the paranoia of the hero – or in all of these. "You?" may be everybody, some or one sick man. At the end of the film you should choose.' The project was presumably inspired by the assassinations of Martin Luther King and Robert Kennedy in 1968, but it failed to find sufficient backing and remained unmade. American financial backing for British film making was evaporating fast (Walker 1986: 441–59; Murphy 1992: 274–5) as the major Hollywood studios suffered serious box office failures with big-budget movies made both at home and overseas. London's position at the centre of international cultural innovation was slipping, and lower budget independently produced films with a focus on American youth culture and audiences seemed the most bankable prospect.

Country Dance (1970, USA: Brotherly Love)

With the Hollywood industry poised to begin financial retrenchment and cultural introspection, Lee Thompson was delighted to learn that his friend Robert Emmett Ginna had secured MGM's backing to produce a property in which Lee Thompson had invested almost a decade earlier. He had bought the rights to James Kennaway's second novel, *Household Ghosts*, soon after publication,[14] and the writer was able to complete the adaptation under the title *Country Dance* just before his death in a car accident in December 1968. MGM was probably given the confidence to back the production by the knowledge that Kennaway had written *Tunes of Glory* and the then current spectacular *The Battle of Britain* (Guy Hamilton, 1969).[15]

For Lee Thompson, making *Country Dance* became a labour of love and a tribute to its dead writer. It is a film which, he says, is 'close to my heart'. Unfortunately, MGM vetoed his return to Perthshire to film the movie. Southern Ireland was now a more attractive financial proposition, as suitable locations could be found near the modern facilities offered by Dublin's Ardmore Studios.[16] The studios were also the favoured venue of the film's star Peter O'Toole, who had made *The Lion in Winter* (Anthony Harvey, 1968) there. O'Toole enthusiastically accepted the role of Sir Charles Henry Arbuthnot Pinkerton Ferguson – familiarly known as 'Pink' – the last in a line of Scottish noblemen and victim of his own refusal to change with the times. Susannah York naturally played his sister Hilary as the part had been written for her by her cousin James Kennaway.[17] In addition, Lee Thompson cast a number of actors he had worked with before: Michael Craig (*Yield to the Night*) played Hilary's husband Douglas; Harry Andrews (*Ice Cold*) played Brigadier Crieff, a local farmer; and Mark Malicz (*Before Winter Comes*) was cast as Benny-the-Pole. In the role of Maitland, the doctor in charge of the genteel mental hospital to which Pink is sent, Lee Thompson cast Cyril Cusack, the Irish actor who had made his screen debut in Reed's *Odd Man Out*.

In the making of *Cape Fear* Robert Mitchum had lived his part as a hard-drinking ex-con. In *Country Dance* Peter O'Toole also took his part as an alcoholic hell-raiser seriously. Lee Thompson remembers:

> 'Peter was going through a very heavy drinking period, and there were times when it was difficult to work with him. He was arrested one night, and Bob Ginna had to go to the police station and get

him out for the next day's shooting. But he was such a great actor that he would come on the set and immediately perform magnificently.'

O'Toole is certainly ideally cast as the crazed, eccentric and irresponsible Pink, a thoroughly degenerate remnant of Scotland's landed gentry. The character is a childish prankster who finds social proprieties a bore and cares little for anyone except himself and his sister Hilary with whom he had had an unnaturally close relationship in boyhood and adolescence. Hilary had married Douglas, one of Pink's ex-employees, who is now the estate manager of his neighbour Brigadier Crieff; but the marriage is in trouble and she has returned to live with her brother on their farm. The country dance of the title is a Young Conservatives' *ceilidh* where, in an adjoining schoolroom, Pink tries to provoke Douglas with suggestions that he and Hilary share an incestuous past. Torn between her too-dull husband and too-manic brother, Hilary turns briefly to promiscuity before deciding to settle for Douglas. Pink reacts with typical extravagance by blowing his ear off at a duck shoot, before intensifying his drinking binges. In an effort to keep her brother out of Montreal House, the local sanatorium for unbalanced gentry, Hilary asks a former dairymaid on the farm (Judy Cornwell) to look after him, but he continues to slide into insanity. As his sister prepares to leave, he confesses that she is the only woman he ever loved. This is sufficient for Douglas to finally take the initiative and, as Hilary has been hoping, assert himself, and she agrees to commit her brother to Montreal House.

The film contains some interesting subtextual comments on the post-war class system – the waning powers of an aristocracy grown decadent and demented due to inbreeding, and the rise of the managerial class[18] – but is more significant in its surfaces. The hills and lowlands of County Wicklow are lovingly photographed by Ted Moore,[19] and Kennaway's lavish and idiosyncratic dialogue gives the cast every opportunity to demonstrate their techniques, a chance which they seize with relish. Always tempted to give gifted actors their head, Lee Thompson allows O'Toole, in particular, to go full-tilt into spells of raving madness so florid that they test the audience's patience. Lee Thompson feels O'Toole 'gave an excellent performance', but he admits that 'it's a film of dialogue, and the dialogue of James Kennaway is very strange – it's an acquired taste, you might say – it's almost poetic, with a very strange rhythm'. He realises that, in a period when cinema was turning away from the adaptation of dialogue-heavy stage plays and towards more dynamic original screenplays, *Country Dance* was 'too wordy for the times', but the real problem lies with the characters. John Russell Taylor in *The Times* (12 March 1971) nailed the point when he complained that, from the viewpoint of the audience, 'the people are tiresome to be with'. Consequently, Ian Christie found it impossible to view the more emotional sequences 'with any concern' (*Daily Express*, 15 March 1971). Like Christie, Cecil Wilson (*Daily Mail*, 12 March 1971), could admire 'the polish of J. Lee Thompson's direction'; but, as for what happens to the characters, at the end of this 'overwrought and overmannered film' he was left asking 'who cares?' But, in spite of reservations about the appeal of Pink and his sister, *Country Dance* represented the sort of sophisticated film making which critics valued. Dilys Powell though that 'the verbal pyrotechnics' might be 'overdone' but the film was 'a welcome change' from an increasingly brutal cinema of exploitation and permissiveness (*Sunday Times*, 14 March 1971). Michael McNey in the *Guardian* (19 March 1971) even considered it 'J. Lee Thompson's finest film for many years'.[20] Critics may have approved, but *Country Dance* never attracted a large audience. It previewed at the 1970 Edinburgh Festival, before opening modestly at the small Ritz Cinema in London in the spring of 1971. 'Unfortunately the film wasn't very successful and played mostly in art houses', Lee Thompson recalls sadly, 'but it's one of my favourite films.'

Simian Allegories

With the completion of *Country Dance* in the late summer of 1969, J. Lee Thompson returned to Los Angeles where he made the well-regarded television movie *A Great American Tragedy*

(1972, UK: *Man at the Crossroads*), with George Kennedy and Vera Miles playing a couple whose comfortable life is disrupted by unemployment.[21] Quinlan (1983: 294) regards it as 'adroitly handled' and a welcome return to 'the more intimate dramas with which Thompson made his name'. More significantly, however, he directed the last two films in *The Planet of the Apes'* quintet. *Conquest of the Planet of the Apes'* was perhaps his most overtly political film since *Yield to the Night*. A violent allegory of African-American struggles for emancipation and equality, the film depicted 'race war' between apes and their human slave-masters in the America of 1991. While the film leaves open questions about the moral and strategic validity of armed insurrection, it injects into the *Apes'* series 'an increased sense of crisis' and gives expression to the frustrated rage of contemporary black nationalists (Greene 1998: 82–112; see also Asch 1994: 38). The controversial ending of the film originally mirrored the closure of *Cape Fear*, as Caesar, the victorious ape leader, vows to enslave humans in revenge for their treatment of apes. In this reversal of the system of domination, the violence and hatred of the oppressor has been transferred to the oppressed, emphasising what Greene (1998: 112) terms 'the recursive nature of brutalism', just as *Cape Fear* had done. However, after observing the reactions of preview audiences, nervous executives at Twentieth Century-Fox insisted (against the protests of Lee Thompson) that the end be softened to avoid alienating white viewers. The revised version ends with an appeal from Caesar to his followers to 'cast out your vengeance' and act in a more human fashion towards the defeated enemy. When Lee Thompson came to make the next and last film in the saga he was told by Fox that no further surprises were wanted and instructed him to make a 'kids' picture' (1998: 115). *Battle for the Planet of the Apes* (1973) was rather more complex than that, but its themes were more integrationist and its narrative emphasised the problems of co-existence rather than the necessity of conflict.

During the 1970s, with British film production sinking deeper into the crisis created by the withdrawal of American finance and the ever-dwindling attendances figures, Lee Thompson's contribution to his native cinema was negligible. He confined his activities largely to Hollywood, working as a jobbing director making films in a variety of genres including a musical (*Huckleberry Finn*, 1974), a macabre fantasy (*The Reincarnation of Peter Proud*, 1974), a hard-boiled thriller (*St Ives*, 1976) and a western (*The White Buffalo*, 1977), the last two films starring Charles Bronson with whom he established a close working partnership. Hollywood, as he put it, is 'where the work is' (Summers 1976). He returned to London in 1976, not to make a film, but to supervise a new stage play he had written called *Getting Away with Murder*, which was produced at the Comedy Theatre in the West End. It was as if his career had come full circle, forty years after *Double Error*. The play was not, however, J. Lee Thompson's final act of creativity in Britain. In 1977 he directed parts of *The Greek Tycoon* (1978), the ill-advised and ill-conceived fictional bio-pic of Aristotle Onassis at Pinewood.

The Passage (1979)

J. Lee Thompson's last 'British' film was *The Passage*, shot entirely in location in the Pyrenees and in the Victarine Studios in Nice, France. Although meeting the requirements for classification as a British film, it is an example of the 1970s' trend towards inter-national production. It has a British director (working from Holly-wood) and cinematographer (Michael Reed, who had shot *On Her Majesty's Secret Service*, directed by Peter Hunt, 1969), three British actors among an international cast, and was financed jointly by the London-based distributors Hemdale and United Artists. It was based on the novel *Perilous Passage* by Bruce Nicolayson who also contributed the screenplay – to which J. Lee Thompson made considerable changes in order to introduce greater suspense into the text.

The Passage is a straightforward story of a rugged Basque resist-ance fighter (Anthony Quinn) who is paid to escort a scientist – Professor Bergson (James Mason) – and his family, wanted by the Nazis for their 'war machine', from German-occupied Toulouse across the Pyrenees to Spain. The man trying to stop the escape is Gunther von Berkow (Malcolm McDowell), a psychopathic SS captain. If the film is remembered today, it is for the mad-eyed campness of McDowell's performance. In his rendition of a sadist with a macabre sense of humour, McDowell goes beyond *Clockwork Orange*'s Alex and seems to be getting into character for his role as *Caligula* (Tinto Brass, 1980). His comic-book Nazi psycho completely overwhelms the other performances – Quinn frowns and grimaces moodily, Mason hardly acts at all and only Christopher Lee as a gypsy leader seems to be in the same film. McDowell's sporting of a swastika jockstrap rests uneasily with the film's striving for social realism through its cinematography. As a piece of self-indulgent theatricality his performance easily rivals Peter O'Toole's in *Country Dance*. Lee Thompson now regrets the absence of a moderating influence:

> 'We weren't good for each other, because we liked to go to extremes, both Malcolm and I, and we overdid it, I think; we overdid the rather comic side of his character. I like to take risks, and I know I was taking a risk with the excess of the character played by Malcolm McDowell. I still like this characterisation but certainly the critics didn't like it and thought it was awfully over the top. Which it was, but I took the risk of doing that hoping it would have a more successful outcome than it did.'

Certainly, *The Passage* would be a pretty dull and colourless film without McDowell's von Berkow, but his manic presence overshadows the hero of the piece, Anthony Quinn's Basque pathfinder, and the glamour of the character also tends to transfer itself to the sadism of his actions.

Thematically, *The Passage* is a classic J. Lee Thompson movie: *The Guns of Navarone* meets *Cape Fear* filmed in the style of *Before Winter Comes*. The tag-lines in the American poster expressed it succinctly: 'An ice-swept escape route in front of them. A cold-blooded killer behind them. The only way out is up.' The narrative describes another hazardous journey (a *Perilous Passage*) out of a tight situation during which the protagonists discover emotions and resources they did not realise they possessed. Like the Bowdens in *Cape Fear*, the Bergson family learn what they are capable of doing to survive. Bergson and his son (Paul Clemens) learn to be 'killers' while his daughter (Kay Lenz) submits to rape by von Berkow.[22] The wilderness through which they are pursued and the obsessive relentlessness of their persecutor are also clear echoes of *Cape Fear*. The tensions between the Basque and the Bergsons recall those between the Anthony Quinn and Gregory Peck characters in *Guns*, and the familiar Lee Thompson distinction between good and bad Germans is also made. The ending, too, where a mortally wounded hunter, von Berkow, refrains from shooting his quarry as his life ebbs away references the restraint shown at the close of both *Cape Fear* and *Conquest of the Planet of the Apes*.[23] Much of the verbal philosophising of the earlier films, however, is eliminated, leaving dialogue which verges on the taciturn, and an unusually muted subtext.

No Regrets?

It is fitting that Lee Thompson's last British film should have drawn together so many of the threads of his cinema, but it is a shame that the pattern they made was not given a more memorable frame than *The Passage*. As British cinema hit rock-bottom in the early 1980s the director it had so successfully groomed turned finally away and concentrated his talents on a succession of tough-guy thrillers with Charles Bronson – *Cabo Blanco. Where Legends are Born...* (1980); *10 to Midnight* (1983); *The Evil that Men Do* (1984); *Murphy's Law* (1986); *Death Wish 4: The Crackdown* (1987); *Messenger of Death* (1988; USA: *The Avenging Angels*); and *Kinjite: Forbidden Subjects* (1989). In between, he found time for a couple of Indiana Jones-inspired adventure yarns – *King Solomon's Mines* (1985) and *Firewalker* (1986) – a psycho-thriller, *Happy Birthday to Me* (1981) and his most critically well-received film of the 1980s, *The Ambassador* (1984) in which he once again directed Robert Mitchum, this time in a version of Elmore Leonard's *52 Pick-Up*, the story of an American diplomat's attempts to mediate in the Israeli–Palestinian crisis. Although the films showed a high level of competence and the odd flash of inspiration, overall they were a disappointing coda to a career which had so quickly risen to distinction.

32 Looking back on sixty-five years in film making: J. Lee Thompson in April 1999

Looking back, Lee Thompson is thankful for the regular work which he was able to find in Hollywood and would have struggled to secure in the British industry. Understandably, he is prepared to offer a modest defence of his 1980s' output, but there remains a strong note of regret. He still rates the films he made between 1955 and 1961 his best work:

'I blame myself for wanting to go to Hollywood and to stay in Hollywood. I think I would have done better films if I had come home ... Hollywood is a machine that demands that you do not try to be too clever. In other words, in Hollywood you are in danger of losing your individuality and, except for one or two Hollywood films, I'm afraid I lost that individuality I had in my early British films. I'm not saying that in America the studios handcuffed me and made me shoot the film in what I'm afraid is rather an obvious way. I had freedom in America in all my films, but you are conscious in America – at least I am – that they need box office successes. You're soon out of the business if you don't produce something that's making money for them. Consequently, I took a lot of films I shouldn't have taken and I didn't shoot them so originally as I did in Britain. In fact, I look upon my Hollywood career as being successful in Hollywood terms: that is I made films right into my 80s. I was perhaps one of the oldest directors working in Hollywood. But, except for one or two instances, I think my best work was done in my early career in England.'

In his review of 1960s' British cinema, *Hollywood England*, Alexander Walker (1986: 462) posed the question: 'Where in the period under review does one look for the British equivalent of Bergman, or Forman, or Rohmer, or Antonioni, or Truffaut, or even Godard?' He was forced to conclude that the answer was 'nowhere'. He went on to bemoan 'the inability, or disinclination, of even established-name directors in Britain to articulate a view of life and society in freshly conceived and individual terms, and to translate these aesthetically to the screen with an unmistakable signature'. The frustrating thing is that, had Lee Thompson continued the creative trajectory that brought him to prominence in the 1950s, he might well have been the director Walker was looking for. Instead, he opted out of an industry whose artistic horizons were limited and whose home market was decaying, and out of a film culture which regarded him with suspicion and undervalued his talent. Critics had been confused by what Raymond Durgnat (1970: 244) so aptly termed 'the ferocity of his films' and his inclination to confront 'brutal moral paradoxes' and deal with 'massive blocks of brute emotion'. So much of his film making ran counter to the prevailing critical orthodoxies in ways which appeared unsubtle, overstated and out of step with intellectual fashion. If he had ridden the punches, rejected Hollywood, and made *Chips With Everything* he might have been embraced as a founding father of the British New Wave rather than merely, in Durgnat's phrase, 'a kind of strayed uncle'.

When Margaret Hinxman came to write a review of one of Lee Thompson's films at the end of the 1960s, she was prepared, on behalf of her fellow-critics, to share some of the blame for the way things had developed:

> The sad thing is that J. Lee Thompson was once a trail-blazing British director who has never been sufficiently praised for making honest films like *Yield to the Night* and *Woman in a Dressing Gown* long before it was fashionable to do so. Maybe it's our fault that he's now opted for the box office safety of *Mackenna's Gold*. (*Sunday Telegraph*, 6 July 1969)

While such inconsistency of critical judgement no doubt contributed to the instability of Lee Thompson's creative vision, it does not fully explain the overall unevenness of his output and his long capitulation to Hollywood populism. For an explanation, we must look to factors specific to Lee Thompson himself – a comfortable lifestyle, the ageing process and a fondness for intoxicants that may have clouded his long-term view – but must also look at a culture of film making which encouraged excess, valued commercial success above all else, and was geared to respond instantly to the latest fads and fancies. Finally, we must look to the times. More than any other post-war decade the 1960s was a period of randomness and cultural volatility in which planning and measured prediction became largely untenable, with seismic shifts in generational relationships, aesthetic sensibilities and the loci of creative energy. It is not surprising, then, that in such an unhinged age a new boy in Tinseltown should be so buffeted by chance and contingency. If, in these circumstances, his aim sometimes faltered from the true, we should perhaps forgive the misses and marvel at the times he hit the target.

Notes

1 On a visit to London to discuss *What a Way to Go* with Robert Mitchum in the summer of 1963, Lee Thompson told *Kinematograph Weekly* (11 July 1963) that he planned to film *Shoes of the Fisherman* with Paul Scofield and Spencer Tracy for MGM the following summer. The film was eventually directed by Michael Anderson with Laurence Olivier and released in 1968.

2 The screenplay by Julius Epstein, in consultation with Lee Thompson, is a considerable elaboration on Monteilhet's lean original, particularly in its ending.

3 Ann Pacey in the *Sun* (2 February 1966), for example, thought the performances good and the climaxes 'cleverly handled', while Ernest Betts in the *People* (6 February 1966) found Samantha Eggar 'brilliantly bitchy' and praised Lee Thompson for keeping 'the suspense at screaming point'.

4 Perhaps he had now had a chance to see *The Ipcress File* (1965) in which Sidney Furie (one of the directors originally considered for *Thirteen*) uses an elaborate visual style similar to that pioneered by Lee Thompson on *Yield to the Night*.

5 To add insult to injury, *Eye of the Devil* was released on the ABC circuit as a co-feature with *The Heroin Gang*.

6 It is worth noting the presence, too, of Lee Thompson's signature shot, a child first seen through bars – in this case the strings of a harp.

7 Lee Thompson described Topol as 'the Frank Sinatra of Israel' (*Daily Mail*, 7 February 1969).

8 When Burnside describes Janovic as 'a professional survivor' and 'too useful to liquidate', he is almost quoting the description of von Braun in *I Aim at the Stars*.

9 Not surprisingly, Gil Taylor thoroughly enjoyed the freedom he was given and regards *Before Winter Comes* as 'the film I loved doing with Lee most'. He admits that it was 'very difficult', but is proud that 'it was very good to look at'.

10 In fact, the origins of Lee Thompson's interest in the ethics of science can be traced further back, to *Woman in a Dressing Gown* in which the Prestons' son (Andrew Ray) prepares a debating paper on whether 'a scientist's loyalty to humanity is more important than his loyalty to his country'.

11 Maddow's script makes frequent references to enslavement. A scientist talks of being 'chained hand and foot to an enzyme' which itself is made up of four chains. The destructive effect of politics is dramatised when an 'oldline' Chinese scientist, goaded by the Red Guard, is driven to suicide.

12 Gadgets like the ludicrously simplistic 'psychological status' gauge do not help the film's believability quotient.

13 In an interview in 1976, Lee Thompson claimed that he originally owned the film rights to *Planet of the Apes*, selling them to Arthur P. Jacobs when he failed to get backing for the movie (Summers 1976). This may well be the case, but is yet to be verified.

14 Lee Thompson had originally tried to develop the property as a West End play, but its suggestion of sibling incest was unacceptable to the Lord Chamberlain. The play was eventually produced at the Hampstead Theatre club in 1967 (*Brotherly Love* exhibitors' merchandising manual, MGM 1970).

15 They were probably yet to realise that Guy Hamilton's film was not the money-maker United Artists expected.

16 The unit did eventually travel to Perthshire to film some exteriors.

17 York had made her screen debut in the Kennaway-scripted *Tunes of Glory*.

18 The follies of the aristocracy were more effectively satirised a year after the release of *Country Dance*, in Peter Medak's *The Ruling Class* (1972). The part of Pink is a near-rehearsal for the madcap earl O'Toole plays in this later film, a role for which he was nominated for an Academy Award.

19 Gil Taylor originally expected to photograph *Country Dance*, and was disappointed to learn that the film's producers had snapped up Ted Moore for half his usual fee by buying out his contract from another company whose project had fallen through (interview with Gil Taylor).

20 *Country Dance* was also praised in the *Daily Telegraph* (24 August 1970), the *Sunday Telegraph* (28 March 1971), the *Daily Mirror* (19 March 1971) and the *New Statesman* (10 March 1971).

21 It was the first of a small number of tele-features Lee Thompson made during the 1970s and early 1980s.

22 Bergson's wife (Patricia Neal) sacrifices herself, Captain Oates-style, by walking out into the snow of the mountains so that the escape will not be slowed by her presence.

23 Lee Thompson deliberately changed the bloody ending of Nicolayson's script which has the Basque's dogs jumping to the rescue and ripping out von Berkow's throat and testicles.

Filmography

AS SCRIPTWRITER

The Price of Folly 1937, 52 min., b/w, 'A'

Production company: Associated British
Studio: Welwyn
Producer–Director: Walter Summers
Screenplay: J. Lee Thompson, Ruth Landon, Walter Summers
Original story: J. Lee Thompson
Leading players: Leonora Corbett (Christine), Colin Keith-Johnson (Martin), Judy Kelly (Frances), Andreas Malandrinos (Gomez), Leslie Perrins (Owen), Wally Patch, The Trocadero Girls

The Middle Watch 1939, 87 min., b/w, 'U'

Production company: Associated British
Studio: Elstree
Producer: Walter Mycroft
Director: Thomas Bentley
Screenplay: J. Lee Thompson, Clifford Grey
Original story: Ian Hay, Stephen King-Hall
Director of photography: Claude Friese-Green
Leading players: Jack Buchanan (Capt. Maitland), Romney Brent (Ah Fang), Fred Emney (Adm. Sir Reginald Hewett), Leslie Fuller (Marine Ogg), Greta Gynt (Mary Carlton), Louise Hampton (Charlotte Hopkinson), Martita Hunt (Lady Hewett), David Hutcheson (Cmdr. Baddeley), Bruce Seton (Capt Randall), Ronald Shiner (Engineer), Kay Walsh (Fay Eaton)

East of Piccadilly (US title: *The Strangler*), 1940, 79 min., b/w, 'A'

Production company: Associated British
Studio: Elstree
Producer: Walter Mycroft
Director: Harold Huth
Screenplay: J. Lee Thompson, Lesley Storm
Original story: Gordon Beckles
Director of photography: Claude Friese-Green
Leading players: Judy Campbell (Penny Sutton), Sebastian Shaw (Tamsie Green), Henry Edwards (Inspector), Cameron Hall (George), George Hayes (Mark Struberg), Martita Hunt (Ma), Niall MacGinnis (Joe), Bunty Payne (Tania), Frederick Piper (Ginger Harris), George Pughe (Oscar Kuloff), Edana Romney (Sadie Jones), Charles Victor (Editor)

For Them that Trespass 1949 (USA 1950), 95 min., b/w, 'A'

Production company: Associated British
Studio: Elstree
Producer: Victor Skutezky
Director: Alberto Cavalcanti
Screenplay: J. Lee Thompson, William Douglas Home
Original story: Ernest Raymond
Director of photography: Derek Williams
Editor: Margery Saunders
Music: Philip Green.
Leading players: Stephen Murray (Christopher Drew), Richard Todd (Herb Logan), Patricia Plunkett (Rosie), Rosalyn Boulter (Frankie), Micheal Laurence (Jim Heal), Mary Merrall (Mrs. Drew), Vida Hope (Olive Mockson), Frederick Leister (Vicar), Michael Medwin (Len Stevens), John Salew (Prosecuting Counsel), Robert Harris (Defence Counsel), Joan Dowling (Gracie), Harry Fowler (Dave), Helen Cherry (Mary Drew), George Curzon (Clark Hall), Valentine Dyall (Sir Archibald), Irene Handl (Mrs Sams), James Hayter (Jocko), Harcourt Williams (Judge)

No Place For Jennifer 1949 (USA 1951), 90 min., b/w, 'A'

Production company: Associated British
Studio: Welwyn
Producer: Hamilton G. Inglis
Director: Henry Cass
Screenplay: J. Lee Thompson
Original story: Phyllis Hambleton
Director of photography: William McLeod
Editor: Monica Kimick

Art Director: Charles Gilbert
Music: Allan Gray
Leading players: Leo Genn (William), Rosamund John (Rachel), Janette Scott (Jennifer), Beatrice Campbell (Paula), Guy Middleton (Brian), Anthony Nicholls (Baxter), Jean Cadell (Aunt Jacqueline), Megs Jenkins (Mrs Marshall), Edith Sharpe (Doctor), Ann Cordington (Miss Hancock), Brian Smith (Martin), Andre Morell (Counsel), Phlip Ray (Mr. Marshall), MacDonald Hobley (Salesman)

Last Holiday 1950, 88 min., b/w, 'U'

Production company: Associated British–Watergate
Studio: Welwyn
Producer: Stephen Mitchell, A.D. Peters, J. B. Priestley
Director: Henry Cass
Assistant director: John Arnold
Screenplay: J. B. Priestley, J. Lee Thompson
Director of photography: Ray Elton
Editor: Monica Kimick
Art director: Duncan Sutherland
Music: Francis Chagrin
Make-up: Bob Clark
Leading players: Alec Guinness (George Bird), Beatrice Campbell (Sheila Rockingham), Kay Walsh (Mrs Poole), Gregoire Aslan (Gambini), Jean Colin (Daisy Clarence), Muriel George (Lady Oswington), Brian Worth (Derek Rockingham), Esma Cannon (Miss Fox), Bernard Lee (Inspector Wilton), Sid James (Joe Clarence), Campbell Cotts (Bellinghurst), Moultrie Kelsall (Sir Robert Kyle), Madam E. Kirkwood-Hackett (Miss Hatfield), Wilfrid Hyde-White (Chalfont), Eric Maturin (Wrexham), Helen Cherry (Miss Mellows), Brian Oulton (Prescott), Ernest Thesiger (Sir Trevor Lampington), Ronald Simpson (Dr Pevensey), Arthur Howard (Burden), Meier Tzelniker (Baltin)

AS DIRECTOR

Murder Without Crime 1951, 97, later 76 min., b/w, 'A'

Production Company : ABPC–Marble Arch
Studio: Welwyn
Producer : Victor Skutezky
Production manager: F. Sherwin Green
Director, screenplay, original story: J. Lee Thompson
Director of photography : Bill McLeod
Editor: E. B. Jarvis
Art director: Don Ashton

Music: Philip Green
Music direction: Louis Levy
Sound: Harry Benson, Stan Jolly
Continuity: Constance Newton
Leading players: Dennis Price (Matthew), Derek Farr (Stephen), Patricia
    Plunkett (Jan) Joan Dowling (Grena)
No release in USA

The Yellow Balloon 1953, 80 min. (USA: 76 min.), b/w, 'X'

Production company: ABPC–Marble Arch
Studio: Elstree
Producer: Victor Skutezky.
Production manager: W. G. Eades
Director: J. Lee Thompson
Assistant director: Cliff Owen
Screenplay, original story: J. Lee Thompson, Anne Burnaby
Director of photography: Gilbert Taylor
Editor: Richard Best
Art director: Robert Jones
Music: Philip Green
Sound: Harold V. King, Les Hammond
Special effects: George Blackwell
Continuity: Thelma Orr
Leading players: Andrew Ray (Frankie), Kathleen Ryan (Em), Kenneth More
    (Ted), William Sylvester (Len), Bernard Lee (Constable Chapman), Veronica
    Hurst (Sunday School Teacher), Hy Hazell (Mary), Sandra Dorne (Iris),
    Campbell Singer (Potter), Peter Jones (Spiv)

The Weak and the Wicked 1954, 88 min., b/w, 'A'

Production company: ABPC–Marble Arch
Studio: Elstree
Producer: Victor Skutezky
Production manager: Gordon Scott
Director: J. Lee Thompson.
Assistant director: George Pollard
Screenplay: J. Lee Thompson, Anne Burnaby, with Joan Henry
Original story: Joan Henry
Director of photography: Gilbert Taylor
Editor: Richard Best
Art director: Robert Jones
Music: Leighton Lucas
Sound: Harold V. King, Leslie Hammond
Continuity: June Faithfull

Make-up: L. V. Clark

Leading players: Glynis Johns (Jean), John Gregson (Michael), Diana Dors (Betty), Jane Hylton (Babs), Sidney James (Syd Baden), Olive Sloane (Nellie Baden), Eliot Makeham (Grandad), A. E. Matthews (Harry Wicks), Athene Seyler (Millie), Sybil Throrndike (Mabel), Jean Taylor-Smith (Prison Governor, Grange), Joan Haythorne (Prison Governor, Blackdown), Anthony Nicholls (Prison Chaplain), Barbara Couper (Prison Doctor), Joyce Heron (P. O. Arnold), Ursula Howells (Pam), Mary Merrall (Mrs Skinner), Rachel Roberts (Pat), Marjorie Rhodes (Susie), Josephine Griffin (Miriam), Simone Silva (Tina), Josephine Stuart (Andy), Thea Gregory (Nancy), Edwin Styles (Seymour), Cecil Trouncer (Judge), Paul Carpenter (Joe), Irene Handl (Waitress)

For Better, For Worse (US title: *Cocktails in the Kitchen*), 1954, 85 min., col., 'U'

Production company: ABPC–Kenwood Films
Studio: Elstree
Producer: Kenneth Harper
Director, screenplay: J. Lee Thompson
Original story: Arthur Watkyn
Director of photography: Guy Green
Editor: Peter Taylor
Art director: Michael Stringer
Music: Wally Stott
Song: Sam Coslow
Sound: Harold V. King, Leslie Hammond
Continuity: June Faithfull
Leading players: Dirk Bogarde (Tony), Susan Stephen (Anne), Cecil Parker (Anne's Father), Eileen Herlie (Anne's Mother), Athene Seyler (Miss Mainbrace), Dennis Price (Debenham), Pia Terri (Mrs Debenham), James Hayter (Plumber), Thora Hird (Mrs Doyle), George Woodbridge (Alf), Charles Victor (Fred), Sidney James (Foreman), Peter Jones (Car Dealer)
Award: British Academy, Best Picture nomination

As Long as They're Happy 1955 (USA 1957), 95 min., col., 'U'

Production company: Rank
Studio: Pinewood
Producer: Raymond Stross
Director: J. Lee Thompson
Screenplay: Alan Melville
Original story: Vernon Sylvaine
Director of photography: Gilbert Taylor
Editor: John Guthridge

Art Director: Michael Stringer
Music: Stanley Black
Songs: Sam Coslow
Sound: John Dennis, Gordon K. McCallum
Continuity: Tilly Day
Choreography: Paddy Stone, Irving Davies
Leading players: Jack Buchanan (John Bentley), Janette Scott (Gwen), Jean Carson
   (Pat), Brenda de Banzie (Stella), Susan Stephen (Corrine), Jerry Wayne (Bobby
   Denver), Diana Dors (Pearl), Hugh McDermott (Barnaby), David Hurst (Dr
   Schneider), Athene Seyler (Mrs Arbuthnot), Joan Sims (Linda), Nigel Green
   (Peter), Dora Bryan (Mavis), Gilbert Harding, Norman Wisdom (Themselves),
   Pauline Winter (Miss Prendergast), Hatty Jacques (Party girl), Vivienne Martin
   (Kay), Leslie Phillips (Office Manager), Charles Hawtrey (Teddy Boy)

An Alligator Named Daisy 1955 (USA 1957), 88 min., col., 'U'

Production company: Rank
Studio: Pinewood
Producer: Raymond Stross
Production controller: Arthur Alcott
Production manager: Jack Swinburne
Director: J. Lee Thompson
Screenplay: Jack Davies
Original story: Charles Terrott
Director of photography: Reginald Wyer
Editor: John B. Guthridge
Art director: Michael Stringer
Music: Stanley Black
Songs: Sam Coslow, Paddy Roberts
Sound: John W. Mitchell, Gordon K. McCallum, Roger Cherrill
Continuity: Tilly Day
Choreography: Alfred Rodrigues
Costume design: Kitty Preston
Special Effects: W. Warrington
Leading players: Donald Sinden (Peter), Diana Dors (Vanessa), Jean Carson
   (Moira), James Robertson Justice (Sir James), Margaret Rutherford (Prudence
   Croquet), Stanley Holloway (The General), Roland Culver (Colonel Weston)

Yield to the Night (US title: *Blonde Sinner*), 1956, 95 min. (USA 70 min.), b/w, 'X'

Production company: ABPC–Kenwood Films
Studio: Elstree
Producer: Kenneth Harper
Production manager: Gerry Mitchell

Director: J. Lee Thompson
Screenplay: Joan Henry, J. Lee Thompson, John Cresswell
Original story: Joan Henry
Director of photography: Gilbert Taylor
Editor: Richard Best
Art director: Robert Jones
Music: Ray Martin
Music Director: Louis Levy
Sound: Harold V. King, A Bradburn, Len Shilton, A. Southgate
Continuity: Thelma Orr
Make-up: L. V. Clark
Leading players: Diana Dors (Mary Hilton), Yvonne Mitchell (PO Macfarlane), Michael Craig (Jim Lancaster), Marie Ney (Governor), Geoffrey Keen (Chaplain), Liam Redmond (Doctor), Olga Lindo (PO Hill), Joan Miller (PO Barker), Athene Seyler (Miss Bligh), Mary Mackenzie (Prison Officer)
Award: British Academy nomination: Best Film and Best British Screenplay

The Good Companions   1957, 104 min., col., 'U'

Production company: ABPC
Studio: Elstree
Producer: J. Lee Thompson, H. G. Inglis
Director: J. Lee Thompson
Screenplay: T. J. Morrison
Additional Dialogue: John Whiting, J. L. Hodson
Original story: J. B. Priestley
Director of photography: Gilbert Taylor
Editor: Gordon Pilkington
Art director: Robert Jones
Music: Laurie Johnson
Songs: C. Alberto Rossi, Paddy Roberts, Geoffrey Parsons
Sound: Harold V. King, A. Bradburn, Len Shilton
Choreography: Paddy Stone, Irving Davies
Leading players: Eric Portman (Jess Oakroyd), Celia Johnson (Miss Trant), Hugh Griffith (Morton Mitcham), Janette Scott (Susie Dean), John Fraser (Inigo Jollifant), Bobby Howes (Jimmy Nunn), Rachel Roberts (Elsie and Effie Longstaff), John Salew (Mr Joe), Mona Washbourne (Mrs Joe), Paddy Stone (Jerry Jerningham), Irving Davies (Jerry's Partner), Thora Hird (Mrs Oakroyd), Anthony Newley (Milbrau)
No release in USA

Woman in a Dressing Gown 1957, 94 min., b/w, 'A'

Production company: Godwin–Willis–Lee Thompson
Studio: Elstree
Producer: Frank Godwin, J. Lee Thompson
Director: J. Lee Thompson
Screenplay and original story: Ted Willis
Director of photography: Gilbert Taylor
Editor: Richard Best
Art director: Robert Jones
Music: Louis Levy
Sound: A. Bradburn, Len Shilton
Leading players: Yvonne Mitchell (Amy Preston), Anthony Quayle (Jim Preston),
    Sylvia Syms (Georgie), Andrew Ray (Brian Preston), Carole Lesley (Hilda),
    Michael Ripper (Pawnbroker), Nora Gordon (Mrs Williams), Marianne
    Stone (Hairdresser), Olga Lindo (Manageress), Harry Locke (Wine Merchant)
Awards: British Academy: Best Actress nomination (Sylvia Syms); Berlin:
    Silver Bear Best Actress (Yvonne Mitchell); International Critics Prize: Best
    Film; USA Golden Globe: Best English Language Foreign Film (1958)

Ice Cold in Alex (US title: *Desert Attack*), 1957, 125 min. (USA: 80 min.), b/w, 'A'

Production company: ABPC
Studio: Elstree
Producer: W. A. Whittaker
Director: J. Lee Thompson
Screenplay: T. J. Morrison, Christopher Landon
Original story: Christopher Landon
Director of photography: Gilbert Taylor
Editor: Richard Best
Art director: Robert Jones
Music: Leighton Lucas
Sound: Leslie Hammond, Len Shilton
Continuity: Joan Kirk.
Leading players: John Mills (Capt. Anson), Sylvia Syms (Sister Diana Murdoch),
    Anthony Quayle (Capt. Van der Poel), Harry Andrews (MSM Pugh), Diane
    Clare (Sister Denise Norton), Richard Leech (Capt. Crosbie), Liam Red-
    mond (Brigadier), Allan Cuthbertson (Brigadier's Staff Officer), David
    Lodge (CMP Captain – tank trap), Michael Nightingale (CMP Captain –
    check point), Basil Hoskins (CMP Lieutenant), Walter Gotell (First German
    Officer), Frederick Jaeger (Second German Officer), Richard Marner (German
    Guard), Peter Arne (British Officer at oasis), Paul Stassino (Barman)
Awards: British Academy nominations: Best Film, Best Actor (Anthony
    Quayle); Berlin: FIPRESCI Award for Best Film

No Trees in the Street 1959 (US title: *No Tree in the Street*, 1964), 96 min., b/w, 'X'

Production company: Allegro (Godwin–Willis–Lee Thompson)
Studio: Elstree
Producer: Frank Godwin
Production manager: Al Marcus
Director: J. Lee Thompson
Assistant director: Ross MacKenzie
Screenplay and original story: Ted Willis
Director of photography: Gilbert Taylor
Editor: Richard Best
Art director: Robert Jones
Music: Laurie Johnson
Sound: Norman Coggs, Len Shilton
Continuity: Joan Kirk
Leading players: Sylvia Syms (Hetty), Herbert Lom (Wilkie), Joan Miller (Jess), Melvyn Hayes (Tommy), Stanley Holloway (Kipper), Liam Redmond (Bill), Ronald Howard (Frank Collins), Carole Lesley (Lova), Lana Morris (Marge), Lilly Kann (Mrs Jackobson)
Awards: British Academy nominations: Best Actress (Sylvia Syms), Best British Screenplay

Tiger Bay 1959 (USA 1960), 105 min., b/w, 'A'

Production company: Julian Wintle–Leslie Parkyn
Studio: Beaconsfield
Producer: John Hawkesworth
Production manager: George Mills
Director: J. Lee Thompson
Assistant director: Chris Noble
Screenplay: John Hawkesworth, Shelley Smith
Original story: Noel Calef
Director of photography: Eric Cross
Editor: Sidney Hayers
Art director: Edward Carrick
Music: Laurie Johnson
Sound: Arthur Cox, Ken Cameron, Len Page
Make-up: Trevor Crole-Rees
Continuity: Susan Dyson
Leading players: Horst Buchholz (Korchinsky), Hayley Mills (Gillie), John Mills (Superintendent Graham), Megs Jenkins (Mrs Philips), Anthony Dawson (Barclay), Yvonne Mitchell (Anya), George Selaway (Det. Sergeant Harvey)
Awards: British Academy: Most Promising Newcomer (Hayley Mills); Nominations: Best Film, Best British Screenplay; Berlin: Special Award (Hayley Mills)

North West Frontier 1959 (US title: *Flame Over India*, 1960), 129 min., col., 'U'

Production company: Rank–Marcel Hellman
Studio: Pinewood
Executive producer: Earl St John
Producer: Marcel Hellman
Production manager: Denis Holt
Director: J. Lee Thompson
Assistant director: Stanley Hosgood
Screenplay: Robin Estridge
Original story: Patrick Ford, Will Price
Director of photography: Geoffrey Unsworth
Editor: Frederick Wilson
Art director: Alex Vetchinsky
Music: Mischa Spoliansky
Sound: E. G. Daniels, Gordon K. McCallum, Roy Fry, Don Sharpe
Costume designer: Yvonne Caffin, Julie Harris
Make-up: W. T. Partleton
Special effects: Syd Pearson
Continuity: Joan Davis
Second unit executive: Frederick Wilson
Technical advisor: Col. R. C. Duncan
Leading players: Kenneth More (Capt. Scott), Lauren Bacall (Catherine Wyatt), Herbert Lom (Van Leyden), Wilfrid Hyde White (Bridie), I. S. Johar (Gupta), Ursula Jeans (Lady Windham), Eugene Deckers (Peters), Ian Hunter (Sir John Windham), Jack Gwillim (Brigadier Ames), Govinda Raja Ross (Prince Kishan), S. M. Asgarilli, S. S. Chowdhary (Indian Soldiers).
Awards: British Academy nominations: Best Film, Best British Screenplay.

I Aim at the Stars USA–West Germany 1960, 106 min., b/w, 'U'

Production company: Morningside Worldwide–Fama
Studio: Columbia
Producer: Charles H. Schneer
Production supervisor: George Van Block
Director: J. Lee Thompson
Screenplay: Jay Dratler
Original story: George Froeschel, U. Wolter, H. W. John
Director of photography: Wilkie Cooper
Editor: Frederick Wilson
Art director: Hans Berthel
Music: Laurie Johnson
Sound: Walter Ruhland
Leading players: Curt Jurgens (Wernher von Braun), Herbert Lom (Anton Reger), James Daly (William Taggert), Gia Scala (Elizabeth Beyer), Victoria

Shaw (Maria), Adrian Hoven (Mischke), Karl Stepanek (Capt. Dornberger), Helmo Kindermann (General Kulp), Eric Zuckmann (Himmler), Austin Willis (John B. Medaris)

The Guns of Navarone 1961, 157 min., col., 'A'

Production company: Open Road
Executive producer: Carl Foreman
Studios: Shepperton, Columbia
Producer: Cecil F. Ford.
Associate producer: Leon Becker
Production manager: Harold Buck
Director: J. Lee Thompson
Assistant director: Peter Yates
Screenplay: Carl Foreman
Original story: Alistair MacLean
Director of photography: Oswald Morris
Additional photography: John Wilcox
Editors: Alan Orbiston, John Smith, Raymond Poulton, Oswald Hafenrichter
Art director: Geoffrey Drake
Special effects: Bill Warrington, Wally Veevers
Music: Dimitri Tiomkin
Orchestrator (uncredited): John Williams
Sound: Vivian C. Greenham, Chris Greenham, John Cox, George Stephenson
Costume design: Olga Lehmann
Leading players: Gregory Peck (Mallory), David Niven (Miller), Anthony Quinn (Andrea), Stanley Baker (Brown), Anthony Quayle (Franklin), James Darren (Pappadimos), Irene Papas (Maria), Gia Scala (Anna), James Robertson Justice (Jensen), Richard Harris (Barnsby), Brian Forbes (Cohn), Allan Cuthbertson (Baker), Michael Trubshawe (Weaver), Percy Herbert (Grogan), George Mikell (Sessler), Walter Gotell (Muesel), Tutte Lemkow (Nicholai), Albert Lieven (Commandant), Norman Woodland (Group Captain), Christopher Rhodes (German Gunnery Officer)
Awards: Academy Award: Best Special Effects (Warrington, Veevers, V. C. Greenham); Academy Award nominations: Best Film, Best Director, Best Screenplay (adapted), Best Sound, Best Score (drama or comedy); Best Film Editing; British Academy Award nomination: Best British Screenplay (Foreman); Golden Globe: Best Motion Picture – Drama, Best Motion Picture Score

Cape Fear USA 1962 (UK 1963), 105 min. (UK 99 min.), b/w, 'X'

Production company: Melville–Talbot
Studio: Universal
Producer: Sy Bartlett
Director: J. Lee Thompson
Screenplay: James R. Webb
Original story: John D. MacDonald
Director of photography: Sam Leavitt
Editor: George Tomasini
Art directors: Alexander Golitzen, Robert Boyle
Set decoration: Oliver Emert
Music: Bernard Herrmann
Sound: Waldon O. Watson, Corson Jowett
Leading players: Gregory Peck (Sam Bowden), Robert Mitchum (Max Cady),
    Polly Bergen (Peggy Bowden), Lori Martin (Nancy Bowden), Martin
    Balsam (Chief Dutton), Jack Kruschen (Grafton), Telly Savalas (Sievers),
    Barrie Chase (Diane Taylor), Paul Comi (Garner), Page Slattery (Deputy
    Kersek), Ward Ramsey (Officer Brown), Thomas Newman (Lt Gervasi),
    Edward Platt (Judge), Will Wright (Dr Pearsall), Joseph Jenkins (Janitor),
    Joan Stanley (Waitress)

Taras Bulba USA 1963, 124 min., col., 'U'

Production company: Harold Hecht
Studio: United Artists
Producer: Harold Hecht
Associate producer: Alexander Whitelaw
Director: J. Lee Thompson
Screenplay: Waldo Salt, Karl Tunberg
Original story: Nikolai Gogol
Director of photography: Joseph MacDonald
Editors: William Reynolds, Gene Milford, Eda Warren, Folmar Blanksted
Set decorator: William Calvert
Costume design: Norma Koch, Izzy Berne, Olive Koenitz
Music: Franz Waxman
Sound: Stan Cooley
Special effects: Howard A. Anderson
Technical adviser: Audrey Tolstoy
Leading players: Tony Curtis (Andrei Bulba), Yul Brynner (Taras Bulba),
    Christine Kaufmann (Natalia Dubrov), Sam Wanamaker (Filipenko), Guy
    Rolfe (Prince Grigory), Brad Dexter (Shilo), Perry Lopez (Ostap Bulba),
    George Macready (Governor), Ilka Windish (Sophia Bulba), Vladimir
    Sokoloff (Old Stepan), Daniel Ocko (Ivan Mykola), Vladimir Irman (Grisha
    Kubenko), Abraham Sofaer (Abbot), Micky Finn (Korzh), Richard Rust
    (Capt. Alex), Ron Weyand (Tymoshevsky)
Awards: Academy Award nomination: Best Score (Franz Waxman)

Kings of the Sun USA 1963 (UK 1964), 107 min., col., 'U'

Production company: Mirisch
Studio: United Artists
Producer: Lewis J. Rachmil
Production supervisor: Allen K. Wood
Director: J. Lee Thompson
Assistant director: Thomas Shaw
Screenplay: Elliott Arnold, James R. Webb
Original story: Elliott Arnold
Director of photography: Joseph MacDonald
Editor: William Reynolds
Art director: Alfred Ybarra
Special effects: Roscoe Cline
Music: Elmer Bernstein
Sound: Bert Hallberg
Costume design: Norma Koch
Leading players: Yul Brynner (Black Eagle), George Chakiris (Balam), Shirly
    Ann Field (Ixchel), Richard Basehart (Ah Min), Brad Dexter (Ah Haleb),
    Barry Morse (Ah Zok), Armando Silvestre (Isatai), Leo Gordon (Hunac
    Ceel), Victoria Vettri (Ixzubin), Rudy Solari (Pitz), Ford Rainey (The Chief),
    Angel Di Steffano (Balam, the (elder) King), Jose Moreno (The Sacrifice).

What a Way to Go USA 1964, 111 min., col., 'A'

Production company: APJACK–Orchard
Studio: Twentieth Century-Fox
Producer: Arthur P. Jacobs
Director: J. Lee Thompson
Assistant director: Fred R. Simpson
Screenplay: Betty Comden, Adolph Green
Original story: Gwen Davis
Director of photography: Leon Shamroy
Editor: Marjorie Fowler
Art directors: Jack Martin Smith, Ted Haworth
Set decoration: Walter M. Scott, Stuart Reiss
Music: Nelson Riddle
Songs: Betty Comden, Adolph Green, Jule Styne
Choreography: Gene Kelly
Sound: Bernard Freericks, Elmer Raguse
Costume design: Edith Head
Leading players: Shirley MacLaine (Louisa), Paul Newman (Larry Flint), Robert
    Mitchum (Rod Anderson), Dean Martin (Leonard Crawley), Gene Kelly
    (Jerry Benson), Bob Cummings (Dr Steffanson), Dick Van Dyke (Edgar
    Hopper), Reginald Gardiner (Painter), Margaret Dumont (Mrs Foster),
    Lou Nova (Trentino), Fifi D'Orsay (Baroness), Maurice Marsac (Rene),
    Wally Vernon (Agent), Jane Wald (Polly), Lenny Kent (Hollywood Lawyer)

John Goldfarb, Please Come Home (USA) 1964 (UK 1965), 96 min., col., 'A'

Production company: Steve Parker –J. Lee Thompson
Studio: Twentieth Century-Fox
Producer: Steve Parker
Director: J. Lee Thompson
Assistant director: John Flynn
Screenplay: William Peter Blatty
Director of photography: Leon Shamroy
Editor: William Murphy
Art directors: Jach Martin Smith, Dale Hennesy
Set decoration: Walter M. Scott, Stuart Reiss
Music: Johnny Williams
Sound: Carleton W. Faulkner, Elmer Raguse
Choreography: Paul Godkin
Costume design: Edith Head
Leading players: Shirley MacLaine (Jenny Ericson), Peter Ustinov (King Fawz), Richard Crenna (John Goldfarb), Scott Brady (Sakalakis), Jim Backus (Miles Whitepaper), Fred Clark (Heinous Overreach), Harry Morgan (Deems Sarajevo), Wilfrid Hyde White (Mustafa Gus), Patrick Adiarte (Prince Ammud), Leon Askin (Samir), Jerome Cowan (Brinkley), Richard Wilson (Frobish), Richard Deacon (Maginot), Milton Frome (Air Force General), Charles Lane (Editor of *Strife*), Jerome Orbach (Pinkerton)

Return From the Ashes 1966, 104 min., b/w, 'X'

Production company: Mirish
Studios: Elstree, Borehamwood
Executive producer: Lewis J. Rachmil
Producer–Director: J. Lee Thompson
Associate producer: Cecil Ford
Production manager: Charles Blair
Assistant director: Kip Gowans
Screenplay: Julius J. Epstein
Original story: Hubert Monteilhet
Director of photography: Chris Challis
Editor: Russell Lloyd
Art direction: Michael Stringer
Music: John Dankworth
Sound: John Bramall
Leading players: Maximilian Schell (Stanislaus Pilgrin), Ingrid Thulin (Dr Michele Wolf), Samantha Eggar (Fabi), Herbert Lom (Dr Charles Bovard), Talitha Pol (Claudine), Valadek Sheybal (Manager of Chess Club), Jacques Brunius (First Detective), Andre Maranne (Second Detective), Yvonne Andre (Woman on Train), John Serret (Man on Train), Pamela Stirling (Mother on Train)

Eye of the Devil 1968 (USA 1967), 90 min., b/w, 'X'

Production company: Filmways
Studios: MGM, Elstree
Producer: Martin Ransohoff
Production supervisor: Ben Kadish
Production manager: Sydney Streeter
Director: J. Lee Thompson
Assistant director: Basil Rayburn
Screenplay: Robin Estridge, Dennis Murphy
Original story: Philip Loraine
Director of photography: Erwin Hillier
Editor: Ernest Walter
Art director: Elliot Scott
Music: Gary McFarland
Sound: A. W. Watkins, Gerry Turner
Costume design: Julie Harris, John Furness
Titles: Maurice Binder
Leading players: Deborah Kerr (Catherine), David Niven (Philippe de Mont-faucon), Donald Pleasence (Père Dominic), Edward Mulhare (Jean-Claude Ibert), Flora Robson (Countess Estelle), Emlyn Williams (Alain de Montfaucon), Sharon Tate (Odile), David Hemmings (Christian de Caray), John Le Mesurier (Dr Monnet), Suky Appleby (Antionette), Donald Bisset (Rennard), Robert Duncan (Jacques), Michael Miller (Grandee)

Mackenna's Gold USA 1968 (UK 1969), 136 min., col., 'A'

Production company: Highroad Productions
Studio: Columbia
Producer: Carl Foreman
Production manager: Ralph Black
Director: J. Lee Thompson
Second unit director: Tom Shaw
Assistant director: David Slaven
Screenplay: Carl Foreman
Original story: Will Henry
Director of photography: Joseph MacDonald
Additional photography: Harold Wellman, John Mackey, Richard Moore, Don Glouner
Editor: Bill Lenny
Production designer: Geoffrey Drake
Set decoration: Alfred E. Spencer
Special effects: Geoffrey Drake, John Mackey, Bob Cuff, Willis Cook, Larry Butler
Music: Quincy Jones
Sound: Derek Frye, William Randall Jr

Costume design: Norma Koch
Narrator: Victor Jory
Leading players: Gregory Peck (Mackenna), Omar Sharif (Colorado), Telly
    Savalas (Sgt Tibbs), Camilla Sparv (Inga), Keenan Wynn (Sanchez), Julie
    Newmar (Hesh-ke), Ted Cassidy (Hachita), Eduardo Ciannelli (Prairie
    Dog), Eli Wallach (Ben Baker), Edward G. Robinson (Adams), Raymond
    Massey (Preacher), Burgess Meredith (Store Keeper), Anthony Quayle (Older
    Englishman), J. Robert Porter (Younger Englishman), Lee J. Cobb (Editor),
    Dick Peabody (Avila), Rudy Diaz (Besh), Robert Phillips (Monkey), Shelly
    Morrison (Pima Squaw), John Garfield Jr (Adams' Boy), Pepe Callahan
    (Laguna), Madeleine Taylor Holmes (Old Apache Woman), Duke Hobbie
    (Lieutenant)

Before Winter Comes 1969, 107 min., col., 'A'

Production company: Windward
Studio: Columbia
Producer: Robert Emmett Ginna
Production manager: Bruce Sharman
Director: J. Lee Thompson
Assistant director: Jake Wright
Screenplay: Andrew Sinclair
Original story: Frederick L. Keefe
Director of photography: Gilbert Taylor
Editor: Willy Kemplen
Art director: John Blezard
Music: Ron Grainer
Sound: Cyril Collick
Leading players: David Niven (Major Giles Burnside), Topol (Janovic), Anna
    Karina (Maria), John Hurt (Lt Francis Pilkington), Ori Levy (Capt. Kamenev),
    Anthony Quayle (Brigadier Bewley), John Collin (Sgt Woody), George
    Innes (Bill), Hugh Futcher (Joe), Tony Selby (Ted), Colin Spaull (Alf),
    Christopher Sandford (Johnny), Larry Dann (Al), Karel Stepanek (Count
    Kerassy), Guy Deghy (Kovacs), Mark Malicz (Komenski), Gertan Klauber
    (Russian Major), Hana-Maria Pravda (Beata)

The Most Dangerous Man in the World (US title: *The Chairman*), 1969, 99 min., col., 'A'

Production company: APJAC–Twentieth Century-Fox
Studio: Pinewood
Producer: Mort Abrahams
Production supervisor: John Merriman
Production manager: David Korda
Director: J. Lee Thompson

Assistant director: Ferdinand Fairfax
Screenplay: Ben Maddow
Original story: Jay Richard Kennedy
Director of photography: Ted Moore
Editor: Richard Best
Art director: Peter Mullins
Music: Jerry Goldsmith
Sound: Dudley Messenger.
Leading players: Gregory Peck (Dr John Hathaway), Anne Heywood (Kay Hanna), Arthur Hill (Lt General Shelby), Conrad Yama (Chairman), Francisca Tu (Soong Chu), Keye Kuke (Professor Soong Li), Alan Dobie (Air Commodore Benson), Zienia Merton (Ting Ling), Eric Young (Yin), Burt Kwouk (Chang Shou), Alan White (Colonel Gardner), Ori Levy (Alexander Shertov)

Country Dance (US title: *Brotherly Love*), 1970, 112 min., col., 'X'

Production company: Windward–Keep–MGM
Studio: Ardmore, Dublin
Producer: Robert Emmett Ginna
Associate producer: Denis Johnson
Production manager: Bernard Williams
Director: J. Lee Thompson
Assistant director: Jake Wright
Screenplay and original story: James Kennaway
Director of photography: Ted Moore
Editor: Willy Kemplen
Art director: Maurice Fowler
Set decoration: John Jarvis
Music: John Addison
Sound: Jim Groom, Simon Kaye, Gerry Humphreys
Costume designer: Yvonne Blake
Choreography: Bobby Watson
Titles: Maurice Binder.
Leading players: Peter O'Toole (Pink), Susannah York (Hilary), Michael Craig (Douglas Dow), Harry Andrews (Brigadier Crieff), Cyril Cusack (Dr. Maitland), Judy Cornwell (Rosie), Brian Blessed (Jock Braid), Robert Urquhart (Auctioneer), Mark Malicz (Benny-the-Pole), Lennox Milne (Miss Mailer), Jean Anderson (Matron), Marjorie Dalziel (Bank Lizzie), Helena Gloag (Auntie Belle), Madeleine Christie (Bun McKenzie), Roy Boutcher (MacLachan-Forbes), Peter Reeves (Alex Smart), Leonard Maguire (Store Keeper), Paul Farrell (Alec), Rona Newton-John (Miss Scott), Ewan Roberts (Mr Hutchison), Frances de la Tour (Nurse), Patrick Gardiner (Ambulance Driver), Bernadette Gallagher (Ina), Maura Keely (Ina's Mother), John Kelly (Ina's Father), Clare Mullen (Barmaid), Eamonn Keane (Fred-who-is-Bob), Desmond Perry (Dr Soames), Tom Irwin (Ramsay), Mary Larkin (Hilary's Friend)

Conquest of the Planet of the Apes USA 1972, 85 min., col., 'AA'

Production company: APJAC–Twentieth Century-Fox
Studio: Twentieth Century-Fox
Producer: Arthur P. Jacobs
Associate producer: Frank Capra Jr
Production manager: William G. Eckhardt
Director: J. Lee Thompson
Assistant director: David 'Buck' Hall
Screenplay: Paul Dehn
Director of photography: Bruce Surtees
Editors: Marjorie Fowler, Allan Jaggs
Art director: Philip Jefferies
Set decoration: Norman Rockett
Music: Tom Scott
Sound: Herman Lewis, Don Bassman
Make-up: John Chambers
Titles: Don Record
Leading players: Roddy McDowall (Caesar), Don Murray (Breck), Natalie
    Trundy (Lisa), Ricardo Montalban (Armando), Hari Rhodes (McDonald),
    Severn Darden (Kolp), Lou Wagner (Busboy), John Randolph (Commission
    Chairman), Asa Maynor (Mrs Riley), H. M. Wynant (Hoskyns), David
    Chow (Aldo), Buck Kartalian (Frank), John Dennis (Policeman), Gordon
    Jump (Auctioneer), Dick Spangler (Announcer), Joyce Haber (Zelda)

Battle for the Planet of the Apes USA 1973, 86 min., col., 'A'

Production company: APJAC
Studio: Twentieth Century-Fox
Producer: Arthur P. Jacobs
Associate producer: Frank Capra Jr
Production manager: Michael S. Glick
Director: J. Lee Thompson
Assistant directors: Ric Rondell, Barry Stern
Screenplay: John William Corrington, Joyce Hooper Corrington
Original story: Paul Dehn
Director of photography: Richard H. Kline
Editors: Alan L. Jaggs, John C. Horger
Art director: Dale Hennesy
Set decoration: Robert DeVestal
Special mechanical effects: Gerald Endler
Music: Leonard Rosenman
Sound: Herman Lewis, Don Bassman
Make-up: John Chambers, Joe Di Bella.
Leading players: Roddy McDowall (Caesar), Claude Akins (Aldo), Natalie
    Trundy (Lisa), Severn Darden (Kolp), Lew Ayres (Mandemus), Paul

Williams (Virgil), Austin Stoker (McDonald), Noah Keen (Teacher), Richard Eastham (Mutant Captain), France Nuyen (Alma), Paul Stevens (Mendez), Heather Lowe (Doctor), Bobby Porter (Cornelius), Michael Sterns (Jake), John Landis (Jake's Friend), John Huston (The Lawgiver)

Huckleberry Finn USA 1974, 118 min., col., 'U'

Production company: APJAC
Studio: United Artists
Producer: Arthur P. Jacobs
Associate producer: Robert Greenhut
Director: J. Lee Thompson
Assistant director: Newton Arnold
Screenplay, music, lyrics: Robert B. Sherman, Richard M. Sherman
Original story: Mark Twain
Director of photography: Laszlo Kovacs
Editor: Michael F. Anderson
Art director: Philip Jefferies
Set decoration: Robert DeVestal
Sound: Larry Jost, Jim Pilcher, Theodore Soderberg
Choreography: Marc Breaux.
Titles: Don Record
Costume design: Donfeld
Leading players: Jeff East (Huckleberry Finn), Paul Winfield (Jim), Harvey Korman (The King), David Wayne (The Duke), Arthur O'Connell (Col. Grangerford), Gary Merrill (Pap), Natalie Trundy (Mrs Loftus), Lucille Benson (Widder Douglas), Kim O'Brien (Maryjane Wilks), Jean Fay (Susan Wilks), Ruby Leftwich (Miss Watson), Odessa Cleveland (Jim's Wife), Joe Boris (Jason), Danny Lantrip (Kyle), Van Bennett (Wayne), Linda Watkins (Mrs Grangerford), Jean Combs (Miss Emmerline), Frances Fawcett (Miss Charlotte), Suzanne Prystup (Miss Maryanne), H. L. Rowley (Horatio), Doris Owens (Marybelle), Frank Mills (Buck), Sherree Sinquefield (Miss Sophia)

The Reincarnation of Peter Proud USA 1974 (UK 1975), 104 min., col., 'X'

Production company: Bing Crosby
Studio: Twentieth Century-Fox
Executive producer: Charles A. Pratt
Producer: Frank P. Rosenberg
Production manager: Hal Polaire
Director: J. Lee Thompson
Assistant director: David 'Buck' Hall
Screenplay and original story: Max Erhlich
Director of photography: Victor J. Kemper

Editor: Michael Anderson
Art director: Jack Martin Smith
Set Decoration: Robert DeVestal
Music: Jerry Goldsmith
Sound: Bernard F. Pincus, Andy Gilmore, David Dockendorf
Costume design: Oscar Rodriguez, Betty Cox
Leading players: Michael Sarrazin (Peter Proud), Jennifer O'Neill (Ann Curtis), Margot Kidder (Marcia Curtis), Cornelia Sharpe (Nora Hayes), Paul Hecht (Dr Samuel Goodman), Tony Stephano (Jeff Curtis), Normann Burton (Dr Frederick Spear), Anne Ives (Ellen Curtis), Debralee Scott (Suzy), Jon Richards (Newspaper Custodian), Steve Franken (Dr Charles Crennis), Fred Stuthman (Pop Johnson), Lester Fletcher (Car Salesman), Brenna Benjamin (Miss Hagerson), Addison Powell (Reeves), Philip Clark (Number Five), Gene Boland (Charlie), Albert Henderson (Police Sergeant), Connie Garrison (Ellie), Sam Laws (Satan's Disciple)

St Ives USA 1976, 94 min., col., 'AA'

Production company: Warner Bros, Kohner–Beckerman–Canter
Studio: Warner Bros
Producers: Pancho Kohner, Stanley Canter
Production manager: Hal Klein
Director: J. Lee Thompson
Assistant director: Ronald L. Schwary
Screenplay: Barry Beckerman
Original story: Oliver Bleeck
Director of photography: Lucien Ballard
Editor: Michael F. Anderson
Art director: Philip M. Jefferies
Set decoration: Robert DeVestal
Music: Lalo Schifrin
Sound: Bill Rivol, Edwin Scheid, Joe Von Stroheim, Bill Mauch, Gene Eliot, Harlan Riggs, Arthur Piantadosi
Special effects: Gene Grigg
Titles: Pacific Title
Stunts: Max Kelven
Leading players: Charles Bronson (St Ives), John Houseman (Abner Procane), Maximilian Schell (Dr John Constable), Jacqueline Bisset (Janet Whistler), Elisher Cook (Eddie), Burr De Benning (Officer Frann), Harry Guardino (Detective Deal), Harris Yulin (Detective Oller), Joe Roman (Seymore), Robert Eglund, Mark Thomas, Jeff Goldblum (Hoods), Dana Elcar (Charlie Blunt), Michael Lerner (Myron Green), Dick O'Neill (Hesh), Val Bisoglio (Finley), Daniel J. Travanti (Johnny Parisi), Tom Pedi (Fat Angi), Joseph De Nicola (No Nose), George Memmoli (Shippo), Don Hanmer (Punch), Bob Terhune (Mike Kluszewski), Norman Palmer (McDuff), Walter Brook (Mickey), Jerome Thor (Chasman), Jerry Brutsche (Jack Boykins), Dar Robinson (Jimmy Peskoe)

The White Buffalo USA 1977, 97 min., col., 'AA'

Production company: Dino De Laurentiis
Producer: Pancho Kohner
Production co-ordinator: Virginia Cook
Production manager: Hal Klein
Location manager: R. Anthony Brown
Director: J. Lee Thompson
Assistant director: Jack Aldworth
Screenplay and original story: Richard Sale
Director of photography: Paul Lohmann
Editor: Michael F. Anderson
Art director: Tambi Larsen
Set decoration: James Berkey
Music: John Barry
Sound: Harlan Riggs, William McCaughey, Lyle J. Burbridge, Michael J. Kohut
Costume design: Eric Seelig
Make-up: Phil Rhodes, Michael Hancock
Special Effects: Richard M. Parker, Ross Taylor
Titles: Dan Perri
Leading players: Charles Bronson (Wild Bill Hickock, 'James Otis'), Jack Warden (Charlie Zane), Will Sampson (Chief Crazy Horse, 'Worm'), Kim Novak (Poker Jenny Schermerhorn), Clint Walker (Whistling Jack Kileen), Stuart Whitman (Winifred Coxy), Slim Pickens (Abel Pinkney), John Carradine (Amos Briggs), Cara Williams (Cassie Ollinger), Shay Duffin (Tim Brady), Cliff Pellow (Pete Holt), Douglas V. Fowley (Amos Bixby), Ed Lauter (Capt. Tom Custer), Martin Kove (Jack McCall), Scott Walker (Gyp Hook-Hand), Ed Bakey (Ben Corbett), Richard Gilliland (Corp. Kileen), David Roy Chandler (Kid Jelly), Philip Montgomery (Wes Pugh), Linda Moon Redfearn (Black Shawl), Chief Tug Smith (Old Worm), Douglas Hume (Aaron Pratt), Cliff Carnell (Johnny Varner), Ron Thompson (Frozen Dog Pimp), Eve Brent (Frieda), Joe Roman (Silky Smith), Bert Williams (Paddy Welsh)

The Greek Tycoon USA 1978, 106 min., col., 'AA'

Production company: ABKCO Films
Studio: Universal
Executive producers: Mort Abrahams, Peter Howard, Les Landau
Producers: Alan Klein, Ely Landau
Co-producers: Nico Mastorakis, Lawrence Myers.
Associate producer: Eric Rattray
Production managers: George Iakovidis (Greece), Roy Parkinson (UK), Jerry Brandt (USA)
Director: J. Lee Thompson

Assistant directors: Ariel Levy, Anthony Mixaleas, Steve Barnett
Screenplay: Mort Fine
Original story: Nico Mastorakis, Win Wells, Mort Fine
Director of photography: Tony Richmond
Second unit photography: Christos Triantafillou
Editors: Alan Strachan, Derek Trigg
Art directors: Michael Stringer, Tony Reading, Gene Gurlitz, Mel Bourne
Set decoration: Vernon Dixon
Music: Stanley Myers
Songs: John Kongos, Mike Moran
Sound: Allan Sones, Dino Di Campo, Bill Trent, Robin Gregory, Gordon K. McCallum
Costume design: Phyllis Dalton
Leading players: Anthony Quinn (Theo Tomasis), Jacqueline Bisset (Liz Cassidy), Raf Vallone (Spyros Tomasis), Edward Albert (Nico Tomasis), Marilu Tolo (Sophia Matalas), James Franciscus (James Cassidy), Camilla Sparv (Simi Tomasis), Charles Durning (Michael Russell), Luciana Paluzzi (Paola Scotti), Robin Clarke (John Cassidy), Kathryn Lee Scott (Nancy Cassidy), Roland Culver (Robert Keith), Tony Jay (Doctor), John Bennett (Servant), Katherine Schofield (Helena), Joan Benham (Lady Allison), Linda Thorson (Angela), Guy Deghy (Tahlie), Jill Melford (Magda), Lucy Gutteridge (Mia), John Denison (Lord Allison), Carolle Rousseau (Camille), Cassandra Harris (Cassandra), Sandor Eles (Lawrence), Bonnie George (Aggie), Henderson Forsythe (Stoneham), Dimitri Nikolaidis (Socrates), Dimos Starenios (Kazakos)

The Passage 1979, 98 min., col., 'X'

Production company: Hemdale–Passage Films; Lester Goldsmith and Maurice Binder for Monday Films
Studio: Victarine, Nice
Executive producers: John Daley, Derek Dawson
Producer: John Quested
Associate producer: Geoffrey Helman
Production manager: Phillip Kenny
Location managers: Arlette Danis, Bernard Mazauric
Director: J. Lee Thompson
Assistant director: Kip Gowans
Screenplay and original story: Bruce Nicolaysen
Director of photography: Michael Reed
Editors: Alan Strachan, Derek Trigg
Art directors: Jean Forestier, Constantin Mejinsky
Music: Michael Bosch
Sound: Allan Sones, Norman Bolland, Ken Barker
Special Effects: Trielli
Costume design: Brian Smith

Make-up: Neville Smallwood
Leading players: Anthony Quinn (The Basque), James Mason (Professor John Bergson), Malcolm McDowell (Capt. von Berkow), Patricia Neal (Ariel Bergson), Kay Lenz (Leah Bergson), Paul Clemens (Paul Bergson), Christopher Lee (Gypsy), Robert Rhys (Gypsy's son), Michael Lonsdale (Alain Renoudot), Marcel Bozzuffi (Perea), Peter Arne (Guide), Neville Jason (Lt Reincke), Robert Brown (Major), Rosa Alba (Madam Alba)

Cabo Blanco: Where Legends Are Born ... USA 1980, 87 min., col., 'R'

Production company: Avco Embassy
Executive producer: Martin V. Smith
Producers: Lance Hool, Paul A. Joseph
Associate producer: Alan Hool
Executive production manager: Joe Cavalier
Production manager: Chico Day
Director: J. Lee Thompson
Screenplay: Milton Gelman, Mort Fine
Original story: Milton Gelman, James Granby Hunter
Director of photography: Alex Phillips
Editor: Michael Anderson
Art director: Jose Rodriguez Granada
Set Decoration: Jaime Perez Cubero
Music: Jerry Goldsmith
Sound: Gregg Landaker
Costume design: William Travilla
Leading players: Charles Bronson (Giff Hoyt), Jason Robards (Gunther Beckdorff), Dominique Sanda (Marie Allasandri), Fernando Rey (Terredo), Simon MacCorkindale (Jim Clarkson), Camilla Sparv (Hera), Gilbert Roland (Dr Ramirez), Dennis Miller (Horst), Clifton James (Lorrimer), Ernest Esparza (Pepe), James Booth (John Bunce)
Released, without a certificate, on video only in UK

Happy Birthday to Me Canada 1980 (UK 1981), 111 min., col., 'X'

Production company: The Birthday Film Company, with Canadian Film Development and Famous Players
Producers: John Dunning, Andre Link
Associate producer: Lawrence Nesis
Production controller: Leo Gregory
Production manager: Gineete Hardy
Location manager: Cary Ross
Director: J. Lee Thompson
Second unit director: Charles Braive
Screenplay: Timothy Bond, Peter Jobin, John Saxon

Original story: John Saxon
Director of photography: Miklos Lente
Editor: Debra Karen
Art director: Earl Preston
Music: Bo Harwood, Lance Rubin
Sound: Peter Thompson, Richard Lightstone, Les Fresholtz
Special effects: King Hernandez, Bill Doane, Warren Keillor, Ron Otteson
Costume design: Hugette Gagne
Special make-up effects: Burbank Studio
Stunts: Max Kleven
Leading players: Melissa Sue Anderson (Virginia Wainwright), Glenn Ford (Dr Faraday), Lawrence Dane (Hal Patterson), Tracy Bregman (Ann), Jack Blum (Alfred), Matt Craven (Steve), Lenore Zann (Maggie), David Eisner (Rudi), Michael Rene Labelle (Etienne), Richard Rebiere (Greg), Lesleh Donaldson (Bernadette), Lisa Langlois (Amelia), Earl Pennington (Lt Tracy), Jerome Tiberghien (Professor Heregard), Maurice Podbray (Dr Feinblum)

10 to Midnight USA 1983, 102 min., col., '18'

Production company: Cannon
Executive producers: Menahem Golan, Yoram Globus
Producers: Pancho Kohner, Lance Hool
Director: J. Lee Thompson
Screenplay: William Roberts
Director of photography: Adam Greenberg
Editor: Peter Lee Thompson
Art director: Jim Freiburger
Set decoration: Cecilia Rodarte
Music: Robert O. Ragland
Sound: Gregory H. Watkins
Costume design: Del Adey-Jones
Make-up: Alan Marshall
Leading players: Charles Bronson (Leo Kessler), Lisa Eibacher (Laurie Kessler), Andrew Stevens (Paul McAnn), Gene Davis (Warren Stacy), Geoffrey Lewis (Dave Dante), Wilford Brimley (Capt. Malone), Robert F. Lyons (Nathan Zager), Bert Williams (Mr Johnson), Ola Ray (Ola), Kelly Preston (Doreen), Cosie Costa (Dudley), Jeana Tomasina (Karen), June Gilbert (Betty), Arthur Hansel (Judge), Sam Chew Jr (Minister), Katrina Parish (Tina), Shawn Schepps (Peg), Barbara Pilavin (Mrs Byrd), James Thor (Medical Examiner), Breck Costin (Tim Bailey), Jean Manson (Margo), Shay Duffin (Nestor), Daniel Ades (Ben Linker)
Released in the UK on video only (96 mins, cut by 1 minute 42 seconds)

The Evil that Men Do USA 1983 (UK 1984), 90 min. (UK 89 min.), col., '18'

Production company: ITC: Capricorn–Zuleika Farms in association with Producciones Cabo
Executive producer: Lance Hool
Producer: Pancho Kohner
Associate producers: Jill Ireland, David Pringle
Production executive: Howard P. Alston
Production supervisor: Marco Aurelio Ortiz
Unit production manager: Gordon A. Webb
Post-production supervisor: James Potter
Director: J. Lee Thompson
Second unit director: Ernie Orsatti
Assistant director: Gordon A. Webb
Screenplay: David Lee Henry, John Crowther
Original story: R. Lance Hill
Director of photography: Javier Ruvalcaba Cruz
Editor: Peter Lee Thompson
Art director: Enrique Estevez
Music: Ken Thorne
Sound: Michael Redbourn, Richard Shorr, Joseph Holsten, John Post, Roberto Camacho, Micheal Minkler
Special effects: Laurencio Cordero
Costume design: Poppy Cannon
Make-up: Alan Marchall
Titles/opticals: CFI
Stunts: Ernie Orsatti
Leading players: Charles Bronson (Holland), Theresa Saldana (Rhiana Hidalgo), Joseph Maher (Dr Clement Molloch), Jose Ferrer (Dr Hector Lomelin), Rene Enriquez (Max Ortiz), John Glover (Briggs), Raymond St Jacques (Randolph), Antoinette Bower (Claire), Enrique Lucero (Aristos), Jorge Luke (Cillero), Mischa Hausserman (Karl), Roger Cudney (Cannell), Constanza Hool (Isabel), Joe Seneca (Santiago), Jorge Zepeda (Victim), Angelica Aragon (Maria), Nicole Thomas (Sarah), Anais de Mello (Dominique), Jorge Humberto Robles (Jorge Hidalgo), Fernando Saenz (Assael)

The Ambassador USA 1984, 95 min., col., '18'

Production company: Cannon–Northbrook Films
Producers: Menahem Golan, Yoram Globus
Associate producer: Isaac Kol
Production co-ordinator: Henia Mandelbaum
Production managers: Avi Kleinberger, Asher Gat
Location manager: Roy Golan
Director: J. Lee Thompson

Assistant director: Gidi Amir
Screenplay: Max Jack
Original story: Elmore Leonard
Director of photography: Adam Greenberg
Lighting director: Avam Leibman
Editor: Mark Goldblatt
Associate editors: Thierry J. Courturier, Peter Lee Thompson
Art director: Yoram Barzilai
Set decoration: David Varod
Music: Dov Seltzer
Sound: Michael R. Sloan, George H. Anderson, Harry B. Miller III, Eli Yarkoni, Gary Bourgeois, Neil Brody, Joe D. Citarella
Sound effects: Michael J. Bateman
Foley editor: Hugo Weng
Special effects: Yoram Pollack
Costume design: Tami Mor
Make-up: Mary Ellen Yitznocov
Titles/opticals: MGM
Leading players: Robert Mitchum (Peter Hacker), Ellen Burstyn (Alex Hacker), Rock Hudson (Frank Stevenson), Fabio Testi (Mustapha Hashimi), Donald Pleasence (Eretz), Heli Goldenberg (Rachel), Michael Bat-Adam (Tova), Ori Levy (Abe), Uri Gavriel (Assad), Zachi Noy (Ze'ev), Joseph Shiloah (Shimon), Shmulik Kraus (Stone), Yossi Virginsky (Asher), Iftar Katzur (Lenny), Shai Shwartz (Gadi), Ran Vered (Rafi), Assi Abaiov (Reuven), Avi Kleinberger (Abba), Dana Ben-Yehuda (Helen), Zehava Keilos (Dvora), Esther Zebco (Marilyn), Bob Stevens (Mike)

King Solomon's Mines USA 1985, 100 min., col., 'PG'

Production company: Cannon
Producers: Menahem Golan, Yoram Globus
Associate Producers: Rony Yacov, Avi Lerner
Production supervisor: John Stodel
Production co-ordinator: Naomi Mayberg
Production manager: Joe Pollini
Location managers: Rory Kilalea, Avner Pelled
Director: J. Lee Thompson
Second unit director: Carlos Gil
Assistant director: Miguel Gil
Screenplay: Gene Quintano, James R. Silke
Original story: H. Rider Haggard
Director of photography: Alex Phillips
Editor: John Shirley
Art directors: Luciano Spadoni, Leonardo Coen Cagli
Set decoration: Nello Giorgetti
Music: Jerry Goldsmith

Sound: Peter Best, Bryan Tilling, Graham Harris, Richard Fettes, Bob Mullins, Eli Yarkoni
Sound effects: Germano Natali, Fred Unger, Franco Scarano, Fabio Traversari
Costume design: Tony Pueo
Make-up: Walter Cossu
Opticals: Westbury Designs, General Screen Enterprises
Stunts: Peter Diamond, Scully Levine
Leading players: Richard Chamberlain (Allan Quartermain), Sharon Stone (Jessica Huston), Herbert Lom (Colonel Bockner), Bernard Archard (Professor Huston), John Rhys-Davies (Dogati), Ken Gampu (Umbopo), June Buthelezi (Gagoola), Sam Williams (Scragga), Shai K. Ophir (Kassam), Fidelis Che A (Mapaki Chief), Mick Lesley (Dorfman), Vincent Van Der Byl (Shack), Bob Greer (Hamid), Oliver Tengende (Bushiri), Bishop McThuzen (Dari)

Murphy's Law USA 1986, 100 min., col., '18'

Production company: Cannon
Executive producers: Menaham Golan, Yoram Globus
Producers: Pancho Kohner, Jill Ireland
Associate producer: Gail Morgan Hickman
Production executive: Jeffrey Silver
Production co-ordinator: Alan Gershenfeld
Unit production manager: George Van Noy
Location manager: Larry Pearson
Post-production supervisor: Michael R. Sloan
Director: J. Lee Thompson
Assistant director: Steve Lazarus
Screenplay: Gail Morgan Hickman
Director of photography: Alex Phillips
Editors: Peter Lee Thompson, Charles Simmons
Art director: William Cruise
Set decoration: W. Brooke Wheeler
Scenic artist: Aimee D. Orkin
Music: Marc Donahue, Valantine McCallum
Sound: George Berndt, Craig Felburg, Dick Portman, Bob Glass
Foley editors: John Duvall, Dave LeBrun, Barry Rubinow
Sound effects: Sancy Gendler.
Costume supervisor: Shelley Komarov
Make-up: Lily Benyair
Special effects: Pioneer FX
Stunts: Ernie Orsatti, Beau van den Ecker.
Leading players: Charles Bronson (Jack Murphy), Kathleen Wilhoite (Arabella McGee), Carrie Snodgrass (Joan Freeman), Robert F. Lyons (Art Penney), Richard Romanus (Frank Vincenzo), Angel Tompkins (Jan), Bill Henderson (Ben Wilcove), James Luisi (Ed Reineke), Clifford A. Pellow (Lt

Nachman), Janet MacLachman (Dr Lovell), Lawrence Tierney (Cameron), Jerome Thor (Judge Kellerman), Mischa Hausserman (David Manzarek), Cal Haynes (Reese), Hans Howes (Santana), Joseph Spallina Roman (Carl), Chris De Rose (Tony Vincenzo), Frank Annese (Kelly), Paul McCallum (Hog), Dennis Hayden (Sonny), Tony Montero (Max), David Hayman (Jack)

Firewalker USA 1986 (UK 1987), 104 min., col., 'PG'

Production company: Cannon
Executive producers: Norman Aladjem, Jeffrey M. Rosenbaum
Producers: Menahem Golan, Yoram Globus
Associate producer: Carlos Gil
Production executive: Rony Yacov
Production co-ordinator: Enid L. Kantor
Unit production manager: Pablo Buelna
Post-production supervisor: Michael R. Sloan
Director: J. Lee Thompson
Assistant director: Russ Harling
Screenplay: Robert Gosnell
Original story: Robert Gosnell, Jeffrey M. Rosebaum, Norman Aladjem
Director of photography: Alex Phillips
Editor: Richard Marx
Supervising editor: Peter Lee Thompson
Art director: Jose Rodriguez Granada
Set decoration: Kleomenes Stamatiades
Music: Gary Chang
Sound: Barney Cabral, Bruce Stambler, Michael Wilhoit
Costume design: Poppy Cannon
Make-up: Alberto Lopez, Ilona Bobak
Opticals: Anne Couk
Titles: Pacific Title
Special Effects: Reyes Abades
Stunts: Aaron Norris
Leading players: Chuck Norris (Max Donigan), Lou Gossett (Leo Porter), Melody Anderson (Patricia Goodwyn), Will Sampson (Tall Eagle), Sonny Landham (El Coyote), John Rhys-Davies (Corky Taylor), Ian Abercrombie (Boggs), Richard Lee-Sung (Chinaman), Alvaro Carcano (Willie), John Hazelwood (Tubbs), Mario Arevalo (Guerrilla Leader)

Death Wish 4: The Crackdown USA 1987 (UK 1988), 99 min. (UK 98 min.), col., '18'

Production company: Cannon
Executive producers: Menahem Golan, Yoram Globus
Producer: Pancho Kohner
Production executive: Rony Yacov

Production supervisor: Marc S. Fischer
Production co-ordinator: Barbara A. Hall
Production manager: John Zane
Location manager: Larry Pearson
Post-production supervisors: Michael Alden, Alain Jakubowicz
Director: J. Lee Thompson
Assistant director: Robert J. Dougherty
Screenplay: Gail Morgan Hickman
Director of photography: Gideon Porath
Second unit photography: Tom Neuwirth
Art director: Whitney Brooke Wheeler
Set decoration: Mark Andrew Haskins
Music: Paul McCallum, Valentine McCallum, John Bisharat
Sound: Mike LeMare, Gary Shepherd, Craig Felburg
Foley editor: Karola Storr
Costume design: Michael Hoffman
Make-up: Carla Frabrizi, Lesa Nielsen
Special effects: Michael Wood
Titles/opticals: LA Effects
Stunts: Ernie Orsatti
Leading players: Charles Bronson (Paul Kersey), Kay Lenz (Karen Sheldon),
    John P. Ryan ('Nathan White'), Perry Lopez (Ed Zacharias), George
    Dickerson (Detective Reiner), Soon-Teck Oh (Detective Nozaki), Dana Barron
    (Erica Sheldon), Jesse Dabson (Randy Viscovich), Peter Sherayko (Nick
    Franco), James Purcell (Vince Montono), Michael Russo (Danny Moreno),
    Danny Trejo (Art Sandella), Daniel Sabia (Al Arroyo), Mike Moroff (Jack
    Romeo), Dan Ferro (Tony Romeo), Tom Everett (Max Green), David Fonteno
    (Frank Bauggs), Tim Russ (Jesse), Hector Mercado (JoJo), Connie Hair
    (Angie), Margaret Howell (Rape Victim), Gerald Castillo (Lt Higuera),
    Bruce Hensel (Dr Rosenblatt), Richard Nugent-Aherne (real Nathan White)

Messenger of Death (US title: *The Avenging Angels*), USA 1988, 91 min., col., '18'

Production company: Cannon
Executive producers: Menahem Golan, Yoram Globus
Producer: Pancho Kohner
Production executive: Marc S. Fischer
Production manager: Sheridan Dar Reid
Director: J. Lee Thompson
Assistant director: Robert C. Ortwin Jr
Screenwriter: Paul Jarrico
Original story: Rex Burns
Director of photography: Gideon Porath
Editor: Peter Lee Thompson
Music: Robert O. Ragland
Costume design: Shelley Komarov

Leading players: Charles Bronson (Garret Smith), Trish Van Devere (Jastra Watson), Laurence Luckinbill (Homer Foxx), Daniel Benzali (Chief Barney Doyle), Marilyn Hassett (Josephine Fabrizio), Charles Dierkop (Orville Beecham), Jeff Corey (Willis Beecham), John Ireland (Zenas Beecham), Penny Peyser (Trudy Pike), Gene Davis, John Solari (Assassins), Jon Cedar (Saul), Tom Everett (Whey), Duncan Gamble (Lt Scully), Bert Williams (Sheriff Yates), Jerome Thor (Jimmy), Sydna Scott (Sarah), Cheryl Waters (Magda), Melanie Noble (Rebecca), Patricia Allison (Florinda), Maria Mayenzet (Esther), Sheila Gale Kandlbinder (Ursula), Margaret Howell (Naomi), Warner Loughlin (Ruth), Kimberly Beck (Piety), Beverly Thompson (Lucy Bigelow), Don Kennedy (Cyrus Pike), Susan Bjurman (Mrs Doyle), Phil Zuckerman (Caleb), Jeffrey Conklin (Joshua, the Priest), Eric Fry (Timothy)
Released in the UK on video only (87 mins)

Kinjite: Forbidden Subjects USA 1989, 97 min., col., '18'

Production company: Cannon
Executive producers: Menahem Golan, Yoram Globus
Producer: Pancho Kohner.
Associate producer: Patricia G. Payro
Production co-ordinator: M. Ginanne Carpenter
Director: J. Lee Thompson
Assistant director: Robert Ortwin Jnr
Screenplay: Harold Nebenzal
Director of photography: Gideon Porath
Editors: Mary E. Jochem, Peter Lee Thompson
Art director: Whitney Brooke Wheeler.
Set decoration: Margaret C. Fischer
Music: Greg De Belles
Sound: Craig Felburg, Tony Garber.
Foley editor: Kurt N. Forshager
Costume design: Michael Hoffmen
Make-up: Carla Fabrizi
Special effects: Burt C. Dalton
Titles/opticals: Pacific Title
Stunts: Ernie Orsatti
Leading players: Charles Bronson (Lt Crowe), Perry Lopez (Eddie Rios), Juan Fernandez (Duke), James Pax (Hiroshi Hada), Peggy Lipton (Kathleen Crowe), Sy Richardson (Lavonne), Marion Kodama Yue (Karuko Hada), Bill McKinney (Father Burke), Gerald Castillo (Capt. Tovar), Nicole Eggert (DeeDee), Amy Hathaway (Rita Crowe), Michell Wong (Setsuko Hada), Sam Chew Jr (McLane), Jim Ishida (Nakata), Leila Lee Olsen (Nobu-Chan), Richard Egan Jr (Vince), Deonca Brown (Louise), Tom Morga (Kriega), Erez Yoaz (Rosario), Elizabeth Chavez (Maria Rios)
Released in the UK on video only (94 mins)

References

Adair, Gilbert (1985), 'The British tradition', in Gilbert Adair and Nick Roddick, *A Night at the Pictures: Ten Decades of British Film*, Bromley: Columbus.

Aitken, Ian (2000), *Strange Realisms: The Cinema of Alberto Cavalcanti*, Trowbridge: Flicks Books.

Aldgate, Tony (1995), *Censorship and the Permissive Society: British Cinema and Theatre*, Oxford: Clarendon Press.

Aldgate, Tony (2000), '*Women of Twilight, Cosh Boy* and the advent of the "X" certificate', *Journal of Popular British Cinema* 3: 59–68.

Anez, Nicholas (1991), '*Cape Fear*', *Films in Review*, Oct./Nov.: 290–301.

Asch, Andrew (1994) 'Ape politic', *Sci-Fi Universe* 1, June/July.

Barker, Martin (1984), *A Haunt of Fears: The Strange History of the British Horror Comics Campaign*, London: Pluto Press.

Barr, Charles (1980), *Ealing Studios*, London: Cameron & Tayleur.

Barr, Charles (1999), *English Hitchcock*, Moffat: Cameron & Hollis.

Bourdieu, Pierre (1993), *Distinction: A Social Critique of the Judgement of Taste*, London: Routledge.

Bourget, Jean-Loup (1978), 'Faces of the American melodrama: Joan Crawford', *Film Reader* 3.

Bourne, Stephen (1996), *Brief Encounters: Lesbians and Gays in British Cinema 1930–1960*, London: Cassell.

Burton, Alan, O'Sullivan, Tim and Wells, Paul (eds) (1997), *Liberal Directions: Basil Dearden and Post-War British Film Culture*, Trowbridge: Flicks Books.

Burton, Alan, O'Sullivan, Tim and Wells, Paul (eds) (2000), *The Family Way: The Boulting Brothers and British Film Culture*, Trowbridge: Flicks Books.

Cardiff, Jack (1996), *Magic Hour: The Life of a Cameraman*, London: Faber.

Caute, David (1994), *Joseph Losey: A Revenge on Life*, London: Faber & Faber.

Chadder, Viv (1999), 'The higher heel: women and the post-war British crime film', in Steve Chibnall and Robert Murphy (eds), *British Crime Cinema*, London: Routledge.

Chapman, James (1998), 'Our finest hour revisited: the Second World

War in British feature films since 1945', *Journal of Popular British Cinema* 1: 63–75.

Chibnall, Steve (1977), *Law-and-Order News*, London: Tavistock.

Chibnall, Steve (1996), 'Counterfeit Yanks: war, austerity and Britain's American dream', in Philip J. Davies (ed.), *Representing and Imagining America*, Keele: Keele University Press.

Chibnall, Steve (1997), 'The teenage trilogy: *The Blue Lamp, I Believe in You* and *Violent Playground*', in Burton, O'Sullivan and Wells (1997).

Chibnall, Steve (1998), *Making Mischief: The Cult Films of Pete Walker*, London: FAB Press.

Chibnall, Steve (1999), 'Alien women: The politics of sexual difference in British sf pulp cinema', in I. Q. Hunter (ed.), *British Science Fiction Cinema*, London: Routledge.

Ciment, Michael (1985), *Conversations With Losey*, London: Methuen.

Connolly, Cyril (1985), *The Condemned Playground*, London: Hogarth Press.

Cook, John (1998), *Dennis Potter: A Life on Screen*, 2nd edn, Manchester: Manchester University Press.

Dors, Diana (1959), *Swingin' Dors*, London: World Distributors.

Dors, Diana (1978), *For Adults Only*, London: W. H. Allen.

Dors, Diana (1979), *Behind Closed Dors*, London: W. H. Allen.

Douglas-Home, William (1954), *Half-Term Report: An Autobiography*, London: Longman Green.

Douglas-Home, William (1979), *Mr Home, Pronounced Hume: An Autobiography*, London: Collins.

Drazin, Charles (1999), *In Search of The Third Man*, London: Methuen.

Durgnat, Raymond (1970), *A Mirror for England: British Movies from Austerity to Affluence*, London: Faber.

Dyer, Richard (1994), 'Feeling English', *Sight and Sound*, March: 16–19.

Ellis, John (1996), 'The quality film adventure: British critics and the cinema 1942–1948', in A. Higson (ed.), *Dissolving Views: Key Writings on British Cinema*, London: Cassell.

Elsaesser, Thomas (1972), 'Tales of sound and fury: observations on the family melodrama', *Monogram* 4: 2–15.

Everett, John (1986), *You'll Never Be 16 Again*, London: BBC Publications.

Ferguson, Ken (1962), 'My battle with the censor, by J. Lee Thompson', *Photoplay*, October.

French, Sean (1993), *Patrick Hamilton: A Life*, London: Faber.

Friedman, Betty (1971 [1963]), *The Feminine Mystique*, London: Victor Gollancz 1971.

Geraghty, Christine (1984), 'Masculinity', in Geoff Hurd (ed.), *National Fictions: World War Two in British Films and Television*, London: BFI.

Geraghty, Christine (1986), 'Diana Dors', in Charles Barr (ed.) *All Our Yesterdays: 90 Years of British Cinema*, London: BFI, 341–5.

Greene, Eric (1998), Planet of the Apes *as American Myth*, Hanover and London: Wesleyan University Press.

Green, Ian (1983), 'Ealing in the comedy frame', in James Curran and Vincent Porter (eds), *British Cinema History*, London: Weidenfeld & Nicholson.

Greene, Graham (1938), 'Subjects and stories', in C. Davy (ed.), *Footnotes to the Film*, London: Lovat Dickinson.

Greene, Graham (1950), The Third Man *and* The Fallen Idol, London: Wm Heinemann.

Greene, Graham (1971), *A Sort of Life*, Harmondsworth: Penguin.

Halliday, Jon (1972), *Sirk on Sirk*, London: Secker & Warburg.

Hancock, Robert (1993 [1963]), *Ruth Ellis, the Last Woman to Be Hanged*, London: Orion Books.

Harper, Sue (1994), *Picturing the Past: The Rise and Fall of the British Costume Film*, London: BFI.

Harper, Sue and Porter, Vincent (1999), 'Cinema audience tastes in 1950s' Britain', *Journal of Popular British Cinema* 2: 66–82.

Harris, Robert A. and Lasky, Michael S. (1976), *The Films of Alfred Hitchcock*, New York: Citadel.

Hatton, Charles (1958), *No Trees in the Street*, London: Corgi.

Henry, Joan (1952), *Who Lie in Gaol*, London: Victor Gollancz.

Henry, Joan (1954), *Yield to the Night*, London: Victor Gollancz.

Higgins, Patrick (1996), *Heterosexual Dictatorship: Male Homosexuality in Post-War Britain*, London: Fourth Estate.

Higham, Charles (1993), *Merchant of Dreams: Louis B. Mayer, MGM and the Secret Hollywood*, London: Sidgwick & Jackson.

Hill, John (1986), *Sex, Class and Realism: British Cinema 1956–1963*, London: BFI.

Hill, John (1999), *British Cinema in the 1980s*, Oxford: Clarendon Press.

Hitchcock, Alfred (1995 [1936]), 'Why I make melodramas', in Sidney Gottlieb (ed.), *Hitchcock on Hitchcock*, London: Faber.

Hoggart, Richard (1957), *The Uses of Literacy*, London: Chatto & Windus.

Holland, Steve (1993), *The Mushroom Jungle: A History of Post-War Paperback Publishing*, Westbury: Zeon Books.

Hopkins, Harry (1964), *The New Look: A Social History of the Forties and Fifties in Britain*, London: Secker & Warburg.

Jancovich, Mark (1997), *Rational Fears: American Horror in the 1950s*, Manchester: Manchester University Press.

Kleinhans, Chuck (1978), 'Notes on melodrama and the family under capitalism', *Film Reader* 3.

Koestler, Arthur and Rolph, C. H. (1961), *Hanged By the Neck*, Harmondsworth: Penguin.

Laing, Stuart (1986), *Representations of the Working Class 1957–1963*, London: Macmillan.

Landon, Christopher (1957), *Ice Cold in Alex*, London: Wm Heinemann.

Landy, Marcia (1991), *British Genres: Cinema and Society 1930–1960*, Princeton, NJ: Princeton University Press.

Lee Thompson, J. (1956), 'The time for courage and experiment', *Kinematograph Weekly*, 13 December: 87.

Lee Thompson, J. (1958), 'The censor needs a change', *Films and Filming*, August: 8.

Lee Thompson, J. (1960), 'I aim at the truth', *Films and Filming*, December: 20.

Lee Thompson, J. (1963), 'The still small voice of truth', *Films and Film-ing*, April: 5–6.

Loraine, Philip (1964), *Day of the Arrow*, London: M. S. Mill.

Macdonald, John D. (1957), *The Executioners*, New York: Random House.

MacKenzie, John M. (ed.) (1992), *Popular Imperialism and the Military 1850–1950*, Manchester: Manchester University Press.

MacLean, Alistair (1957), *The Guns of Navarone*, London: Collins.

McArthur, Colin (1972), *Underworld USA*, London: Secker & Warburg.

McArthur, Colin (1980), 'War and anti-war', *The Movie* 45.

McFarlane, Brian (1996), *Novel to Film: An Introduction to the Theory of Adaptation*, Oxford: Clarendon Press.

McFarlane, Brian (1997), *An Autobiography of British Cinema*, London: Methuen.

McFarlane, Brian (1999), *Lance Comfort*, Manchester: Manchester University Press.

Medhurst, Andrew (1984), '1950s' war films', in Geoff Hurd (ed.), *National Fictions: World War Two in British Films and Television*, London: BFI.

Mills, John (1981), *Up in the Clouds, Gentlemen Please*, London: Penguin.

Monteilhet, Hubert (1963), *Return From the Ashes*, London: Hamish Hamilton.

More, Kenneth (1978), *More or Less*, London: Hodder & Stoughton.

Morley, Sheridan (1986), *The Other Side of the Moon – David Niven: A Biography*, London: Coronet.

Moss, Robert F. (1987), *The Films of Carol Reed*, London: MacMillan.

Mulvey, Laura (1977), 'Notes on Sirk and melodrama', *Movie* 25.

Murphy, Robert (1992), *Sixties' British Cinema*, London: BFI.

Murphy, Robert (1997), 'Fifties' British war films', *The Electronic Journal of British Cinema: www.shu.ac.uk/services/lc/closeup/fifties.htm*

Nellis, Mike (1988), 'British prison movies: the case of *Now Barabbas*', *The Howard Journal* 27(1): 2–31.

Niven, David (1972), *The Moon's a Balloon*, London: Coronet.

Parish, James (1991), *Prison Pictures From Hollywood*, North Carolina: MacFarland.

Prothero, David (2000), 'Interview with Derek Hill', *Journal of Popular British Cinema* 3: 133–42.

Pyle, Ernie (1945), *Here Is Your War*, New York: World Publishing.

Quinlan, David (1983), *The Illustrated Guide to Film Directors*, London: B. T. Batsford.

Rattigan, Neil (1994), 'The last gasp of the middle class: British war films of the 1950s', in Wheeler Winston Dixon (ed.), *Re-Viewing British Cinema 1900–1992*, Albany: State University of New York Press.

Richards, Jeffrey (1973), *Visions of Yesterday*, London: Routledge & Kegan Paul.

Richards, Jeffrey (1984), *The Age of the Dream Palace: Cinema and Society in Britain 1930–1939*, London: Routledge.

Richards, Jeffrey (1998), *Films and British National Identity: From Dickens to Dad's Army*, Manchester: Manchester University Press.

Roach, William (1993), *Ken and Me*, London: Simon & Schuster.

Robertson, James (1999), 'The censors and British gangland 1913–1990', in Steve Chibnall and Robert Murphy (eds), *British Crime Cinema*, London: Routledge.

Robertson, James (2000), 'Unspeakable acts: the BBFC and *Cape Fear* (1962)', *Journal of Popular British Cinema* 3: 69–76.

Sarris, Andrew (1968), *The American Cinema: Directors and Directions*, New York: Dutton.

Sellar, Maurice, Jones, Lou, Sidaway, Robert and Sidaway, Ashley (1987), *Best of British*, London: Sphere.

Selwyn, Francis (1991), *Nothing But Revenge: The Case of Bentley and Craig*, London: Penguin.

Silverman, Stephen M. (1989, revised 1992), *David Lean*, New York: Harry N. Abrams.

Sinden, Donald (1982), *A Touch of the Memoirs*, London: Hodder & Stoughton.

Sitkoff, Harvard (1981), *The Struggle for Black Equality 1954–1980*, Toronto: Collins.

Slide, Anthony (1999), *Banned in the USA: British Films in the United States and Their Censorship 1933–1960*, London: I. B. Tauris.

Spoto, Donald (1983), *The Life of Alfred Hitchcock: The Dark Side of Genius*, London: Collins.

Stern, Lesley (1995), *The Scorsese Connection*, Bloomington: Indiana University Press.

Stern, Michael (1979), *Douglas Sirk*, Boston, MA: Twayne.

Stoddart, Lothrop (1922), *The Revolt Against Civilization: The Menace of the Underman*, New York: Charles Scribner's Sons.

Summers, Sue (1976), 'The workmanlike J. Lee Thompson', *Screen International*, 31 July.

Tanitch, Robert (1993), *John Mills*, London: Collins & Brown.

Taylor, Eric (1997), *Front-Line Nurse: British Nurses in World War Two*, London: Robert Hale.

Thumin, Janet (1991), 'The "popular", cash and culture in the post-war British cinema industry', *Screen* 32(3): 244–71.

Walker, Alexander (1986), *Hollywood England. The British Film Industry in the Sixties*, London: Harrap.

Wapshott, Nicholas (1990), *The Man Between: A Biography of Carol Reed*, London: Chatto & Windus.

Warren, Patricia (1983), *Elstree: The British Hollywood*, London: Elm Tree.

Warren, Patricia (1995), *British Film Studios: An Illustrated History*, London: B. T. Batsford.

Webster, Jack (1991), *Alistair MacLean: A Life*, London: Chapman.

Willeman, Paul (1971), 'Distanciation and Douglas Sirk', *Screen* 12:(2).

Willeman, Paul (1972), 'Towards an analysis of the Sirkian system', *Screen* 13(4).

Williams, Melanie (1999a), 'Woman in a Dressing Gown', unpublished paper, University of Hull.

Williams, Melanie (1999b), 'Why Sylvia Syms is in *Ice Cold in Alex*', unpublished paper, University of Hull.

Williams, Raymond (1979), *Politics and Letters*, London: New Left Books.

Willis, Ted (1959), *Woman in a Dressing Gown and Other TV Plays*, London: Barrie & Rockcliffe.

Willis, Ted (1991), *Evening All*, London: Macmillan.

Wise, Damon (1998), *Come By Sunday: The Fabulous Ruined Life of Diana Dors*, London: Sidgwick & Jackson.

Yallop, David (1971), *To Encourage the Others*, London: W. H. Allen.

Yorke, Edmund J. (1996), 'Cultural myths and realities: the British Army and Empire as portrayed on film 1900–90', in Ian Stewart and Susan Carruthers (eds), *War, Culture and the Media: Representations of the Military in 20th Century Britain*, Trowbridge: Flicks Books.

Zalcock, Bev (1998), *Renegade Sisters: Girl Gangs on Film*, London: Creation Books.

Index

Page numbers in bold refer to illustrations